TEACHING & LEARNING
THROUGH
MULTIPLE
INTELLIGENCES

LINDA CAMPBELL

BRUCE CAMPBELL   DEE DICKINSON

ACF-1379

Vice President, Education: Nancy Forsyth
Editorial Assistant: Kate Wagstaffe
Editing: Dorothy Bestor
Book Design: Jean Lilley
Production Editor: Catherine Hetmansky
Cover Administrator: Suzanne Harbison
Manufacturing Buyer: Aloka Rathnam
Electronic Production: MediaLink Associates, Inc.

Copyright © 1996 by Allyn & Bacon
A Simon & Schuster Company
Needham Heights, Massachusetts 02194

ISBN: 0-205-16337-8

Printed in the United States of America

10 9 8 7 6 5 4 3   99 98 97 96

*To Dr. Howard Gardner we extend our deepest thanks
for his thoughtful reading and recommendations
as each part of this book has taken form.
The Theory of Multiple Intelligences has become the
framework for our work in bringing about positive
change in education over the past ten years.
This theory is redefining the goals of education.*

This book is dedicated

to discovering the gifts

in every child.

ACKNOWLEDGEMENTS

This book represents the combined efforts of theorists, teachers, administrators, students, researchers, and interested lay people whose work, questions, and comments have helped us understand and articulate the Theory of Multiple Intelligences.

First and foremost, our thanks are extended to Dr. Howard Gardner for his inspiration and critique of this book. In addition, we are especially grateful to those who shared their expertise with us on the book's contents. These individuals include: Nancy Murphy for her impressive knowledge and suggestions for the logical-mathematical chapter; Lowell Hovis and Mark Wahl who also provided helpful feedback on the logical-mathematical chapter; Kristen DeWitte for her ideas for the linguistic chapter; Sarah Welsh for her beautifully drawn mindmap in the visual chapter; Carol Scott-Kasner for her thoughtful contributions to the musical chapter; Pat Guild for her contribution entitled Appreciating Differences in the interpersonal chapter; and to Kate McPherson for her wealth of information on service learning in the interpersonal chapter.

We also thank those who helped the book take its early pilot edition form: Dorothy Bestor for editing, Roz Pape for book design, and Cheryl Senecal for graphics. We feel fortunate, indeed, to have found Jean Lilley, who as teacher-turned-graphic-artist created the cover and book design for its final version. We appreciate as well the support for this book from numerous publishers and authors who graciously permitted us to include their work in ours.

CONTENTS

CHAPTER TWO:

CHAPTER THREE:

CHAPTER FOUR:

CHAPTER FIVE:

CHAPTER SIX:

CHAPTER 7

CHAPTER 8:

CHAPTER 9:

CHAPTER 10:

INTRODUCTION:
MANY KINDS OF INTELLIGENCE

In what ways are your students smart?

Do you have some who can create beautiful pieces of visual art? Are others gifted in sports, making complex series of physical movements appear graceful and effortless? Some may play a musical instrument so well that listening touches chords within. A few may thrill to the challenge of mathematical precision. Others may love writing and have already learned the excitement of seeing their own stories or poems in print. Several may be natural leaders offering positive role models and trusted guidance to their classmates. And a few may possess penetrating personal insights about who they are and what they stand for, while pursuing important life goals. Among the students mentioned, who would be the most intelligent? The question is impossible to answer because each of the examples represents students who have developed different intelligences. Each student is unique and all in individual ways offer valuable contributions to human culture.

A DEFINITION OF HUMAN INTELLIGENCE

Dr. Howard Gardner, Co-Director of Project Zero and Professor of Education at Harvard University, has for many years conducted research on the development of human cognitive capacities. He has broken from the common tradition of intelligence theory which adheres to two fundamental assumptions: that human cognition is unitary and that individuals can be adequately described as having a single, quantifiable intelligence. In his study of human capacities, Gardner established criteria by which to measure whether a talent was actually an intelligence. Each intelligence must have a developmental feature, be observable in special populations such as prodigies or "idiots savants," provide some evidence of localization in the brain, and support a symbolic or notational system.

While most people possess the full spectrum of intelligences, each individual reveals distinctive cognitive features. We possess varying amounts of the seven intelligences and combine and use them in highly personal ways. Restricting educational programs to focusing on a preponderance of linguistic and mathematical intelligences minimizes the importance of other forms of knowing. Thus many students who fail to demonstrate the traditional academic intelligences are held in low esteem and their strengths may remain unrealized and lost to both the school and society at large.

Not only did Gardner's research reveal a wider family of human intelligences than previously believed, but he also generated a refreshingly pragmatic definition of the concept of intelligence. Instead of viewing human "smartness" in terms of a score on a standardized test, Gardner defines intelligence as:

- **The ability to solve problems that one encounters in real life.**

- **The ability to generate new problems to solve.**

- **The ability to make something or offer a service that is valued within one's culture.**

Gardner's definition of human intelligence underscores the multicultural nature of his theory.

A DESCRIPTION OF THE SEVEN INTELLIGENCES

In his 1983 book, *Frames of Mind*, Gardner presented his Theory of Multiple Intelligences that reinforces his cross-cultural perspective of human cognition. The intelligences are languages that all people speak and are influenced, in part, by the culture into which one is born. They are tools for learning, problem-solving, and creating that all human beings can use. A brief description of Gardner's seven intelligences follows:

 Linguistic intelligence consists of the ability to think in words and to use language to express and appreciate complex meanings. Authors, poets, journalists, speakers, and newscasters exhibit high degrees of linguistic intelligence.

 Logical-mathematical intelligence makes it possible to calculate, quantify, consider propositions and hypotheses, and carry out complex mathematical operations. Scientists, mathematicians, accountants, engineers, and computer programmers all demonstrate strong logical-mathematical intelligence.

Spatial intelligence instills the capacity to think in three-dimensional ways as do sailors, pilots, sculptors, painters, and architects. It enables one to perceive external and internal imagery, to recreate, transform, or modify images, to navigate oneself and objects through space, and to produce or decode graphic information.

Bodily-kinesthetic intelligence enables one to manipulate objects and fine-tune physical skills. It is evident in athletes, dancers, surgeons, and craftspeople. In Western societies, physical skills are not as highly valued as cognitive ones, and yet elsewhere the ability to use one's body is a necessity for survival as well as an important feature of many prestigious roles.

 Musical intelligence is evident in individuals who possess a sensitivity to pitch, melody, rhythm, and tone. Those demonstrating this intelligence include composers, conductors, musicians, critics, instrument makers, as well as sensitive listeners.

 Interpersonal intelligence is the capacity to understand and interact effectively with others. It is evident in successful teachers, social workers, actors, or politicians. Just as Western culture has recently begun to recognize the connection between mind and body, so too has it to come to value the importance of proficiency in interpersonal behavior.

 Intrapersonal intelligence refers to the ability to construct an accurate perception of oneself and to use such knowledge in planning and directing one's life. Some individuals with strong intrapersonal intelligence specialize as theologians, psychologists, and philosophers.

Gardner is careful to explain that intelligence should not be limited to the ones he has identified. He believes that the seven, however, provide a far more accurate picture of human capacities than do previous unitary theories. Contrary to the small range of abilities that many standard IQ tests measure, Gardner's theory offers an expanded image of what it means to be human. He also notes that each intelligence contains several sub-intelligences. For example, there are sub-intelligences within the domain of music that include playing music, singing, writing musical scores, conducting, critiquing, and appreciating music. Each of the six other intelligences also encompass numerous components.

Another aspect of the Multiple Intelligences is that they may be conceptualized in three broad categories. Three of the seven, spatial, logical-mathematical, and bodily-kinesthetic, may be viewed as "object-related" forms of intelligence. These capacities are controlled and shaped by the objects which individuals encounter in their environments. On the other hand, the "object-free" intelligences, consisting of verbal-linguistic and musical, are not shaped by the physical world but are dependent upon language and musical systems. The third category consists of the "person-related" intelligences with inter- and intrapersonal intelligences reflecting a powerful set of counterbalances.

Each intelligence appears to have its own developmental sequence, emerging and blossoming at different times in life. Musical intelligence is the earliest form of human giftedness to emerge; it is a mystery as to why this is so. Gardner suggests that excelling at music as a child may be conditioned by the fact that this intelligence is not contingent upon accruing life experience. On the other hand, the personal intelligences require extensive interaction with and feedback from others before becoming well-developed.

Gardner believes that since each intelligence can be used for good or ill purposes, all seven are inherently value-free. Goebbels and Gandhi both had strong interpersonal intelligence but applied it in dramatically different ways. How an individual goes about using his intelligence within society is a moral question of crucial importance.

It is evident that creativity can be expressed through all the intelligences. Gardner notes, however, that most people are creative within a specific domain. For example, although Einstein was gifted mathematically and scientifically, he did not exhibit equal genius linguistically, kinesthetically, or interpersonally. Most people appear to excel within one or two intelligences.

This book is about how to create open systems of education to make it possible for the human mind—which can be the most open of systems—to flourish. Not all human beings will become great artists, or musicians, or writers, but every human life will be enriched through developing many kinds of intelligence to the greatest extent possible. When individuals have opportunities to learn through their strengths, unexpected and positive cognitive, emotional, social, and even physical changes will appear.

ABOUT THE AUTHORS

The authors of this book have shared with teachers exciting breakthroughs in learning students experience when instructional strategies engage the seven intelligences. They themselves have been classroom teachers at all levels from elementary through university. Many experiences from their work are interwoven throughout the text as illustrations of what can happen when the repertoire of teaching strategies is expanded and the opportunities for learning in different ways are increased. By engaging their strengths, students can bridge into other ways of learning and growing.

As a public school teacher, **Linda Campbell** was elected teacher of the year three times. She has applied what she has learned during her many years of elementary and secondary teaching to a new model of teacher preparation she designed for Antioch University Seattle. In this graduate program, mid-career adults who are studying to become elementary and middle school school teachers, learn how to apply all seven intelligences in each lesson they teach. These future educators not only acquire lesson planning and assessment strategies that utilize the seven intelligences, but they all learn project-based, interdisciplinary models of curriculum development, as well as how to recognize the diverse intelligences in the students they teach.

In order to understand the Theory of Multiple Intelligences on a personal as well as theoretical basis, Linda's certification students must identify their current intelligence strengths as well as intelligences that are under-developed. Each then creates a personal plan to develop competency in an intelligence that is seldom-used. Throughout a ten month timeframe, the prospective teacher nurtures a latent area of potential. To do so, students pursue music or

singing lessons, implement diet and exercise programs, start daily journal writing, volunteer for community agencies, learn a foreign language, begin computer programming, or take art lessons. One of the goals of this personal exploration of the Multiple Intelligences is to learn as a teacher what it feels like as a child to develop new skills. Additionally, as the prospective educators increase their competence in a greater number of intelligences, they become "literate" in a variety of symbol systems and better able to communicate with the diverse students they encounter. These pre-service educators also report that not only do they value their new-found skills, they desire to tackle other areas as well, pursuing what some have referred to as the "Renaissance ideal."

Dee Dickinson, as head of a language arts department, taught a survey course in English literature for many years. In an attempt to create a rich context for understanding the literature of each period, she created a learning environment which engaged all of the intelligences. As students entered the room each day, music of the period was playing. Slides were shown of the great works of art of each period. The philosophical and political thinking of the time entered into class discussions, along with important historical events.

For each literary period, the head of the science department was invited in to explain what was then known about the human body, the physical environment, and the solar system, as well as what methods were used to make scientific discoveries. The head of the math department explained mathematical theories of the era and gave students problems to solve in ways that would then have been available to them.

Students sight-read and sang Gregorian chants and English madrigals. They tried their hands at writing adventures in the style of Beowulf and Chaucer. They "became" Samuel Pepys writing a diary of their own times, or a news reporter interviewing a classmate as Thoreau. They role-played William Wordsworth writing poetry in the lake country of England and wrote poems in the manner of Robert Frost. In order to accomplish these tasks, the students read more literature more deeply and with greater motivation than might otherwise have been the case. And as adults, now many years later, these former students still remember their studies in detail and with much enthusiasm.

It was such successful experiences that in 1980 led Dee to found New Horizons for Learning, an international education network devoted to helping all students become more successful at learning. In 1984, the network began focusing on implementing Gardner's Theory of Multiple Intelligences. Numerous New Horizons for Learning Conferences have been built around his theory, publications have presented examples of how it is being implemented, and the new NHFL electronic network offers ongoing conferences focused on classroom applications of MI theory.

Bruce Campbell has applied Gardner's theory to his elementary third/fourth/fifth grade, multi-age classroom for six years. This instructional model involved seven learning centers, each devoted to one of the intelligences. The students spent approximately two thirds of their school day rotating through the centers. The morning started with a brief lecture and discussion of the classroom's current theme. Students then divided into seven groups to begin their center work, spending about 25 minutes at each center. The last third of the day students worked on independent projects of their choice and shared their work with their classmates.

Once again, the application of Gardner's ideas with Bruce's students resulted not only in higher test scores, but in improvements in other areas of the children's lives as well. In a year-long, action research project Bruce undertook, numerous effects of this curricular model were documented: students discover diverse areas of strength and apply numerous intelligences to classroom work. Behavior problems are minimized; self-concept is enhanced; cooperation and leadership skills develop and above all, the children's love of learning is increased.

At the beginning of the school year, when students began working at all seven centers, many of them expressed discomfort. By midyear, however, all students gave multimodal presentations of their independent projects by singing, performing, building, interacting with their audience, displaying charts and diagrams, and reflecting upon their own learning experiences. Additionally, the teacher discovered that after working multimodally for six years, his own abilities to think and plan in the seven intelligences have developed substantially. As a result of the success of this classroom model, similar programs have been implemented in classrooms and districts throughout the country. Recently, Campbell was selected to serve as the "Teacher on Sabbatical" at Western Washington University where he taught education students what he has learned in his pioneering program. Bruce currently is serving as a learning and restructuring specialist in his school district assisting K-12 teachers in expanding learning opportunities for all students.

A PERSONAL INVENTORY

Before surveying the strategies in this book, it may be helpful to self-assess one's current personal and professional use of each of the seven intelligences. Everyone relies on one or more intelligences for successful daily living. It is likely that heredity, the environment, and one's culture all influence our intelligence preferences. In our professional lives as educators, we also rely on one or more intelligences in our instructional approaches. Such inclinations may be determined by our individual preferences, our training as educators, and the "cultural norms" of our schools.

The inventory below enables readers to identify their strengths as well as the intelligences they seldom use. We hope that such an assessment will serve as a guide in discovering intelligence areas that may be more fully developed. The inventory features the seven intelligences and boxes in which to assess the current level of professional and personal use. Assign a 3 to any intelligence used extensively, a 2 for moderate use, a 1 for infrequent use, and a 0 if never used. The total for each intelligence then can range from a low of zero to a high of six.

A PERSONAL INVENTORY			
INTELLIGENCE	PROFESSIONAL USE	PERSONAL USE	TOTAL
Logical/ Mathematical			
Verbal/ Linguistic			
Visual/ Spatial			
Bodily/ Kinesthetic			
Musical			
Interpersonal			
Intrapersonal			

After completing this brief assessment, reflect on the results. Are there differences between intelligences used in your personal and professional life? Are there other intelligences you would like to develop for professional use? How were your areas of strength nurtured as a child and as an adult? How might you go about developing other intelligences of interest? Could you establish a timeline for such work? What kinds of intelligences do you perceive in your students? Which intelligences do you feel are most highly developed in teachers in general?

Reflecting on such questions might deepen your awareness of your unique capacities as well as expand appreciation for those gifted in other domains.

This inventory serves as a simple introduction to recognizing and respecting differences in intelligence among students and colleagues. Such awareness can motivate us to seek equitable ways of teaching diverse groups of children so that they in turn may have more equitable opportunities for learning and succeeding in school.

INTELLIGENT ENVIRONMENTS

Not only is it important for teachers to recognize the intelligence in our mind/body systems, but also to realize that it is possible to create "smart environments" in which to live and learn. The new field of research on "distributed cognitions" suggests that intelligence extends beyond individuals and is enhanced through interactions with other people, through resource materials in books and databases, and through the tools we use to think, learn, and problem-solve such as pencils and paper, notebooks and journals, calculators, and computers.

Take a moment to reflect upon your classroom environment. How is it "smart?" Are there sufficient opportunities for students to interact with each other in pairs, small groups, or as a whole class? Are resources available in the form of books, magazines, other publications, bulletin boards, art work, posters, computers, databases and networks? Are there plenty of tools to use in learning and problem-solving? Do students have their own journals? Throughout this book you will find ways to create environments that foster the development of all the intelligences.

It is well to remember that neurophsyiologists such as Marian Diamond at the University of California at Berkeley have discovered that the brain can change physiologically as a result of learning and experience—for better or worse. Throughout life we can continue to develop enhanced mental abilities in environments that are positive, nurturing, stimulating, and interactive.

WHAT THIS BOOK OFFERS

Written for educators, this book offers practical classroom applications of the Theory of Multiple Intelligences. Philosophically, the authors maintain that students must have opportunities for the cre-ative exploration of their individual interests and talents while also learning valued skills and concepts through multimodal means. Not all children exhibit the same intelligence profile, nor do they share the same interests. In an age of exploding information, none of us can learn everything; choices ultimately must be made about what and how we will learn. In making such choices, the students' individual inclinations and interests should guide some of their curricular options.

The basic knowledge that all students must master, such as language arts, mathematics, history, and science does not need to be taught in the same manner for everyone. Frustration and academic failure might be greatly reduced if teachers presented information in numerous ways, offering students multiple options for success. This book, then, was written to assist teachers in acquiring "intelligence fair" methods of perceiving students and their talents, of designing curriculum and assessment approaches, and of nurturing individual capacities so that each child may experience the pleasure of gaining skill in an area of intrinsic interest.

As you browse through the book, you will notice that each of the chapters on the seven intelligences are organized in the same manner: each begins with a story of an individual who exemplifies a particular intelligence. This is followed by a definition of the intelligence, suggestions for enhancing the classroom environment, and numerous instructional strategies. The final three chapters are dedicated to curriculum and assessment issues and what has been learned from pilot Multiple Intelligence school programs.

The authors offer this collection of practical applications of the Theory of Multiple Intelligences to reinforce the fine work that many teachers are already doing and to serve as a resource of ideas that may be new to some. All of these suggestions are founded upon the same goal: to free the learning potential and creative expression of each student.

CHAPTER 1

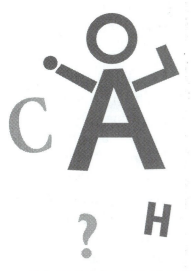

WRITING THROUGH A LIFETIME

The introduction to Carl Sandburg's *Complete Poems* quotes the great poet as saying, "At the age of six, as my fingers first found how to shape the alphabet, I decided to become a person of letters. At the age of ten I had scrawled letters on slates, on paper, on boxes and walls and I formed an ambition to become a sign-painter."

A WAY WITH WORDS: VERBAL-LINGUISTIC INTELLIGENCE

"The poet possesses a relation to words beyond our ordinary powers, a repository, as it were, of all the uses to which particular words have been put in previous poems. That knowledge of the history of language use prepares— or frees—the poet to attain certain combinations of his own as he constructs an original poem. It is through such fresh combinations of words, as Northrup Frye insists, that we have our only way of creating new worlds."

— *Howard Gardner, Frames of Mind*

Even though his failure in entrance exams in mathematics and grammar kept Carl Sandburg from being admitted to West Point, he graduated from Lombard College and went on to a brilliant career as a writer. He collected American folk-songs into an anthology, *The American Songbag*, and his four-volume biography of Abraham Lincoln led to doctoral degrees at twelve universities. Yet never satisfied with his writing skills, even into his eighties, Sandburg wrote:

"I am still studying verbs and the mystery of how they connect with nouns. I am more suspicious of adjectives than at any other time in all my born days. I have forgotten the meaning of twenty or thirty of my poems written thirty or forty years ago. I still favor several simple poems published long ago which continue to have an appeal for simple people. I have written by different methods and in a wide miscellany of moods and have seldom been afraid to travel in lands and seas where I met fresh scenes and new songs. All my life I have been trying to learn to read, to see and hear, and to write. At sixty-five I began my first novel, and the five years lacking a month I took to finish it, I was still traveling, still a seeker. I should like to think that as I go on writing there will be sentences truly alive with verbs quivering, with nouns giving color and echoes. It could be in the grace of God, I shall live to be eighty-nine, as did Hokusai, and speaking my farewell to earthly scenes, I might paraphrase, "If God had let me live five years longer I should have been a writer.""

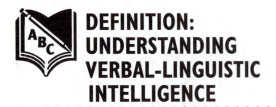 ## DEFINITION: UNDERSTANDING VERBAL-LINGUISTIC INTELLIGENCE

Sandburg's statement exemplifies verbal-linguistic intelligence as he describes both his keen sensitivity to the sound, rhythm, and meaning of words and his lifelong passion for learning to express himself in his writing. Gardner suggests that language is a "pre-eminent instance of human intelligence" that has been indispensable to human society. He notes the importance of the rhetorical aspect of language, or the ability to convince others of a course of action; the mnemonic potential of language, or the ability to use words in remembering lists or processes; the capacity of language to explain concepts, and the value of metaphor in doing so; and the use of language to reflect upon language, or to engage in "metalinguistic" analysis.

The use of words to communicate and document, to express powerful emotions, to set to music in song sets human beings apart from other animals. Early in the history of humankind, language changed the specialization and function of the human brain by offering possibilities for exploring and expanding human intelligence. The spoken word made it possible for our ancestors to move from concrete to abstract thinking as they progressed from pointing to objects to naming them and to talking about objects not in their presence. Reading has made it possible for human beings to know about objects, places, processes, and concepts that we have personally not experienced, and writing has made it possible to communicate with people the speaker has never met. It is through the ability to think in words that human beings can remember, analyze, problem-solve, plan ahead, and create.

Since the normal fetus develops hearing while still in the womb, the foundation of verbal-linguistic intelligence is laid before birth. Many studies, including those of neonatologists such as Thomas Verney, indicate that babies who have been read to, sung to, and talked to before birth have a head start on the development of verbal-linguistic intelligence.

Verney, as well as the National Association for the Education of Young Children, point out the importance of creating language-rich environments in which parents or other caregivers engage young children in verbal interaction, including playing with words, telling stories and jokes, asking questions, stating opinions, and explaining feelings and concepts. Children should be involved in discussions and provided with opportunities to make meaningful choices and decisions. Small wonder that a child born into such an environment has a leading-edge on becoming a competent listener, speaker, reader, and writer.

Classrooms in every subject matter area, at every grade level, must also be language-rich environments in which students frequently speak, discuss, and explain—and above all are encouraged to be curious. Interest in learning grows when students feel secure enough to ask questions and debate viewpoints Expressing ideas verbally is an important metacognitive exercise, for it is often in hearing ourselves speak or reading what we have written that we gain insights into what we really think and know.

Self-confidence grows when students learn to defend their position in discussions and debates. They understand their lessons more deeply when they have opportunities to discuss or teach others what they have learned. Yet observations of classrooms by such researchers as John Goodlad reveal that in most cases teachers are the ones who speak the vast majority of the time—to groups of passive students.

Even in classrooms where students are primarily listeners, that skill is rarely taught. Yet, it is through listening that one learns to use the spoken word correctly, effectively, even eloquently. Ineffective listening skills account for many failed lessons, misunderstandings, and even physical injuries. Speaking is another essential skill that does not develop effectively without a great deal of practice and encouragement. Effective writing requires practice as well as broad, thoughtful reading. In the successful classroom, in any subject, all four of these skills are seamlessly and actively developed. The development of these four components of verbal-linguistic intelligence can have a significant effect on success in learning any subject—throughout life.

✔ CHECKLIST OF VERBAL-LINGUISTIC INTELLIGENCE QUALITIES

Early in the history of our country in the schools of the Massachusetts Bay Colony, reading and writing composed two-thirds of the curriculum. Today, the curriculum has vastly expanded, yet reading and writing, along with listening and speaking, remain essential tools for learning in all subjects.

In *Planning and Assessing the Curriculum in English Language Arts*, author Stephen Tchudi, past president of the National Council of Teachers of English and professor of English at the University of Nevada, discusses the importance of the "growth-through English" movement. Terms such as "student-centered," "naturalistic," "developmental," "organic," "integrated," "language experience," and "whole language" are commonly associated with this kind of teaching and learning. Tchudi notes that each of these terms hints at one of the central features of the personal growth model, which:

- looks to the students' language as the starting point for instruction;

- allows for natural progression of language skills development instead of prescribed sequences;

- builds skills developmentally, meshing instruction with students' cognitive and linguistic growth;

- organically connects language and literature;

- integrates the various components of language arts— reading, writing, listening, and speaking;

- uses youngsters' own experiences with life as the entry point for reading and writing; and

- treats language as a whole, rather than dividing instruction into discrete skill components.

This approach to language arts instruction draws on the research in learning and thinking of such educational pioneers as Lev Vygotsky, Susanne Langer, James Britton, and James Moffett, as well as successful models of progressive education in both England and the United States.

The following list suggests some indicators of verbal-linguistic intelligence. We recognize that the hearing, speaking, or sight-impaired will develop language and communication skills in other ways, often through other intelligences discussed in later chapters. It is likely that a person with well-developed verbal-linguistic intelligence exhibits the following characteristics:

1. **Listens and responds to the sound, rhythm, color, and variety of the spoken word.**

2. **Imitates sounds, language, reading, and writing of others.**

3. **Learns through listening, reading, writing, and discussing.**

4. **Listens effectively, comprehends, paraphrases, interprets, and remembers what has been said.**

5. **Reads effectively, comprehends, summarizes, interprets or explains, and remembers what has been read.**

6. **Speaks effectively to a variety of audiences for a variety of purposes, and knows how to speak simply, eloquently, persuasively, or passionately at appropriate times.**

7. **Writes effectively: understands and applies rules of grammar, spelling, punctuation, and uses an effective vocabulary.**

8. **Exhibits ability to learn other languages.**

9. **Uses listening, speaking, writing, and reading to remember, communicate, discuss, explain, persuade, create knowledge, construct meaning, and reflect upon language itself.**

10. **Strives to enhance his or her own language usage.**

11. **Demonstrates interest in journalism, poetry, storytelling, debate, speaking, writing, or editing.**

12. **Creates new linguistic forms or original works of writing or oral communication.**

VERBAL-LINGUISTIC LEARNING PROCESSES

Throughout this book, you will find connections between each of the other intelligences and the development and use of language.

The tendency of some teachers in attempting to teach verbal skills in isolation or out of context may be one reason that many students do not master them. Although we discuss each of these skills separately in the following list, they are closely linked and must be well integrated into the curriculum.

Because so much has been researched and written on the subject of verbal skills, this chapter does not discuss the introduction and teaching of fundamentals, but rather highlights important ways to exercise and develop these skills. The specific strategies described in this chapter include:

ESTABLISHING A VERBAL-LINGUISTIC LEARNING ENVIRONMENT

LISTENING TO LEARN
  Keys to Good Listening
  Listening to Stories and Reading Aloud
  Listening to Poetry
  Teachers as Storytellers
  Listening to Lectures

SPEAKING
  Students as Storytellers
  Classroom Discussions
  Memorizing
  Reports
  Interviews

READING
  Finding Materials
  Words in the Classroom
  Reading for Understanding

WRITING
  Categories of Writing
  Writing across the Curriculum
  Getting Started with Writing
  The Real Work of Writing
  Writing Groups

TECHNOLOGY THAT ENHANCES VERBAL-LINGUISTIC INTELLIGENCE

SUMMARY

ESTABLISHING A VERBAL-LINGUISTIC LEARNING ENVIRONMENT

Verbal-linguistic intelligence is deeply rooted in our feelings of competence and self-confidence. The more young children exercise this intelligence in a secure setting, the more easily they develop the verbal skills that will serve them throughout life. Teachers can provide strong models by playing with words, sharing their favorite written works, engaging in discussions with enthusiasm, providing field trips to local theatrical productions, and telling stories.

Storytelling is one of the oldest and most engaging of the language arts. This educational strategy is not used nearly as much as it might to motivate students, explain processes or events, or simply create a hospitable environment. Stories in the form of parables have been used effectively by every religion in the world to convey important principles and teachings. Myths were invented and told in all primitive societies to explain scientific phenomena, and legends entertained, inspired, and motivated listeners. The oral tradition is an ancient one, and bears recognition as one of the most effective ways of communicating. Later in this chapter, you will find suggestions for incorporating storytelling into the classroom.

Reading aloud carries the sound, rhythm, and music of language into the ear. Recordings or videotapes of actors interpreting the works of great playwrights, poets, and short story writers bring the written word to life. Authors reading their own works often foster in-depth understanding of their writings. Teachers reading some of their favorite written works aloud with enthusiasm and feeling can inspire interest that lasts a lifetime. Students reading to each other before reading aloud to the whole class can develop greater self-confidence.

Teachers can model effective listening skills by paying careful attention to the comments of students or guests in the classroom. Students are encouraged to listen more carefully to others when they themselves are listened to attentively. Numbers of ways to develop these skills are described in this chapter.

Extensive opportunities for individualized reading, writing, and speaking have positive effects on achievement and tend to carry over into leisure-time activities. Students who have little knowledge of the great body of available literature need to be guided and motivated to become enthusiastic readers. Their interest can best be engaged when parents or teachers suggest books or articles that are related to their interests; however, they must be introduced to other reasons for reading as well.

The study of great stories, plays, poetry, or novels can be complemented by challenging writing assignments. Requiring a book report that lists the characters and summarizes the plot does not generate student enthusiasm. An essay on a poem's meaning or a play's underlying theme may not stimulate interest either. Teachers do well to suggest topics they would enjoy writing about themselves, and ones they know are interesting to their students.

In order to make sense of what might otherwise be a fragmented educational experience, it is important for teachers to help students see connections between subjects. Teachers of math and science must demand the same high standards of listening, speaking, reading, and writing as do language arts instructors. And teachers of literature may create a meaningful context for reading a book by relating it to studies in other subjects.

Students require a wide variety of experiences to engage verbal-linguistic intelligence as exemplified throughout this book. Exercising listening, speaking, reading, and writing skills leads to fuller human development and to the mastery of skills important throughout life: thinking, learning, problem-solving, communicating, and creating as contributing members of society.

10 KEYS TO EFFECTIVE LISTENING

These keys suggest ways to improve listening. In fact, they're at the heart of developing better listening habits that could last a lifetime.

10 KEYS TO EFFECTIVE LISTENING	WEAK LISTENERS	STRONG LISTENERS
1. **Find areas of interest**	Tune out "dry" subjects	Opportunize: ask "what's in it for me?"
2. **Judge content, not delivery**	Tune out if delivery is poor	Judge content, skip over delivery errors
3. **Hold your fire**	Tend to enter into argument	Withhold judgement until comprehension is complete
4. **Listen for ideas**	Listen for facts	Listen for central themes
5. **Be flexible**	Take intensive notes using only one system	Take fewer notes. Use 4-5 different systems, depending on speaker
6. **Work at listening**	Fake attention	Work hard, exhibit active body state
7. **Resist distractions**	Are easily distracted	Fight or avoid distractions; tolerate bad habits; know how to concentrate
8. **Exercise your mind**	Resist difficult material; seek simple material	Use dense material as exercise for the mind
9. **Keep your mind open**	Agree with information if it supports pre-conceived ideas	Consider diverse points of view before forming opinions
10. **Capitalize on fact since *thought* is faster than speech**	Tend to daydream with slow speakers	Challenge, anticipate, summarize, weigh the evidence; listen between the lines

LISTENING TO LEARN

For those able to hear, the human voice provides the first introduction to language. It has been estimated by such researchers as Dr. Lyman Steil, professor of rhetoric at the University of Minnesota, that individuals spend 80 per cent of their waking hours communicating, and that 45 per cent of that time is devoted to listening. Steil estimates that in many traditional classrooms students spend over 70 per cent of classroom time in listening, yet there is little time spent helping them learn effective listening strategies.

Steil contends that the majority of people are inefficient listeners. After hearing a ten minute oral presentation most listeners hear, understand, evaluate, and retain only half of what was said. They lose another 25 per cent during the following 48 hours. In other words, most people retain only about a quarter of what they hear unless they have developed the skills to listen more efficiently.

KEYS TO EFFECTIVE LISTENING

Some ten years ago, the Sperry Corporation hired Dr. Steil to help their employees improve their listening skills. These skills can be developed at any age and are appropriate for students to practice in the classroom. With Dr. Steil's help, the Sperry Corporation developed ten keys to effective listening that can provide learning tools useful throughout life. Teachers may wish to discuss the ten keys with their students and to intentionally practice one or more of them as appropriate.

Since there is a definite time-lag between the number of words the average speaker says in a minute (200) and the average number of words a listener can process in a minute (300 to 500),

good listeners use the extra time to activate their thinking. When students are listening to an explanation, a lecture, or a guest speaker, they can use this time-lag to identify the speaker's purpose, main points, and central themes. They can review and evaluate what has been said, anticipate what may be coming, and think about what is of personal importance to themselves. They may take notes of significant points, using as few words as possible, or they may make mindmaps. (Several kinds are suggested in the chapter on visual-spatial intelligence.) If teachers want students to remember what they hear, students should be given opportunities to summarize or discuss the content with someone else within the next eight hours.

LISTENING TO STORIES AND READING ALOUD

Telling stories and reading aloud are useful ways to engage interest and facilitate learning in all subject matter areas. For example, a history lesson may be brought to life through anecdotes, or through letters or journals of well-known historical figures such as explorers or the authors of the Constitution. Science lessons might be prefaced with stories of important discoveries, such as those of Madame Curie, George Washington Carver, or Thomas Edison. For example, by learning about Edison's life, teachers could read selected passages from any one of numerous biographical sources or turn the information into a story. The following illustrates one potential story to be read or memorized and told to students:

Thomas Edison: An Inventor throughout His Life

Thomas Edison began conducting experiments during his childhood. Assuming that

birds could fly because they ate worms, Edison cut up worms, mixed them with food, gave the concoction to an unsuspecting woman, and waited to see if she would fly. Another experiment he unsuccessfully attempted when he was young was to sit on a batch of eggs to see if he could make them hatch.

While undertaking hundreds of unsuccessful experiments, Edison eventually invented and patented 2500 items, including the electric lamp and phonograph. He was determined to "give laughter and light" to people, but most people scoffed at him. Without losing hope, Edison attempted over 1000 unsuccessful experiments in his efforts to make an electric lamp. When people told him he was wasting his time, energy, and money for nothing, Edison exclaimed, "For nothing! Every time I make an experiment, I get new results. Failures are stepping stones to success."

Determined to give people electric lamps, Edison said he'd meet his goal by early 1880. In October, 1879, he created his first electric lamp, and in so doing, received much praise. People realized that Edison's invention was impervious to rain or wind, remaining constant through bad weather. Just as he had hoped, Edison provided people with light and laughter.

Sharing such biographical information brings people and their work to life. Not only do students see the human side of invention, they also learn about important qualities creative individuals possess. In so doing, they may discover similar qualities within themselves or identify new ones to pursue.

Biographical Resources as Subject Matter

An excellent resource to assist teachers in learning about the lives of others is the book *Great Lives* compiled by Simon Boughton. This volume includes biographies of over 1000 men and women from around the world who have made important contributions to humankind. The book is arranged both as a dictionary of famous individuals, and as a chronological timeline; it includes a subject index as well.

Another similar resource is *Cradles of Eminence* by Goertzel and Goertzel which describes the childhoods of 400 famous men and women. There are also educational series that feature biographies of artists, mathematicians, scientists, and others such as *American Women of Achievement, Black Americans of Achievement,* and *World Leaders of Achievement* published by Chelsea House and the Creative Lives Series published by Zephyr Press.

LISTENING TO POETRY

Just as storytelling or reading aloud the lives of famous men and women can enliven learning, so too can the use of poetry. Short poems can introduce many curriculum units. Teachers might want to compile and share poems with each other that can complement any subject matter area. An excellent resource for poems across the curriculum is Koch's and Farrell's *Talking to the Sun: An Illustrated Anthology of Poems for Young People.* Other sources of colorful poems includes Hill's *Time for Poetry—A Teacher's Anthology,* or Bennett's *Noisy Poems.*

Many students write poems that they will gladly share. Two student poems are printed below. The first was written by a 16 year old and may be appropriate when introducing a lesson on cycles of night and day or on literary character development.

Dawn
Yvonne MacRae

The death of a star
Is secretly hidden in
The birth of a day.

The next poem was written by a fourth grade student who had recently learned about the Multiple Intelligences. She wrote the poem "for fun" one evening and brought it to her teacher the next morning. This poem serves as an excellent introduction to Gardner's theory for students or adults. Indeed, the authors frequently use the poem at workshops to introduce MI to teachers.

The Intelligence Rap
by Shawna Munson

The seven intelligences are really cool.
We all have them so no one is a fool.

Linguistic deals with writing and with words.
We have language - we're not like animals or birds.

Logical-mathematical doesn't need to be a shock.
If you study real hard, you'll be smarter than Spock!

Spatial involves seeing, drawing, and art,
Creating different things and taking them apart.

In case you didn't know, kinesthetic is P.E.
Get fit and coordinated athletically!

All of these so far are really neat,
But I like musical 'cause it has a beat.

Sometimes, I feel lonely, without any friends,
But interpersonal skills put that to an end.

Intrapersonal skills are when you want to reflect.
For yourself, you should always have respect.

Now, I've come to the end of my rap.
Learn in many ways and you'll never be a sap.

TEACHERS AS STORYTELLERS

When resources are not readily available, or when a teacher wants to explore teaching content in various ways, storytelling offers an option that delights young and old learners alike. Any topic or subject springs to life when told as a story. Additionally, people of all ages find it easy to remember information when it is encoded in a story. Even though many of us would claim we are not storytellers, all of us already are! Each of us has stories from our own lives we enjoy sharing, many of us like telling jokes, recounting dreams, or even gossiping about others—a practice that may be the basis for future folktales or legends.

Subject Matter Stories

Where can classroom stories come from? Often from our own life experiences. Remembering our own reactions as children when encountering school subjects can provide teachers with real life stories to share with students who are learning similar content. Taking subject matter content and reworking it for storytelling is another option which is easier than it might at first appear. By identifying key characters and a challenge for them to undertake story lines can quickly develop. Teachers may want to reflect on content they plan to teach and consider what characters and plot emerge for storytelling possibilities. Additionally, students are often eager to create and tell stories that incorporate academic content.

The Cultural Dimensions of Storytelling

Storytelling is also a powerful way to provide students with insight into history and diverse cultures. Students may be interested to learn that storytelling is older than written history. Before reading and writing were common, stories transmitted the oral history of a culture—including the hopes, fears, values, and accomplishments of its people.

For example, during the time of slavery in the United States, stories assumed another purpose as well. Since slaves were not allowed to gather in groups larger than five, nor speak or write in their native African languages, nor write in English, they created animal stories to forge a sense of community they were denied. The animal they chose for many of their tales was the rabbit—a creature as powerless as the slaves, but one who also knew everything happening around him, yet out of necessity remained silent. The rabbit was called Brer Rabbit. By hearing stories of Brer Rabbit, students might empathize with the slaves who created him as a central character in their folklore.

Multicultural Storytelling Resources

There are numerous resources available for the teacher who wants to introduce students to other cultures, in part, through storytelling. When multicultural stories are told, teachers can ask students to listen for and gather information about diverse cultures. Upon hearing a story, teachers and students might discuss the structure and message of the story as well as its cultural implications. Suggested questions include:

What is the setting in the story?

What values are conveyed through the story?

How is language used in the story?

Are there stereotypes that the story reinforces?

Are there stereotypes that the story diminishes about this culture?

School and local librarians are usually knowledgeable of a variety of storytelling resources. They will often eagerly identify stories to accompany any cultural study. The authors have included a partial list of multicultural storytelling books below:

African-American Stories:
Giant Treasury of Brer Rabbit by Anne Hessey
Mules and Men by Zora Hurston
The People Could Fly: American Black Folktales by Virginia Hamilton
Shukin' and Jivin' by Daryl Cumber Dance

American Indian Stories:
The Legend of the Indian Paintbrush Retold by Tomie De Paola
Native American Stories from Puget Sound by Vi Hilbert
Once Upon a Totem by Christie Harris
Stories of California Indians, by Anne Fisher

Asian Stories:
Asian Laughter by Leonard Feinberg
The Courtesan's Jewel Box by Gladys Yang and Xianyi
Floating Clouds, Floating Dreams: Favorite Asian Folktales by I.K. Junne
How the Ox Star Fell from Heaven by Lily Toy Hong
Tales from the Japanese Storytellers by Post Wheeler

Hispanic Stories:
Mexican Folk Tales by Anthony Campos
Tales from the Amazon by Martin Elbl
The Woman Who Outshone the Sun by Alejendro Cru

Jewish Stories:
Such A Noise! by Aliana Brodmann
A Treasury of Jewish Folklore by Nathan Asubel

Female Heroine Stories:

Cut from the Same Cloth: American Women of Myth, Legend and Folktale by Robert Sansouci

Tatterhood by Ethel Phillips

The Woman in the Moon and Other Forgotten Heroines by James Riordan

Collections of Stories from Diverse Cultures:

Folktales of the World by Richard Dorson

Pleasant Journeys: Twenty-two Tales from Around the World by Pleasant de Spain

The Stolen Fire: Legends from Around the World by Stella Humphries

Resources on the art of storytelling:

Handbook for Storytellers by Caroline Bauer

Storytelling: Art and Technique by A. Baker and E. Greene

The World of Storytelling by Ruth Sawyer

LISTENING TO LECTURES

Although there will be fewer lecture-discussion formats in classrooms of the future, we recognize that lecture is still one effective means of presenting information to a large group of older students. As such, lectures will continue to be used in many learning settings, and it is important for students to discover the best ways to listen and learn from them. While such skills are rarely taught, some suggestions are offered below to sharpen your students' listening abilities:

1. Teachers might want to present a mini-lecture to students on a meaningful topic with which they are not familiar. To begin, give the title of the talk and ask students to use the following active listening practices by writing:

   - **what they already know about the subject**
   - **what questions they have about it**
   - **how they feel about listening to this talk**

   Then, when the lecture begins, ask students to:
   - **outline or mindmap the significant points**
   - **underline the most important ideas**
   - **note in some way, such as with asterisks or stars, any point that is unclear or that is particularly interesting**
   - **put in the margin questions they wish to have answered. After ther mini-lecture is finished, ask students to write or explain:**
   - **what they learned that was new**
   - **how this topic relates to what they already knew**
   - **its relevance to their lives**

   Answer any questions students might pose after the mini-lecture, suggesting that they make note of the answers. Then ask the students to discuss the results of this task with a partner.

2. Another useful exercise is to ask students to listen to a mini-lecture without taking notes or making mindmaps. Immediately following the lecture, request that they

mindmap everything they remember, and categorize their information into topics. Then suggest they work with a partner to compare maps and fill in any points they omitted from their own. This is a useful exercise in developing both listening and memory skills. (Mindmapping is explained in the visual chapter.)

3. Teachers may want to provide students with a listening guide with blanks to fill in as information is presented. This is a useful framework for helping students to focus their listening, to think in an organized way, and to learn more about how to structure a future presentation of their own. A sample guide follows:

LISTENING GUIDE

Student name: _____

Speaker's name: _____

Title or subject of talk: _____

Introductory ideas: _____

_____

First main point: _____

_____

Supporting details or examples _____

_____

Second main point: _____

_____

Supporting details or examples: _____

_____

Third main point: _____

_____

Supporting detail or examples: _____

_____

Concluding ideas: _____

_____

Other ideas: _____

_____

Questions this presentation raised: _____

_____

SPEAKING

Effective speaking involves not only the words we use, but the way we say them, our tone of voice, facial expressions, posture, and gestures. Albert Mehrabian, author of *Silent Messages*, suggests that only seven per cent of what we communicate in speech has to do with the words we use, 38 per cent has to do with tone of voice, and 55 per cent with our facial expressions and body language. If this is so, then effective speaking involves all the intelligences!

It is essential for teachers to model effective speaking skills, since good modeling has a profound effect on the speaking habits of students. Teachers may make a point of using colorful or unusual vocabulary frequently, playing with puns, jokes, and riddles, or eloquently describing a personal experience.

The classroom can provide a supportive environment for learning to speak effectively as teachers create a relaxed and positive atmosphere for students to converse and discuss ideas. These are not classrooms in which the teacher is doing most of the talking! Questions that stimulate discussion should be thought-provoking and not easily answered in a few words. It is also important for teachers to ask open-ended, interesting questions to which they may not know the answer. As a result, stimulating discussions can take place that may lead to surprising insights and new possibilities for learning for all involved.

Clearly, students benefit from practicing and developing speaking skills through such exercises as the following:

STUDENTS AS STORYTELLERS

Some students will enthusiastically volunteer for opportunities to tell stories to their peers. Others will find the idea daunting. Yet listening to stories involves numerous listening skills, while telling stories requires linguistic stretches. Storytelling, both an entertaining and powerful form of linguistic communication, teaches students about the rhythm, pitch, and nuances of language. Educators interested in encouraging storytelling in their classrooms might want to consider the following guidelines:

Storytelling Guidelines:

1. *Model storytelling yourself.*

2. *Identify local storytellers to visit your classroom.* You may want to learn whether there is a storytelling guild near you or perhaps, as in Philadelphia, an official storyteller for the city.

3. *Help students find stories*—from class content, dreams, family or school events, stories they already know, anthologies, or interviews with senior citizens.

4. *Teach students some of the skills of storytelling such as:*

   • beginning with an interesting opening

   • keeping the number of characters manageable

   • making sure the story contains images that listeners can "see" or imagine

   • encouraging the use of simile and metaphor

   • animating key points in the story with sound effects, voice, hands, and body movements

   • keeping the voice clear, expressive, and well-paced

   • making eye contact with the audience

   • considering whether or not there will be audience participation

5. *Practice storytelling with the whole class.* The teacher can select one story and read it part by part to the class, asking students to suggest embellishments to make the story vivid and entertaining. The whole class could divide into groups. Each group could be assigned a section of the story to learn and then tell in sequence.

6. *For beginning storytellers, anxiety can be relieved when students tell their stories to small groups of four or five peers rather than to the whole class.* Students who volunteer may tell their stories to larger groups. Also telling stories to younger children often relieves unnecessary tension.

CLASSROOM DISCUSSIONS

Classroom discussions occur in nearly every subject at all grade levels. There are logistics to address such as the arrangement of physical space and ways to involve everyone in the conversation before discussions will be positive and satisfying. For example, teachers might consider how student desks or tables are arranged in the classroom. Does the current arrangement facilitate or impede student discussions? Might a U shape or a circle better accommodate student interaction?

There are numerous human dynamics that influence the quality of classroom discourse. Some students must learn to refrain from dominating the conversation. Others need encouragement to participate. It is challenging to keep a discussion on track, to pose higher level questions, and to teach students how to assume greater responsibility for leading classroom discussions. To address these and other issues, some suggestions follow for initiating, implementing, and debriefing discussions as well as involving everyone equally in the process.

The Five Stages of a Classroom Discussion

As Richard Arends indicates in *Learning to Teach* effective classroom discussions typically consist of five stages. These stages, when intentionally planned for, strengthen student discourse and reveal where intervention might be warranted. Some teachers assume that discussions require less planning than lectures or cooperative learning activities. Even though spontaneity and flexibility are important aspects of discussions, it is prior planning by the teacher that makes these features possible. When discussions are to be conducted in a classroom, teachers may want to plan for the five following stages to insure meaningful dialogue with and among their students.

1. *Explain the purpose of the discussion:* Teachers should explain what will be discussed as well as appropriate standards of student behavior. Questions can be posed, issues raised, or a puzzling situation presented to initiate the conversation.

2. *Hold the discussion:* Teachers can ask students specific questions or request volunteers to initiate student conversation. It is important to ensure that responses are listened to with courtesy. On the blackboard, a flip chart, or the overhead projector, a student volunteer might list or mindmap discussion contributions. Such processes keep the discourse on track as well as prevent redundant contributions.

Teachers can model effective discussion skills by responding to student questions in diverse ways. For example, to reflect on student ideas, statements such as, "I heard you say…" or "that is interesting because…" are helpful. In attempting to encourage students to consider diverse perspectives or alternative possibilities, a teacher might assume the role of devil's advocate, or ask, "You have provided one point of view about this topic. Are there other points of view? "How do your ideas compare with…?" David Perkins, Harvard psychologist, calls such questioning "unpacking your thinking."

Wait time should also be provided. When students are asked a question approximately one to three minutes of time should be provided before responses are considered. The teacher should also observe student participation carefully, encouraging those who are not comfortable speaking and keeping others from monopolizing discussions.

3. *Keep the discussion on track:* Students will often bring up issues not related to the topic at hand. Teachers can gently state that the focus of the conversation has shifted, and that the discussion should revert to the original topic. If many students appear interested in a subject raised by a peer, the teacher may choose to set aside classroom time for students to pursue the other topic later.

4. *End the discussion:* Discussions, like other lessons, should be brought to closure. The teacher may want to summarize what has been said, relate the discussion to other classroom learnings, or use it as a bridge to highlight new information.

5. *Debrief the discussion:* Teachers and students will both benefit from talking about how how the discussion proceeded. Questions such as, "How did the discussion work today?" "What would have made it more effective?" "Did everyone have a chance to participate?" "Did we listen effectively to everyone?"

Once students see discussions modeled effectively by the teacher and understand the stages of such discourse, they can then assume responsibility for leading either small or whole-group discussions themselves.

Involving Everyone in Discussions

In whole-class discussions many teachers find that only a small percentage of students actively participate. To encourage equitable participation, Richard Arends suggests the following strategies:

1. *One student can be assigned the role of discussion monitor.* This student keeps track of everyone's participation. If she notices that one student talks repeatedly, she might give that student a note asking that he refrain from speaking until others have had turns.

2. *Each student can be provided with three or four "talking tokens."* A token must be relinquished whenever a student makes a contribution. When all of a student's tokens are gone, she must refrain from speaking which encourages students who have tokens left to enter into the conversation.

3. *An additional technique that promotes one person talking at a time includes throwing a ball or passing a "talking stick" or rock to one student who volunteers to initiate the discussion.* Students are told that if they want to participate they must raise their hands and receive the object before making their contributions.

Facilitating Small Group Discussions

Many students and adults are hesitant to participate in large, whole-group discussions and prefer instead to talk with fewer people. One way to broaden participation for all students is to use the collaborative strategies offered below:

Think-Pair-Share

To encourage student reflection on the content of a lecture, a film, or a provocative question, the teacher can pose a question or raise an issue. Students are given one to two minutes to think individually. They are then paired with classmates to discuss their thinking for approximately five minutes. For the final step, each pair shares with the whole class what they have discussed.

Buzz Groups

Teachers can arrange students in groups of three to six to discuss ideas about a particular topic. Each group assigns one person to serve as the recorder who lists all of the ideas suggested by the group. After several minutes of discussion, the teacher asks the recorders to summarize the ideas and opinions expressed in his or her group.

Fishbowls

Fishbowls are effective group processes to use during the middle or end of a unit. To conduct a fishbowl, classroom chairs or desks are arranged in a large circle, with a smaller, inner circle of chairs provided for four to six students. Those sitting in the inner circle are in "the fishbowl," and they have the task of discussing a topic while the rest of the students watch. Any student in the fishbowl, after having contributed whatever she wanted to the conversation, vacates her seat. Observers are free to fill any vacancy in the inner circle. The fishbowl continues until the discussion reaches a natural conclusion or the teacher brings closure to the process.

MEMORIZING

Although memorization has fallen out of favor in many classrooms, there is no better way to free the mind to concentrate on oral presentation or writing skills than to memorize basic facts, a poem, or lines in a play. The fringe benefit is that many of these pieces remain in the memory for life and provide solace, amusement, or inspiration when recalled.

Young students may memorize nursery rhymes, jingles, or short, lively poems, such as those in Jill Bennet's *Noisy Poems*, to say first as a group to inspire confidence, and then as solo volunteers. Older students may wish to memorize longer pieces, such as Poe's "The Raven" or Langston Hughes' "The Dreamkeeper" to present to the class, perhaps choosing to use sound effects, background music, or costumes. Choral reading at any age develops greater flexibility in range and tone of voice, and conveys the rhythm of language while encouraging emotional expression. Since singing often enhances the quality and flexibility of the voice, it is useful to have the class sing poems that have been set to music.

Poems or jingles can also be written by students or the teacher to use as mnemonic devices to remember information in many subjects such as history, science, or geography. For example, jingles can be made up to remember the order of the stars in the solar system or the process of the water cycle. Medical students have for generations used rhymes to remember the names of bones in the hand and other parts of the human body. Memory tricks can even improve spelling.

Improving Memory

When students are asked to memorize any kind of content, it is important to realize that repetition alone has little value unless accompanied by active student involvement. Information will, quite literally, go in one ear and out the other without strong memory encoding. To help students memorize important information, the following strategies can be suggested:

1. Students might first review the entire piece they are to memorize. This gives an overview of the task and provides mental hooks for later learning.

2. Students can "cluster" or "chunk" portions of the content to memorize it, and create visual images for each section. Their visual images can be drawn or simply imagined.

3. Content can also be set to music to help facilitate long-term memory.

4. Students might tape record what they want to memorize. They can play the tape back frequently to enhance recall of the content.

5. Short memorizing sessions are often more productive than long ones. Explain to students that memory work should not exceed more than 30 minutes at a time.

6. Review schedules are necessary for information to be retained. Explain to students that memory is greatly reinforced when items are reviewed the following day, a week later, a month later, and so on.

REPORTS

Students are often asked to give reports in class. Report-giving typically begins in early elementary grades with "Show and Tell' and progresses to formal research reports often required in high school classes. The kinds of reports

teachers assign vary greatly both in content, format, and assessment criteria. Students benefit by explicitly knowing how to format their presentations. Typical guidelines for formal reports often include:

Guidelines for Reports:

- select a topic suitable for the audience
- organize the presentation
- plan an attention-grabbing opening
- use colorful anecdotes and specific examples
- involve the audience in some activity, and
- plan an effective conclusion.

Further points include suggestions for oral reports:

- choose appropriate vocabulary for the topic and audience
- engage the audience with eye-contact and body-language
- use clear diction and good grammar
- avoid speaking in long, rambling sentences
- use effective and varied expression, and
- avoid using "a's" and "ums."

To help stimulate interest in conducting research for their reports, students can identify the facts, suppositions, and questions they have about their selected topic. Questions can be posed such as:

> **What do I know for sure?**
> **What do I think I know and**
> **What do I want to know?**

As with peer-review of written work, the response of the audience to an oral report should first of all be positive. Feedback can be given in an "appreciation sandwich" format by first specifying what was good about the presentation, then offering suggestions for improvement, and ending with another positive comment.

INTERVIEWS

Interviewing others is one way for students to develop oral information-gathering skills. Before conducting interviews, students need to distinguish between an interview and a conversation. While both are forms of oral communication, conversations consist of informal talk or the exchange of ideas on topics of interest to those speaking. By contrast, interviews have a pre-determined goal; the interviewer seeks specific information and avoids topics that may be considered irrelevant. For example, doctors interview patients about their symptoms; reporters interview people to gather information for a story; high school students interview pro-fessionals to learn about different careers; personnel directors interview prospective employ-ees. Teachers and students may want to brain-storm lists of interview situations and discuss the purposes inherent in each. It may be appro-priate for students to interview those of diverse cultures, careers, or expertise to complement their academic studies.

It is helpful for students to know what consti-tutes effective interviewing skills. Some suggestions follow which may be used to prepare for or assess student interviews once completed:

EFFECTIVE INTERVIEWING SKILLS

- **Be prepared for the interview. Know what you want to ask and what the purpose of the interview is.**

- **Schedule the interview at a mutually agreed upon time.**

- **Know how you are going to take notes. If you are tape-recording the interview, secure permission from the interviewee before proceeding.**

- **Encourage the interviewee to talk.**

- **Maintain a friendly facial expression, adopt positive body language, and be polite.**

- **Be a careful listener, and avoid asserting your own opinions or comments.**

- **Ask open-ended questions that elicit more than a simple "yes" or "no" response.**

- **Keep the interview on the subject.**

- **Keep the interview within preset time limits.**

- **Once the interview has ended, review what was said to help retain the information in your long-term memory.**

- **Write a thank-you note to the person you interviewed.**

To prepare students for interviewing, the teacher may want to divide the class into small groups to role play different interview circum-stances. Perhaps students will be interviewing younger children at their school, famous athletes or artists, community activists, school board members, or even each other. In their small groups, students can brainstorm appropriate questions for each circumstance, as well as role play interviews. While two students role play, other group members can observe the effective-ness of the interview and suggest improvements. Such activities assist students in developing the skills for the real-life interviews they are about to conduct.

READING

Literature provides the foundation for exercising and developing the whole gamut of verbal-linguistic intelligence. Stories, novels, biographies, essays, plays, and poems provide the starting point for developing active listening skills, speaking projects, and creative or analytical writing. Such materials offer food for thought since they model the effective use of language and stimulate intellectual development.

An increasing number of curriculum planners and teachers are replacing textbooks with real books that offer examples of the finest writing in various genres and that may prove to be more interesting and relevant to student interests.

FINDING MATERIALS

Stephen Tchudi, author of *Planning and Assessing the Curriculum in English Language Arts*, suggests that teachers seeking appropriate reading materials for their classrooms should "become specialists in books for children and young adults, exploring and reviewing new and classic titles in fiction and nonfiction."

Developing a Classroom Library:

Tchudi suggests that teachers may develop their classroom libraries by:

- **working closely with school librarians and media specialists,**
- **involving parents in recommending and donating books**
- **forming liaisons with education directors of area newspapers**
- **meeting with paperback book distributors to work out special price deductions**
- **creating a review group of students**
- **asking other faculty members to suggest appropriate reading materials**
- **conducting community "scavenger hunts" for good reading materials from such sources as garage sales**

- **introducing students to electronic databases or the Internet in order to access current information on topics they find interesting.**

Even with large classes, it is important for teachers to identify the developmental levels and interests of individual students. Reluctant readers may perk up when they have opportunities to read books related to specific interests such as their heroes, hobbies, pets, inventions, scientific discoveries, favorite sports, music groups, or foreign countries. Every attempt should be made to have resources at hand to capitalize on their interests with reading materials that are appropriate for their diverse developmental levels.

WORDS IN THE CLASSROOM

In every classroom there are words on the walls, bulletin boards, and blackboards explaining classroom rules, listing assignments, and describing daily schedules. Teachers can intentionally pay attention to the use of language in their classrooms and can identify how to capitalize upon the essential skill of reading. Some teachers have developed effective motivators to encourage students to read which follow:

Motivating students to read:

1. Post daily quotations or questions and weekly curricular vocabularies to enrich literacy and student interest in academic content.

2. Hang word and concept mobiles from the classroom ceiling.

3. Add names or labels to classroom posters, blackboards, and student papers.

4. Set aside classroom space for a note and message board or have a notebook positioned on a podium to spark informal reading and writing. Students are usually curious about what classmates and teachers write, and will avidly read what's newly posted.

Other important reading resources in the classroom are the worksheets students use. As often as possible, teachers should prepare their own worksheets and exercises based on classroom experiences and vocabulary. Such materials are more relevant for students than impersonally written textbooks. Since students learn at varying rates and in different ways, textbooks and workbooks have to be adapted and extended regardless of their quality.

Many students suffer from poor reading skills or may have little motivation. Fortunately, there are ways teachers can enhance the quantity and quality of reading in all content areas. While each teacher must make adaptations appropriate for his students, content, and teaching style, the questions offered below may assist educators in determining how best to teach reading across the curriculum.

Reflecting on Classroom Reading

1. What kinds of classroom activities naturally incorporate reading and how might I capitalize on them?

2. How can I accommodate the reading differences among my students?

3. What can I share from my own knowledge and interests that might motivate students to read course materials?

4. What do I know about my students that I can use to enhance their reading?

5. How might I effectively link classroom experiences with required reading?

6. How can I teach specific reading skills appropriate for my subject matter?

7. How might I assist students who struggle with reading?

READING FOR UNDERSTANDING

There are numerous approaches to teaching reading that are effective with some students but not others. While programs abound with claims for improving reading skills and specifically reading comprehension, James Moffett, a noted language arts specialist and co-author of *Student-Centered Language Arts K-12*, maintains that many reading problems are due to lack of student motivation. To improve comprehension, Moffett emphasizes the importance of providing opportunities for students to attend to what is read, recall content, and infer the author's meaning. Such skills can be taught in ways that are engaging and motivating. Some of Moffett's suggestions follow.

Improving Reading Comprehension:

1. To help students pay attention to and recall information from their readings in any subject matter area, it is beneficial to organize the class into small groups for interactive discussions. Whenever possible, use role plays to enliven the text. This requires students not only to read the information, but also to synthesize and communicate it.

2. Both dramatization and small group discussions are helpful in teaching students how to draw inferences. Students can be asked to cite evidence from the text to support their discussion or role play ideas. The process of building and canceling inferences teaches students about their own thought processes while revealing the reasons for misunderstanding. Assuming numerous points of view identified in the text offers another approach to addressing inference.

3. Students, as writers, can experience inference in action. Students can mutually explore the intentions of the writer and the assumptions of the reader by writing about their readings and then sharing their summaries and cri-

tiques with classmates. In either case, the original text should be readily available for easy reference. Writing activities provide insight into how both composition and comprehension are dependent upon the reader completing the text. When students are writers they must make decisions about what to include, omit, emphasize, or downplay. This helps clarify that when reading, students must actively round out the text to discern the author's intentions.

WRITING

Writing cannot be segregated from other language acts. It is reinforced by speaking, listening, and reading. Fully incorporating language arts activities into all content areas helps students communicate more effectively as well as learn more thoroughly. As in speech, writing carries ideas from one person to another, with distinct purposes and meanings. Students, through a variety of writing activities, can develop a sense of audience and perceive writing as a relevant act occurring between themselves, others, and society.

As with other areas of verbal-linguistic intelligence, it is essential for teachers and parents to model effective writing skills, demonstrating pleasure in the writing process and efforts to refine their skills. Teachers interested in improving their writing ability can find support and inspiration in such sources as William Zinsser's *On Writing Well*, Natalie Goldberg's *Writing Down the Bones*, or Henriette Klauser's *Writing on Both Sides of the Brain*. A dictionary, thesaurus, Strunk and White's *Elements of Style,* and the *New York Times Stylebook* ought to be accessible in any classroom.

Teachers can model specific writing skills for students whenever they think out loud about how to choose a topic, read samples of their own writing for students to critique (this takes courage), or write occasional lengthy comments on student papers with great care. They may wish to share with their students a piece of their writing at various stages, pointing out the number of revisions and corrections on subsequent drafts.

CATEGORIES OF WRITING

James Britton, in his classic book *Language and Learning,* categorizes writing in a way that offers insight for teachers into the kinds of written work they assign. Teachers may want to read the following descriptions of Britton's four categories to identify diverse writing approaches that may be appropriate for their lessons:

Britton's categories include the **mechanical** uses of writing such as multiple-choice exercises, fill-in-the blank, short-answer, math calculations, transcription from written or oral material, and translation. This form of writing predominates in many classrooms.

The second category has to do with the **informational** uses of writing, such as note-taking, recording of experience (in a report or diary), summary, analysis, theory, or the persuasive uses of writing.

The third includes the **personal** uses of writing, such as diaries and journals, letters, and notes.

The last includes the **imaginative** uses of writing such as in stories and poetry.

Although it is important that students write accurately and correctly on tasks related to the first category, it is also important to focus on increasing the number of experiences in the other three categories since these hold the greatest promise for exercising and developing verbal-linguistic intelligence.

WRITING ACROSS THE CURRICULUM

Many content-area teachers are hesitant to assume the role of writing and reading teacher when they already have an abundance of content to teach in their disciplines. There are, however, numerous ways to promote linguistic activities in all disciplines that will promote subject matter understanding. A brief survey of language-based activities is offered below:

History and Social Studies:

1. Students can conduct local history projects and then create newspapers or news broadcasts of what they learn.

2. In some schools, students with special expertise in technology are doing research on computer networks for their state legislatures and senates. Letter writing about local social or political issues can also be e-mailed to prominent citizens or groups.

3. Correspondence among students in urban or rural schools can provide insight into the similarities and differences both groups encounter.

Foreign Language and Bi-Lingual Education:

1. After listening to songs in another language, students can use new and familiar vocabulary to make their own word games by writing short definitions, antonyms, homonyms, or synonyms for some of the lyrics.

2. Students might take photographs of their school and local environments, bring the pictures to school, and then write about what the photos portray. At some schools, such activities have evolved into school guidebooks for newly arrived, non-English speaking students and their families.

3. Teachers can bring folklore, poems, riddles, and puzzles from various cultures into the classroom, read part way through a selection, and then ask the class to complete the piece. Student-suggested endings can be compared with the original literature.

Science and Mathematics:

1. Journals or logs can serve as notebooks for students to record explanations and examples given in class, to list their questions, confusions, or criticisms, and to offer suggestions to improve classroom learning experiences.

2. Take-home writing projects for math and science might focus on community growth issues. Students can research and write about local development and its challenges.

3. Students can watch science fiction programs on television and write brief analyses of what is fact and what is fiction.

Language Arts:

English teachers are often hesitant to include science or social studies content in their curriculum. However, there are many scientific and social issues that provide stimulating topics for students to consider. Possibilities include the environment, social and political issues, the space program, genetic engineering, computers, video games, energy alternatives, and the modern diet. In addition, some students would enjoy writing about popular culture or the current or future job market.

WRITING OPTIONS FOR ALL CONTENT AREAS

In any subject matter area, students may be especially motivated to write after a field trip, seeing a demonstration or video, or listening to an interesting guest speaker. When debriefing such experiences, the teacher can record student comments on the board, and categorize them into separate topics. For example, after an early elementary grade's trip to the zoo, the teacher might ask what animals were seen, what their environments were like, and what students learned as they observed the different animals. Students can use the recorded vocabulary (which has already been correctly spelled) and add their own ideas to write in any one of several formats.

Other Stimuli

Students also enjoy writing to taped sound effects, or lively, dramatic, or mysterious music, as suggested in the musical chapter. Pantomime and creative dramatics activities, as described in the chapter on kinesthetic intelligence, lead to interesting writing options as well. Students of any age can generate possible topics by doing a "quick-write," starting with a "fuse" such as "On the first day of the year 2000, I…" "You will never believe this, but…" and writing for five or ten minutes as fast as possible without attention to mechanics. These processes often access ideas lurking in the deep sources of creativity.

Teachers can suggest numerous alternatives for writing assignments. Instead of traditional procedures where every student completes the same assignment, students can make their own decisions about which options best suit their topics and their interests. Some writing suggestions follow that may be useful for various content areas:

Student Writing Options:

scripts for dramas, television, or radio productions
slogans or bumper stickers
petitions
imaginary diaries
directions
excerpts from one's own experience
writing from another perspective
songs
graffiti walls
bulletin boards
labels and captions
scrolls
advertisements
classroom newsletters
poems
how-to-manuals
collections of folklore, riddles, jokes, explanations,
pamphlets, brochures
letters
dialogues
awards
posters
bookmarks, or book jackets
prescriptions for help in a content area
free writing samples
self-evaluations
checklists
sequels
interviews
booklets
dictation
editorial essays

The above list of options, as well as samples of previous student work can suggest numerous ways for students to approach the same topic.

Presenting one's written work to the class provides a powerful learning opportunity for the author as well as for fellow students to view the same topic through numerous linguistic lenses.

GETTING STARTED WITH WRITING

Even though they may have interesting ideas for possible topics, writers of any age often have difficulty starting their work. Professional writers have suggestions for overcoming this obstacle. One author begins each session by turning on lively music and dancing out her ideas. Another makes "clusters" or mindmaps filling pages as quickly as she can with free flowing ideas. This author writes her books directly from mindmap to computer. Others like to write with certain kinds of paper and pencils or other special tools. Still others find it useful to change environments—by going into another room, exercising briefly, or working in a place that feels comfortable and inviting. One well-known writer spends ten or fifteen minutes reading one of his favorite authors before he begins writing. He says it gives him a running start for the day.

Other possibilities to jumpstart writing include foregoing the beginning by writing the middle of the piece, or writing the ending first, writing with or without music, jotting down notes with colored pens or pencils or on colored paper, quick writing on the computer, stream-of-consciousness writing, talking ideas over with a friend, talking into a tape-recorder, or brainstorming ideas with a classmate.

Another idea for writing is so unusual that it often produces startling results. Glossalalia is made-up language or gibberish. Students might attempt writing an entire paragraph in glossalalia (the weirder the words the better) and then translating it. It may be helpful to provide them with the following sentences to "translate" before writing their own:

> **Weinsth guek einc ei! Ptionsiu dfetkj, atin et tetp slier ae ads etioj aseint. "Laeltij, iaeltij, iaelti," giaj Skloiae. "Lawei di Ieti?"**

Possible to do in pen or pencil, this jumpstarter is even more fun on a computer and provides a unique warm-up for writers of all ages.

THE REAL WORK OF WRITING

Many students have experienced the humiliation of receiving corrected papers covered with red marks. It may have appeared to them that correcting errors in grammar, spelling, or punctuation is the final step in writing a paper. Yet, as all of us know from our own efforts, writing is a process, with each draft warranting not only corrections but numerous revisions and refinements. It is important for students to realize that most professional writers spend a good deal of time rewriting, revising, deleting, adding, changing paragraphs, and polishing before they submit their work to an editor. There are many ways to involve students in the process of writing. Some suggestions follow:

Nurturing an Appreciation for the Process of Writing

1. Teachers can review samples of professional writing with their students. They may wish, for example, to duplicate an article such as an 800 word newspaper column that is crisp and succinct and encourages the reader to read further. Students can analyze what makes the selection lively and suggest the choices the author may have made to create her well-written piece.

2. Local writers might be provide earlier drafts of their published works and explain how and why they made the changes they did. Students might then analyze drafts of their own writing to determine ways to improve upon their initial efforts.

3. Timely and frequent feedback is important as students practice their writing skills. Students may initially receive feedback from their peers or even write collaboratively, but individual appointments with the teacher at various stages of their work provide important opportunities for feedback and guidance.

4. Teachers may offer constructive suggestions on first drafts and withhold grading until final revisions are made. It is often in the process of discussing revisions and corrections that students are the most receptive to learning about the mechanics of language. Lessons in punctuation, parts of speech, and grammatical usage are seldom retained when they are presented out of context. A quick lesson at a "teachable moment" when students are struggling with some problem may be the most relevant and lasting way for them to learn.

5. Students who use word processors can produce written work that looks deceptively polished when nicely formatted on a computer; yet most likely, it still requires reworking. Students will find it useful to print out the first draft double-spaced, then do the revising by hand. In this way, they will have a record of the revisions they have made.

6. Keeping all drafts in sequence in a portfolio provides both students and teachers with comprehensive records of writing progress. Specific information about portfolios can be found in the assessment chapter.

! preposition

noun ;

vocabulary ?

: adjective

adverb

"

WRITING GROUPS

Most teachers do not have time to correct all the written work their students produce. Since there is no better way for students to learn to write than by writing, managing student feedback is an important challenge. One way to ensure that students receive feedback as well as develop editing skills is to use writing groups. Such groups typically consist of three to four students who work together for the duration of a project, quarter, or in some cases for longer periods of time. The group serves as a sounding board for ideas about a writing topic, gives feedback on rough drafts, listens to readings, makes suggestions for improvement, and sees the writing project through from beginning to end. Above all, the writing group offers support and encouragement for the difficult task of improving written work.

As writing groups are formed, it is important to discuss how students can offer constructive feedback to one another. Teachers can explain the negative effects of "rejection slip trauma" and how important it is to phrase suggestions in positive ways.

Together, the students and teacher may identify appropriate ways to respond to the writing of others. Some suggestions follow:

- Listen carefully and thoughtfully as the piece is being read.

- Note what is especially good about the writing, being as specific as possible in regard to content, mechanics, theme, tone, vocabulary, form, and general effect.

- Note ways in which the writing might be improved, once again making specific suggestions.

- Take turns reporting back to the author, always beginning with positive comments.

- As the author, listen carefully and take notes that may be used in revising the piece.

Writing groups, like many other strategies suggested throughout this book, shift the role of the teacher to that of a "guide on the side." As students shoulder more responsibility for their academic work, they must organize, manage, and refine their learning as well as provide assistance to their peers. When given such responsibility, students usually rise to the occasion, much to their personal benefit and their teacher's delight.

TECHNOLOGY THAT ENHANCES VERBAL-LINGUISTIC INTELLIGENCE

Just as the printing press revolutionized learning and thinking in the 15th century, so the computer has created a similar revolution today. Through worldwide databases and computer networks students have direct access to current information. In every field of knowledge, educational systems are transforming as both teachers and students learn to use multimedia technology. Children who cannot yet read are writing stories on the computer with software that in some cases reads back to the students what they have written. New programs allow children to write and insert graphics in rebus-like texts such as Wings for Learning/ Sunburst's "Muppet Slate." Other programs, such as Microsoft's "Fine Artist and Creative Writer," make it possible to format writing projects in different shapes, write words in unusual forms and sizes, add accompanying sound effects, and wrap illustrations around the text. Such programs are highly motivating for both beginning and more accomplished writers.

Today's computer banks filled with information on every conceivable subject, plus on-line experts including university professors, researchers, and scientists, offer students an inexhaustible supply of information. Course content in any subject can be enriched and updated from such sources, and it is frequently the students themselves who access and share the information.

A high school student talks about "surfing the Net" one evening and coming across the Magna Carta. He had never seen the document even though he had read about it in many of his history books. Excitedly he printed it out and took it to school the next day with a strong sense of ownership. Such discoveries make learning personal and exciting as students make knowledge their own.

Increasingly user-friendly computer programs are making it possible to combine information in different forms, including words, images, and sounds. Students can store, sort, and cross-reference information, notes, bibliographies, and create multimedia reports to make an adventure of learning. Teachers are able to develop their own courseware, create databases linking documents, present preprogrammed slide presentations from videodiscs, and enrich their courses with a wealth of the technology described in the chapters on each of the other intelligences.

The computer encourages students to revise and rewrite compositions and thus develop greater fluency and a more effective style. Recopying by hand or typewriter often inhibits ongoing correction and revision, but the computer facilitates these processes and gives students a greater sense of control over their writing. When students see their work in professional-looking formats they become more interested in studying and mastering the mechanics that will give it final polish. Some of the most popular word processing programs include Microsoft Word, Word Perfect, and Ami Pro for Windows.

Learning keyboarding in early elementary school today is as important as learning to write with a pencil, and learning to use a word processor is as important for students as learning to type. Children are encouraged to use these skills in communicating and collaborating with distant students on a variety of projects, through an increasing number of electronic networks. Telephones and modems essential to this process should be standard equipment in every classroom.

Electronic technology is having an enormous impact on the development of speaking skills, as children find it possible to communicate with new friends around the country and world. Most school districts have access to projects such as the National Geographic Kids Network. Just as the computer has enhanced writing skills, so audiotape-recording, video-taping, and video-conferencing are having positive effects on oral fluency. When students observe and hear themselves speaking, they learn to express themselves effectively.

Technology offers new communication and learning opportunities to students with multiple handicaps and "different abilities." For example, students who are physically unable to move can talk into a computer that writes as they speak. Others who are able to move but not speak can write on computers that then "say" what was written. Specific examples include:

- for deaf students: Microflip's "Full Talk," LTJ Design's "Wee Talk"

- for physically-handicapped students: "Smart Keyboards" fit the body shape of their users and are developed by Arjan Khalsa for Unicorn

- for blind students: Eduquest's "talking mouse"

- for hearing-impaired students: EduQuest's "Speech Viewer" and "Phone Communicator"

- for visually-impaired students: EduQuest's "Screen Reader" and "Voice Type"

The development of linguistic skills for all populations can be catalyzed by remarkable new electronic tools for accessing and managing information and communicating, learning, and developing intelligence in unprecedented ways.

SUMMARY

How do we help students fall in love with words? A passion for language can lead students to savor the sound of words, to respect and use their power responsibly, to explore their subtle shades of meaning, and to draw upon them in endless ways to express love or sympathy, win an argument, explain a complex task, teach a younger child, or simply to enjoy communicating with others.

Some years ago, Robert Frost was speaking to an entranced group of students who with furrowed brows were seriously trying to take down every word he said. Suddenly, in mid-sentence, he stopped and said, "Put down your pencils and just listen! Doesn't matter whether you are going to be a writer or mathematician or scientist or artist—If you can't play with ideas and get the fun of it, you just 'ahn't' gettin' it!"

This thought has been a hopeful one for many of those who listened that evening. Writing and speaking effectively, listening sensitively, and reading for deep understanding are hard work. It is not worth the effort, however, unless there are bountiful rewards and fun in the process. We must help all students to enjoy these

rewards early on, since they build from one small success to the next while gathering sustenance for further efforts.

This chapter offers suggestions for creative language experiences as well as practical applications in listening, speaking, reading, and writing. Through these experiences, educators can help students appreciate the value of their literary work not only in their own lives but also as contributions to their community and the greater world around them.

In a recent article, Leon Botstein, president of Bard College, writes that "the key instrument in our tradition of education is literacy and the use of language." He notes that "hope is contingent on the possession of language. The animal can't hope because it does not possess language. Hope is not an emotion but a function of language, and is thus contingent on education. To create hope in a society, there must be education."

In order to help the reader to summarize, reflect upon, and synthesize the contents of this chapter, the following is offered:

APPLYING VERBAL-LINGUISTIC INTELLIGENCE:

1. Important ideas or insights gleaned from this chapter: _____
_____
_____
_____
_____
_____
_____
_____

2. Areas I'd like to learn more about: _____
_____
_____
_____
_____
_____
_____
_____

3. Ways I can use this information in my teaching. Please note that the strategies mentioned in this chapter are listed below with space provided to note how each strategy might be incorporated into classroom instruction:

VERBAL-LINGUISTIC STRATEGY   **CLASSROOM APPLICATION**

**Establishing a Verbal-Linguistic
Learning Environment:**   _____

Listening to Learn:
    Keys to Effective Listening   _____
    Listening to Stories and Reading Aloud   _____
    Biographical Resources   _____
    Listening to Poetry   _____
    Teachers as Storytellers   _____
    Cultural Dimensions of Storytelling   _____
    Multicultural Storytelling Resources   _____
    Resources on the Art of Storytelling   _____
    Listening to Lectures   _____

Speaking:
    Students as Storytellers   _____
    Storytelling Guidelines   _____
    Classroom Discussions   _____
    The Five Stages of Classroom Discussions   _____
    Involving Everyone in Discussion   _____
    Facilitating Small Group Discussions   _____
    Think-Pair-Share   _____
    Buzz Groups   _____
    Fish Bowls   _____
    Memorizing   _____
    Improving Memory   _____
    Report Writing   _____
    Guidelines for Reports   _____
    Interviews   _____
    Effective Interviewing Skills   _____

Reading:

Finding Good Materials

Words in the Classroom

Motivating Students to Read

Reflecting on Classroom Reading

Reading for Understanding

Improving Reading Comprehension

_____

_____

_____

_____

_____

_____

Writing:

Categories of Writing

Writing across the Curriculum

History and Social Studies

Foreign Language and English
  as a Second Language

Science and Math

Language Arts

Writing Options for All Content Areas

Other Stimuli

Student Writing options

Getting Started with Writing

The Real Work of Writing

Nurturing an Appreciation for the
  Writing Process

Writing Groups

_____

_____

_____

_____

_____

_____

_____

_____

_____

_____

_____

_____

_____

Technology that Enhances Verbal-Linguistic Intelligence:

_____

VERBAL-LINGUISTIC REFERENCES

Arends, R. (1994). *Learning to Teach*. N.Y. McGraw-Hill Inc.

Applebee, A. N. (1981). *Writing in the Secondary School*. Urbana, Il: National Council of Teachers of English.

Bennett, J. (1987). *Noisy Poems*. Oxford: Oxford University Press.

Britton, J. (1970). *Language and Learning*. Harmondsworth, England: Penguin.

Burley-A. (1982). *Listening, the Forgotten Skill*. N.Y.: John Wiley and Sons, Inc.

Chenfeld, M. B. (1978). *Teaching Language Arts Creatively*. N.Y.: Harcourt and Brace.

Christensen, M. (1992). *Motivational English for At-Risk Students*. Bloomington, Indiana: National Educational Service.

Dean, J. F. (1983). *Writing Well: 60 Simply-Super Lessons to Motivate and Improve Students' Writing*. Belmont, CA: David S. Lake Publishers.

Elbow, P. (1981). *Writing with Power: Techniques for Mastering the Writing Process*. N.Y.: Oxford University Press.

Forester, A. D., and Reinhard, M. (1989). *The Learners' Way*. Manitoba, Canada: Peguis Publishers.

Forester, A.D. and Reinhard, M. (1991). *On the Move*. Manitoba, Canada: Peguis Publishers.

Gardner, H. (1983). *Frames of Mind: The Theory of Multiple Intelligences*. N.Y.: Basic Books.

Goldberg, N. (1986). *Writing Down the Bones: Freeing the Writer Within*. Boston: Shambhala Publications.

Hill, M. *Time for Poetry—a Teacher's Anthology*. (1951). Glenview, Il: Scott Foresman.

Jacobs, L.B. (1971). *Animal Antics in Limerick Land*. Champaign, Il: Garrard.

Klauser, H. (1986). *Writing on Both Sides of the Brain: Breakthrough Techniques for People Who Write*. San Francisco: Harper and Row.

Kobrin, Beverly. (1988). *Eyeopeners: How to Choose and Use Children's Books About Real People, Places and Things*. N.Y.: Viking Penguin.

Langer, J. A. and Applebee, A.N. (1987). *How Writing Shapes Thinking: A Study of Teaching and Learning*. Urbana, Il: National Council of Teachers of English.

McCracken, R.A. and Marlene J. (1987). *Stories, Songs, and Poetry to Teach Reading and Writing*. Winnipeg: Peguis Publishers.

Means, B. and Lindner, L. (1988). *Clear and Lively Writing: Creative Ideas and Activities, Grades 6-10*. Englewood, CO: Libraries Unlimited, Inc.

Moffett, J. and Wagner, B.J. (1992). *Student-Centered Language Arts, K-12*. Portsmouth, NH: Heinemann.

Piaget, Jean. (1926). *The Language and Thought of the Child*. N.Y.: Harcourt Brace.

Piening, E. and Lyons, N. (1979). *Educating as an Art: The Rudolf Steiner Method*. N.Y.: The Rudolf Steiner Press.

Rico, G. L. (1983). *Writing the Natural Way: Using Right-Brain Techniques to Release Your Expressive Powers*. Los Angeles: J.P. Tarcher.

Sandburg, C. (1950). *Complete Poems*. N.Y.: Harcourt Brace.

Smagorinsky, P., McCann, T., and Kern, S. (1987). *Explorations: Introductory Activities for Literature and Composition, 7-12*. Urbana, Il: ERIC Clearinghouse on Reading and Communication Skills and the National Council of Teachers of English.

Smagorionsky, P. (1991). *Expressions: Multiple Intelligences in the English Class*. Urbana, Il.: National Council of Teachers of English.

Smith, F. (1971). *Understanding Reading*. N.Y.: Holt, Rinehart and Winston.

Strunk, W. and White, E.B. (1979). *The Elements of Style*. N.Y.: Macmillan Publishing Co., Inc.

Tchudi, S. (1991). *Planning and Assessing the Curriculum in English Language Arts*. Alexandria, VA: Association for Supervision and Curriculum Development.

Troyka, L. Q. and Nudelman, J. (1975). *Taking Action: Writing, Reading, Speaking, and Listening Through Simulation Games*. Englewood Cliffs, N.J.: Prentice-Hall.

Williams, L. (1981). *The Oak Meadow School Curriculum Guide: Third Grade*. Ojai, CA: Oak Meadow Publications.

Zinsser, W. (1988). *On Writing Well*. N.Y.: Harper and Row.

CHAPTER 2

THE CALCULATING MIND:
LOGICAL-MATHEMATICAL INTELLIGENCE

"That vast book which stands forever open before our eyes, the universe, cannot be read until we have learned the language and become familiar with the character in which it is written. It is written in mathematical language, without which means it is humanly impossible to comprehend a single word."

— Galileo, 1663

FOR THE LOVE OF NUMBERS

When he was two years old, Daniel squealed with delight every time his mother uttered any random string of numbers such as 21, 47, 63, 150, 2,679.

Not only was the sound of numbers pleasing, but the abstract symbols themselves conveyed mysteries to be solved. Pieces of cereal in the cereal bowl had to be counted and numerically written, the rocks outside on the driveway, and the toys in the toy box had to be known by quantity. By the time Daniel was three, questions of time, sequence, and the concept of multiplication dominated his interest. To him, a half hour meant how long it took to watch a favorite television program or to drive to the grocery store. To the surprise of his parents, he could open a computer program in a series of steps he memorized as he watched them work. Multiplication grew more interesting

than random numbers as he perceived and manipulated predictable patterns. When he was playing toddler basketball, Daniel assigned each basket a number and practiced the times tables as he played. His basketball scores mounted quickly as did Daniel's memorization of the multiplication facts.

In first grade, he was fascinated by the concept of negative numbers. Daniel's teacher accommodated his advanced skills by providing him with fourth and fifth grade math textbooks and by asking him open-ended questions that challenged his higher-level thinking skills. Throughout his elementary years, math was, expectedly, the boy's favorite

For the love of numbers ...continued

subject. Outside of school, new facets of interest emerged: computing sports statistics, classifying objects into similar categories, figuring out time differences across the globe, and posing questions about space.

Today, as a middle schooler, Daniel's interest in math is evident not only in the advanced math classes he takes, but also in his joy in problem-solving real world issues. For fun, he asks his mother to "quiz him" with mathematical story problems, and enjoys helping his family make decisions about household budget matters. At 13, Daniel has developed numerous shortcuts to mathematical problem-solving easily beating adults and sometimes calculators at computational tasks. He often spends leisure hours sorting and pricing a sports card collection, measuring distance, and at school, scores among the highest in national math competitions. He is exacting about issues with time, scoffs at faulty reasoning, and still smiles at the sound of numbers whenever they are used in conversation. Whatever studies Daniel will pursue in high school and beyond, it is likely that math will be at the core of his interests.

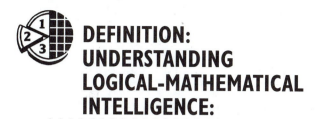

DEFINITION: UNDERSTANDING LOGICAL-MATHEMATICAL INTELLIGENCE:

Gardner suggests Piaget's model of cognitive development progressing from sensori-motor activities to formal operations, was, perhaps, a description of development in one domain, that of logical-mathematical intelligence. Piaget mapped the progression of logical intelligence beginning with a child's interactions with objects in the environment, to the discovery of number, to the transition from concrete objects to abstract symbols, to the manipulation of abstractions, and, finally, to the consideration of hypothetical statements with their relationships and implications. Gardner doubts that Piaget's ideas of cognitive development apply equally well to other realms of human competence.

As is evident in the story about Daniel, logical-mathematical intelligence involves numerous components: mathematical calculations, logical thinking, problem-solving, deductive and inductive reasoning, and the discernment of patterns and relationships. At the core of mathematical ability is the ability to recognize and solve problems. While this intelligence has been of great importance to Western society and is often credited with guiding the course of human history, Gardner contends that logical-mathematical intelligence is not necessarily superior to other intelligences nor is it universally perceived with the highest esteem. There are other problem-solving and logical processes inherent in each of the intelligences. Each intelligence possesses its own ordering mechanism, principles, core operations, and media that logical-mathematical intelligence cannot reveal.

CHECKLIST OF LOGICAL-MATHEMATICAL INTELLIGENCE QUALITIES:

Gardner describes logical-mathematical intelligence as encompassing many kinds of thinking. He suggests that this intelligence encompasses three broad, but interrelated fields: mathematics, science, and logic. While it is impossible in a single list to capture the range of mathematical expression in an individual, some suggested descriptors follow. It is likely that a person with well-developed logical-mathematical intelligence:

1. **Perceives objects and their function in the environment.**

2. **Is familiar with the concepts of quantity, time, and cause and effect.**

3. **Uses abstract symbols to represent concrete objects and concepts.**

4. **Demonstrates skill at logical problem-solving.**

5. **Perceives patterns and relationships.**

6. **Poses and tests hypotheses.**

7. **Uses diverse mathematical skills such as estimating, calculating algorithms, interpreting statistics, and visually representing information in graphic form.**

8. **Enjoys complex operations such as calculus, physics, computer programming, or research methods.**

9. **Thinks mathematically by gathering evidence, making hypotheses, formulating models, developing counter-examples, and building strong arguments.**

10. **Uses technology to solve mathematical problems.**

11. **Expresses interest in careers such as accounting, computer technology, law, engineering, and chemistry.**

12. **Creates new models or perceives new insights in science or mathematics.**

LOGICAL - MATHEMATICAL LEARNING PROCESSES:

For the last two decades, numerous reports and position papers generated by professionals and academic organizations call for new forms of mathematics instruction. The National Council of Teachers of Mathematics recommends that mathematics instruction emphasize the awareness and appreciation of the role of mathematics in society, the ability to reason and communicate mathematically, to problem-solve, and to apply mathematics to students' everyday lives.

Similar recommendations are evident in science education as well. Many groups such as the National Science Teachers Association and the National Academy of Science, the organization that is coordinating the creation of National Science Education Standards, are struggling to identify what is of most worth in science education. Some suggestions include teaching the process skills of science inquiry, applying the basic concepts of science as appropriate, using science in everyday decision-making, and helping students recognize that science, technology, and society influence one another. Both science and math educators are calling for the development of higher-order thinking on the part of students as well as the teaching of problem-solving and decision-making skills.

This chapter does not suggest ways to improve the instruction of mathematics or science. Nor does it assume that these subjects do not need to be taught as discrete subject matter areas in their own right. Rather, the intent of this chapter is to suggest instructional strategies that integrate mathematical and logical thinking into diverse subject areas. In so doing, logical intelligence may play a larger role in thinking and learning. Graphing, for example, can

be used to present information in any classroom. Probability theory might predict the outcomes of physical exercise or current events. These and other strategies described in this chapter include:

ESTABLISHING A LOGICAL-MATHEMATICAL LEARNING ENVIRONMENT

THE TEACHING OF LOGIC:
   The Scientific Method
   Thinking Scientifically
      across the Curriculum

DEDUCTIVE LOGIC
   Syllogisms
   Venn Diagrams

INDUCTIVE LOGIC
   Analogies

ENHANCING THINKING AND LEARNING
   Mediating Learning
   Questioning Strategies

MATHEMATICAL THINKING PROCESSES:
   Patterning
   Pattern Blocks
   Patterns in Data
   Codes
   Graphs

WORKING WITH NUMBERS
   Averages and Percentages
   Measurement
   Calculation
   Probability
   Geometry

STORY PROBLEMS ACROSS THE CURRICULUM

SEQUENCING

MATH THEMES FOR ALL SUBJECT AREAS

TECHNOLOGY THAT ENHANCES LOGICAL-MATHEMATICAL INTELLIGENCE

SUMMARY

ESTABLISHING A LOGICAL-MATHEMATICAL LEARNING ENVIRONMENT

In 1989, the National Council of Teachers of Mathematics released an extensive report called The Curriculum and Evaluation Standards for School Mathematics which describes new math standards and curriculum In addition to recommending curricular and pedagogical changes, new student roles were also suggested:

> "Learning should engage students both intellectually and physically. They must become active learners, challenged to apply their prior knowledge and to experience new and increasingly more difficult situations. Instructional approaches should engage students in the process of learning rather than transmit information for them to receive."

The emphasis in the NCTM report shifts the traditional student role from being a passive to an active learner. This single recommendation serves as a guideline for teachers wanting to enhance the logical-mathematical nature of their classrooms. In any classroom the following active learning processes enhance logical thinking:

- Using diverse questioning strategies
- Posing open-ended problems for students to solve
- Constructing models of key concepts
- Having students demonstrate their understanding using concrete objects
- Predicting and verifying logical outcomes
- Discerning patterns and connections in diverse phenomena
- Asking students to justify their statements or opinions
- Providing opportunities for observation and investigation

- Encouraging students to construct meaning from their studies
- Connecting mathematical concepts or processes to other subject matter areas and real life.

As the reader will find later in this chapter, certain math manipulatives can be used throughout all curriculum areas. By working with concrete objects, students become actively engaged in problem-solving. Teachers may find it valuable to have pattern blocks, games, puzzles, graph paper, rulers, compasses, protractors, calculators, computers, and a variety of computer software available in their classrooms. Since these items are not considered essential supplies in all subject matter areas, especially at the secondary level, such manipulatives can be borrowed from math teachers and made easily transportable. Placing the needed items in a plastic tub with an inventory list attached can tell teacher and students at a glance what is available as well as what might be missing. Student representatives might also be responsible for regularly inventorying the materials.

Such suggestions as well as the learning processes that follow expand the concept of traditional mathematics education. Replacing the perception of math as a subject that develops only computational and algebraic skills, mathematics today includes problem-solving, reasoning, and making connections, which are skills that benefit any field of study. The authors hope that the following learning processes augment the work of math and science educators by assisting students in applying logical thinking more confidently to all of their learning opportunities.

THE TEACHING OF LOGIC

Logic as an academic discipline was invented by Aristotle and is concerned with argument, validity, proof, definition, and consistency. Undoubtedly before formal logic was recognized, people were reasoning in consistent and logical ways. Nevertheless, Aristotle was the first philosopher to identify and formalize rules for this branch of philosophy. During the Middle Ages, Arabic and European cultures contributed to the field and during the nineteenth and twentieth centuries, there were numerous developments in mathematical logic.

To introduce formal logic to students, it is useful to explain that logic examines how arguments are constructed. Logical arguments typically consist of two kinds of statements: premises that state evidence and conclusions that are drawn from the premises. Logic attempts to tell us what is true if the premises are true. By teaching logical reasoning processes, students are exposed to exacting mental discipline and can learn whether chains of reasoning are valid or invalid.

There are several kinds of logic, the most common of which are deductive and inductive logic. In deductive logic, the conclusion follows from the stated premises. In inductive logic, the conclusion is developed step-by-step from the particular to the general. The scientific method uses both types of logic; hypotheses are often developed through deductive reasoning and theories are built on inductive thinking.

THE SCIENTIFIC METHOD

The scientific method, a way of thinking about problems and solving them, involves extensive use of logic. Scientists have worked out the general process of the empirical scientific method, a series of five steps that attempt to explain a problem and its solution in an orderly manner. The five steps of the scientific method are:

> **STATING THE PROBLEM**
>
> **FORMING THE HYPOTHESIS OR EXPLANATION**
>
> **OBSERVING AND EXPERIMENTING**
>
> **INTERPRETING THE DATA**
>
> **DRAWING CONCLUSIONS**

The scientific method attempts to explain phenomena by examining cause and effect. An experiment typically involves manipulating one variable, while holding all other variables constant, thus isolating the effects of the one manipulated variable. If after repeated trials the results are predictable, then the scientific method allows scientists to answer the question: "What are the grounds for our beliefs?" Scientists attempt to design experiments with as few variables as possible because we consider our beliefs reliable when based on experiments that minimize the number of uncontrollable variables.

THINKING SCIENTIFICALLY ACROSS THE CURRICULUM

How can this kind of empirical thinking be incorporated into the classroom?

Regardless of the subject area, information can be presented, hypotheses or explanations formed, examples found through research, experimentation, or observation, data examined, and relevant conclusions drawn. The following sample premises may be used to engage students in thinking scientifically across the curriculum. The students' tasks would consist of testing such premises to determine if their hypotheses are supported and to explain how they arrived at such decisions.

Premises to be Researched Using the Scientific Method

(i.e. manipulating one variable and looking at the results in a responding variable):

- Putting an aspirin or a penny in a vase of flowers keeps them fresh longer.
- Cats always purr when you pet them.
- Aerobic exercise reduces resting heart rate.
- Blue lighting reduces tension.
- Mixing yellow with blue creates green.
- Bees are attracted to yellow.
- Smoking cigarettes makes people more popular.
- Higher interest rates result in slower realty markets.
- Boys have faster reaction times than girls.

In addition to the empirical research method, there are numerous types of logic problems that question whether inferences are true. In using deductive logic, students can employ syllogisms and Venn Diagrams to determine if premises are valid, while in using inductive logic, they might create analogies to reveal proportional relationships. These three logic problems, syllogisms, Venn Diagrams, and analogies can be applied to many subject areas. For example, analogies in science might assist students with concept development, and syllogisms or Venn diagrams in social studies might be used to compare or contrast different cultures or geographic regions.

DEDUCTIVE LOGIC

Deductive reasoning begins with a general rule and attempts to prove that data are consistent with the generalization. Students frequently see such logic in action. If the principal announces that anyone throwing snowballs on the playground will suffer the consequences of his actions and Andy proceeds to throw snowballs, the results are predictable. Or, if directions in one's art class state that using too much glue will cause tissue paper to bleed, and Molly uses large amounts of glue, she should then not be too surprised when she gets bright colored dye on her hands and shirt. This kind of reasoning represents syllogisms in action. Syllogisms are structured arguments composed of two premises and a conclusion, and are examples of deductive logic.

Syllogisms

Aristotle is the earliest known philosopher to use syllogisms as a form of logical problem-solving. He taught that the syllogism was the main instrument for reaching scientific conclusions. Aristotle determined that certain propositions could be inferred as true if their premises were true. For example:

> All men are mortal.
> Socrates is a man.
> Therefore, Socrates is mortal.

The structure of syllogisms is always consistent. The first line provides one piece of information or premise that describes the noun (men) as a member of a set (mortal). The second line provides an additional premise that describes a new noun (Socrates) in relation to the subset (man). The conclusion is the third statement in a syllogism which allows us to draw logical conclusions based upon set/subset membership (since men are mortal and Socrates is a man, then Socrates must be mortal). In this case, the conclusion is supported or proved by the premises, and the syllogism is considered valid.

Syllogisms are carefully worded. For example, premises begin with all, none, or some. The verbs used in premises consist of is, are, or are not. The conclusion begins with the word, therefore. The challenge when working with syllogisms is to determine whether the conclusion is valid. Many syllogisms are invalid. For example,

> **All weeds are plants.**
> **The tree is a plant.**
> **Therefore, all trees are weeds.**

In the above syllogism, the conclusion is not supported by its premises and is considered invalid. Note that syllogisms are valid if the object of the second premise refers to the subject of the first premise. Students can diagram this to show increasingly small subsets based upon these premises:

Valid Premise

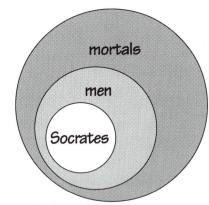

Invalid Premise

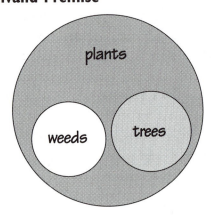

Syllogisms teach students about establishing premises and determining either logical or illogical conclusions. For example, teachers and students can apply syllogisms to different subjects. In a social studies unit on European geography, a teacher might pose the following problem:

> **All countries in Europe are north of the Equator, Spain, Italy, and Greece are in Europe.**
>
> **Therefore _____.**

Or in a life science or biology class:

> **All reptiles have cold blood**
>
> **_____ are reptiles.**
>
> **Therefore, _____ have cold blood.**

Solving syllogisms requires determining their validity or invalidity. The above examples are both valid, but when assessing students a teacher might provide them with a number of syllogisms, some valid, some invalid, to determine the effectiveness of their learning. The logic in a syllogism can be valid even though the content of the syllogism is invalid. Be careful to evaluate content knowledge and logical reasoning separately when using syllogisms.

Venn Diagrams

Venn Diagrams are visual syllogisms. John Venn designed Venn Diagrams using overlapping circles to compare or contrast sets of information. Generally, two intersecting circles are drawn resulting in three individual areas:

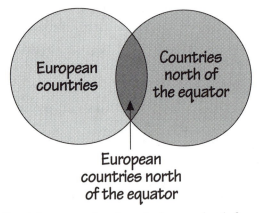

In this example, the circle on the left represents all European countries. The circle on the right represents all countries north of the equator. The area created by the overlap must represent countries that contain both attributes

(European and north of the equator). Countries that are north of the equator and non-European would be placed outside of the diagram.

Venn diagrams are especially effective to help students focus on attributes and to help them compare similarities and differences. Students should gain experience fitting objects into pre-created Venn diagrams. When they master this skill they should be challenged to design Venn diagrams of their own. Some suggested attributes are:

> **characteristics of plants - characteristics of animals**
> **short stories - novels**
> **you - classmate**
> **democracy - dictatorship**
> **editorials - documentaries**
> **words used as nouns - words used as verbs**
> **rules for soccer - rules for rugby**

In more complex Venn diagrams, three overlapping circles can be drawn resulting in seven individual areas. (Actually, the number of circles can extend indefinitely). The following example asks students to place geometric figures into a more complex Venn diagram:

Place a trapezoid, square, rhombus, parallelogram, and rectangle in the right spot:

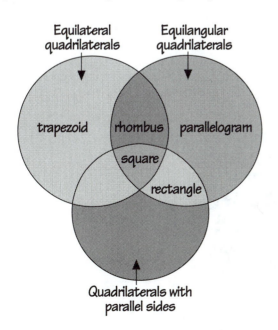

Students enjoy occasional challenges such as "What's My Rule." Draw two large intersecting circles on the classroom floor. As students enter the classroom, sort them into secret categories (such as long-sleeved tops, tennis shoes, and both). Let them guess what attributes you are using to place them in the sections.

INDUCTIVE LOGIC

Aristotle, the Father of Logic, referred to inductive logic as "a passage from individuals to universals." Inductive logic involves reasoning from particular facts to a general conclusion. We use inductive logic whenever we try to solve a problem for which there is not a single answer, for example, where to go to college, how to decide the best time to harvest a crop, or how to introduce a new unit to students on Monday. When inductive thinking is used, pieces of information can be formed into a generalization.

One type of inductive reasoning is the analogy. An analogy reveals proportional relationships such as A is to B as C is to D. It is a method that compares one known item or circumstance to another. Analogies are commonly used to test reasoning on standardized tests and they are effective classroom tools to engage logical thinking.

ANALOGIES

Analogies are structured as two pairs or sets of words. The first pair reveals a relationship. The second set, when completed, reveals a similar relationship. The subjects of the two pairs may be different but the relationships are the same. To solve an analogy, look at the first pair of words to determine their relationship. Then look at the third word to determine how it relates to the first and what the missing word should be. When a word is identified to fill in the blank, it must reveal the same relationship as in the first set. For example: Car is to land as boat is to _____ [water]. An additional item to note in analogies is that the words in both sets must be in the same order.

In mathematics the symbol ":" represents "is to" and the symbol "::" represents "as." So: Bird : nest :: bee : _____ [hive].

Analogous thinking can be applied to various topics such as the following:

1. Churchill : England :: Stalin : _____

2. Electron : Nucleus :: Planet : _____

3. Bear : Mammal :: Rattlesnake : _____

4. Albany : New York :: Tallahassee : _____

5. Nick Bottom : A Midsummer Night's Dream :: Falstaff : _____

6. Monet : Impressionism :: Braque : _____

7. Hydrogen : Element :: Water : _____

8. Moby Dick : Herman Melville :: Little House on the Prairie : _____

9. Five : Ten :: Fifty : _____

10. Three : Triangle :: Five : _____

This same technique can be used with pictures instead of words or a combination of both. A student might picture an analogy in the following ways:

The analogies on standardized tests are usually closed-ended, multiple-choice options in which there is only one right answer. Both students and teachers can create more open-ended analogies to share in the classroom. Initially, it is often easier for students to begin by adding the second set rather than creating an entire analogy. For example,

Light is to dark as _____ **is to** _____ .

Minute is to hour as _____ **is to** _____ .

2/5 : 10/25 :: _____ : _____ .

Madagascar : Africa :: _____ : _____ .

Students can then progress to creating their own analogies simply by filling in the blanks as follows:

_____ **is to** _____ **as** _____ **is to** _____ .

_____ : _____ :: _____ : _____

ENHANCING THINKING AND LEARNING

Some students may find syllogisms, analogies, or other structured thinking processes difficult. In such cases, teachers often experience frustration over how best to assist a student who is struggling with his or her learning. The problem is further compounded when teachers cannot specify which cognitive skills require strengthening. Dr. Reuven Feuerstein, an Israeli clinical psychologist, has identified essential cognitive skills that underlie human thinking and learning. Feuerstein and others who have worked with his programs that teach the skills of intelligence, such as Instrumental Enrichment and the Learning Potential Assessment Device, claim that intentional mediation of fundamental intellectual processes results in great cognitive gains. In many cases, Feuerstein's methods appear to jump-start learning when it has stalled. To improve the thinking of their students, educators around the world are looking to one of Feuerstein's cognitive programs called Mediated Learning.

MEDIATING LEARNING

Feuerstein initially developed his revolutionary Mediated Learning Experience (MLE) to address the educational needs of tens of thousands of traumatized refugee children who survived the Holocaust or impoverished conditions in North Africa. Finding their cognitive skills severely deficient as a result of their deprived environments and life experiences, Feuerstein created learning strategies to greatly enhance the logical thinking and learning abilities of these young people. During the last 40 years, Feuerstein's methods have proved consistently effective with multicultural populations as well as with those of all ages and ability levels.

Students with learning disabilities as well as those who are highly capable have made impressive academic gains through Mediated Learning. Feuerstein's system has been implemented in countries around the world and most states in the U.S. now include his methods in schools, districts, and corporate training programs. In 1990, Feuerstein was awarded the highest medal of honor bestowed by the president of France to acknowledge his retraining of the work force of 250 French corporations. In 1991, he received the Humanitarian Award from the International Variety Clubs, also in recognition of his work to improve learning at all ability levels. What is this method that has received such wide acclaim?

Feuerstein describes Mediated Learning as "a quality of interaction…when I interpose myself between the learner, the child and the whole world, and I make the world accessible to the child." MLE occurs whenever an individual deliberately intervenes between stimuli and learner to transmit or mediate understanding.

Many parents, teachers, and trainers intuitively or explicitly mediate learning for others. Unfortunately, many do not, thus limiting the effective cognitive functioning of an individual. Feuerstein asserts that all people require the same basic intellectual skills to make sense of information and the world.

Feuerstein's theory is broad and complex. However, an American professor and researcher, Dr. Katherine Greenberg, has adapted the theory to make it accessible to parents and helping professionals. Greenberg's program, entitled COGNET (The Cognitive Enrichment Program), is based at the University of Tennessee in Knoxville.

Greenberg notes that Feuerstein originally identified more than 28 cognitive functions, the skills upon which thought processes are based. In using Mediated Learning, the mediator evaluates the learner's cognitive competencies and seeks to develop any that are weak. Greenberg has condensed the number of cognitive competencies to ten which she refers to as "Building Blocks of Thinking." One of the many ways in which the COGNET program applies the theory of mediated learning is through its emphasis upon helping students understand and use the ten Building Blocks of Thinking which include:

Greenberg's Ten Building Blocks of Thinking

Approach to Task—refers to how one initiates, sustains, and completes a task. Gathering information, thinking about the situation, and expressing thoughts or actions about one's learning efforts are also components of approach to task.

Precision and Accuracy—refers to the ability to use language accurately, to imitate correctly when necessary, and to be exact and correct in understanding what constitutes the learning activity at hand.

Space and Time Concepts—refers to understanding basic spatial ideas about how things relate in size, shape, distance, and sequence. This building block also includes the ability to understand time and/or changes that occur over time.

Thought Integration—refers to pulling together and using multiple sources of information at the same time.

Selective Attention—refers to the ability to choose relevant pieces of information when considering thoughts or events, as well as the ability to ignore what is irrelevant.

Making Comparisons—refers to the ability to determine what is the same and what is different.

Connecting Events—refers to the ability to associate one activity with another and to use this association in a meaningful manner.

Working Memory—refers to the ability to encode and recall information from memory as well as to make connections among the information gathered.

Getting the Main Idea—refers to the ability to find a fundamental element that related pieces of information have in common.

Problem Identification—refers to the ability to experience and define within a given situation what is causing a feeling of imbalance.

Learners may experience difficulty with several of the above Building Blocks especially when they face a new or troublesome task. When frustration, anxiety, or a lack of motivation is present, such feelings frequently indicate that one or more of the blocks may be underdeveloped or misused. The following checklist created by the authors of this book identifies the Building Blocks of Thinking that students may struggle with or master. The teacher may use the checklist to observe a student in the process of learning, or the student may be asked to respond to the list independently. Interventions might be created to respond to any perceived cognitive weakness.

BUILDING BLOCKS OF THINKING

Name: _____

Assess whether each building block was used proficiently or inefficiently by checking the appropriate boxes below. The student demonstrated:

	Proficient	Inefficient
APPROACH TO TASK BY:		
Gathering information needed to complete the activity.	_____	_____
Making a plan to complete the task.	_____	_____
PRECISION AND ACCURACY BY:		
Asking for help if something was not clear or understood.	_____	_____
Expressing ideas clearly and accurately.	_____	_____
Meeting the goals of the task with precision and accuracy.	_____	_____
SPACE AND TIME CONCEPTS BY:		
Using size, shape, and distance adequately.	_____	_____
Sequencing appropriately.	_____	_____
Explaining how things change over time.	_____	_____
THOUGHT INTEGRATION BY:		
Clustering thoughts effectively.	_____	_____
Combining bits of information into a whole thought.	_____	_____
Retaining the relevant bits of information needed in a situation.	_____	_____
SELECTIVE ATTENTION BY:		
Identifying important information.	_____	_____
Ignoring unimportant information or stimuli.	_____	_____
MAKING COMPARISONS BY:		
Identifying similar items.	_____	_____
Identifying dissimilar items.	_____	_____
CONNECTING EVENTS BY:		
Connecting past, present, and future events.	_____	_____
Identifying cause and effect.	_____	_____
Perceiving that events are related.	_____	_____
WORKING MEMORY BY:		
Encoding information in memory.	_____	_____
Retrieving information from memory.	_____	_____
Making connections between parts of information.	_____	_____
GETTING THE MAIN IDEA BY:		
Identifing the fundamental element that relates pieces of information.	_____	_____
PROBLEM IDENTIFICATION BY:		
Articulating a problem.	_____	_____
Developing an approach to address the problem.	_____	_____

The checklist on the previous page may reveal one or more cognitive functions that need strengthening. Frequently, teachers encounter children who are struggling with learning, but have found it difficult to identify what was wrong. The Building Blocks of Thinking help teachers and students recognize specific cognitive weaknesses and provide important clues for ameliorating learning difficulties. Mediated Learning can be integrated into classroom lessons on any subject; however, it requires fine-tuning of many everyday classroom interactions.

Math and science teachers will probably recognize that Greenberg's Building Blocks of Thinking resemble the mathematical reasoning skills of the National Council of Teachers of Mathematics Standards and the process skills of science. The Building Blocks of Thinking basically reword those thinking processes in a fully interdisciplinary manner. Teachers can use the Building Blocks as ways to encourage the development of mathematical-logical intelligences regardless of the subject matter or theme of instruction.

QUESTIONING STRATEGIES

"In the skillful use of the question, more than anything else lies the fine art of teaching; for in such use we have the guide to clear and vivid ideas, the quick spur to imagination, the stimulus to thought, the incentive to action."

—Charles DeGarmo, 1911

Long before Socrates, questioning has served as one of teaching's most common practices. Questions commonly asked in classrooms vary greatly placing different demands on children and their thinking. Many questions can be answered by a single right answer: When did the Spanish-American War take place? What is the chemical symbol for hydrogen? What is the definition of a prepositional phrase? Since children's cognitive performance is linked to a teacher's pedagogical skill, it is important to find ways to challenge student thinking and responses. Questions that elicit factual recall are necessary since children must master basic information. However, to engage higher level thinking processes, a variety of questioning strategies must be used.

Benjamin Bloom's Taxonomy is a well-known resource that identifies and evaluates different kinds of thinking while offering a framework for questioning as well. Bloom's taxonomy identifies six cognitive domains which include: recall, comprehension, application, analysis, synthesis, and evaluation. By reflecting on the quality of questioning to be used in classroom discussions or in students' assignments, teachers can elicit higher level thinking by intentionally posing questions from each of Bloom's domains.

Certain follow-up strategies also improve the quality of classroom thinking. Teachers, on the average, wait less than three seconds after asking a question before asking another student to respond or answering the question themselves. If, however, a teacher waits ten seconds or longer, student responses improve as do teacher reactions. The benefits of wait time include enhanced participation in discussions, increased use of reasoning to justify answers, and more speculative responses. Similar benefits also occur when wait time is used before a teacher comments after a student response.

The quality of responses can also be enhanced by asking students to query each other in pairs before they respond in the whole group. This strategy makes it possible for more students to participate, allows students to "hear" their own thinking, and encourages them to listen to and understand other points of view.

Jay McTighe and his colleagues at the Maryland State Department of Education have developed a simple cueing device, a bookmark, for teachers to use during class discussion and question and answer sessions. One side of the bookmark features question starters based on the book *Dimensions of Thinking* by Bob Marzano. Discussion strategies are listed on the other side. The bookmark is included below. Copy and use it as a tool for easy referencing during class activities.

QUESTIONING
FOR QUALITY THINKING

RECALLING
Who, what, when, where, how _____?

COMPARING
How is _____similar to/different from____?

IDENTIFYING ATTRIBUTES AND COMPONENTS
What are the characteristics/parts of _____?

CLASSIFYING
How might we organize _____into categories?

ORDERING
Arrange ____into sequence according to ____.

IDENTIFYING RELATIONSHIPS AND PATTERNS
Develop an outline/diagram/web of _____.

REPRESENTING
In what other ways might we show/illustrate __?

IDENTIFYING MAIN IDEAS
What is the key concept/issue in _____?
Retell the main idea of ____in your own words.

IDENTIFYING ERRORS
What is wrong with _____?

INFERRING
What might we infer from _____?
What conclusions might be drawn from _____?

PREDICTING
What might happpen if _____?

ELABORATING
What ideas/details can you add to _____?
Give an example of_____.

SUMMARIZING
Can you summarize _____?

ESTABLISHING CRITERIA
What criteria would you use to judge/evaluate__?

VERIFYING
What evidence supports_____?
How might we prove/confirm _____?

STRATEGIES
TO EXTEND THINKING

REMEMBER "WAIT TIME I AND II"
Provide at least five seconds of thinking time after a question **and** after a response.

ASK "FOLLOW-UPS"
e.g., "Why? How do you know? Do you agree? Will you give an example? Can you tell me more?"

CUE RESPONSES TO "OPEN ENDED" QUESTIONS
e.g., "There is not a single correct answer to this question. I want you to consider alternatives."

USE "THINK-PAIR-SHARE"
Allow individual thinking time, discussion with a partner, and follow with whole-group discussion.

CALL ON STUDENTS RANDOMLY
Avoid the pattern of only calling on those students with raised hands.

ASK STUDENTS TO "UNPACK THEIR THINKING"
e.g., "Describe how you arrived at your answer."

ASK FOR SUMMARY TO PROMOTE ACTIVE LISTENING
e.g., "Could you please summarize our discussion thus far?"

PLAY DEVIL'S ADVOCATE
Require students to defend their reasoning against different points of view.

SURVEY THE CLASS
e.g., "How many people agree with the author's point of view?" (thumbs up, thumbs down)

ALLOW FOR STUDENT CALLING
e.g., "Richard, will you please call on someone to respond?"

ENCOURAGE STUDENT QUESTIONING
Provide opportunities for students to generate their own questions.

Maryland State Department of Education

MATHEMATICAL THINKING PROCESSES

Mathematics, a subject typically thought of as abstract and exacting, can actually serve as an exciting integrating focus of many lessons and curricular units. For students previously uninterested in math, the following activities such as patterning, graphing, and making and breaking codes, may reawaken a curiosity about how things work and how problems are solved. Teachers may want to pick and choose from among the numerous processes suggested below and adapt any that might encourage an appreciation of mathematical thinking processes.

PATTERNING

By observing and solving problems that involve patterns, students begin to notice the underlying relationships which pervade logic, nature, and the universe. Patterns exist in everything from floor tiles to the shapes of galaxies, from bee hives to modern paintings, from the cross-section of a tree to the layout of the orchard, and from the eggs in a carton to atoms in a molecule. Mathematics is founded on patterns. The skill of recognizing and using patterns is a valuable problem-solving tool. Through working with patterns in any subject, students can explore, discover, and create a harmony of design while they deepen their appreciation for this vital mathematical theme.

Pattern Blocks

Pattern blocks, sets of wooden or plastic geometric shapes that fit together forming infinite configurations, are common manipulatives in elementary mathematics classes. Some pattern blocks serve as stamps or plastic stencils so that students can draw or "stamp" their designs on paper. Such manipulatives concretely represent abstract mathematical symbols, and are motivating to students who prefer to learn through touching, seeing, and experimenting.

Although generally used to introduce geometry or symmetry, pattern blocks are effective tools for numerous hands-on, problem-solving activities. For example, one creative chemistry teacher asked his students to replicate the atoms of elements in the periodic table with pattern blocks. Brightly colored blocks might also depict cubist art, covered wagons crossing the prairie, or electrons surrounding a nucleus. When students are confronted with open-ended problem-solving activities, they may use countless visual configurations to portray possible solutions. The following list suggests only a few of the possible ways to weave pattern blocks throughout the curriculum:

1. **Demonstrate the configuration of different types of galaxies in space.**

2. **Show the internal geometry of a beehive.**

3. **Make a map of the continents.**

4. **Invent a musical notation system.**

5. **Design a building in which colors or shapes represent different rooms or stories.**

6. **Recreate what cells look like under a microscope.**

7. **Write a rebus story which includes pattern blocks.**

8. **Create a Venn diagram for sorting pattern blocks.**

9. **Represent a particular syllogism using pattern blocks.**

10. **Create analogies using pairs of pattern blocks.**

If pattern blocks are available in the classroom, students will find ways to put them to use. For example, in one school, fifth grade students created a replica of the Mayflower, and eighth-graders used blocks to demonstrate an aquatic food chain. In another school, students enjoyed creating repetitive symmetrical patterns which prepared them for their future study of geometry.

Patterns in Data

From the recurrence of wars throughout history to changes in the stock market, from weather patterns to school enrollment, there are observable patterns in the institutions and phenomena around us. Students or teachers who wish to discover or analyze such patterns need look no further than the daily newspaper or readily available reference materials, or any group of students or teachers.

Many classrooms track the weather by noting temperature, rainfall, or the number of sunny days. Such data can be analyzed quantitatively to discern monthly or seasonal trends. In many locations, birds leave or return at predictable times which might lead students to observe patterns or cycles in their lives. Graphing data is one way to help students identify patterns.

Patterns are evident in all of the core disciplines. In the life sciences, there are patterns in the cross section of a tree, the water cycle, and the arrangement of cells. In the arts, patterns are evident in modern paintings, the couplets of Victorian poetry, the structure of novels, and in musical compositions. There are patterns in architecture, quilts, clothing design, braille letters, and the treads on new tires. Regardless of the subject, teachers can identify or ask students to discover patterns evident in their studies. Students might create collages of patterns they observe, perhaps dedicating each collage to a different theme such as patterns in nature or literature.

Codes

Some of the most valued members of the military during wartime are the code breakers. There are, however, other uses for codes besides those for military purposes. Governments may send memos to each other or to their consulates in foreign countries using codes. Businesses often use codes to prevent their rivals from accessing information on new products. Some retail stores have coded information on price tags so that fluctuating prices are retrievable during sales.

Codes can liven up learning in the classroom and involve students in active pattern-seeking. Students enjoy breaking codes and decoding messages that contain content information. A coded message sent from one revolutionary war general to another might provide students with important information about geography, battle strategies, or significant historical figures. Another coded message might provide information about the rules of grammar or spelling. The notes on a musical score could easily be turned into a code for music students to decipher a tune. Art students might create clever glyphs with which to communicate.

Teachers will find it easy to make codes with some of the sample formulas provided below:

- **Alphabetic codes can be made so that each letter in the alphabet stands for the letter which comes before it, after it, or two letters before it.**

- **Numerical codes can have 1 represent A, 2 represent B, etc. Infinite variations are possible. The numbers might go backwards or count by 5's.**

- **Morse code, the traditional dot-dash language of the telegraph, can be used with sound, flashing light, or electronic pulses.**

- **Symbol codes feature icons or glyphs that represent letters or numbers. The optional symbol system on most computer keyboards as well as certain symbolized fonts in word processors make excellent codes.**

GRAPHS

Graphs can make almost any information more easily understood. A graph generally consists of two variables on two coordinates. When information is plotted on the different axes, mathematical relationships become easier to understand. This process can be used by the teacher to present factual information or by the student to demonstrate information acquired through research or surveys. Samples of information that can be represented by either line or bar graphs follow:

- **The number of students attending a particular school during the last ten years.**

- **The national budget under each president during this century.**

- **The quantities and kinds of animals native to one's locale.**

- **The most common kinds of writing mistakes students make.**

- **The growth of the use of pesticides during the last 25 years.**

Some graphs plot two or more curves over one time period. This is valuable for studying the relationship of the two curves. Two examples follow: one that plots population growth and one that demonstrates skill in shooting baskets.

- **The population of major cities during each ten year census period over the past 70 years. Has one grown faster?**

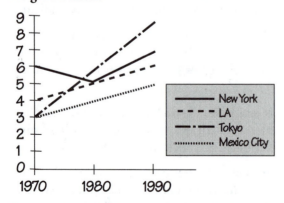

- **The number of points made on a basketball court by two players can easily be plotted. Ten shots by each player could be attempted at** increments of three feet from the basket. Does each have an optimal distance?

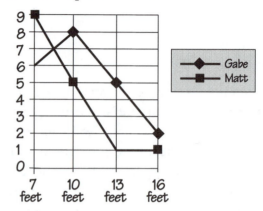

Some graphs are simply frequency charts that can be easily created by most students. Here are some examples that students might graph:

- **Different activities and the number of hours students spend doing them in a week.**

- **The number of times each letter of the alphabet shows up on the page of a storybook.**

- **The number of days it rains each month.**

Bar graphs or pie charts can also represent such information. They may serve the same purposes as line graphs but are often used to represent categorical information (information that allows you to compare different categories). Instead of following a line across a graph, the viewer need only look at the relative lengths or sizes of the bars. For young children, bar graphs are the easiest kind of graph to understand and produce because of the ease of providing a developmentally-sequenced experience from concrete graphs (putting the candy bars on a grid) to representational graphs (drawing the candy bars on a grid) to abstract graphs (such as the one listed below):

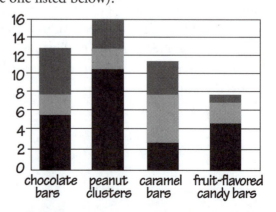

WORKING WITH NUMBERS

Since most school curriculum is organized into discrete subject matter areas, students rarely encounter number problems unless they are studying math and working in their math textbooks. In reality, however, numbers and numerical thinking abound in all academic subjects. Since some students enjoy the precision involved in mathematics, they find it especially enjoyable to work with the numerical aspects of diverse subject areas. The following activities including averages and percentages, measurement, calculating across the curriculum, probability, and story problems provide students with a numerical entry point into the humanities or other subjects not normally associated with the study of mathematics.

AVERAGES AND PERCENTAGES

Calculating averages and percentages are mathematical procedures that can be applied in numerous everyday situations. An artist may carefully compute the percentage of warm colors in relation to cool colors to achieve the desired effect in a painting. The young sports fan is often busy calculating batting averages, percentages of free throws made, the average number of shots stopped by a goalie during the season, or the percentage of first serves made in a tennis match. Some students find that a quantitative approach to information helps them readily grasp relationships and quantities. Averages or percentages can be calculated for the following as well as other content areas:

- **The percentage of states in the United States that border oceans.**

- **The average number of cells in a square millimeter of a leaf.**

- **The percentage of spelling words spelled correctly each day of the week.**

- **The percentage of walkers, bus riders, and car riders to school each day.**

- **The percentage of paintings that are portraits, landscapes, still-lives.**

- **The average number of symphonies composed by great composers.**

- **The percentage of specific instruments in the school band.**

- **The percentage of democracies and dictatorships in the world.**

MEASUREMENT

Size, shape, weight, liquid measurement, distance, speed or motion, temperature, and time are some of the ways we measure or quantify the world around us. To develop students' measurement skills, ask them to determine which units are most appropriate to measure and how to convert between different types of units. It is also valuable for students to know when to measure accurately or when to estimate. Measurement and estimation can be extended into numerous subject areas:

1. **Determine how to measure acceleration as marbles roll down a track in a physics lesson.**

2. **Measure how much classroom bean plants grow on a daily basis.**

3. **Learn simple triangulation to measure the heights of trees.**

4. **Time laps walking, running, or bike-riding around the playground.**

5. **Measure distance on maps that different explorers traveled.**

6. **Record daily temperatures, wind speeds, or barometric pressure.**

7 **Weigh a clay sculpture before and after the clay dries.**

8. **Measure the lengths of shadows from a simple sundial on the playground.**

9. **Measure on a map how far birds or whales migrate each year.**

When conducting measurements, it is often helpful to record information on a table. Tables make it easy to compare and contrast information. Sample tables follow:

A Table for Recording Weights of Items Before and After Drying To Determine Moisture Content

	Name of object	Weight before drying	Weight after drying	Change in weight	Percentage Moisture
1.					
2.					
3.					
4.					
5.					
6.					
7.					
8.					
9.					

A Table for Recording Laps and Times

	Student's Name	Number of Laps	Total Time
1.			
2.			
3.			
4.			
5.			
6.			
7.			
8.			
9.			

CALCULATION

The use of calculators in the classroom is still a topic of debate, but most educators now agree with the National Council of Teachers of Mathematics that calculators should be integrated into the school program at all grade levels in class work, homework, and evaluation. Calculators are used far less in schools than they are "in the real world."

The NCTM recommends that all students use calculators to:

- **concentrate on the problem-solving process rather than on the calculations associated with problems**

- **gain access to mathematics beyond the students' level of computational skills**

- **explore, develop, and reinforce concepts including estimation, computation, approximation, and properties**

- **experiment with mathematical ideas and discover patterns**

- **perform those tedious computations that arise when working with real data in problem-solving situations.**

When they are available in the classroom, calculators can be used for problem-solving, the development of higher level thinking, for understanding mathematical operations, and for learning estimation. In general, students find it useful to work with calculators since they simplify time-consuming mathematical tasks. They free students to exercise higher order thinking skills, such as identifying number patterns, or testing estimates and hypotheses. Teachers often appreciate calculators because they allow them to focus more on the processes of problem-solving than on the rote application of calculation methods. Calculators are capable of providing many possibilities for mathematical learning and can be used to:

1. **Calculate averages and percentages.**

2. **Solve mathematical problems in subject areas. For example:**

   If there were two tons of tea thrown overboard during the Boston tea party, and 32 men were involved, how much tea did each man throw overboard if they all threw the same amount?

   If it takes 12 seconds for a skin cell to divide through the process of cell division, how many daughter cells will be formed from a single cell in 36 seconds? In one minute? In 3 minutes?

   If 56 Americans a day are infected with the HIV virus, how many will be infected in a year? If 42% are women, how many women will that be? If 23% of those women have babies who are infected, how many babies is that?

   If the sun is 93,000,000 miles from Earth, and light travels at 52,600 miles per second, how long does it take light from the sun to reach earth. If Neptune is 8,000,000,000 miles from the sun, how long will it take the sun's light to get there?

3. **Practice cumulative addition or subtraction. For example:**

   Add the total number of minutes that students in the class spend reading after school and on weekends. As each student individually reports, other class members keep a running tally on the calculator. Or, after estimating a large number such as how many beans in a jar, some students

maintain a running tally as others count the beans.

4. **Figure out grade point averages.**

5. **Plan class or individual budgets.**

6. **Create numerical problems based upon students' personal interests or experiences and use calculators to find solutions to their own or each others' work.**

7. **Play calculator games. For example:**

   ### Elimination
   (A game for two players with one calculator)

   a. Players start by entering 15 into the calculator

   b. Players take turns by subtracting 1, 2, or 3 and pressing "=."

   c. The player who causes the calculator to go to "0" or below (a negative number) loses.

8. **Code and send messages, or write story problems for each other that have challenging mathematical puzzles built into them. Students then answer each others' questions in order to decode the problem. Try the following.**

   After school yesterday, I hid $1.00 under a rock. The rock is in the front yard of a house on Maple Street. The address of the house is:

   37982 - 5514 + 80174 - 96225 + 1003 - 8502 = _____Maple Street.

9. **Undertake a personal challenge. Ask students to carry a small hand-held calculator with them for a week to explore how many real-life uses they can find for such a tool.**

   While knowing how to use a calculator is a valuable skill, it does not substitute for the mastery of math facts. This knowledge remains essential and throughout this book we suggest various ways to facilitate the learning of math facts.

PROBABILITY

Most of us take chances of one kind or another. Similarly, most of us have ideas about what might or might not happen. Taking chances and speculating upon the future have much to do with what mathematicians call probability, the likelihood of an event occurring. If you buy a lottery ticket, put the top down on your convertible, purchase insurance, or simply flip a coin, you are putting your own theory of probability into action.

Although probability involves guessing, the intention is to make good guesses or estimates which require logical thinking. Scientists rely upon probability as do army generals, politicians, artists, and composers. Teachers as well depend on the probability that their lesson plans will be effective.

Begin working with the intuitive probability of certain outcomes with students. Have them determine the likelihood of a particular outcome by using the following scale before working with mathematical models of probability:

Likelihood that something will occur:

0% ← → 100%

Here are some sample questions that can help students to think in terms of intuitive probability:

- **If two bar magnets are facing each other, will they attract or repel?**
- **What is the likelihood of the polar ice caps melting?**
- **Are nuclear power plants safe?**
- **Will the gray whales migrate past California in March this year?**
- **Will the next president be a Democrat, Republican, or Independent?**

The mathematical probability of a certain outcome is represented as:

probability = (the number of ways the event can occur one way)
_____
(the total number of possible outcomes).

For example, if you flip a coin once, the probability that it will be heads is 1/2 or 50%. (one heads flip) / (two possible outcomes: heads or tails).

Sample questions to help students determine this simple one-stage event include:

- **What is the likelihood that you will draw an ace from a deck of cards?**
- **What is the likelihood that the stop light will be green when you first see it?**
- **What is the likelihood that the new baby in your family will be a boy?**

One-stage events can involve combinations of outcomes which makes it necessary to look at all of the possible combinations before determining the probability. The following charts show all of the possible combinations of some simple events:

THROWING TWO COINS		
	Coin 1: HEADS	Coin 1: TAILS
Coin 2: HEADS	heads, heads	tails, heads
Coin 2: TAILS	heads, tails	tails, tails

Total possible outcomes:
heads, heads: 1 • heads, tails: 2 • tails, tails 1
Probability that it will be two heads = 1/4 = 25%:

ROLLING A PAIR OF DICE:						
	1	2	3	4	5	6
1.	1,1	1,2	1,3	1,4	1,5	1,6
2.	2,1	2,2	2,3	2,4	2,5	2,6
3.	3,1	3,2	3,3	3,4	3,5	3,6
4.	4,1	4,2	4,3	4,4	4,5	4,6
5.	5,1	5,2	5,3	5,4	5,5	5,6
6.	6,1	6,2	6,3	6,4	6,5	6,6

Probability that it will be a 6 and a 3 = 2/36 = 5.5%

Two-stage events require a different mathematical model. If you toss a coin once and it is heads, what is the probability that you will get heads the second time? There is a 50% probability that you would get heads the first time. The second time the coin is tossed, you also have the same 50% chance of getting heads. Getting heads the first time doesn't make it more likely that you will get tails because the events are independent. Other examples of independent events are whether or not it rains each day or finding pearls in oysters. However, the math changes if you ask the question "What is the probability that I will toss two heads in a row?" In this case, we multiply the probabilities of each event happening in a sequence:

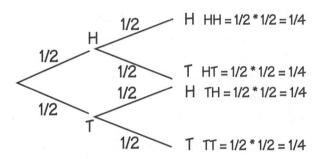

Using this logic we can address questions such as :

• **If I win once, does that affect the probability that I will win again?**

• **What is the probability that three events will occur simultaneously (clear sky, full moon, Friday night)?**

GEOMETRY

From Cubism to cathedrals, from cells to skyscrapers, from the Parthenon to the pyramids, and from sand dunes to starfish, we find the principles of geometry exemplified. Both the world of nature and the world that human beings have created reflect symmetry, topology, points, lines, planes, curves, solids, and of course, measurement and mathematics. In both,

we find circles, hexagons, rectangles, spheres, triangles, cubes, cylinders, cones, pyramids, and prisms.

The word *geometry* comes from the Latin words meaning "earth" and "measure." Originally, geometry involved the measurement of farmland in places such as Egypt where the Nile flooded the valley each year and boundaries had to be re-established. Even today, surveying is an extension of the earliest forms of geometry.

Architects, mechanics, fashion designers, engineers, builders, pilots, navigators, artists, and seamstresses all use geometry in their work. With the prevalence of geometry in our world, its applications throughout the school curriculum are extensive. Some suggestions are offered on how to incorporate geometric awareness into diverse subject matter areas:

1. **Study the geometric designs on flags of the world and have students create their own flags using common geometric shapes.**

2. **Look at architectural structures throughout history (pyramids, temples, mosques, government buildings, cathedrals, domes, or skyscrapers) and compare styles as well as similar and different geometric characteristics.**

3. **Use straight edges, compasses, and protractors to recreate designs in nature such as a forest of straight, tall trees, round rocks on the beach, rays of the setting sun on the horizon, jagged mountain peaks in the distance, the circular pattern of a sunflower, close up of an eye, ripples formed by a pebble dropped on a smooth pond, snowflakes, rectangular rock outcroppings, reeds or blades of tall grass, the moon in different phases, the distant shore of a lake, the veins in a leaf, a tornado, a feather, a jellyfish, a spider web, or the cellular infrastructure of a rotten piece of wood.**

4. **Create symmetrical silhouettes of the profiles of famous historical figures.**

5. **Study the stylistic uses of geometry in cubism or other art forms incorporating explicit geometric shapes.**

6. Write triangle poems with three lines, each leading into the next e.g.:

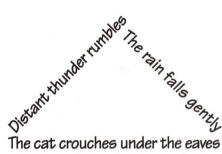

In triangle poems, there is no predetermined starting or ending point; any line can be the first or last. After they have attempted triangle poems, students might want to experiment with square, hexagonal, or pentagonal poems. They may be curious to determine how many sides would exist on a dodecagon poem.

7. Challenge students to find hidden geometric shapes. Using pictures from any subject area (Eli Whitney's cotton gin, the circulatory system of the human body, a tropical rain forest, the Spanish armada, the Great Wall of China, an Atlas booster rocket, London Bridge, or a city skyline) ask students to locate regular or irregular polygons or polyhedrons in the picture. For younger students, the teacher may want to draw hidden shapes into a nature scene or other picture, duplicate copies for the students, and ask them to locate the hidden geometric shapes.

8. Ask students to make flash cards to learn vocabulary words, states and capitals, parts of speech, molecular compounds or any other information by putting the facts on geometrically shaped card stock. Rectangular cards are common, but how about hexagonal or oval cards? A variation could be normal rectangular flash cards with geometric shapes drawn onto them as visual cues serving as a mnemonic device.

9. Make a collage of geometrical shapes by cutting out circles, triangles, parallelograms, or rhombuses from different colors of construction paper, then paste them into an artistic arrangement. The work of Mexican-American artist Carlos Merida could be presented as an example.

10. Study the history of geometry. It dates back to ancient times when the Babylonians and Egyptians used geometry to study the planets and stars, lay out cities, measure angles, and build large structures. Later, the Greeks used the principles of geometry to develop the reasoning and logic involved in proving mathematical statements that we still use today.

11. Cut out electrons, protons, and neutrons from various colors of paper to create different atoms with the shapes of the electrons' orbits sketched around the nucleus. The same could be done with atoms in various molecules or different planets orbiting the sun.

STORY PROBLEMS ACROSS THE CURRICULUM

The very name "story problem" strikes fear into the hearts and minds of many students. However, by making story problems interesting and meaningful, teachers can incorporate logical-mathematical thinking into almost any area of the curriculum. Here are a few examples:

• Winston Churchill called Franklin Roosevelt on the telephone. It was 1:00 AM in London. Roosevelt was in Washington D.C. They talked for two hours. What time was it in Washington when Roosevelt hung up?

• If it takes 22 days for a frog's egg to hatch into a tadpole, how many days does it take for 10 frogs' eggs to hatch into tadpoles?

• If Jeff has to diagram eight sentences every night for an entire week but his girlfriend, Melissa, does half of them for him and his sister does 14 for him, and he lost half of one daily assignment, how many sentences did Jeff diagram?

• If Monet, Gaugin, and Van Gogh began mixing paint together and Monet mixed the primary colors, Gaugin mixed the secondary colors, and they ended up with 23 containers of paint, then how many colors did Van Gogh mix?

- If the Pinta and the Nina left Spain on Tuesday and the Santa Maria left Spain one day later, and the Pinta sailed 500 miles by the following Monday and the Nina sailed 560 miles in the same time, then how far behind was the Santa Maria if she sailed at the same speed as the Nina?

- October 17 falls on a Saturday. List the dates of all Saturdays in April.

SEQUENCING

Putting things in logical order is a skill relevant to almost any undertaking. From making a tuna fish sandwich to planting a garden, it is important to follow the appropriate sequence. In school, we write in a certain logical order, we perform a play sequentially, we build things in order, we conduct experiments following a prescribed order, and we proceed through the school day in a predetermined manner. Below are several exercises for students to practice the skill of sequencing. Such activities can be made as simple or complex as the situation demands.

WRITING A BUSINESS LETTER
Put the following items in the correct order.

a. Type or write the date.
b. Type or write the closing.
c. Take an envelope from the desk.
d. Fold the letter and put it in the envelope.
e. Type the name and address of the person to whom the letter will go.
f. Seal the envelope.
g. Explain the purpose of your letter.
h. Mail the letter at the post office.
i. Put a postage stamp on the envelope.
j. Type or write the greeting.
k. Write the name and address on the envelope.

Your order: ___ ___ ___ ___ ___ ___

___ ___ ___ ___ ___

HOW A BILL BECOMES LAW IN THE UNITED STATES
Put the following items in the correct order.

a. The bill goes to the Senate.
b. The bill goes to the President.
c. Introduction of the bill to the House of Representatives.
d. The bill is printed by the government printing office.
e. An idea for a new law is proposed.
f. A conference committee from both houses works out details.
g. The bill is sponsored by a member of the House or Senate.
h. The bill becomes law.
i. The Speaker of the House signs the bill.

Your order: ___ ___ ___ ___ ___ ___

___ ___ ___ ___

HOW FOOD IS DIGESTED IN THE HUMAN BODY
Put the following items in the correct order.

a. Salivary glands make saliva.
b. Gall bladder stores bile made in liver.
c. Large intestine stores and finally disposes of waste.
d. Food passes to stomach through esophagus.
e. Duodenum receives bile and pancreatic juice.
f. Teeth chop food.
g. Small intestine completes digestion; sends food into blood stream.
h. Liver and pancreas make digestive juices for use in small intestine.
i. Stomach churns food and adds digestive juice.

Your order: ___ ___ ___ ___ ___

___ ___ ___ ___

MATH THEMES FOR ALL SUBJECT AREAS

While educators frequently discuss reading and writing across the curriculum, it is less common to hear of mathematics across the curriculum. Mathematics is often isolated from other areas of study even though its central functions include thinking processes valuable to all disciplines such as identifying and representing patterns and relationships, problem-solving, and communicating precisely. One way to introduce logical-mathematical thinking into any subject area is through rich themes drawn from mathematical concepts. Teachers might organize a curriculum unit around such themes or ask students to research these topics as they relate to classroom content:

SYMMETRY	RANDOMNESS
PERSPECTIVE	SYMBOLIZATION
ITERATION	MULTIPLICATION
MODELING	INFINITY
SPACE	OPPOSITES
BALANCE	PROGRESSION
GROWTH	CHAOS
CONVERGENCE	DIVISION
INFINITESIMAL	EQUALITY

By emphasizing mathematical themes throughout the curriculum, students can see beyond their math and science textbooks into the real world of building and design, keeping records and allocating resources, playing sports and games, and exploring the physical universe.

TECHNOLOGY THAT ENHANCES LOGICAL-MATHEMATICAL INTELLIGENCE

Logical-mathematical intelligence can be exercised and developed through many challenging and innovative kinds of multimedia technology. Students of every ability level can learn effectively through interesting software programs that offer immediate feedback and go far beyond drill and practice and "workbooks on computers." Many of them offer challenging opportunities to exercise and develop higher order thinking skills that are essential in problem-solving. Following are a few examples of the many outstanding programs that are now available.

Edmark's "Millie's Mathhouse" is a delightful and successful computer program that introduces number and math concepts to preschool and early elementary children. It is alive with color, sounds, and graphics and works with a touch screen. Children are introduced to essential math concepts as they build animated bugs, operate a cookie machine, count wiggling critters, and make patterns with talking animals and shapes. As they explore and discover, children learn about numbers, shapes, sizes, patterns, and problem-solving.

For primary students, IBM's "Math and More" programs introduce students to patterns and relationships, geometry, probability, and statistics through highly motivating video, manipulative, and printed materials.

Wings for Learning/Sunburst's "King's Rule" and "Safari Search" for older children develop sequencing abilities and logical-mathematical thinking through visual-spatial, manipulative tasks that are in the form of thought-provoking and challenging games.

Broderbund's "Geometry, Physics and Calculus" software make abstract and sometimes difficult subjects more concrete and easily understandable as students manipulate colorful graphics. Videodiscovery's multimedia video-discs, "The Physics of Auto Collisions" and "The Tacoma Narrows Bridge Collapse," use real events to relate physics to practical applications. As students analyze real world events in scientific and mathematical terms, the principles of physics become more meaningful and relevant.

"The Adventures of Jasper Woodbury," developed by Vanderbilt University's Cognition and Technology Group, provides additional rich contexts for developing mathematical thinking and problem solving about real-world situations through what is being called "anchored instruction." At the present time, there are six dramatic episodes on videodisk (with six more to come), that present complex mathematical problems for students to solve.

One of the first adventures, "Rescue at Boone's Meadow," presents the task of transporting a critically wounded eagle to a veterinary 65 miles away as quickly as possible. Because of the difficult terrain, students must figure out optimal combinations of using a truck, ultralight aircraft, and hiking, taking into consideration fuel, payload, weight, and different starting points. The students use a combination of the random-access videodisk, maps, and computers to generate alternative solutions. Fifth-grade students of average ability have been fascinated with the task, and have been motivated to solve it with solutions that require over 15 steps.

In many of these new "authentic learning" projects, learners become contributors to the collaborative knowledge base of the community. In the Global Lab project organized by the Technical Education Research Centers (TERC),

an international group of teachers, high school students, and global-change researchers are collaborating in studying local and world ecological change using instruments such as ozonometers, ion-selective probes for soil and water monitoring, and field data loggers. Students learn to collect, analyze, and report data that is used by the scientists. And in the MicroObservatory project at Harvard University, secondary school students are using remote computer-controlled optical telescopes to do their own research projects in astronomy.

The "Wireless Coyote," a joint project of Apple Classrooms of Tomorrow and the Orange Grove Middle School in Tucson, Arizona, involved middle school students in using electronic technology to learn more about the ecology of Sabino Canyon in Tucson. Twenty-one sixth grade students used a variety of scientific instruments to measure soil and water temperature, wind speed, and soil. They also used mobile computers connected to a wireless local area network and a wide-area network and voice-activated walkie-talkies to collaborate with each other and communicate the data they collected.

The students, teachers, and technicians were divided into three groups to gather data in different locations. They communicated the data to another base-camp group that provided equipment, coordinated the activities, and transmitted the findings to yet another group in the school 15 miles away where students built a database of the results. A naturalist worked with this group to increase their understanding and offer information which they communicated back to students in the field.

Increasing numbers of multimedia software programs are focused on developing the critical and creative thinking skills of students. IBM's "Modern Solutions" and "Wrinkers" (combination of thinking and writing) offer challenging projects that utilize logic, analysis, synthesis, and evaluation in creating and problem-solving. Seymore Papert's "Lego Logo" program, also offers an opportunity for students to develop the skills of analysis and logic as they learn to use a new computer programming language and apply it to controlling the movement of Lego "machines" that they create.

"Learn Smart" is a new software program developed by Key Technologies that is based on Guilford/Meeker's Structure of Intellect methods of developing intellectual skills. The program assesses individual strengths and weaknesses in cognition and offers strategies to strengthen intellectual powers. It is appropriate for students at all ability levels.

Stanley Pogrow's "HOTS" (Higher Order Thinking Skills) program combines Socratic thinking in small groups with activities utilizing computer technology. This program, focused on learning how to understand and problem-solve, demonstrates clearly that most students, including the "at risk" and "learning disabled," are capable not only of learning the basic skills, but of developing and applying higher order thinking skills in the process.

The programs described above are consistent with the current recommendations of the National Council of Teachers of Mathematics and with current research on "situated cognition." The focus of this research is on demonstrating that learning and thinking are always situated in a context, that knowing and doing are strongly linked, and, as a result, that authentic learning activities and direct experience provide rich opportunities for successful learning.

SUMMARY

In 1267, the English scientist Roger Bacon wrote, "Mathematics is the gate and key of the sciences." Today, scientists who use powerful computers in a physics lab or electron microscopes in a genetics experiment, and mathematicians who create formulas for forecasting economic trends or population growth, use logical-mathematical thinking and its abstract symbolic language system to solve many challenges confronting humanity.

Many other professions also depend on the mastery of this subject. Industry and business, agriculture, the arts, and technical fields all depend on the logical-mathematical thinking of those involved. And on a daily basis, most of us use logical intelligence to calculate household budgets, remember where we left a misplaced item, make decisions, and solve problems. Yet many students avoid the study of math and

science, disdaining the drill and practice frequently associated with such courses.

This chapter offers a variety of strategies to help students master the basic skills as well as develop the higher order thinking skills related to logical-mathematical intelligence. Mind-numbing and boring drill and practice exercises are not included. Students will have rich opportunities to develop their logical-mathematical intelligence as they exercise deductive and inductive logic, practice graphing and patterning, use the tools of electronic technology, and participate in authentic learning experiences as well as stimulating games and activities. They may also become more interested in continuing their studies of math and science and preparing for careers in which they can utilize what they have learned.

In order to summarize, reflect, and synthesize the content of this chapter, the following is offered:

APPLYING LOGICAL-MATHEMATICAL INTELLIGENCE

1. Important ideas or insights gleaned from this chapter: _____

   _____

   _____

   _____

2. Areas I'd like to learn more about: _____

   _____

   _____

   _____

3. Ways I can use this information in my teaching. Please note that all of the strategies mentioned in this chapter are listed below with space provided to note how each strategy might be incorporated into classroom instruction:

LOGICAL-MATHEMATICAL STRATEGY	CLASSROOM APPLICATION
Establishing a Logical-Mathematical Learning Environment:	
The Teaching of Logic:	
The Scientific Method	
Thinking Scientifically across the Curriculum	
Deductive Logic:	
Syllogisms	
Venn Diagrams	
Inductive Logic:	
Analogies	
Enhancing Thinking and Learning:	
Mediating Learning	
Greenberg's Ten Building Blocks of Thinking	
Questioning Strategies	
Mathematical Thinking Processes:	
Patterning	
Pattern Blocks	
Patterns in Data	
Codes	
Graphs	
Working with Numbers:	
Averages and Percentages	
Measurement	
Calculation	
Probability	
Geometry	
Story Problems Across the Curriculum:	
Sequencing	
Writing a Business Letter	
How a Bill Becomes Law	
How Food is Digested	
Math Themes for All Subject Areas:	
Technology that Enhances Logical-Mathematical Intelligence:	

LOGICAL - MATHEMATICAL REFERENCES

Baratta-Lorton, M. (1976). *Mathematics Their Way.* Menlo Park, CA: Addison-Wesley Publishing Company.

Bennett A., Foreman, L. (1991). *Visual Mathematics Course Guide, Volume I.* Portland, OR: Math Learning Center.

Boldrin, P. (1992). *Positive Perspectives on Calculators.* Issaquah, WA: Issaquah School District.

Black, H., Black S. (1984). *Building Thinking Skills — Book 1.* Pacific Grove, CA: Midwest Publications.

Burns, M. (1975). *The I Hate Mathematics! Book.* Boston: Little Brown & Company.

Burns, M. (1976). *The Book of Think.* Boston: Little Brown & Company.

Burns, M. (1987). *A Collection of Math Lessons From Grades K through 3.* White Plains, N.Y.: Math Solutions Publications.

Burns, M. (1987). *A Collection of Math Lessons; From Grades 3 through 6.* White Plains, N.Y.: Math Solutions Publications.

Burns, M. (1990). *A Collection of Math Lessons; From Grades 6 through 8.* White Plains, N.Y.: Math Solutions Publications.

Burns, M. (May/June 1993). "Math Standards in Action." *Instructor*, Vol 102, No. 9.

Dosey, J. (November, 1989). "Transforming Mathematics Education." Alexandria VA: *Educational Leadership.* Association for Supervision and Curriculum Development.

Exner, et al. (1980). *Elements of Mathematics, Book 0, Operational Systems.* Aurora, CO: Comprehensive School Mathematics Program: Mid-Continent Regional Educational Laboratory.

Fuerestein, R., Rand, Y., Rynders, J. (1988). *Don't Accept Me As I Am: Helping Retarded People to Excel.* N.Y.: Plenum Press.

Feuerstein, R. (1980). *Instrumental Enrichment: An Intervention Program for Cognitive Modifiability.* Baltimore: University Park Press.

Gardner, H. (1983). *Frames of Mind: The Theory of Multiple Intelligences.* N.Y.: Basic Books.

Greenberg, K. (1989). The Cognitive Enrichment Network *(COGNET)funded in part by the U.S. Department of Education Follow Through Program (grant #S014C10013).* The University of Tennessee Follow Through Sponsor Project, Katherine Greenberg, Ph.D., Director.

Gilbert, A. (1977). *Teaching the Three R's through Movement Experiences.* N.Y.: MacMillan Publishing Company.

Horne, S. (1970). *Patterns and Problems in Mathematics.* Chicago: Franklin Publications, Inc.

Jacobs, H.R. (1982). *Mathematics: A Human Endeavor.* N.Y.: W.H. Freeman and Company.

Kaye, Peggy. (1987). *Games for Math.* N.Y.: Pantheon.

Kennedy, J.G. (1959). *A Philosopher Looks at Science.* N.Y.: Van Nostrand.

Kleiman, G. (October, 1991). "Mathematics Across the Curriculum." *Education Leadership*, Vol. 49, No.2. Association for Supervision and Curriculum Development.

Liem, Tik. (1987). *Invitations to Science Inquiry.* Science Inquiry Enterprises. 14358 Village View Lane, Chino Hills, CA 91709.

Lovell, R. (1993). *Probability Activities for Problem Solving and Skills Reinforcement.* Berkeley, CA: Key Curriculum Press.

Marzano, R., Brandt, R., Hughes,C., Jones, B.F., Presseisen, B., Rankin, S., Suhor,C. (1988). *Dimensions of Thinking: A Framework for Curriculum and Instruction.* Alexandria, VA: Association for Supervision and Curriculum Development.

McAnallen, R. (1993). *A Catalog of Materials for Math Maniacs.* Institute for MathMania, P.O. Box 910, Montpelier, VT 05601.

Merseth, K. (March 1993). "How Old Is the Shepherd? An Essay about Mathematics Education." *Kappan*, Vol. 74, No.7: Bloomington IN: Phi Delta Kappa.

National Council of Teachers of Mathematics, Commission on Standards for School Mathematics. (1989). *Curriculum and Evaluation Standards for School Mathematics.* Reston, VA: NCTM.

Post, B., Eads, S. (1982). *Logic, Anyone?* Belmont, CA: David S. Lake Publishers.

Seymour, D. Beardslee, E. (1988). *Critical Thinking Activities in Patterns, Imagery, Logic.* Paloalto, CA: Dale Seymour Publications.

Wahl, M. (1989). *A Mathematical Mystery Tour.* Tucson: Zephyr Press.

Willoughby, S. (1990). *Mathematics Education for a Changing World.* Alexandria, VA: Association for Supervision and Curriculum Development.

Wonderful Ideas. A Math Newsletter. P.O. Box 64691, Burlington, VT 05406.

CHAPTER 3

MOVING TO LEARN: KINESTHETIC LEARNING

Ah, if you could only dance all that you've just said, then I would understand.

— *ZORBA THE GREEK*
Nikos Kazantzakis

PAULA'S DANCE

In first grade, Paula was assessed as learning disabled. For the next four years, she was placed in special education classrooms and experienced little if any academic success.

Paula consistently lagged two or more grade levels behind her peers in the basic skills. Her self-esteem decreased and, understandably, her dislike of school increased. By the end of the fifth grade, Paula hid under her bed in the morning to avoid going to school, and during the summer before her sixth grade year, she attempted suicide. Her parents, aware that it was necessary to provide her with a successful sixth grade experience, mainstreamed her into a classroom with an empathetic teacher.

Observing the girl for the first couple of days, the teacher noticed an exceptional grace. Paula moved with poise and dignity. Tall for her age, she walked and ran with ease, her long hair mirroring her movements. Whenever the teacher watched Paula, she imagined a dancer and one day, asked the girl if she had ever studied dance. Paula explained she had indeed taken ballet lessons, which she greatly enjoyed but had to discontinue because of their cost. This information made the teacher wonder if Paula would learn more efficiently through movement.

Although Paula was in sixth grade, her spelling skills approximated those of a second grader. She refused to read, write, or practice spelling word lists. Following her hunch that Paula was kinesthetically talented, the teacher suggested that the girl create a movement alphabet using her body to form each of the 26 letters. For example, to demonstrate the letter "t," Paula could stand erect, with her legs together and her arms outstretched. Some letters would obviously be challenging to create, such as an *m*, *b* or a *w*, but they'd be thought-provoking

Paula's Dance ...continued

and interesting to tackle. Paula said she would think about the teacher's suggestion.

Before school the next day, Paula hurried to her classroom telling the teacher she had something to show her. Paula began her demonstration, dancing the letters of the alphabet one at a time and then sequencing all 26 into a unified performance. The ballet, performed with confidence and skill, was accomplished in total silence. Paula was unabashedly pleased with her efforts and the teacher was awestruck. The girl was a dancer. The instructor asked Paula if she could dance her first name. The dance was done effortlessly with Paula adding her last name as well. Next, she danced the words on the board and that evening, Paula practiced a list of spelling words at home and danced them for her classmates the following day.

Within a week Paula quickly moved from dancing to writing. First, she performed individual words, then wrote them. Then she danced entire sentences. Paula's spelling and writing scores began to increase as did her self-confidence in learning.

After four months, to everyone's chagrin, Paula no longer danced her writing. She simply remained seated and wrote her assignments along with the rest of the class. By the end of her sixth grade year, Paula was writing and reading at grade level.

Four months of kinesthetic learning, of learning through an inherent strength, transformed Paula's school experience and her self-image. For her seventh grade year, Paula attended the local junior high school where, mainstreamed in all classes, she earned above-average grades. ▲

DEFINITION: UNDERSTANDING KINESTHETIC INTELLIGENCE

Paula is not alone in her need to experience physically what she learns. Many children and adults find visual and auditory modes insufficient sensory channels for understanding and remembering information. Such individuals rely on tactile or kinesthetic processes and must manipulate or experience what they learn in order to understand and retain information. Tactile students learn through touch and manipulation of objects, while kinesthetic learners involve their whole bodies in their activities or prefer to work with concrete, real-life experiences. Both tactile and kinesthetic individuals learn through "doing" and through multi-sensory experiences.

Kinesthetic learning processes are frequently undervalued in school since other problem-solving approaches are held in higher esteem. In *Frames of Mind*, Gardner notes that a separation between mind and body has emerged in recent cultural traditions. He bemoans a loss of the Greek ideal of "…a harmony between mind and body, with the mind trained to use the body properly, and the body trained to respond to the expressive powers of the mind."

Bodily-kinesthetic intelligence includes the ability to unite body and mind to perfect physical performance. Beginning with control of automatic and voluntary movements, kinesthetic intelligence progresses to using our bodies in highly differentiated and skilled ways. All talented performances require an acute sense of timing and the transformation of intention into action. Highly developed kinesthetic intelligence is easily discerned when we observe actors, athletes, or dancers. It is also evident in inventors, jewelers, mechanics, and others who work skillfully with their hands or objects. Bodily-

kinesthetic intelligence is the foundation of human knowing, since it is through our sensory-motor experiences that we experience life.

Physical activities focus student attention in the classroom and aid memory by encoding learning throughout the body's neuro-musculature. We all possess "muscle memory" which can be effectively applied to the learning of academic subjects.

Robert McKim in his book *Experiences in Visual Thinking* describes the power of kinesthetic thinking as follows:

> **Consider the sculptor who thinks in clay, the chemist who thinks by manipulating three-dimensional molecular models, or the designer who thinks by assembling and rearranging cardboard make-ups. Each is thinking by seeing, touching, and moving materials, by externalizing his mental processes in a physical object.**
>
> **Externalized thinking has several advantages over internalized thought. First, direct sensory involvement with materials provides sensory nourishment—literally "food for thought." Second, thinking by manipulating an actual structure permits serendipity—the happy accident, the unexpected discovery. Third, thinking in the direct context of sight, touch, and motion engenders a sense of immediacy, actuality and action.**
>
> **Finally, the externalized thought structure provides an object for critical contemplation as well as a visible form that can be shared with a colleague or even mutually formulated.**

Unfortunately, learning becomes increasingly internalized and less externalized as students move into higher grade levels. Since there are fewer opportunities for active, participatory learning, many students become less motivated when taught through passive and abstract learning processes. Physical education—in the fullest sense—belongs in every classroom. The activities suggested in this chapter can be utilized in any setting to help make learning more stimulating, dynamic, and memorable.

CHECKLIST OF TACTILE-KINESTHETIC QUALITIES:

According to Gardner, those who have the ability to use their whole bodies or parts of their bodies such as their hands to solve problems have well-developed kinesthetic intelligence. Athletes, dancers, choreographers, mimes, actors, surgeons, and craftspeople exhibit high degrees of bodily-kinesthetic intelligence. It's important to remember that being skilled in one kinesthetic realm does not necessarily indicate talent in another. For example, an individual may be gifted in the art of mime and yet reveal little if any talent in sports or handcrafts.

The following list identifies potential characteristics of individuals with kinesthetic aptitude. Please note, however, that not every learner will exhibit all of the following characteristics. Some areas may be more developed than others. It is likely that a person with well-developed kinesthetic intelligence:

1. **Explores the environment and objects through touch and movement. Prefers to touch, handle, or manipulate what is to be learned.**

2. **Develops coordination and a sense of timing.**

3. **Learns best by direct involvement and participation. Remembers most clearly what was done, rather than what was said or observed.**

4. **Enjoys concrete learning experiences such as field trips, model building, or participating in role play, games, assembling objects, or physical exercise.**

5. **Shows dexterity in working by means of small or gross motor movements.**

6. **Is sensitive and responsive to physical environments and physical systems.**

7. **Demonstrates skill in acting, athletics, dancing, sewing, carving, or keyboarding.**

8. **Demonstrates balance, grace, dexterity, and precision in physical tasks.**

9. **Has the ability to fine-tune and perfect physical performances through mind and body integration.**

10. **Understands and lives by healthy physical standards.**

11. **May express interest in careers such as those of an athlete, dancer, surgeon, or builder.**

12. **Invents new approaches to physical skills or creates new forms in dance, sports, or other physical activities.**

All of us express some kinesthetic tendencies and needs; however, those who literally must hold ideas in their hands to learn rarely have opportunities to do so. Multi-sensory learning seldom exists in classrooms, since most teachers are still unfamiliar with such processes. As educators, we lack role models to emulate and have few resources to turn to. Yet it is kinesthetic learning that frequently offers the most potent, enjoyable and memorable educational experience for ALL learners. John Goodlad, one of the nation's leading educational researchers, notes in his book *A Place Called School*:

> **Regardless of subject, students reported that they liked to do activities that involved them actively or in which they worked with others. These included going on field trips, making films, building or drawing things, making collections, interviewing people, acting things out, and carrying out projects.**

Students want to be active participants in their learning, not passive recipients of information. The next section describes several processes that encourage learning by doing.

TACTILE AND KINESTHETIC LEARNING PROCESSES:

There are a wide variety of tactile-kinesthetic activities that enhance instruction for students of all ages. In this chapter, we describe physical learning experiences from the following categories:

THE PHYSICAL ENVIRONMENT
  Classroom Zones
DRAMA:
  Formal Theatre
  Role-Play
  Creative Dramatics
  Simulations
CREATIVE MOVEMENT
  Understanding Bodily-Knowing
  Introducing Creative Movement Activities
  Applying Creative Movement to Basic Skills
  Creating Content-Specific Movement Activities
DANCE
  Elements of Dance
  A Sequence for Learning through Dance
MANIPULATIVES
  Task Cards
  Task Card Puzzles
  Junk Drawer Manipulatives
  Making Classroom Stamps
CLASSROOM GAMES
  Scavenger Hunts
  Large Floor Games
  Total Physical Response Games
  Generic Review Game
PHYSICAL EDUCATION
  Characteristics of a Physically-Educated Person
  Adventure Education
  The Spider Web
  The Ten-Person Pyramid
  Classroom Adventures
EXERCISE BREAKS
  Quick Energizers
  Ten Shin Go So
  The Eight Treasures
  Eye Exercises
  Waking Up
  Calming Down
FIELD TRIPS
  Field Trip Guidelines
ENHANCING KINESTHETIC INTELLIGENCE THROUGH TECHNOLOGY
SUMMARY

Ths list is far from exhaustive. Instead, it introduces teachers to a variety of kinesthetic processes that may be incorporated easily into any academic area. Once teachers become familiar with such techniques, they often gain the confidence to add kinesthetic opportunities to many classroom lessons.

ESTABLISHING THE PHYSICAL LEARNING ENVIRONMENT

The environments we live and work in affect us physiologically and psychologically. Most of us pay a significant amount of attention to our home environments. We determine the neighborhood to live in, the colors used to paint interior and exterior walls, the furniture, photographs, and art work in each room, the lay-out and design of the interior space as well as the yard. Such considerations are equally important for classrooms, and yet there is often little attention given to the design of school environments.

When it has been thoughtfully organized or designed, the four-walled, self-contained classroom has tremendous potential to contribute to the learning process. Anne Taylor, an architect specializing in learning environments at the University of New Mexico, maintains that a classroom can serve as "an active, three dimensional textbook or teaching tool, rather than a passive space housing a disarray of things."

Classrooms can be transformed into learning-enhancing environments with thought, enthusiasm, and design planning. Taylor and the other architects, recommend establishing several "zones" appropriate for K-12 classrooms. Each zone in the classroom might serve a specific function and be visually and functionally distinct. By redesigning classrooms into zones, educators might better accommodate the tactile and movement needs of kinesthetically-oriented children. Simply providing students with the opportunity to walk from one work space to the next satisfies the need to stretch, move and be active. Potential zones appropriate for either elementary or secondary classrooms might ideally include the following:

CLASSROOM ZONES:

Entry Zone: Upon arrival at the classroom, students can be welcomed with an entry space that includes plants, hanging fabric, partitions filled with student art, or the day's schedule of events.

Work Zone: To accommodate multi-modal instruction, several work zones might be established around the classroom with spaces for private, small-group, and whole-group work. Learning centers or stations can be established if appropriate. For an aesthetic touch, decorating the room with carpeting, student art samples, fine art prints, or plants creates a comfortable, home-like atmosphere. Copies of art work, posters, photographs, or quotations that reinforce classroom lessons can be visually displayed. The humming, flickering neon bulbs in traditional light fixtures might be replaced with full-spectrum lighting. Teachers and students might consider whether desks or tables provide the most appropriate work spaces. If possible, equipment such as easels, large paper pads, lap boards, colorful markers and paints, pencils, paper, and construction items should be readily accessible.

Storage Zones: Storage systems can be delineated with individual desks, bins, or colorful, plastic stacking trays that serve as "classroom lockers." Rules about responsibility for maintaining the classroom environment will need to be clearly communicated and followed.

Display Zones: To avoid visual overload, selected spaces should be identified for the display of art work, messages, or photographs. The display walls or partitions can attain a museum-like quality by the way in which works are hung and through the use of negative space.

Library Zone: Classroom reference materials, literature, video machines, typewriters, and computers can be well organized in this zone. This is often an appropriate place for independent or small group work.

Soft Zone: Many students enjoy a classroom if it conveys a living-room atmosphere. In the soft zone, students may read, lounge, play quiet games, or participate in small group discussions or creative dramatics. The soft zone can accommodate the needs of those students who like to stretch out on the floor or on a couch to read.

Movement Zone: A space should be designated in the classroom for students to conduct role plays or skits or to do energizing or calming exercises. In such a zone, it is preferable if furniture can be moved aside easily to accommodate small or large group physical activities. Teachers may also want to reflect on the existing traffic patterns in the classroom and consider how students move from one place to another. With intentional planning, movement around the classroom can be made more efficient.

From the suggested zones above, it is evident that classroom environments can better accommodate the physical, academic, and psychological needs of students and teachers alike. Educators may want to identify appropriate for their classrooms. Foregoing fixed rows of student desks by intentionally planning classroom space can transform schools into healthy, humane, and exciting places to learn. When provided the opportunity, students often are willing architects, who take delight in designing an environment tailor-made to suit their needs.

DRAMA

Drama has served as a method of learning and remembering from the beginning of recorded history. Pictures on cave walls depict the enactment of great hunts and heroic deeds. The plays of ancient Greece were written not only to entertain and provide emotional catharsis, but to educate as well. The dramas performed on the steps of medieval churches and temples taught illiterate people the morality and history of their religion. Today's theatres and television are also powerful educational forces in society—for better or worse.

The authors, as classroom teachers, have often wondered how anything could be taught without drama! It provides students with opportunities to almost become what they are studying and is a powerful way to bring academic content to life. Learning through drama is valuable at any grade level, but most especially in the middle school years when hormonal, physical, and psychological changes make learning in abstract ways even more difficult.

Whether students present a formal play before an audience or participate in theatre games not intended for an audience, enhanced learning often results.

FORMAL THEATRE

Formal theatre productions involve all of the intelligences in dynamically related ways. Reading the play, assuming the roles, memorizing lines and actions, creating costumes and sets, practicing music and at times choreography, and finally, performing before an invited audience all result in memorable experiences, enhanced self-confidence and poise, and learning that lasts throughout life.

Memorizing lines written by great playwrights can begin early. A second grade class recently performed with great gusto their own abridged version of Shakespeare's *A Midsummer Night's Dream*. Their parents were astonished to hear Shakespeare quoted at the dinner table. What a rich foundation for later studies of such plays in greater depth!

An eighth grade French class spent an entire quarter translating the songs of Hansel and Gretel into French, creating sets and costumes, choreographing the dances, and memorizing the songs and dialogue. Their performance for the rest of the school revealed their unprecedented gains in vocabulary and fluency in the process.

Some teachers have used a single Shakespearean play such as *Romeo and Juliet* or *King Lear* as the theme for a year-long interdisciplinary curriculum. In such classrooms, math assignments are integrated into set construction, history is based on Elizabethan times, science on what was then known about astronomy, anatomy and biology, art on costume design, and health on contagious diseases of the period.

Teachers who are committed to incorporating traditional theatre in their classrooms explain that students learn far more than the script, stage presence, and integrated academic content. The mental, physical, and technical discipline required to succeed on stage are also needed to succeed in life. Additionally, important cognitive skills are developed through rehearsing and performing, including the ability to organize thought, to perceive and analyze, to evaluate and reason, to discern the whole as well as the parts, to address complexity and ambiguity, and to collaborate with others to achieve a common goal. Theatre provides students with a rigorous educational experience that prepares them well for real-world problem-solving.

Two useful sources of scripts are Samuel French, Inc. at 7623 Sunset Blvd., Hollywood, CA. 90046, (213) 876-0570, and Baker's Plays, c/o Walter Baker Co., 100 Chauncey Street, Boston, MA 02111, (617) 482-1280.

ROLE-PLAYING

Less formal than theatre, role-playing gives teachers and students the freedom to create plays from topics studied in class. Unlike formal theatre, the process is more important than the product. Nearly any subject area can be transformed into role-plays, including mathematical story problems, scientific processes, the parts of speech, or historic events. Role-plays add action to language, are powerful tools for teaching information, and also develop interpersonal, intrapersonal, and problem-solving skills.

For teachers unfamiliar with the process, there are three main steps in preparing role-plays: planning, rehearsal and performance, and evaluation. Guidelines are provided below to assist teachers in their preparation:

Step 1: Planning

1. To ready students for a role-play, it is first necessary for the teacher to determine the desired educational objectives. Specify the learning outcomes for students to attain.

2. After the objectives are determined, the teacher or students can outline the role-play. The situation, the problem, or the fundamental issue must be identified.

3. Next, develop the roles and a process for selecting performers.

4. Determine whether the actors will have set lines to memorize or make up their own scripts.

5. Specify the amount of preparation time needed.

6. If there are student observers of the role-play, explain the audience's role and appropriate behavior.

7. Arrange the physical environment as appropriate.

8. Secure necessary resources such as equipment, costumes, or props.

Step 2: Rehearsal and Performance

Once the scenes are designed and the class informed of the objectives and content, students are ready to rehearse. An adequate amount of time is needed for preparation before the plays are performed. All non-performing students should be reminded to be supportive audience members as well as constructive evaluators.

When the rehearsals are complete, specify a time, date, and place for the performances. Ask the actors if they would like to have other classes or parents observe. If not, honor their requests to perform for their classmates only.

Occasionally, a teacher may want to intervene during a performance if an actor is in distress or if the interaction is inappropriate. In such cases, the teacher can offer a brief reflection on what has occurred and then allow the group to resume its role-play with the noted adjustments or with additional rehearsal time.

Step 3: Evaluation

After the performances, have students debrief their experiences. Questions can address the academic content, performance skill, student reactions to their experiences, and the audience's reactions as well since student observers can highlight what was done well and what might be improved. The teacher may or may not choose to have a role in the evaluation.

Role-plays are easily devised for nearly any subject. Students can role play individuals addressing prejudice and its impact, scientists at a press conference after the discovery of a medical breakthrough, or a child having difficulty learning to regroup in subtraction with a helper explaining the process. Assuming the roles of diverse life forms and their dependence on the environment can be role played as well as individuals addressing social or behavioral issues. And, certainly current or historical events are easily enacted.

One example of a role-play that addresses diverse points of view is the enactment of the confirmation of a political appointee. The class begins by discussing the appointment, its ramifications, and the fact that there are pros and cons to the individual's political agenda. Next, students identify the various characters involved in the confirmation process and "cast" the appropriate parts, ready the scene, including the confirmation panel, and determine whether the "audience" might actually serve as an interactive gallery in the process. The role-play starts with the appointee defending herself and the various panel members questioning or supporting her. The class would then be asked whether they would approve the appointment based upon the role-play.

A second example, at the elementary level, addresses an unpopular rule on the playground. Students disagree with a rule prohibiting the use of "hard" balls such as baseballs during school hours. Roles include students who support their use, impartial students, the school nurse, administrators, parents, and neighbors. A discussion follows with each participant explaining his point of view. It is often useful to have students represent an opinion different from the one they actually believe. Upon completion of the role-play, the class might compose and send a recommendation to the school administration.

CREATIVE DRAMA

Creative drama is less formal than role-plays since lines and actions are improvised as the play or scene develops. Re-enacting a scene to incorporate suggestions for improvement is an important component of this kind of theatre experience. Working without an audience is often necessary to allow students to concentrate and perform without self-consciousness.

One easy way to begin working with creative drama in the classroom is to ask students to play "group characters." For example, the teacher may read a story that has characters such as an old man, a little girl, and a giant. The children as a group can pantomime each of the characters, perhaps to appropriate music, and begin to develop confidence to play the part individually.

After the teacher has read the story, students then review the "plot," discuss how it could be performed, volunteer to play the different characters, plan the setting, and set the stage for action. A stage manager may be in charge of calling "Curtain" at the beginning and ending of the scenes. Following the performance, all students may participate in a critique discussing what was particularly successful and what could be improved.

Once a class gains experience in such activities, they can begin to improvise and dramatize more open-ended situations such as the organization of state offices with appointed and elected officials, the causes and effects of extinction, magnets attracting or repelling each other, or predicting what will happen as the adult population ages in the United States.

One example of the power of creative drama emerged in a fourth grade science class when the teacher realized her students did not understand photosynthesis as it was described in their textbooks. Deciding to try a kinesthetic approach, the instructor asked student volunteers to act out the five main "characters" involved in the process of photosynthesis: a plant, chloroplasts, water, carbon dioxide, and sunlight.

Simple signs made out of notecards were pinned onto each character. The teacher served as the narrator with the volunteer performers dramatizing chloroplasts resting on a leaf of a plant whose roots were drinking water from the ground. The water character sprinkled water on the ground and "feet" of the plant. Suddenly, sunlight shone on the leaf (portrayed with a flashlight) which caused the chloroplasts to absorb energy (flexed muscles). The chloroplasts, powered by sunlight, took the water and a gas from the air called carbon dioxide, twirled these two around to make sugar (candy bar) which then nurtured the entire plant.

This brief performance was repeated three times by different student volunteers, required approximately five to six minutes of time, and greatly improved the students' understanding of the concept. After the performances, students drew the process of photosynthesis on a piece of notebook paper and verbally explained the process to their partners. A week later, 90% of the students in the class accurately described photosynthesis on a written quiz.

As another example, a class of eleventh grade English students recently embarked on the study of Chaucer with less than enthusiastic attitudes until they brought Chaucer's *Canterbury Tales* to life through creative drama. Their teacher read the Prologue aloud with much feeling and humor and engaged the class in a discussion of the characteristics of these colorful people. Next, the teacher put student names in a medieval hat and let the students each draw one. The following day, after rereading the material, the students came into the classroom as the character they had chosen. In groups of four, they planned a meeting at a likely place—on the road or at a wayside tavern—and improvised dialogue keeping in mind everything they knew about the characters they were playing. Within a few days, they requested help in speaking Middle English!

SIMULATIONS

Simulations are also powerful learning tools since they place students in an environment or situation they must further develop for themselves. Simulations can be easily and quickly developed as appropriate for each classroom's content. Sample simulations used in classrooms have included:

- Visiting a French restaurant where students order food in the foreign language
- Spending a class period "living" during a significant time in history such as the Renaissance, the Civil War, or under the rule of Stalin
- Conducting a trial on the Salem witch cases, new senate bills, or involvement in war efforts
- Experiencing a variety of economic or social class systems
- Establishing a mini-classroom United Nations
- Decision-making for medical or environmental crises
- Living in a lunar space colony with limited numbers of people and resources.

Designing Simulations

Teacher-generated or commercial simulations can be used or adapted to teach a variety of academic content. The following steps outline how to create simulations:

1. First, determine the learning goals as with role-plays.

2. Next, identify simulation rules so that the constraints inherent in the real life situation are reproduced.

3. Gather and organize any resources or materials that will be needed.

4. Predetermine the logistics of the simulation such as dividing the class into small groups, assigning work spaces, and allotting time.

5. Schedule a discussion or writing session in which students debrief their completed simulation experiences.

Thoroughly prepared commercial science and social studies simulations are available that cover a wide range of content areas appropriate for elementary through high school students. One helpful resource is Interact, Box 997, Lakeside, CA 92040.

Whether working with formal theatre, role-plays, creative dramatics or simulations, planning is essential to avoid classroom chaos. Freedom to create must exist within clear structure guided by well- defined expectations. The main objective in using theatre-based strategies is to encourage students to enact the information they are learning. For some, this will be the way they will truly absorb and understand the content. For most, it will be the way they will remember it.

CREATIVE MOVEMENT

Movement theorists such as Rudolf Laban and Henri Bergson underscore the relationship between non-verbal, movement experiences and abstract, symbolic thought. Through movement we can both perceive and express the meaning in our experiences. By incorporating creative movement in the classroom, students are asked to problem-solve and analyze physically, while engaging their creative imagination in the process.

As Edward T. Hall, a noted anthropologist states in his book, *Beyond Culture*, "…Western man has created chaos by denying that part of his self that integrates while enshrining the parts that fragment experience." In order to integrate body and mind, it may be necessary to re-introduce ourselves to physical knowing.

Often teachers are uncomfortable using movement in the classroom. This may be because they do not personally value the importance of physical activity, or because of their own physical limitations, or because they are simply unfamiliar with such processes. The following creative movement strategies introduce such concepts in ways that are comfortable and practical for teacher and student alike. The range of strategies includes reflecting on bodily knowing, initial creative movement activities,

theatre games, and applying creative movement to basic skills instruction. We suggest you read through all the strategies and then select those that appear most applicable.

Peggy Hackney, a nationally recognized authority in Laban Movement Analysis, recommends that teachers and students address the following questions to heighten kinesthetic sensitivity and to increase body awareness:

UNDERSTANDING BODILY-KNOWING

1. **On a piece of paper, jot down associations, images, sounds, feelings, thoughts, concepts, beliefs, and "shoulds" for the word "body."**

2. **Draw a picture of yourself. Indicate on the drawing where on your body different parts of your life are represented such as school, home, sports, family, friends, pets, hobbies, and work.**

3. Next, consider unique forms of body knowing:

   Where in your body does sensation register when you and another person are in disagreement?

   Observe another person for a moment. What is his or her body communicating non-verbally?

   When you make a decision, where do you sense its right or wrongness?

   When you are creating ideas for teaching or doing a school project, where do the ideas come from?

The above questions hint at dimensions of kinesthetic intelligence and the wisdom of bodily-knowing. When involved in any activity, it is often beneficial to reflect for a moment on how the body is engaged, its sensations, and its own form of physical insight. Knowledge is felt kinesthetically and can be accessed by listening to the body and by moving to learn.

In addition to getting in touch with physical knowing, it is also possible to use creative movement to learn. Hackney offers suggestions for introducing moving to learn in the classroom as follows:

INTRODUCING CREATIVE MOVEMENT ACTIVITIES

1. Through individual or small group movement physically represent an animal, cloud, tree, concept, or event. Such identification enables students to perceive relationships and deepens their knowing of the object or event being considered. Movement experiments can be linked directly to subject-matter such as the water cycle, a historical event, a mathematical formula, or the structure of a short story.

2. Identify habitual movements in school and life situations. Learn to notice when your body is feeling physically tense, when your breathing stops, or when you divert your eyes. Such indicators signal discomfort and may compound physical stress. Conversely, notice situations that make you feel energized, eager, and comfortable. Reflect on what can be gleaned from such awareness to enhance other activities in life.

3. Imagine how ideas move. Catch an idea and encode it in physical movement. Provide students with five or so minutes during class to express through movement the concepts being learned. If students are initially hesitant, ask them to use only their arms and hands. Afterwards, ask them to explain what they learned about their topic by experiencing it kinesthetically.

It is important for the teacher to model physical activities as methods of enhancing learning and personal awareness. If the teacher feels uncomfortable doing so, explain the discomfort to the students, enlist their suggestions and support, or bring a guest into the classroom to assist both the students and teacher with such activities.

APPLYING CREATIVE MOVEMENT TO THE BASIC SKILLS

Creative movement activities are totally absorbing for many students. Teachers might initiate movement activities by asking such questions as, "How could movement reinforce this concept?" "How can classroom space be used to introduce today's math problems?" "How might you express what you have learned through movement?" As the teacher becomes accustomed to using movement as a tool for learning, answers will appear more readily.

To begin integrating creative movement into the teaching of basic skills, suggestions are provided below for math and language arts:

Language Arts: Students can study vocabulary through charades. They might role play parts of speech, proper outline form, the elements of literature, or characters and their motives. Individually they can develop finger or body alphabets or use macaroni, shaving cream, yarn, and glue for spelling-word practice. The whole class can silently pantomime stories as they are read. Students can physically punctuate written work by jumping out of their seats for exclamation marks, holding two fingers up on each hand for quotation marks, and arching an arm for a comma.

Mathematics: Story problems can be enacted with small groups of students. Students can draw flow charts explaining subtraction, division, or algebraic, problem-solving processes on carpeting or a cement floor. Once drawn, they can walk through the mathematical process in sequential steps. Geometry can be studied through kite-making, role playing theorems and axioms, and using one's arms to demonstrate right, obtuse and acute angles. Area and perimeter can be learned by measuring distances within the classroom or on school grounds, and the metric system might be studied through paper airplane-building and flying to scale.

For teachers who want to teach academic content with creative movement, the following questions can help formulate appropriate activities:

Creating Content-Specific Movement Activities:

1. How can physical movement be added to this lesson? How can the students use their bodies to "become" the topic under study?

2. What learning opportunities can be provided for students who need to move to learn while accommodating the needs of non-kinesthetic learners at the same time?

3. What kind of directions will clearly explain what is to be done kinesthetically?

4. How can students be encouraged to describe what they have learned after their kinesthetic experience?

5. How might students be involved in brainstorming their own kinesthetic opportunities to help themselves learn more efficiently?

6. What classroom management strategies will encourage appropriate participation?

DANCE

Another form of creative movement is dance. Through dance, students have the opportunity to learn, synthesize, and demonstrate their knowledge by means of choreography. For those interested in incorporating dance into the classroom, two excellent resources are *Teaching the Three R's through Movement* by Anne Green-Gilbert, published by MacMillan and *A Moving Experience: Dance for Lovers of Children and the Child Within* by Teresa Benzwie, published by Zephyr Press. Both books illustrate how teachers can help children discover qualities of space, time, numbers, and rhythm, while integrating cognitive learning with dance.

As with any form of creative movement, warm-ups are important before students explore dance. The following warm-ups not only help prepare students for kinesthetic activity, they also introduce the elements of dance. They are

provided by Debbie Gilbert, Executive Director of Very Special Arts in Washington State, and Co-Director with Joanne Petroff of the Whistlestop Dance Company,

ELEMENTS OF DANCE WARM-UPS:

Time:

1. To work with the element of time, ask students to walk at different speeds such as fast, medium, and slow. Suggest the use of other locomotive movements such as slide, jump, crawl, and leap. Select and play taped music with different speeds, play a drum at varying rates, or find a musician to accompany the movement.

2. From student work, select a "character" that is either a person, place, or thing. Ask students to move across the room as that character using motions that seem most fitting.

Space:

1. Ask students to use their bodies to create and explore a small space, a large space, a high and a low one.

2. Suggest that students explore an imaginary cave with tiny passageways, large caverns, high ledges, and low tunnels. Musical instruments or voices can be used for sound effects.

Shape:

1. While music is playing, ask students to move through the space in the room and freeze when it stops, noting the shapes of their frozen musical sculptures.

2. Together as a group, suggest that students make 25 shapes, changing with each beat of a drum or music.

3. In small groups, let students create shapes taken from classroom lessons, such as an isosceles triangle, a hydrogen molecule, quotation marks, or an historical date.

4. From students' academic studies, select a large complex shape for students to create

in groups such as a geometric theorem, a governmental system, a molecular structure, the parts of an essay, or the spread of a contagious disease.

Energy:

1. As music plays or a drum beats, students move first with "swinging" energy, then with "shaking" energy, and finally with "smooth" energy, inventing sounds to go with each energy quality.

2. In a circle so that everyone can see one another, each student takes a turn as dance leader. The "leader" chooses an energy quality, and demonstrates it, after which the others imitate this spontaneous choreography.

3. Select "actions" from class lessons such as dividing, borrowing, exploring, researching, or editing, and use any or all of the energy qualities to turn the actions into dance.

Once students have practiced the warm-ups, they can use the elements of dance to choreograph stories, poems, historical events, and mathematical formulas. A simple procedure follows:

A SEQUENCE FOR LEARNING THROUGH DANCE

1. Select a story, event, or process to transform into a dance. Have musical selections or a drum available for student use.

2. Divide the selection into scenes or sections.

3. Assign a small group to each section.

4. Let the small groups explore ways to use the elements of dance and provide time for choreographing their sections.

5. As a whole group, have students create a beginning shape or entrance and an ending shape or exit.

6. Select a narrator to read or explain each section.

7. Put it all together. As the narrator explains the action, the students dance the information. The narrator may want to use a handheld drum or play a musical selection to highlight the content, cue movements, set the mood, or inspire the dancers. Videotape the dance for later viewing and show the live or taped performance to an audience.

Many classrooms have discovered creative ways to incorporate dance into traditional curriculum areas. One third grade teacher, during a unit on space, created a dance of the planets. Students spun imitating the rotation of the planets while correctly moving counterclockwise in orbit. Students portraying the sun, moon, comets, and meteors all moved in appropriate relationship to each other.

A fifth grade teacher combined European folk dances with creative movement to teach spelling words. Students learned the basic steps and rhythms of traditional dances and then created their own variations. Additionally, they had to weave the spelling of their weekly words into the choreography.

A high-school Spanish teacher had students write rap songs in Spanish and combine them with street dancing. Vocabulary increased rapidly and test scores improved particularly among many of the students who previously had difficulty with a new language.

Students of all ages love to move rhythmically. Reluctance to "dance" in front of one's peers can be overcome by beginning simply and using warm-ups and movement games. Above all, however, creative movement should begin with the teacher, his subject area, and a splash of creativity. There is no right way to move or dance. Each of us can discover our own preferred ways to move, to dance, and to learn.

MANIVES

In third grade, Jason loved to build with blocks, legos, toothpicks, popsicle sticks, anything that fit together. During a unit on ancient history, Jason built an object for every culture studied. He fashioned Babylonian ziggurats out of legos, Egyptian pyramids with toothpicks and small marshmallows, the Great Wall of China from miniature clay bricks which he made, the Greek Parthenon from styrofoam computer-packing, Roman bridges out of popsicle sticks and brads, and Mayan temples with molded plastic strips resurrected from an old science kit. While appearing apathetic during most classroom activities, Jason was highly animated during his building projects. History came alive for Jason when he could build the structures of each era and culture studied.

Piaget and others have noted the importance of experiential materials in the learning process. Frequently, the use of pattern blocks, plastic cubes, colored rods, geoboards, tangrams, and other manipulatives meet not only tactile requirements of students but their developmental needs as well. Such manipulatives can be used to replicate anything from geometric shapes to Greek architecture to complex sugar molecules. What a student can see and manipulate in his environment ensures learning in ways that reading and lecture cannot.

Many ready-made materials exist to improve the teaching of math, spelling, science, reading, or geography. At times, however, teachers need materials for a particular unit that are not commercially available. The task cards and puzzles described below provide one option for making inexpensive classroom manipulatives.

TASK CARDS

Rita and Kenneth Dunn in their book, *Teaching Students through Their Individual Learning Styles*, recommend the creation of task cards as instructional aids. Task cards can augment the teaching of any subject and can introduce, reinforce, or review learning. Easy to make, these manipulatives satisfy the desire to see and touch at the same time.

Few materials are required to make task cards. Notecards (3"x 5" or 4"x 6"), scissors, and a set of colored markers are the necessary supplies. Each card is cut into two pieces in a jigsaw puzzle manner. A question can be written on one side of the card with the matching puzzle piece providing the answer. Or, one side might have a vocabulary word with the corresponding definition similar to flash cards. Some samples follow:

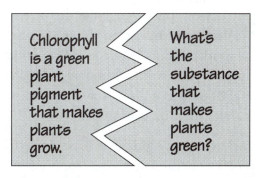

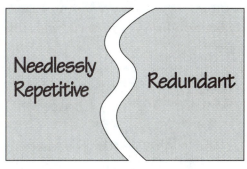

Once a set of cards is prepared, students take turns in pairs or small groups fitting the puzzle pieces together and quizzing each other on the information. In addition to fitting the cards together spatially and tactilely, students should be able to explain verbally each completed puzzle piece to reinforce their learning. In some cases, students might put the cards in order while providing a verbal rationale.

After the first set of task cards is complete, many ingenious ways of making future ones will be evident. Some might include movable parts, color-coding, or self-correcting options. Students can volunteer to create their own sets to reinforce their learning or to use to teach their peers. Sets of cards can be stored in decorated or labeled boxes.

TASK CARD PUZZLES

A variation of the task card is the task card puzzle which requires a sheet of cardstock either 8 x 11 or larger. The topic is written in the center with sub-topics or supporting details arranged around the central theme. The puzzle is cut into jigsaw pieces and scrambled. As a student fits the puzzle together, he or she has time to learn and reflect on the information at hand. Students can also be asked to embellish each puzzle piece with additional information, to paraphrase the information provided, or to create task card puzzles of their own.

One large jigsaw puzzle of kinesthetic learning processes addressed in this chapter is offered as a sample. Again, any content area could quickly be introduced or reviewed with this tactile strategy.

JUNK DRAWER MANIPULATIVES

Other manipulatives can be found by scouring drawers at home. Maria Montessori found her classroom materials in the junk piles of Rome! Buttons, beans, pebbles, poker chips, and pennies are just a few of the items that can be used for math counters. Toothpicks connected by marshmallows or dried peas soaked overnight make wonderful building materials for geometric shapes, houses, or spaceships.

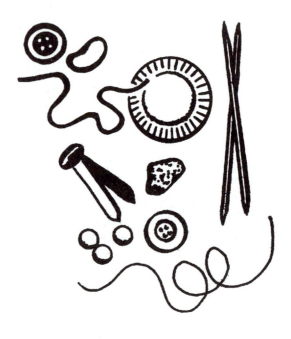

Colored electrical wire can be bent and twisted into diverse shapes for use in many subject areas. Telephone companies frequently give such wire away. This easy-to-manipulate material can replicate the anatomy of plants, animals, or structures enabling students to sculpt them according to scale. Old shoe boxes make fine backgrounds for dioramas of all sorts. Play dough or clay can also recreate scenes or characters from stories. With a little imagination, manipulatives can be found or made to add a tactile dimension to almost any lesson.

STAMPS

Stamps and block print devices are simple classroom manipulatives to make. They can be made from everyday materials such as vegetables, plants, sponges, styrofoam, egg cartons, plaster, linoleum, and cardboard. By gluing string onto a dowel, spool, roller, or rolling pin, a "running" stamp can be made. Even fingers make effective stamps.

Making Classroom Stamps and Block Prints

One of the least expensive and easiest ways to make durable, long-lasting stamps is to use inner tube rubber. Old inner tubes are free at any tire store.

1. **Cut rubber into 2 inch squares with scissors and distribute the squares to students.**

2. **Cut up small blocks of wood, one for each student. 1 x 2's from the lumber yard work well, as do thick sticks cut into 2 inch lengths.**

3. **Students first draw a model stamp design or stencil on paper. When the stencil is complete, it can be cut out of the rubber with an Exacto knife.**

4. **Next, glue designs on blocks of wood. (Remember, just as reflected in a mirror, they print in reverse of what is seen.) Students may put a stamp on both ends. Most types of glue work well, however, adequate drying time is essential, preferably overnight.**

5. **For printing ink, stamp pads work effectively, requiring the least clean-up. Block printing ink is the most permanent and professional looking, while tempera paint is cheap but messy. Elementary students can use markers applied directly to the stamp to create simple prints.**

From simple inner tube stamps to commercial selections, endless possibilities exist for their uses. Once made, ask students to use their stamps in a variety of ways: in math, problems and solutions can be stamped; "signature" stamps can identify student work; patterns can be studied in art, music, or math; in science, stamps can create molecular chains, electrical circuits, cell parts; in language arts stamps can be used for punctuation. Any art history or multi-cultural unit would be incomplete without stamps, since cultures throughout time have used them for everything from calligraphy in manuscripts to the decoration of wedding garments. Everyday designs like arrows, stars, hearts, and other symbols can serve as student logos or simply beautify classroom work.

Examples of stamp designs printed by third graders follow. The first are Chinese characters. The second is a traditional design from Ghana, West Africa.

One class used storm, sun, and rain stamps on state and United States maps to track, analyze, and predict weather patterns. Another used stamps to create Rebus stories for younger children. Although commercially-made stamps are available in educational supply outlets, catalogs, and stationery stores, students usually enjoy the process of making stamps as much as they do using them.

CLASSROOM GAMES

Game-based teaching has had numerous advocates. John Dewey claimed games were integral to schooling since they provided active and positive learning experiences. George Herbert Mead, a colleague of Dewey's, acknowledged their importance for the healthy socialization of children. Through games, children learn to imitate and assume diverse social roles. Certainly, too, Jean Piaget stressed the importance of game-playing in cognitive development.

Games involve students in imaginative and challenging situations that increase factual knowledge, decision-making, and interpersonal skills. When learning through games, most students eagerly and enthusiastically pursue their studies.

Games exist in many forms and can be elaborate technological simulations or as simple as "Simon Says." There are many ready-made classroom games such as "Take Off" or "Yotta." Teachers, however, frequently want games that teach specific academic content. The ones described in the following section are easy-to-make and adaptable to any subject matter area. They include scavenger hunts, large floor games, total physical response games modeled after the foreign language learning method developed by James Asher, and a generic review game.

SCAVENGER HUNTS

One game eagerly played by elementary and secondary students alike is a revised version of the scavenger hunt. Scavenger hunts can serve as fun-filled research processes appropriate for gathering data on any topic. Guidelines for creating scavenger hunts follow:

Creating a Classroom Scavenger Hunt

To create a scavenger hunt, the teacher first identifies a topic the students are about to study. It is necessary to list 10 to 30 essential concepts the unit will cover. This list, once compiled, serves as the basis of the scavenger hunt and directs student research. When the "hunt" is distributed, students are organized into small groups. Working in teams, each student is responsible for collecting approximately two to six items on the list. Once all data has been gathered, the teams present what they have learned to the other groups in the class. Points may be assigned to each item to turn the activity into a class competition or omitted to emphasize collaboration.

One high school history teacher wanted students to study the fall of Rome and make generalizations about the cycle of civilizations. Some of the sample scavenger hunt items she created included:

1. **Find three written resources that describe the decline of the Roman Empire. Compare and contrast their versions of what happened.**

2. **Identify and watch a film or videotape about the fall of Rome.**

3. **Identify and interview a knowledgeable adult about the reasons for the decline. Such adults may include other social studies teachers at the high school, community members, or history professors from the local university.**

4. **Gather data on Rome's monetary systems and its weaknesses.**

5. **Gather data on Rome's leaders and the military.**

6. **Gather data on the countries surrounding Rome and their increasing strength.**

7. **Pool all relevant information from the above items.**

8. **Make a chart that explains the potential causes and effects involved in Rome's downfall.**

9. **Make an educated guess as to the decline of Rome other than the reasons cited above and substantiate the claim.**

10. **Create a visual that explains your group's perception of the cycles of civilization.**

11. **Compare and contrast your group's theory of civilization with American culture today.**

Scavenger hunts are an extremely effective kinesthetic research process. Students may need two to three weeks to gather information and to prepare a group presentation for their classmates. Teachers will find it necessary to set aside classroom space on bulletin boards, desks, or tables for students to display their data.

LARGE FLOOR GAMES

Large floor games can reinforce any kind of academic content. Simple materials such as paper plates and colored markers are the only supplies needed to create the games described below:

Paper Plate Games

One effective physical learning format is a paper plate game. Teachers write facts on paper plates that are placed on the floor about two feet apart. For example, a science teacher might want to devise a game to review the names and symbols of the chemical elements. He would write C (for carbon) on three to four plates, Ca (for calcium), H (for hydrogen), and Mg (for magnesium) on several additional plates. It is necessary to write each symbol on three or four plates so that there are multiple copies. Next, the teacher picks a small group of approximately four to six student volunteers to play the game.

Two simple rules for game-playing must be explained: students must not talk or touch anyone else while playing. They are to silently hop onto the answer they think is correct. When they are ready to begin, the teacher calls out the element and students jump onto the paper plate with the correct symbol. The audience verifies whether the game players have selected the correct answers.

Students enjoy playing this game which can be readily adapted to science, math, language arts, foreign language, health, or art.

Kinesthetic Flow Charts

Numerous large floor games of all types can be created from simple flow chart formats. The best kind of academic content for this game is sequential as is found in plot structure, math formulas, recipes, scientific processes, or historical events. Teachers or students first design flow charts on notebook paper and then transfer them onto large sheets of butcher paper or vinyl. To begin creating a kinesthetic flow chart, first consider information to be placed into each of the boxes below:

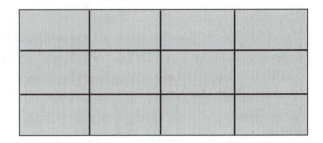

Cut out the boxes and arrange them in a logical sequence. Use arrows to indicate the order of steps involved. Once you are satisfied with the mock-up of the flow chart, transfer it to a large piece of vinyl or butcher sheet as follows:

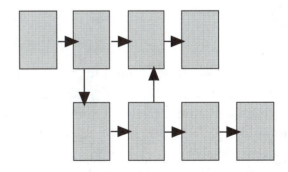

When the chart is ready, students actually walk or hop through it while explaining the information they step on. Such verbalization reinforces the kinesthetic learning of the academic content. For sample flow charts, refer to the visual chapter.

Total Physical Response Games

Dr. James Asher, a professor at San Jose State University, developed a foreign language learning method called "Total Physical Response" outlined in his book, *Learning Another Language through Action*. This movement-based method involves students in games and kinesthetic activities for second language learning. Asher's approach mirrors the way infants acquire their native language through verbal commands and corresponding movements that explain and reinforce the commands. The teacher's gestures and manipulation of objects convey the meaning of the spoken words. Students replicate the instructor's movements and are encouraged to use words when they feel confident doing so. TPR is currently used extensively both in this country and abroad for foreign language learning. An additional foreign language learning TPR resource is Jo Ann Olliphant's book entitled, *Total Physical Fun*, listed in the resources at the end of this chapter. The book contains 100 games to energize language learning.

Because of its success, TPR components have been adapted for general teaching. Its gamelike nature readily transfers to the teaching of all content areas. Some simple games in the basic skills areas follow:

Math: Divide students into three groups such as decimals, fractions, and percents. Give each group approximately 10 minutes to determine the physical benefits of being a fraction, percent, or decimal. Each group then attempts to convince the other two about the superiority of their mathematical process.

Students form a circle and a ball is tossed to one. A student or teacher calls out a math problem; students who know the answer raise their hands; the ball is tossed to one who must give the correct answer. Another question is asked. The student with the ball throws it to a classmate with a raised hand. The ball is tossed each time an additional question is asked and someone responds correctly. Those students who have difficulty generating correct answers can be assigned as the question givers before the game begins. The point of the game is to help everyone experience success in learning.

Science: Groups of students can volunteer or be elements that form to become different molecules. For example, one group might be methane (CH_4), another water (H_2O), another sulfur trioxide (SO_3). Each group must decide how many atoms of carbon, and hydrogen to enact for the rest of the class. As the formulas of the molecules are demonstrated, the audience guesses the identity of each, and students quickly draw a picture of the formula as well.

Any curriculum area: Draw a large hopscotch grid on a concrete floor or on a carpeted floor in chalk. Inside each square, write a vocabulary word students are learning. In groups, students proceed through the hopscotch taking another turn only if they offer a correct definition for the vocabulary word in their square.

If asked, students will eagerly generate game ideas based upon their studies. Teachers might occasionally include creating a classroom game as an optional assignment.

A Generic Review Game

To involve students in a kinesthetic review of academic material, gather a few simple resources together and prepare the following game. The required materials include one notecard per student, colored markers, and one large ball of twine. On each notecard, students write one vocabulary word, fact, or name they recently learned from a classroom lesson. Each card ideally contains information distinct from every other card.

Once the cards have been prepared, the game is ready to begin. Gather and redistribute the cards, giving one to each person in class. Students then form a large circle. The teacher begins by throwing a ball of twine to a student in the circle. That student starts the game by stating what's written on her card and expanding upon that information in some manner. If a student is stuck, she may ask someone to her right or left for assistance. Once the information is shared, other students in the circle raise their hands if they can explain how their cards relate to what was just said. The student holding the ball wraps the twine around a finger and tosses the ball to a student with her hand raised. The second student explains how the information on her card relates to what was just shared and adds any other additional information as well. Other students then raise their hands to continue the game.

For the initial round, each student should only have one opportunity to contribute and catch the ball of twine. Additional rounds can be added if the students and teacher desire. The interconnecting twine demonstrates visually and kinesthetically how the information is interrelated while offering an enjoyable review activity.

During the game, the teacher can change the level of questioning to engage higher-level thinking skills. After six or seven students have played, or during a second round, the teacher might request that students explain how their card differs from what was just stated, whether or not the preceding comments were correct, and/or create new responses that are unique and imaginative. After everyone has contributed and the game is over, assign a student at the end of the review to rewind the ball of twine for future use.

PHYSICAL EDUCATION

New definitions of physical education are emerging from sport and educational associations. Rather than viewing physical education as a class that takes place in the gym three or more times a week, many groups call for a broader perspective of the field. In 1986, the Outcomes Committee of National Association for Sport and Physical Education established a definition of the "physically-educated person." This definition emphasizes an essential aspect of kinesthetic intelligence: the importance of knowing and participating in health-enhancing activities. Four main characteristics of the physically-educated person were identified and include:

CHARACTERISTICS OF A PHYSICALLY-EDUCATED PERSON

1. **A physically-educated person has learned the skills necessary to perform a variety of physical activities. He moves using concepts of body awareness, space awareness, effort and relationships; he demonstrates competence in a variety of individual and group skills, has proficiency in a few forms of physical activity, and has learned how to learn new physical skills.**

2. **A physically-educated person is physically fit and can assess, achieve, and maintain such fitness by designing personal programs in accordance with appropriate training and conditioning principles.**

3. **A physically-educated person regularly participates in health-enhancing activity at least three times a week and selects and participates in lifetime physical activities.**

4. **A physically-educated person identifies the benefits, costs, obligations, risks, and safety factors involved in his physical activities. Such a person knows the rules, strategies, and appropriate behaviors for selected activities, and understands that wellness involves more than being physically fit. Additionally, he will recognize that participation in physical activity can enhance multi-cultural and international understanding and provide the opportunity for enjoyment, self-expression, and communication.**

While the definition of physical education is expanding, important work has been done in refining performance in specific physical endeavors. Peak performance researchers have learned much about educating for and perfecting physical and academic skills. One additional outcome they emphasize in physical education is the necessary union of body and mind to enhance any physical skill. Some of this information is shared in the intrapersonal chapter.

ADVENTURE EDUCATION

"Adventure learning" programs which can include "initiatives," ropes courses, new games, or Outward Bound activities confront students with physical challenges. In small cooperative groups, students engage in problem-solving situations that entail physical, social, emotional, and/or intellectual risks. Claiming that most school curriculum is unnecessarily dull, adventure education proponents suggest that significant learning occurs when risk and problem-solving are involved.

Adventure curriculums contain a sense of unpredictability, drama, and suspense. This is often achieved through the situation itself, such as problem-solving in a forest, slum, or on a canoe trip. Adventure is also established in the classroom by a teacher who builds mystique, suspense, and anticipation into the learning experience. By overcoming adventure challenges, students learn about their self-imposed limitations and their potential capabilities. By working in small groups, they also learn about collaboration, and by confronting fear, change, and uncertainty, students learn important coping skills useful in daily living.

Sample Adventure Activities

Most adventure activities follow a similar format. Students are presented with an adventure, confront the challenge, debrief what they have experienced, and generalize the event to better understand themselves and others. An excellent resource of adventure activities is Karl Rohnke's book, *Silver Bullets: A Guide to Initiative Problems, Adventure Games and Trust Activities*. Two sample adventure activities adapted from Rohnke's book are described below: the "Spider Web" and the "Ten-Member Pyramid."

The Spider Web

The object of the "Spider Web" is to move a group of students through a nylon web without touching the web material. Touching the web activates an imaginary spider, and anyone who does touch it must begin again. The web, constructed of nylon cord and anchored between two trees or vertical supports, contains as many openings as the number of group members and in sizes appropriate for different group members. Once the web is in place, participants determine a way to pass everyone through its openings. When one person has reached the other side of the web, he is no longer able to assist the others.

Although students cannot dive through the web, they can go under it. One or more adults who are silent observers and safety guides are present with each group and intervene only if web activities appear unsafe. It is up to the group members to do all of the problem-solving.

The Spider Web can be mastered only if students collaborate and support each other through the activity. During debriefing, issues such as leadership, trust, and decision-making should be addressed. Students can also reflect on the intellectual, physical, and emotional concerns that were present as well as take pride in what was accomplished and learned. In processing the experience, students might reflect on what they have learned from this activity that can extend to everyday life.

The Ten-Member Pyramid

Another adventure education activity is called "The Ten-Member Pyramid." The goal is to build a symmetrical pyramid with a group of ten people as quickly and efficiently as possible. The following four simple rules must be followed:

1. If possible, the group should be co-ed.

2. Timing begins when the final rule has been given and ends when the last person tops off the horizontal or vertical apex of the pyramid.

3. The exercise should be undertaken only on soft mats inside or on soft ground outdoors.

4. The only acceptable pyramid is a 4-3-2-1 person one.

To resolve the pyramid problem, groups typically begin with a frenzied, problem-solving approach. Actually, this activity could be completed in five seconds by groups simply lying down or lining up in the assigned sequence; however, during debriefing, participants learn that thoughtful planning is necessary to achieve an efficient solution. They can also discuss decision-making, leadership, and cooperation, as well as issues or concerns that may arise for individual members.

Classroom Adventures

Classroom-based adventures can also be created. Students might assume the task of building a loft in a classroom to meet certain specifications, to plan, plant and grow enough vegetables for the school cafeteria, to write and perform plays that will appeal to younger students, or to learn essential course content in two months or less. A sense of challenge, risk, drama, and real-world problem-solving integrated into classroom work adds a missing ingredient for students who seek adventure and excitement in their lives.

EXERCISE BREAKS

Students often sit at desks for long periods of time in positions that prevent adequate, easy breathing. Shallow breathing is enough to sustain life, but not enough to keep the body relaxed and the mind alert! Brief exercise breaks with windows open—even for a few minutes—can bring new alertness and energy. It can also help refocus attention.

The kinesthetic activities which follow are not intended to mirror the content of academic lessons, although in some cases they might do so. Their goal is to energize the mind/body system and in so doing equip students for enhanced learning. It is recommended that teachers first select and practice the recommended exercises before sharing them with students.

QUICK ENERGIZERS

When students appear to be lethargic such as at the beginning of the school day or after lunch, a minute or two of physical exercise can quickly refresh bodies and minds. Use any or all of the following familiar activities. Students can take turns leading their classmates through:

HIP ROTATIONS

KNEE ROTATIONS

NECK ROLLS

SHOULDER ROLLS

PICKING APPLE STRETCHES—reach one arm and hand up at a time, making a grasping motion; alternate with the other arm

DEEP BREATHING—extend arms with open hands; pushing with palms, inhale and reach way up. Exhale and reach down to the floor.

TEN SHIN GO SO

A simple, yet powerful physical and mental focusing activity is called Ten Shin Go So. This exercise was developed jointly by Tai Chi and Aikido masters. The physical movements tell a story of offering one's talents in service to others. Initially, the storyline may be recited, since it assists in memorizing the sequence of movements. For those who prefer, the story may be omitted as unnecessary. Ten Shin Go So gently energizes the body, calms and directs mental attention, and requires about three minutes.

> **Begin by standing with your feet and big toes touching. Your left thumb is clasped in your right hand. Your head is lowered, your mind is at ease and peaceful.** *Storyline: You assume the position of the unborn.*

> **Inhale and spread your feet to shoulder width. Arms circle up and back with fingers open and outstretched.** *Storyline: You greet life.*

> **Exhale and bring your arms down, drawing a mountain shape (or triangle) in the air in front of you. Relax your shoulders and bring your arms down until they are behind you.** *Storyline: You view your mountain to climb in life.*

> **Inhale, pulling your arms forward. Bring your hands together, link your index fingers and thumbs together as your hands move up, forming a triangle. Look through the triangle, while continuing to push your palms upwards.** *Storyline: You see your path to walk in life.*

> **Bring your arms up and back. Exhale and spread your arms backward and downward bending slightly forward as you gather energy until hands reach waist level.** *Storyline: You prepare yourself for your life's work.*

> **Inhale and bring your hands up and together at the wrists with open palms and fingers pointing down. Raise your outstretched arms to chest level with palms making an offering motion.** *Storyline: You offer your talents in service to others.*

> **Exhale and relax. Return to the beginning position with head bent slightly, left thumb clasped in right hand, feet together, shoulders relaxed, and mind peaceful.** *Storyline: You rest from your efforts.*

Some teachers use Ten Shin Go So at the beginning of a class session to focus student energies, or during class to provide a needed stretch break. Telling the storyline the first couple of times as the sequence is learned helps commit the movements to memory. After the process is known, however, it is best done silently.

THE EIGHT TREASURES

Some ancient Tai Chi warm-up exercises, called The Eight Treasures, are described below. These exercises have been used with people of all ages in China for hundreds of years. They are useful with students of all ages early in the morning to wake up the mind and body, when attention of the group starts to wander, and after lunch when energy wanes.

1. *Uphold the Heaven with two hands:* Begin by bending over with knees slightly bent. Fold fingers of both hands together like a basket and gradually begin straightening up the body, breathing in deeply. When the hands are at waist level, turn palms upward and continue raising arms until they are overhead with palms pressing upwards. When lungs are full, fill them fuller. Unclasp hands, lower arms, and repeat.

2. *Open the bow to the left and right:* With feet shoulder-width apart, bend knees and hold an imaginary bow in one hand. Place an imaginary arrow on it with the other, and draw across the chest, all the while breathing in deeply. Repeat on other side.

3. *Raise the hands separately with one palm up and one palm down:* Raise one hand overhead with the palm facing upwards, and the other hand down at the side, with the palm facing the floor. Stretch while breathing deeply, then reverse hands and repeat.

4. *Looking backwards over both shoulders:* Slowly turn one's head to one side, stretching the eyes as though looking behind you. Breathe in slowly, and breathe out as one's head returns to the front. Repeat over other shoulder.

5. *Hold the fists tightly and gaze with angry eyes:* With feet shoulder width apart, bend knees, and bring both fists into the chest. Extend one, breathing out, and widening the eyes. Breathe in as the fist comes back in towards the chest, and repeat with the other fist. (Make sure students are as far apart as possible on this one, and suggest that no one "gaze" at anyone else with the angry eyes!)

6. *Jump lightly:* Jump up and down on toes ten times, lightly. (Have students imagine they are jumping on clouds, and you'll be surprised how quietly this can be done.)

7. *Shake the head and wave the tail:* With feet shoulder width apart, make a circular motion with the upper body, breathing out as you go down one side of the circle, then breathing in as you go up the other side. Repeat several times, then reverse directions.

8. *Hold the toes with two hands:* Flop over and let the hands hang downwards. Bend the knees slightly, and try to touch toes or go as far down as you can bend easily without straining the back. Breathe in deeply as you come up slowly.

These exercises may be done in sequence, or just a few at a time. You will be surprised at how they relax the body and refocus the mind.

EYE EXERCISES

Eye exercises are useful after extensive reading or computer work. Cup the hands over the eyes and look into the blackness for a minute or two. Then open the eyes wide and circle in a clockwise direction without moving the head. Reverse directions. Extend the arm in front with thumb up, circumscribe a large circle and let the eyes follow the thumb, first clockwise, then counter-clockwise. Bring the hand to the nose, and slowly extend the arm and hand outwards, following with the eyes. Move in and out several times. Alternate looking at distant and close objects. Such exercises relax the eyes, and help strengthen the eye-accommodation muscles involved with reading.

WAKING UP

When students are sleepy or losing focus, try this brief exercise. Extend arms in front and shake hands vigorously. At the same time, say, "Zzzzzzzzzz," like a hive of bees, until the top of your head vibrates. Keep shaking your hands as you extend arms overhead, out to the side, down in front, one up and one down, the other up and other down, overhead again, and repeat the sequence. End with several deep breaths, extending arms overhead, and breathe out as arms come down.

CALMING DOWN

There may be times when students are hyperactive, perhaps overstimulated by a field trip or other activity, and you may wish to calm or quiet their energy. Slow, deep breathing and stretching exercises with eyes closed and quiet music playing in the background can be remarkably effective. Or, ask students to imagine swimming slowly with breast-strokes in warm water, breathing deeply in rhythm with the arm movements.

FIELD TRIPS

Well-planned field trips offer meaningful learning experiences for many students, particularly when the trips are integrated with areas studied in the classroom. From simple nature walks or guided museum tours to an international exchange program, field trips provide concrete, experiential learning opportunities. Camping and discovery trips to wilderness areas and field trips to businesses, cultural organizations, and research centers all vitalize learning. Students who are reluctant to work in the classroom are often highly motivated to gather information from a field trip to present later in reports, visuals, databases, or follow-up research.

To be successful, learning goals must be well-planned and communicated before the excursion. When unaware of the goals, many students view field trips as entertainment and overlook their value. By engaging in both preparatory as well as follow-up activities, students will better appreciate the value of such hands-on, real-world learning. Some guidelines for organizing effective field trips are offered below:

Field Trip Guidelines

1. **Identify the purpose and expected outcomes of the experience.**

2. **Provide logistical information such as the location, time, appropriate clothing, and materials. Secure required signatures from students, parents, school district personnel, and the field trip agency if needed.**

3. **Organize student groups and specify their responsibilities. Establish behavior expectations.**

4. **Assign a task to complete or let students devise their own tasks. Distribute any materials the students might need on the field trip.**

5. **Debrief the event with class or small group discussions, journal sharing, or art work.**

6. **Encourage sharing of the experience with other classes, administrators, parents, or community members.**

Since many schools limit the number of field trips because of budgetary or transportation reasons, teachers must often find creative ways to expand learning beyond the four walls of the classroom. One German teacher led her students on weekly walks during which the class conversed in German, identified items in the environment, and even conjugated verbs to a marching beat as the class made its way down the street.

An elementary art teacher routinely takes her class outdoors to gather materials for class art projects: tall grasses for weaving, rocks for painting, sticks and other articles (including litter) for mobiles, and a variety of leaves, flowers, and bark for printing and textures.

An elementary music teacher has his students go outside after a big storm to gather fallen tree limbs to cut up or break up for rhythm sticks. Every student finds his own personal pair of sticks and uses them regularly as percussion for learning rhythms.

A high school American history teacher takes his class on walks to survey the community in its present form. Upon returning to class, students write about any changes that they notice in the community. Similar "walking field trips" are effective for whole language classrooms with students writing descriptions or stories about objects observed during their walks. Whether in the city, the suburbs, or the country, walking field trips as well as bus or car excursions offer a variety of opportunities for science, social studies, and language experiences.

TECHNOLOGY THAT ENHANCES KINESTHETIC INTELLIGENCE

Learning through technology is a highly active and interactive process when used appropriately. Computers rely mostly on eye-hand coordination for their operation—keyboarding and the use of the mouse or touch-screen. This kinesthetic activity reinforces learning and makes the student an active participant in the learning process.

The popularity of video games is due to the total engagement of the player and skillful physical response to the challenges. Games such as "Pong" and "Breakout" were among the first to demonstrate the appeal of this kind of technology. Later, "Tetris" was designed by Alexey Pajitnov, a Russian mathematician, researcher in artificial intelligence, and member of the USSR Academy of Sciences; it is now published in Apple software. It demands fast decision-making and hand-eye coordination, along with quick testing of hypotheses. Undoubtedly, it is these action-packed challenges which engage students who might otherwise be bored in conventional math classes even though they call for the same kind of spatial and logical thinking.

Programs such as "Lego Logo" offer ways to connect the computer to external manipulatives, such as Lego blocks with gears, wheels, and motors. Starting with these, students can invent innumerable kinds of machines to control through computer programs they develop themselves.

Other kinds of programs that combine kinesthetic activity with the development of analytical thinking are Brøderbund's "Science Toolkit" and IBM's "Personal Science Lab." The student creates physical or scientific experiments, the results of which are analyzed and displayed on a computer screen. These are just the beginning of a whole new series of computer programs that are connected to physical activities.

Some computer simulations enable students to experience events seldom encountered in everyday life. Observing and responding to nuclear plant malfunctions, emergence of new life forms, operation of different vehicles or machines, or the passage of geological epochs provide students with enriched classroom experiences.

"Electronic field trips" may not involve the physical body, yet students feel as if they are actually exploring the depths of the sea or the inside of a volcano as they accompany researchers in areas where very few can go. Recently, classrooms of students, linked electronically to explorers investigating the tectonic plates in the depths of the Mediterranean, were able to communicate with the scientists, ask questions, or request the viewing of areas or objects more closely. The students were almost there.

For teachers interested in learning about microcomputer simulations, software reviews can be found in *The Computing Teacher* and *Electronic Learning*. Additionally, the Northwest Regional Educational Laboratory located in Portland, Oregon, publishes a review entitled *Microsift* that contains software ratings generated by teachers who have used the programs.

Multi-media technology also involves much actual physical activity as information is gathered from databanks, books, and photos, as new information is generated by camcorders, and finally as all of it is pieced together electronically through hypermedia programs such as Hypercard or LinkWay. Needless to say, the production of filmed plays or dance programs also involves and exercises kinesthetic intelligence.

Shirley Ririe and Joan Woodbury, co-directors of the Ririe-Woodbury Dance Company in Salt Lake City, have found exciting uses of technology in teaching dance. They enhance dance with computer-generated slide images or have a camera operator videotape and instantly edit a performance, while projecting the edited version on screens behind the dancers. This kind of collaboration among choreographer, recorder, and dancers creates a whole new dance form. Dramatic productions are also making use of these combinations of technology and physical activity. For example, in a recent production of *Macbeth* a hologram (a laser-produced image which seems to hang in the air) of Banquo appeared with the live actors on-stage.

At a time when technology makes it very easy to become a passive observer or only a recipient of information, it is not only possible but essential for students to become actively engaged in learning, as these foregoing examples demonstrate.

SUMMARY

When asked to remember an educational experience, most of us recall a lesson that directly engaged us—an activity that stimulated our senses, one that provided hands-on learning, and one filled with meaning or insight. Such learning occurs kinesthetically, with the mind remembering well what the body experiences.

In her book *A Moving Experience*, Teresa Benzwie explains,

"The more we know about education and how the brain processes information, the more we understand that movement is central to learning. However, we often tend to immobilize children behind desks instead of utilizing the potential of their tremendous natural vitality. To understand symbols such as numerals and letters, or ideas in science and social studies, children can use not only eyes and ears, but the entire being. How far is far and how near is near is experienced from the perspective of the child's own body. Through such relatedness, abstractions become more concrete, and learning becomes an internal process."

This chapter has highlighted a variety of hands-on instructional strategies easily incorporated into classroom lessons. Many students who do not learn well in traditional ways find it easier to understand and remember difficult abstractions kinesthetically.

In order to reflect on the strategies and identify ones that may be appropriate for an individual educator's classroom, we offer the following inventory:

APPLYING KINESTHETIC INTELLIGENCE TO INSTRUCTION

1. Important ideas or insights gleaned from this chapter: _____

_____

_____

_____

_____

_____

2. Areas I'd like to learn more about: _____

_____

_____

_____

_____

_____

3. Ways I can use this information in my teaching. Please note that the strategies described in this chapter are listed below with space provided to note how each might be incorporated into classroom instruction.

KINESTHETIC STRATEGY   **CLASSROOM APPLICATION**

The Physical Environment:
   Classroom Zones _____

Drama:
   Formal Theatre _____
   Role-Play _____
   Creative Dramatics _____
   Simulations _____

Creative Movement:
   Understanding Bodily-Knowing _____
   Introducing Creative Movement Activities _____
   Applying Creative Movement to Basic Skills _____
   Creating Content-Specific Movement Activities _____

Dance:
   Elements of Dance _____
   A Sequence for Learning through Dance _____

Manipulatives:
   Task Cards _____
   Task Card Puzzles _____
   Junk Drawer Manipulatives _____
   Making Classroom Stamps _____

Classroom Games:
   Scavenger Hunts _____
   Large Floor Games _____
   Total Physical Response Games _____
   Generic Review Game _____

Physical Education:
   Characteristics of a Physically-Educated Person _____
   Adventure Education _____
   The Spider Web _____
   The Ten-Person Pyramid _____
   Classroom Adventures _____

Exercise Breaks:
   Quick Energizers _____
   Ten Shin Go So _____
   The Eight Treasures _____
   Eye Exercises _____
   Waking Up _____
   Calming Down _____

Field Trips:
   Field Trip Guidelines _____

Technology That Enhances Kinesthetic Intelligence: _____

KINESTHETIC REFERENCES

Asher, J. (1988). *Learning Another Language through Action*. Los Gatos, CA: Sky Oaks Productions.

Barbe, W. and Swassing, R. (1979). *Teaching through Modality Strengths*. Columbus, OH: Zaner-Bloser.

Benzwie, T. (1988). *A Moving Experience: Dance for Lovers of Children and the Child Within*. Tucson: Zephyr Press.

Dewey, J. (1900). *The School and Society*. Chicago: University of Chicago Press.

Dunn, R. and Dunn, K. (1978). *Teaching Students through Their Individual Learning Styles*. Reston, VA: Reston Publishing Co.

Gilbert, A. G. (1989). *Teaching the Three R's through Movement*. N.Y.: MacMillan.

Gilbert, A. G. (1992). *Creative Dance for All Ages*. Reston, VA: National Dance Association.

Goodlad, J. (1984). *A Place Called School: Prospects for the Future*. N.Y.: McGraw Hill Book Company.

Hackney, P. (1988). "Moving Wisdom" in *In Context Quarterly*. No. 18, Bainbridge Is., WA: In Context.

Horn, R. E. and Cleaves, A. (eds.). (1981). *The Guide to Simulations/Games for Education and Training*. Beverly Hills, CA: Sage.

King, M. (1988). *Dare to Imagine: An Olympian's Technology*. Aurora, CO: Midcontinental Regional Educational Laboratory.

MacRae-Campbell, L., McKisson, M. and Campbell, B. (1990). *Our Only Earth Series: The Ocean Crisis*. Tucson, AZ: Zephyr Press.

McKim, R. (1972). *Experiences in Visual Thinking*. Monterey, CA: Brooks Cole.

National Standards for Arts Education. (1994). *Dance, Music, Theatre, Visual Arts: What Every Young American Should Know and Be Able to Do in the Arts*. Reston, VA: Music Educators National Conference.

Olliphant, J. (1994). *Total Physical Fun*. 11004 111th St. SW, Tacoma, WA 98498.

Rohnke, K. (1984). *Silver Bullets: A Guide to Initiative Problems, Adventure Games, and Trust Activities*. Dubuque, Iowa: Kendall/ Hunt Publishing.

Spolin, V. (1963). *Improvisation for the Theater*. Evanston, IL: Northwestern University Press.

Spolin, V. (1986). *Theater Games for the Classroom*. Evanston, IL: Northwestern University Press.

Taylor, A., Aldrich, R., Vlastos, G. (1988). "Architecture Can Teach." in *In Context Quarterly*, No. 18, Bainbridge Is., WA: In Context.

Thornburg, D. (1989). *Education, Technology, and Paradigms of Change for the 21st Century*. Starsong Publications.

Vitale, B. M. (1982). *Unicorns Are Real: A Right-Brained Approach to Learning*. Rolling Hills Estates, CA: Jalmar Press.

CHAPTER 4

EVERYONE IS AN ARTIST:
VISUAL-SPATIAL INTELLIGENCE

*I found that I could say things with color
and shapes that I had no words for.*

— *Georgia O'Keefe*

SARAH'S STORY
Sarah appeared unmotivated, lacking pride in her school work and turning in papers that were not indicative of her true capabilities.

The one area where she excelled was drawing, yet such skills were rarely needed for most classroom tasks. Sarah was usually obligated to draw on the sly, adorning the margins of her papers with artistic flourishes or filling blank sheets of paper with complex imagery. Teachers often requested that Sarah refrain from doing art work so that she could better pay attention.

Throughout her early elementary years, Sarah was described as restless and disruptive; moreover, she seldom recalled information from a day's study. By the time she was in fifth grade, her teacher noticed that when Sarah was allowed to draw during a lesson, she was not only quiet, but also appeared attentive to class material. Her hand went up occasionally to answer questions and her recall was sharp.

One day as the teacher was speaking with Sarah about a science unit on the structure of the earth, Sarah excitedly showed her a drawing of the morning's lecture. There, in a visual language developed and understood by the girl, were images that represented the earth's core, the mantle, and crust with appropriate features and proportions displayed in an artistic code. Sarah's drawings captured the essence of the subject matter itself.

Whenever Sarah could draw, chart, or visually symbolize information, learning came to life for her. She possessed diverse cognitive skills that enabled her to visualize information and synthesize data and concepts into visual metaphors. Such abilities indicate some of the components of visual-spatial intelligence.

DEFINITION: UNDERSTANDING VISUAL-SPATIAL INTELLIGENCE

Visual imagery is a means of knowing the world that is older than linguistic symbolism. Fossil records indicate that long before the human mechanisms for speech had evolved, the organs of vision were highly developed, serving as important tools of knowledge for early human beings. It was visual-spatial intelligence that inspired the earliest record of human drawings. During the Ice Age, between 60,000 to 10,000 B.C., cave dwellers in France, Spain, Africa, and Scandinavia painted drawings of animals and scenes from their own experience. Such pictorial imagery eventually led to the development of writing and mathematics. Language evolved from images to pictographs to symbolic codes becoming increasingly abstract. Today, most educational programs stress the importance of abstract symbols in reading, writing, and arithmetic, often overlooking other aspects of visual-spatial intelligence.

Visual-spatial intelligence includes an aggregate of related skills including visual discrimination, recognition, projection, mental imagery, spatial reasoning, image manipulation, and the duplication of inner or external imagery, any or all of which may be expressed by a single person. In individuals such as Leonardo da Vinci, visual-spatial intelligence manifests itself in great works of art. In others, such as Newton, who visualized the universe as a machine-like collection of interrelated parts, it is evident in subtle inner imagery.

Although visualization is central to spatial intelligence, it is not directly related to sight, and in fact, can be highly developed in those who are blind. In this chapter, we refer to this intelligence as both visual and spatial since people perceive and process information through both modalities.

In elementary and secondary classrooms, many visually-oriented learners respond well to movies, television, slides, posters, charts, diagrams, computers, and color-coded materials. Besides observation, learning can also be enhanced with visual tools such as computers, telescopes, video cameras, stencils, signs, artistic media, and building and drafting supplies. Some visually-capable learners arrive at unique, unconventional solutions to artistic problems through tools that allow them to express their unique vision.

Classroom environments can be made more supportive and inviting when visual humor is part of the setting. Cartoons, witty posters, and humorous pictures, or photographs related to the subject matter convey pleasant messages about learning to students. Visual-spatial intelligence can also be developed when students are encouraged to try their hand at cartooning or other humorous illustrations.

✔ CHECKLIST OF VISUAL-SPATIAL QUALITIES

Robert McKim in his book, *Experiences in Visual Thinking*, suggests that visual thinking pervades all human activity. It is not solely the domain of artists but also of surgeons, engineers, business people, architects, mathematicians, carpenters, mechanics, football coaches, persons planning what to wear for the day, and daydreamers.

Visual-spatial thinking underlies moving figures in a chess game, organizing one's schedule for a day, moving furniture within a room, or reading maps on a trip. Not all visually-capable learners exhibit the same skills. Some may be talented in painting, others at building three-dimensional models, and still others at critiquing fine art. It is likely that a person with well-developed visual-spatial intelligence:

1. Learns by seeing and observing. Recognizes faces, objects, shapes, colors, details, and scenes.

2. Navigates self and objects effectively through space, as when moving one's body through apertures, finding one's way in a forest without a trail, moving a car through traffic, or paddling a canoe on a river.

3. Perceives and produces mental imagery, thinks in pictures, and visualizes detail. Uses visual images as an aid in recalling information.

4. Decodes graphs, charts, maps, and diagrams. Learns with graphic representation or through visual media.

5. Enjoys doodling, drawing, painting, sculpting, or otherwise reproducing objects in visible forms.

6. Enjoys constructing three-dimensional products, such as origami objects, mock bridges, houses, or containers. Is capable of mentally changing the form of an object—such as folding a piece of paper into a complex shape and visualizing its new form, or mentally moving objects in space to determine how they interact with other objects, such as gears turning parts of machinery.

7. Sees things in different ways or from "new perspectives" such as the negative space around a form as well as the form itself or detects one form "hidden" in another.

8. Perceives both obvious and subtle patterns.

9. Creates concrete or visual representation of information.

10. Is proficient at representational or abstract design.

11. Expresses interest or skill in being an artist, photographer, engineer, videographer, architect, designer, art critic, pilot, or other visually-oriented careers.

12. Creates new forms of visual-spatial media or original works of art.

These are only a few of the possible expressions of visual-spatial intelligence. It is important to acknowledge that spatial intelligence underlies all human activity and cannot adequately be confined to a single list of qualities or characteristics.

VISUAL-SPATIAL LEARNING PROCESSES

In academic settings, visual intelligence is often relegated to the domain of the visual arts. As such, many students forego opportunities to develop perceptual, imaging, and aesthetic skills. In McKim's book, *Experiences in Visual Thinking*, the author identifies three broad components of visual imagery: external imagery we perceive, internal imagery we dream or imagine, and the kind of imagery we create through doodling, drawing, or painting. According to McKim, visual thinking consists of what we see, imagine, or draw. The instructional strategies in this chapter suggest activities for each of these three capacities and include:

ESTABLISHING A VISUAL LEARNING ENVIRONMENT

With a little forethought, effort, and assistance from the students themselves, classrooms can be transformed into aesthetically pleasing environments. Lighting might be improved with full-spectrum bulbs and a floor lamp or two. Crescent or circular seating patterns are often preferable to rows of desks, since students can more readily see and interact with one another. Pieces of inviting furniture such as a comfortable couch, chairs, or pillows can be welcome classroom additions. Colorful fabric or floor covering, bright, as well as nicely displayed art work, posters or charts, and cut flowers or a plant or two establish a positive ambiance that greets students with visual vitality. With time, effort, and respect devoted to the visual environment, teachers might effectively engage the classroom as a powerful learning tool. Some suggestions follow for enhancing the visual dimension of the classroom.

VISUAL TOOLS

A variety of tools including paper, chalk, pencils, markers, paints, cameras, computers, videos, and overhead projectors should be readily available for students' and teachers' use. Organized storage is a necessity for maintaining supplies and limiting visually distracting clutter.

INTENTIONAL DISPLAY AREAS

To avoid visual overload, selected spaces might be identified for the display of art work, messages, or photographs. Walls, bulletin boards, or partitions selected for display can attain a museum-like quality by the way in which works are hung.

PERIPHERAL STIMULI

Accelerated learning theory suggests that the rate and quantity of learning can be greatly increased. One accelerated strategy taps human peripheral perception both to instruct and to facilitate long-term memory. Dr. Georgi Lozanov, the creator of accelerated learning methods, claims that peripheral visual material is subconsciously registered in the mind and can be recalled readily when activated later in a lesson. In Bulgarian studies of adult foreign language learning classes as well as elementary reading and math classes, students were able to recall increased quantities of information when peripheral stimuli were present in the room, even though their conscious attention was not directed at such visuals. The use of peripherals in accelerated learning is considered an important visual component in immersing students in subject matter.

Teachers who are interested in experimenting with peripheral stimuli will need to collect and then display copies of art work, posters, photographs, charts, maps, or quotations that reinforce the topics taught. It should be realized, however, that once displayed, visual information quickly loses its interest and impact. In order to remain intriguing, such visuals need to be either changed or transformed in some manner once a week. This task can be time- consuming unless it is shared by students or other teachers. At the Horton Elementary School in San Diego teachers have a weekly meeting during which they share visuals and other instructional materials they have developed.

CHANGING PERSPECTIVE THROUGH ROTATING SEATING

It is common for many students to sit or work in the same part of the classroom. By asking students to change their seating placement, their visual and social perspectives of the classroom also change. The room assumes a new appearance depending on one's visual perspective; moreover, group dynamics transform as students regularly interact with a variety of classmates. Teacher/student interaction is also likely to alter with new seating arrangements. Additionally, teachers may want to experiment with changing the configuration of classroom furniture, working with circles, U shapes, or with tables or chairs arranged in small groups.

NON-VERBAL COMMUNICATION

The teacher's physical presence and gestures project countless messages as students silently observe and interpret what is being said through body language. Achieving consistency between one's gestures and words can have a positive effect on teaching and communicating in general. When a teacher is enthusiastic about working with students and the topic, her gestures reflect her feelings and encourage enjoyment among students. Conversely, when a teacher is feeling tired or stressed, gestures, posture, and facial expression reveal such feelings and evoke similar emotions in students.

People are often not aware of the many kinds of body language through which they "speak." Students daily observe a teacher's facial expression, gestures, body posture, body space requirements, eye contact, voice tone and inflection, rate of speaking, habitual mannerisms, laughter or other utterances, all of which reveal attitudes and feelings. To insure that appropriate non-verbal messages are being communicated, teachers may want to videotape themselves. Reflecting on one's gestures reveals what students observe every day and may indicate ways to make one's non-verbal communication more purposeful, thereby enhancing both teaching and learning.

PICTORIAL REPRESENTATION

By supporting written or spoken language with charts, diagrams, or photographs, learning can be facilitated and retention reinforced for many students. The phrase "One picture is worth a thousand words" certainly has application in classrooms. Graphic representations of information offer valuable educational functions: they present, define, interpret, manipulate, synthesize, and demonstrate data. Visuals enhance instruction as they clarify concepts teachers are explaining; they provide students with visual means to understand and to communicate what they have learned. Many teachers and students, however, are hesitant to use pictorial representation because of their unfamiliarity with graphic techniques and an incorrect assumption that such images must be artfully done. Rather than emphasizing polished aesthetic displays, both students and teachers can use such tools to probe the subject matter at hand.

There are many forms of pictorial representation that can be employed effectively in the classroom. The ones described in this section include flow charts, visual outlines, unit charts, visual chart stencils, and numerous noting strategies.

FLOW CHARTS

Flow charts describe the structure of concepts and symbolize the direction of flow between ideas. Any "cause-effect" phenomenon whether in math, history, science, health, literature, or instructions can be easily illustrated in flow chart formats. Some students will more readily grasp concepts when illustrated in this form.

Flow charts, whether simple or complex, can be of any size and shape. A large flow chart drawn on butcher paper, a shower curtain, or other fabric might be placed on the floor for students to experience kinesthetically and visually as they walk through its steps. A geometric or free-form shape including rectangles, circles, triangles, or clouds can also be used to "chart" the flow of the concept being explained. Additionally, rather than a flow chart leading only from one step to the next, there can be dual or multiple extensions coming from any one component of the chart as demonstrated below. The first describes the procedure for the addition of numbers larger than one digit, and the second offers a simplified explanation of the causes leading up to the Civil War.

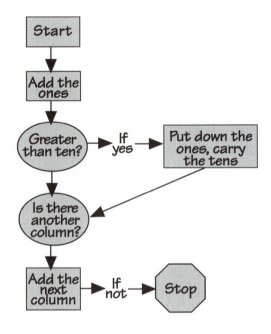

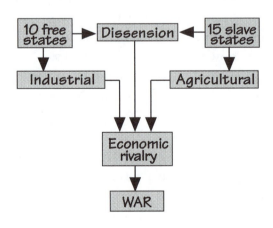

Teachers can transform information to be taught into flow charts, or students can use them to demonstrate their understanding of any conceptual sequence. Making them is a simple process. To create a flow chart, begin with a rectangle or square divided into smaller boxes. Decide upon a concept to display visually. The facts of the concept should be identified and then written one at a time in each of the boxes. Once all the facts are noted, the boxes can be cut out and arranged sequentially, adding arrows or other symbols to indicate the flow of ideas.

VISUAL OUTLINES

Another approach to charting is to ask students to "fill in the boxes" of a paragraph, report, or essay in preparation for writing. Such visual outlines assist many students in identifying the necessary components of writing assignments and clarifies what it is they are expected to write.

Two visual outlines are offered below. The first explains the components of a paragraph and the second the components of a report. Teachers should feel free, however, to develop ones that more appropriately suit their needs.

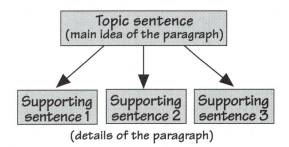

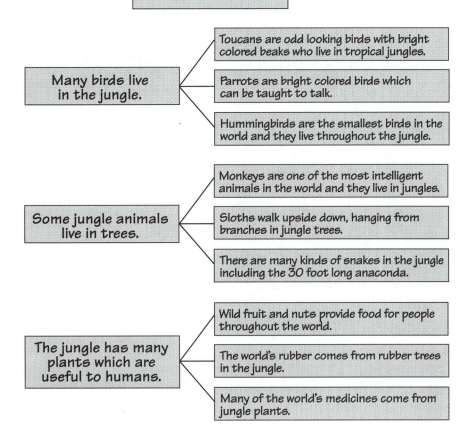

A sample visual outline follows. Elementary students who are studying the jungle might enter "jungle" in the title box at the top. Under topic sentences, their entries could include birds, animals living in the trees, and plants that are useful to humans. Supporting sentences next might be added as demonstrated. Later, an introduction and conclusion can be included and the entire chart transferred to conventional writing formats. Many students, initially daunted by writing assignments, are less threatened when they organize their thoughts in a visual format as a rough draft and then rewrite the draft into a standard written report. When using such visual processes, students not only clarify their understanding of a writing assignment and of the teacher's expectations, but they also learn visual approaches to organizing their thinking.

Students who are capable of extended writing may find the following outline helpful for organizing a written report or essay:

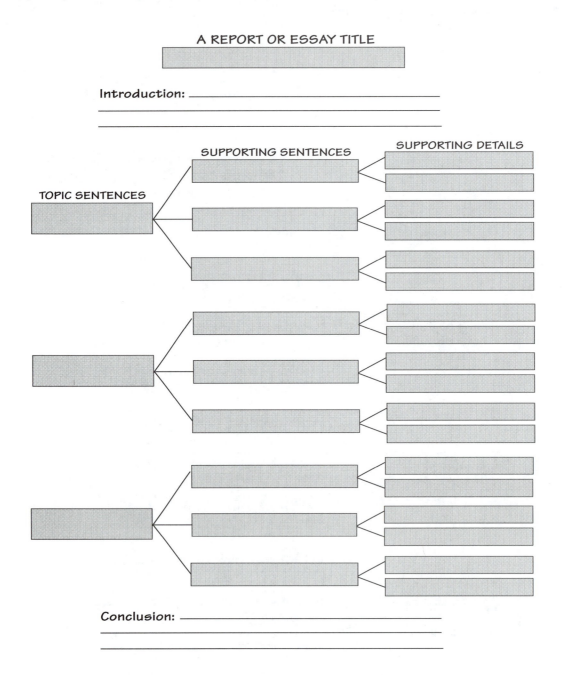

UNIT CHARTS

Large visual charts can be displayed on the blackboard, bulletin board, or in student notebooks to track progress through units of study. As a new topic or unit is introduced, a classroom chart can identify the specific information students will cover. For example, to preview an upcoming unit, list the topic and its major concepts in a flow chart or visual outline format. As the unit progresses, students can assume responsibility for filling in additional information as the new information is available. With such a learning tool, students can tell at a glance where their studies are going, what has been covered, and what yet remains to be learned. An example of a classroom or notebook chart follows:

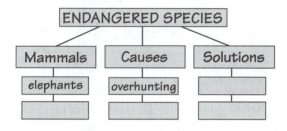

VISUAL CHART STARTERS

There are countless ways of representing information graphically. By learning several simple chart "stencils," teachers and students readily expand their options for manipulating and communicating information visually.

How can students and teachers work with multiple forms of graphic expression when they are usually unfamiliar with charts and diagram formats? One approach is to learn and adapt several "stencils" that can be applied to any content area.

Numerous simple-to-use visual "thinking frames" have been developed by Beau Fly Jones, Program Director of the North Central Regional Educational Laboratory. These graphic representations are useful tools for enhancing the comprehension of academic material. Jones points

out that graphic organizers must appropriately reflect the structure of the text being studied. For example, with ordinary chapter assignments, students might first skim the material to determine how it is structured. Questions can be asked about whether the information is presented as a hierarchy, a comparison or contrast, or as a timeline. Once an appropriate graphic structure is determined, the material can be read with the visual format in mind. Next, students can create the visual image on paper, compare their graphic structure with others, and finally summarize or critique it in an oral or written report.

On the following pages are a number of graphic organizers that teachers and students can adapt to academic material.

Such graphic starters provide both students and teachers with options to visualize written information; however, once one achieves skill with these strategies, it is then important to generate original charts and diagrams. Designing one's own graphic representations requires a synthesis and expression of information in a format that best suits individual needs. By reviewing student visuals, teachers have the opportunity to identify incomplete or incorrect thinking and offer suggestions for improvement. For some lessons, teachers may also find it helpful to request that students create both a graphic representation of information as well as a "white paper" which explains in written form the information contained in the pictorial.

An additional resource for graphic organizers is *Patterns of Thinking*, written by John Clarke, the Director of the Learning Cooperative at the University of Vermont. Clark's book contains a collection of visual strategies for unit planning, test design, independent research, whole class inquiry projects, and small group discussions. It also features many examples of graphics developed by teachers from kindergarten through college.

Graphic representations are visual illustrations of verbal statements. **Frames** are sets of questions or categories that are fundamental to understanding a given topic. Here are nine "generic" graphic forms with their corresponding frames.

Spider Map

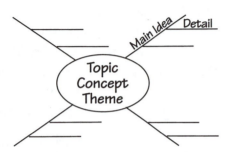

Used to describe a central idea: a thing (a geographic region), processes (meiosis), concept (altruism), or proposition with support (experimental drugs should be available to AIDS victims).

Key frame questions: What is the central idea? What are its attributes? What are its functions?

Series of Events Chain

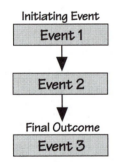

Used to describe the stages of something (the life cycle of a primate); the steps in a linear procedure (how to neutralize an acid); a sequence of events (how feudalism led to the formation of nation states); or the goals, actions and outcomes of a historical figure or character in a novel (the rise and fall of Napoleon)

Key frame questions: What is the object, procedure or initiating event? What are the stages or steps? How do they lead to one another? What is the final outcome?

Continuum/Scale

Used for timelines showing historical events or ages (grade levels in school), degrees of something (weight), shades of meaning (Likert scales), or ratings scales (achievement in school).

Key frame questions: What is being scaled? What are the end points?

Compare/Contrast Matrix

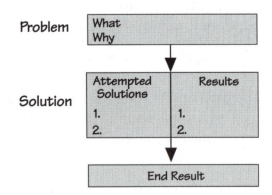

Used to show similarities and differences between two things (people, places, events, ideas, etc.).

Key frame questions: What things are being compared? How are they similar? How are they different?

Problem/Solution Outline

Used to represent a problem, attempted solutions, and results (the national debt).

Key frame questions: What was the problem? Who had the problem? Why was it a problem? What attempts were made to solve the problem? Did those attempts succeed?

Series of Events Chain

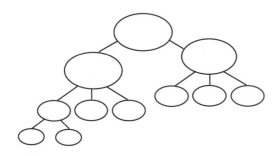

Used to describe the stages of something (the life cycle of a primate); the steps in a linear procedure (how to neutralize an acid); a sequence of events (how feudalism led to the formation of nation states); or the goals, actions, and outcomes of a historical figure or character in a novel (the rise and fall of Napoleon)

Key frame questions: What is the object, procedure or initiating event? What are the stages or steps? How do they lead to one another? What is the final outcome?

Fishbone Map

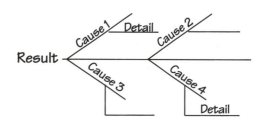

Used to show the causal interaction of a complex event (an election, a nuclear explosion) or complex phenomenon (juvenile delinquency, learning disabilities).

Key frame questions: What are the factors that cause X? How do they interrelate? Are the factors that cause X the same as those that cause X to persist?

Series of Events Chain

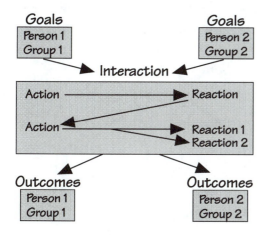

Used to show the nature of an interaction between persons or groups (European settlers and American Indians).

Key frame questions: Who are the persons or groups? What were their goals? Did they conflict or cooperate? What was the outcome for each person or group?

Cycle

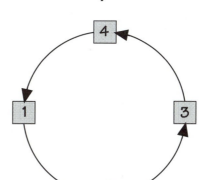

Used to show how a series of events interact to produce a set of results again and again (weather phenomena, cycles of achievement and failure, the life cycle).

Key frame questions: What are the critical events in the cycle? How are they related? In what ways are they self-reinforcing?

VISUAL NOTE-TAKING AND BRAINSTORMING TOOLS

Most people find that note-taking insures better recall of information. One researcher, Michael Howe, at Exeter University, conducted a study of students and note-taking. He found that noted material was six times more likely to be remembered than unnoted material. Note-taking, as opposed to verbatim copying, can serve several valuable functions including storing information, encoding and organizing data, encouraging associations, inferences, and interpretations, and focusing attention on what is important.

Conventional note-taking that usually consists of grammatically correct phrases and sentences is often cumbersome and inefficient when compared with key word noting. Key words, which consist of nouns and verbs that stand out more readily in written or spoken material, generate stronger images and are frequently remembered for longer periods of time. If one reflects on how a young child begins to speak, the importance of key words is apparent. For example, a two year old may state, "Dan, ball" uttering only the essential words to communicate his desire. Later, the same child will become capable of filling in his request with non-key words such as, "I want to play with the ball."

Some estimates claim that only five to ten per cent of language consists of key words. Students who rely on conventional, long-hand, or outline-formatted notes may be at a disadvantage. Time and energy are wasted in such note-taking, information is lost, reviews are too lengthy and the key words are disconnected visually from important relationships.

Recently, visual forms of note-taking have emerged that offer many advantages over conventional formats. Such approaches capitalize on several factors that enhance recall. Essential key words are noted, associations and relationships are highlighted, conscious involvement is required and subjective visual organization is imposed. Four visual noting techniques are described below including mindmapping, clustering, and mindscaping.

CONCEPT MAPPING

Joseph Novak and Bob Gowin in their book, *Learning to Learn*, suggest the use of a graphic organizer they call "concept mapping." Novak, a professor of biology at Cornell, uses this visual technique to teach scientific processes to his students as well as indicate the sequence and relationships in the concepts. Novak also uses concept maps as an assessment device since they reveal whether there is clear understanding of a biological process. While originally developed for the sciences, this strategy is useful in other subjects as well. Two sample concept maps are included below. One was written by a team of seventh grade science students and the other by a history student. Note the use of verbs and key words in both:

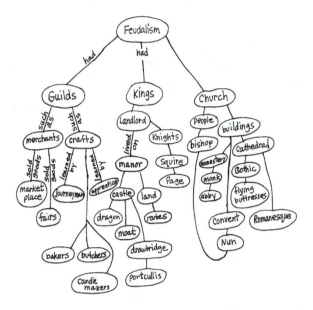

To create concept maps, students may skim a text or listen to a lecture and identify the key concepts presented. They then might compile a list of the major concepts, ranking them from the most general, all-inclusive concept to the most specific. Rank-ordering the concepts requires students to discern what the information is explaining and helps them read or listen for meaning.

Concept maps are constructed as tree-like shapes, with the most inclusive concept presented at the top. The two to five next most general concepts are connected with lines to the first concept. These connecting lines are labeled with appropriate verbs to reinforce the meaning of the relationships. A third level of the hierarchy may be added until all important ideas are included and key relationships identified. Cross-linking may also be added to reveal relationships between one section of the concept map and another. Both teachers and students will find concept maps to be useful tools for identifying salient concepts and their relationships within academic content.

MINDMAPPING

One effective visual note-taking strategy is Tony Buzan's mind-mapping technique presented in his book *Use Both Sides of Your Brain*. Buzan recommends a spatial, non-linear approach to note-taking since it taps the mind's natural ability to work in an integrated, interlinked, complex manner. Similar to concept maps described above, mindmaps feature tree-like branches of information that display key concepts as well as relationships. Differing from more linear concept maps, however, mindmaps are more global in their approach. Beginning with a central idea, students quickly create a "big picture" of their topic.

Mindmaps are useful for several purposes. They assist in organizing and remembering written or verbal information, preparing to write essay questions, planning and evaluating projects or events, or making a visual record of a meeting in progress. When used in a meeting, they can be extremely useful in recording discussions, keeping the meeting on track, eliminating redundancy, and helping people to "piggy-back" on others' ideas. Both students and teachers will find this strategy useful. Buzan stresses the importance of color and graphics as well as form to make the information memorable.

Many visually-talented students enjoy mindmapping and will create symbols or images to illustrate their concepts as well as to beautify their work. For all students, however, mindmapping can be appealing, since the details are organized in categories, and a visual pattern unifies the separate parts into a whole.

An example of a mindmap by Sarah Welsh follows. It reviews the contents of this chapter:

To create a mindmap either for note-taking or brainstorming purposes, a central concept should be placed in the middle of a page. Working outward from the center all directions, key words or images can be quickly recorded and color-coded in the appropriate topic areas. The words in a mindmap should be printed (since this heightens visual recall), and placed on the connecting lines. Colors, images, and codes can be used as mnemonic devices, for individual expression, and for transforming and synthesizing information in a visual format. An example of a mindmap by Sarah Welsh follows. It reviews the contents of this chapter.

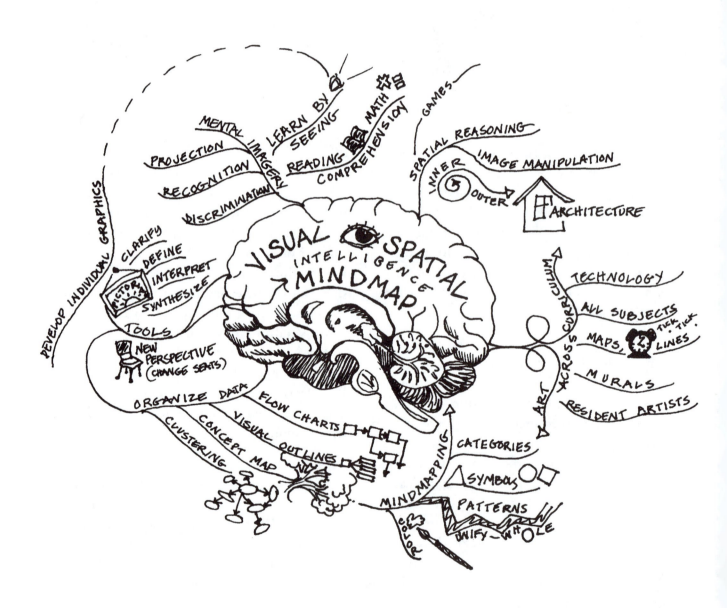

CLUSTERING

Clustering, as developed by Gabriele Rico in her book, *Writing the Natural Way*, is an open-ended process for generating creative ideas. As an effective preliminary to almost any form of writing, clustering can be used to jump-start thinking for creative writing projects, articles, reports, term-papers, even books. Rico writes her own books by creating clusters then writing directly from them on a word processor.

To use clustering for creative writing, place the main concept in the center of the page, then draw a circle around it. Using this topic as a springboard, freely and quickly associate as many ideas as possible, circling each and connecting it to the central concept. As in any brainstorming process, it is important to put down everything that comes to mind, even though it may seem irrelevant. Often irrelevant ideas later trigger useful ones. When the page has been filled—neatness is not important here!—a theme may emerge. Rico calls this a "felt shift." At that point, move to writing a few lines below the cluster. For many, the clustering process is an enormously valuable approach to creative writing, which is often unusually rich in metaphors and insights. A student cluster with its resultant writing sample follows:

Runner

He is still,
Frozen by the photographer's lens
As he is about to break through the tape.
Look more closely;
Look at his expression,
His face contorted
In agony.
Look at his body,
His muscles tight
As steel bars,

His flesh soaked
in sweat,
His arms dangling with indifference.
Look at his stride,
The small stride of a tired runner.
He is almost at the end
Of his strength,
Almost,
But not quite.
He is still,
Frozen by the photographer's lens.

Steve Sano

MINDSCAPING

A method of recording abstract information from lectures or books in the form of images with few words has been developed by Nancy Margulies. Her book entitled *Mapping Inner Space* teaches non-artists how to create visual images that transform information from a verbal to a visual format. Margulies, herself, often "mindscapes" conferences, with her easel beside the podium, creating visual records of each presentation. These colorful creations are posted around the room and offer a graphic review of each presentation as the conference unfolds.

Mindscaping not only enhances learning and memory, it also can be used to map out the day, plan individual lessons, create interesting resumes, or promote new ideas. Margulies offers the following visual symbols that are easily reproduced by most people who want to begin working with graphic imagery:

Each graphic approach—visual outlines, spatial organizers, concept maps, mindmaps, clusters, or mindscapes—is clearly useful for different purposes and preferences. Some of the processes are more linear in nature and lend themselves to analytic tasks; whereas others are more global, and are useful for creative purposes. None is difficult to teach or to learn, and they all offer both teachers and students an array of tools for the variety of tasks involved in the learning process.

VISUALIZATION

Visualization is the ability to mentally construct or to recall visual imagery. Many great discoveries begin with an insight, a clear image, or vision. For example, Einstein first conceived his general theory of relativity "day dreaming" on a sunny day, imagining riding on a beam of light through space. The German chemist Fredrich August Kekule solved another scientific problem one evening as he gazed into the fireplace and imagined a ring of snakes, each with its tail in the mouth of another. This image revealed the molecular structure of benzene. Leonardo da Vinci imagined and drew such technological wonders as the helicopter hundreds of years before it was invented. Diverse fields of human endeavor have been advanced through insights gleaned from inner imagery. By intentionally working with visualization in the classroom, students may gain tools for learning, knowing, and discovering. Encouraging students to produce their own mental imagery also insures their ability to do so as the world grows increasingly visual with the imagery of others on television, movie, computer, and video screens.

CLASSROOM IMAGERY

Simple visualizations can be employed spontaneously in most learning situations. At any point in a lesson, students can be asked to generate and manipulate images. For example, in a French class, students might imagine the Cathedral of Notre Dame from different angles; in a science class, the anatomy of a bird; in math, an isosceles triangle; and in reading, pictures of key words. Such moments provide students with the opportunity to visually experience and assimilate the information at hand.

Significant gains have been reported in reading comprehension when students create mental images of what they have read. One study conducted by Marjorie Pressley in Escondido, California, taught children how to identify key words in reading and create mental images of such words. Even though the program ran for only nine weeks, reading test scores made dramatic gains. Reading comprehension nearly tripled gains from previous years, speed and accuracy doubled, and recall was twelve times greater.

In math, combining visualization with rote memory also offers powerful learning opportunities. One fifth grade student had not yet mastered her multiplication tables and her progress in math was seriously hindered. Knowing that Suni was a talented visual artist, her teacher assumed that if the multiplication facts were learned artistically, Suni would experience success. Following a hunch, the teacher asked the girl to close her eyes and visualize what 81 or 9x9 looked like artistically. Suni readily explained that 81 looked like turquoise, pink and purple lines going in different directions. The teacher asked Suni to draw what she visualized on a notecard. The design was quickly reproduced and the teacher requested that 9 x 9 be written on top of the design with the answer 81 on the back of the notecard. Suni's visualization of 81 is shown at left.

Encouraged with her first math visualization, Suni went on to picture other multiplication facts and their images. At the end of the two weeks, Suni had completed a set of beautiful math art cards, each with its own unique visual symbol. In the process, she easily memorized the multiplication tables.

Many other students, inspired by Suni's example, have since made their own sets of art flash cards for a variety of subject areas. By creating both internal and external images, these students are not only learning academic content, they are also creating and expressing their own visual and symbolic language systems.

VISUAL MEMORY TECHNIQUES

The ancient Greeks explained the phenomenon of human memory in the myth of the great goddess Mnemosyne. The myth recounts that in the beginning of time, the Elder Gods reigned supreme in the universe and were of enormous size and enormous ability. Mnemosyne, one of the original goddesses, possessed a special gift: memory that was as long as her hair. As the goddess of memory, Mnemosyne knew each event that had taken place from the beginning of time. One day, deciding she must share her knowledge, Mnemosyne gathered her daughters, the nine Muses, about her and told them the stories of the universe. She explained the creation of the earth, the stars, and the moon. She talked of the glorious gods and the brave heroes and heroines on earth. The nine Muses, cherishing what their mother taught them, desired to preserve the wondrous stories. To do so, the Muses turned Mnemosyne's tales into poems, stories, and song to insure they would never be forgotten. Through such means, the Muses were able to share their knowledge with mortals so that humankind could know and remember all that was important.

From this explanation of memory, the Greeks created techniques using stories and associations to improve memory and to achieve what appeared to be superhuman feats of memorization. The ancient orators could remember hundreds of items such as decks of cards placed in any order, backwards, forwards, or randomly, dates and numbers, and indeed, entire domains of knowledge. Such skills were possible because of the use of mnemonics, from the Greek word, *mneme*, meaning memory. Mnemonics are techniques that facilitate retention and recall of information by exercising visual-spatial intelligence. These processes also facilitate the ability to work with mental images that is often a characteristic of great creative thinkers.

The success of the ancient memory systems was based upon one common principle, association. Association consists of taking one idea or image and linking it to another. By learning memory techniques that stress interconnections, studies demonstrate the capability to store and recall far more information than we generally expect. Two excellent books explaining memory systems are *The Memory Book* by Harry Lorayne and Jerry Lucas, and *Use Your Perfect Memory* by Tony Buzan.

In the classroom, associative techniques can be used when committing to memory the names of the fifty states, the dynasties of China, the Dewey Decimal System, the Articles of the Bill of Rights, or lists of spelling or vocabulary words. To begin teaching students a memory device, take a list and together generate a class "story" for memorizing the items using clear and distinct images.

For example, students might be asked to memorize the Dewey Decimal System. This classifying system divides books into ten main groups:

000-099	Generalities (encyclopedias, periodicals, journalism)
100-199	Philosophy
200-299	Religion
300-399	Social Sciences
400-499	Language
500-599	Sciences
600-699	Technology
700-799	The Arts
800-899	Literature
900-999	Geography and History

To memorize the above, the following story-line comprised of association and imagery was quickly created:

I went to the general (Generalities) store to buy up to 99 items. The first person I saw was Phil (Philosophy), the owner of the store, who showed me two hundred new Bibles (Religion). I said what I needed was three boxes of SOS (Social Science) pads. When I walked down the fourth aisle, I noticed all sorts of people speaking different languages (Language) and bought five science kits (Science). In the sixth aisle, I saw computers (Technology) but decided to buy seven paintings (The Arts) instead. There were eight big wads of litter (Literature) on the floor. I bought nine world maps (Geography) and then left for the day.

Such a story, when generated by students, can serve as a powerful memory booster. The images might be discussed to bring them into greater clarity, and the storyline rehearsed once or twice. Later, the students should find it relatively easy to silently recall the story while accurately writing the Dewey Decimal System including both the numbers and classification categories.

Associating items with parts of one's home or room is another effective associative device based on an ancient Greek memory system. By mentally picturing each item of a list with an object in one's room, a mental tour of the room usually aids recall. For example, one teacher assigned students a few extra credit words from a short story which included:

trapeze

juggler

equestrian

acrobat

grease paint

Students were asked to memorize the above list of words by imaging their bedrooms containing these items. The trapeze might be suspended from the ceiling, the juggler on the bed, the equestrian coming out of the closet, the acrobat in front of the dresser, and the grease paint on top of a night stand. When asked to recall the words, the students mentally walked through their rooms noting the location of the extra items and writing the respective words on a piece of paper.

Ultimately, such techniques are most effective when students individually create their own imagery. As the above example demonstrates, once students have mastered the technique, the classroom teacher should cease providing lists for quizzes or exams, requiring that students produce such lists from memory instead. For example, on Fridays in classrooms around the country, students take spelling tests. Usually, the teacher reads the words to be spelled. When students have learned the association memory techniques, they can then assume responsibility for recalling the list as well as the accurate spelling of their words. Students can be instructed to get their papers out for the spelling test, silently recall their memory story, and then list and accurately spell the words. In this way, students are tested on both their memory and spelling skills.

Since students frequently find that such memory stories are retained for long periods of time, some have wondered whether their minds will become too cluttered with silly storylines. They can be assured that there is no such possibility. Some researchers claim that if human brains were fed ten new bits of information every second of our lives, we would still have memory room to spare. Associative techniques do not begin to tax our memory skills; they only strengthen them.

Memory techniques, effective for recalling and storing facts, are particularly valuable when students must learn the multiplication tables, spelling and vocabulary words, principles, and formulas. Although drill and practice are useful for memorizing certain facts and skills, they can minimize the importance of meaning and understanding. It is important to teach facts, skills and concepts as part of rich multisensory and interactive experiences. Memory techniques can be embedded in such study and should not, themselves, comprise the sole agent of instruction. Complex, experiential learning opportunities engage the vast realms of human memory while making learning fascinating and meaningful.

VISUAL VARIETY IN LEARNING MATERIALS

Interest and excitement in learning materials can be generated by the visual alteration of color, shape, and imagery. Color is an important component of visual thinking. It distinguishes ideas, guides attention, and enhances recall. Color can highlight information on dittos, student packets, lecture overheads, chalkboard visuals, bulletin boards, class notes, and assignments.

HIGHLIGHTING WITH COLOR

Color can also serve as an important instructional tool. Steps in solving mathematical problems can be clarified through the use of color. For example, the first step in long division can be written in red, the second in blue, and the third in green.

Spelling mistakes can also be corrected through the use of color. The letters of the word that were written correctly appear in one color with the corrections in red or orange to highlight what must be remembered. While it is important for teachers to model color usage in the classroom, students will often establish personal visual language systems when they are free to choose the colors and approaches with which to work.

The steps of open-ended, creative problem-solving can also be highlighted with color as follows:

1. **Black - The first step of creative problem-solving is determining the who, what, when, and where of a situation. Such data can be written in black ink.**

2. **Red - The second step is defining the major problem(s) which can be written in red.**

3. **Green - Numerous solutions can be generated in green.**

4. **Blue - The best solution is selected and circled in blue.**

5. **Orange - An orange-colored action plan is developed.**

Similar sequential color procedures can be used in following directions, note-taking, or memorizing sequences in any content area. When working with color in these sequential ways, teachers can tell at a glance where students are stuck in a problem-solving process.

VARYING SHAPES

The computer provides another convenient way to add visual variety to classroom lessons. It is a simple process to add graphics, font variations, larger and smaller letters, boxes, signs, and banners to learning materials. For example, to remedy a student's misspelling of certain words, misspelled letters can be enlarged to visually "grab" attention and improve recall.

rec**e**ive   **a**isle   conven**ie**nce

It is also easy to help students focus on key words, concepts, or spelling practice by suggesting they visualize such words and their shapes. The shapes or configurations of the words can be highlighted as follows:

Students can draw the outer configurations of words and later have others fill in what is missing. They might also create sentences or math theorems of configurations which they "read" and give to others to read as well.

VISUAL ACCOMPANIMENT FOR LECTURES, DISCUSSIONS, OR READINGS

While many teachers are uncomfortable with their own drawing skills, some students will volunteer to "illustrate" what is being learned as well as create classroom posters for display. Occasionally, a teacher may identify a student who can quickly draw images of spoken information. Such a student might be encouraged to volunteer to sketch at the blackboard, capturing the words of a speaker during a lecture or discussion.

Students can also be encouraged to embellish their own written work with color, doodles, symbols, and varying shapes. Before a reading

assignment begins, suggest that students preview the photos and graphs in written materials since visual scanning creates mental "hooks" for written information and increases understanding. Once students begin reading, suggest that they transform key words or events into their own personal "mind movies" to improve later recall.

BOARD AND CARD GAMES

One of the oldest known pastimes is playing board games. About 2500 B.C., Egyptian carvings on tombs depicted board games in process. A wall painting on the tomb of Nefertari shows the queen playing a board game with movable pieces. The ancient Babylonians, Chinese, Romans, and Aztecs all played games which were often instructional and required logical thinking skills. Some games were spatial, teaching the way around the city or the ways to stalk an animal. Since board games are as popular today as they were in ancient times, they can often ignite students' enthusiasm for learning.

Games with movable pieces often challenge a player's foresight and imagination as well as exercising memory skill and visual-spatial intelligence. Chess is an ancient game that originated in Asia, spread to Persia in the fifth century A.D., then into the Middle East, Spain, and throughout the rest of Europe. Today, while chess is well known as a favorite pastime, some educators are perceiving its value as a tool to enhance students' thinking and learning abilities. Studies in Venezuela have shown that students seven years of age and older who frequently played chess at school experienced IQ gains on traditional measures of intelligence. Perhaps such gains were due to the exercising of a variety of higher order skills demanded in chess, which include critical thinking, decision-making, spatial reasoning, and strategizing.

While there are many prepared games for classroom use, teachers frequently require curriculum-specific ones not readily available in stores. Fortunately, board games can easily be made for any subject area.

For those interested in creating their own classroom games, the easiest kind to design is a Monopoly-style game in which players travel along a path encountering obstacles or boons relating to the subject matter in question. Simple statements such as "Meet British soldiers, go back 5 spaces," or "Name the square root of 169 and take an extra turn," or "Huck Finn and Jim are recognized. Lose your next turn," or "Copernicus makes an important discovery. Draw a bonus card," all teach important facts or reinforce learning. To demonstrate how such games are constructed an example follows.

This game was made by an elementary teacher whose students were studying the continent of Africa. For teachers interested in designing their own games to introduce a topic, to teach subject matter, or to review student learning, see the guidelines on the next page.

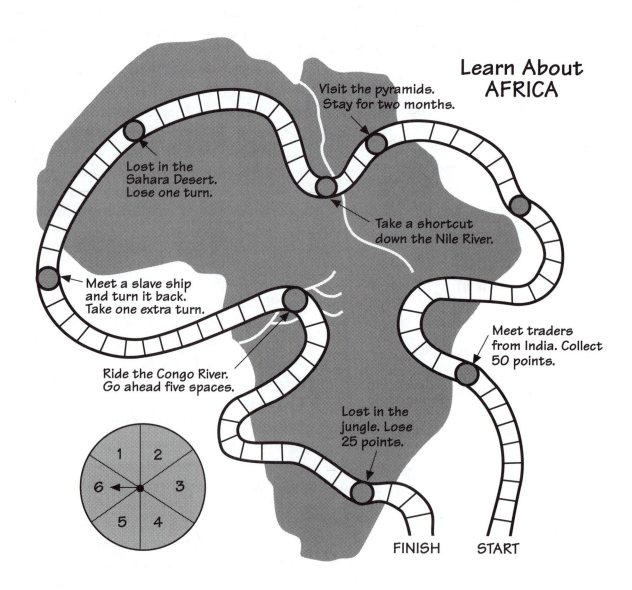

Learn About
AFRICA

Visit the pyramids.
Stay for two months.

Lost in the
Sahara Desert.
Lose one turn.

Take a shortcut
down the Nile River.

Meet a slave ship
and turn it back.
Take one extra turn.

Meet traders
from India. Collect
50 points.

Ride the Congo River.
Go ahead five spaces.

Lost in the
jungle. Lose
25 points.

1 2 3 4 5 6

FINISH   START

GUIDELINES FOR MAKING BOARD GAMES

1. Determine the learning objectives and purpose of the game. Is it to acquaint students with new information, review old information, evaluate a unit, or all of these?

2. Consider how the information and skills might be taught through a game. Commercial games can inspire the structure and format of many classroom games such as Concentration, 20 Questions, and Scrabble. Is there a commercially available game that, with modification, would provide a workable structure? Is there an original format that is more appropriate?

3. To make the board game, draw a rough draft on large paper, creating a path or design to fit the needs of the topic. Game boards can assume the shape of a world map, a DNA molecule, the solar system, a maze, a town or city, or a simple path.

4. Once the path or design is made, determine how the game will end. Will it be the first player to complete the path, the first to accumulate a quantity of points or objects, or the first to visit a certain number of locations on the board by correctly answering questions?

5. Players will need a way to move around the game board. This is often done with spinners that are easily constructed as circles divided into numbered, pie-shaped sections. Fasten the spinner directly to the game board with a brad and draw an arrow on the board. Students spin the wheel and the arrow indicates the number of steps to move. Movement around the board can be accomplished by dice or cards with directions on them, or directions on the board itself.

6. If movement around the game board with dice is preferred, students can make their own dice out of cubes of wood. With sandpaper and markers, number dice can be easily fashioned as can special purpose pieces that best meet the needs of a particular game. For example, dice might feature different kinds of animals on each side, countries, presidents, punctuation marks, or symbols such as the letters for chemical elements.

7. If needed, cut cards from cardstock for questions, bonuses, or penalties.

8. The final step is to transfer the rough draft of the game to large cardstock, cardboard, plywood, or another more permanent surface.

Teachers can benefit by sharing games with colleagues, and students will often enthusiastically create ones based upon material they are studying. When student games are created, ask students to share them with classmates so that the opportunities for playing to learn are increased.

CARD GAMES

Card games also serve as effective visual learning tools. The game "Authors" has helped many children and adults learn literary figures and the titles of their written works. In "Authors," players attempt to collect sets of four cards for each author, each card having the name of a different piece of literature as well as a picture of the writer. The player with the most sets at the end wins.

The same type of card game can be adapted for most subject areas. Instead of different authors, an algebra game might have quadratic equations or polynomial expansions. Players would have to collect sets of four of each. Another example for a simple card game could be parts of speech. Players would have to collect four verbs, four adjectives, four nouns, and four adverbs. Students might decorate their own cards for additional visual appeal and laminate the finished decks for durability. When time is an obstacle, commercial educational card games for a wide range of topics, including endangered species, math facts, and vocabulary words are available for numerous subjects and can be found in educational supply catalogues.

ARCHITECTURE

On a field trip one day, Alec stopped as his schoolmates were halfway across the parking lot on their way to the museum. He was gazing at a high span bridge arching over a nearby waterway. The teacher went to retrieve the boy who excitedly explained without any technical terminology, how the configuration of the steel beams distributed the load and carried the enormous weight of the structure. Alec's fascination with bridges did not quickly subside. During the subsequent two months, he drew a series of complex bridges. Alec's interest piqued the teacher's and one day, she asked her students to think about what makes it possible for buildings and bridges to stand up. This launched a search for explanations that included the exploring of math and physics principles rarely discussed in fifth grade classrooms.

The goals of architecture-in-school curriculums extend beyond training future architects or enhancing aesthetic awareness. Some educators claim that architecture provides an effective means for students to learn and apply mathematics, physics, critical and creative thinking skills, spatial reasoning, problem-solving, and collaboration—all through hands-on projects. For many students, architecture offers entry points into content that previously was abstract or unrewarding. For example, students learning the calculation of area and volume find that such abstractions take tangible form in architectural models.

The study of architecture can be integrated into numerous subject areas and made appropriate for all grade levels. Linkages to architecture can be discovered when teachers consider how the built environment is involved in various instructional units. Additionally, by viewing humankind as part of the environment, architecture becomes integral to all of life's activities, and is no longer perceived as a separate subject.

Numerous architecture-in-the-schools programs have emerged, all teaching students how to acquire an architect's spatial thinking skills while applying and demonstrating their learning through real world applications. Anne Taylor, Professor of Architecture at the University of New Mexico, and her partner, architect George Vlastos, have created an innovative program entitled Architecture and Children. This program uses architecture, design, and creative problem-solving to teach basic skills and subject matter content through the built, natural, and cultural environment. Interweaving math, science, and art, students creatively problem-solve as they suggest and build design activities for the physical environment.

LEARNING TO THINK LIKE AN ARCHITECT

Anne Taylor's Architecture and Children curriculum guides students through a series of problems teaching the steps of the design process. This cognitive apprenticeship approach to learning does not train students in the skills of an architect but rather, through real-life projects, helps children approach problem-solving as experts do. Some of the program's initial "think like an architect" activities ask students to visualize structures that might contain a ping pong ball, a fast-food restaurant, or a theatre for children. Students are also asked to symbolically draw what happens to a bubble as it emerges, floats, and pops. While the teacher blows at least ten or more bubbles, students scrutinize their form and function. Instructed not to draw the bubble itself, students are asked to schematically represent what happens during its "life cycle." A similar task, "The Great Balloon Race," involves the catapulting of four balloons in diverse directions around the classroom with students drawing arrows and lines depicting the objects moving in space as well as their spatial relationships.

To increase spatial reasoning, students learn how to develop a plan for an architectural structure which they later construct in model form. The first task is to draw bubble diagrams of the areas of a house. Next, students develop the bubble diagram into a plan view for their structure, which is then turned into an elevation view to visualize what the building would look like if it were standing. Next, students draw a two-point perspective sketch to capture the illusion of space and depth on a sheet of paper. After this is accomplished, students take their plan views and develop a three-dimensional model of their structures. If resources permit, some students may draw their models on computers with computer-aided design software. Once students complete their models, they present them to their peers. This important step of the design process encourages peer feedback, student self-assessment, and results in a visual portfolio.

Many educational architectural programs involve students in redesigning their classroom space. One fifth grade teacher in White Plains, New York, gave his students free reign in altering their classroom environment. To carry out this project, students had to measure, make scale drawings and three-dimensional models, develop a budget, and implement their plans. Before their foray into architecture, students were below grade level in math. After their classroom redesign efforts, average math scores on both teacher-made and standardized tests increased. Such scores, however, don't begin to measure the students' positive attitudes or motivation towards classroom learning.

A different approach to environmental design is evident at the Meredith School in Philadelphia. Students studied the school district administration building, documenting its history, architectural design, interior design, construction materials, and landscape elements. Their project culminated in the production of a book that included student drawings, interviews, and observations. Additionally, students baked a cake resembling a blueprint of the floor plan.

Doreen Nelson, a former classroom teacher, has created the City Building Education program, in which students reorganize their classroom to run like a city. Classroom traffic patterns are identified and furniture placed accordingly. Storage and retrieval systems for school supplies are analyzed and forms of class government established. In a five-year study conducted by the Los Angeles Superintendent's office, 175 students participating in the City Building Education program scored higher in reading and math than the control group. In addition, Nelson's research showed students in her program learn faster, retain information longer, and transfer knowledge from one discipline to another more fluently than students in conventional programs.

GETTING STARTED WITH ARCHITECTURE IN THE CLASSROOM

Teachers interested in integrating architecture into their classrooms will find several resources currently available. By getting in touch with local chapters of the American Institute of Architects, teachers may identify architects who are willing to work in the schools or offer technical assistance. Some states arts councils fund architect-in-the-schools residency programs. Diverse training programs in architecture and design for educators are also available. Some of these include the Salvadori Center for the Built Environment at New York's City College, Architecture and Children with Anne Taylor at the University of New Mexico and the University of Washington, Teach the Teachers in Kansas City, and Nelson's City Building Education workshops. Other useful resources for teachers include the books, *Architecture Is Elementary: Visual Thinking Through Architectural Concepts* by Nathan Winters, and *Architects Make Zigzags, Looking at Architecture from A to Z* by Diane Maddex.

THE VISUAL ARTS

Schools across the country are reinstating arts programs after many had been cut in the "back to basics" movement. The arts are increasingly recognized as basic to student motivation, higher level thinking skills, positive school climates, and increased academic achievement. Over half of the states now require high school credits in the arts as a graduation requirement. Eliot Eisner, Professor of Education at Stanford says, "Artistic tasks, unlike so much of what is now taught in schools, develop the ability to judge, to assess, to experience in a wide range of meanings that exceed what we are able to say in words. The limits of language are not the limits of our consciousness."

Many schools approach the arts in two ways: by teaching them as discrete subjects in their own right, and by integrating the arts into all subjects as tools of teaching and learning. The visual arts of drawing, painting, sculpting, designing, and collage are often integrated into elementary classrooms. As children grow older, however, such activities are typically omitted from their studies and are offered only as separate art classes usually attended by those students brave enough to claim some artistic talent.

ART AS AN INSTRUCTIONAL TOOL

Two New York City programs called *Learning through an Expanded Arts Program* (LEAP) and *Reading Instruction through the Arts* (RITA) have found that hands-on art experiences help students learn academic content at both the elementary and secondary levels. Components of these two programs are described below and may serve to inspire educators to turn to the arts to improve instruction.

LEAP is a nonprofit educational organization whose mission is to improve the quality of kindergarten through twelfth grade education in the five boroughs of New York City. During its fifteen year history, LEAP has served nearly one half million students through its 85 consultants who work directly with teachers and their classes. All LEAP projects are geared to improve language arts and math achievement through arts-based activities.

BLENDING THE VISUAL AND LANGUAGE ARTS

To improve literacy among elementary students, literature, puppetry, and mural painting all serve to actively engage children in reading, writing, speaking, and performing. One arts-based LEAP project begins with teacher and students reading a story aloud together. Students then volunteer to work in one of two groups: some elect to make puppets, while others become mural painters.

All the students are taught how to draw quick figures and make storyboards that visually capture the main idea of each scene. The story is next reread slowly, with pauses inserted at the end of each scene. While listening, students create their storyboards scene by scene and then proceed to retell the whole story sequentially. Once able to recall the sequence of the story, students are next asked to identify the main ideas of each scene. If this task proves difficult, students are referred to their storyboards for potential answers. The instructor also suggests that when asked about the main idea of a scene or story, students might consider how they would draw it as a single picture. Next, they select the most important event in the story and defend that choice.

Additional lessons for the puppet makers include rereading of the story, making puppets, or drawing the main characters to reflect personality traits as well as physical characteristics. Students are asked to imagine how the story might change if the personality of the main character changed, or to assume the points of view of various characters. Such activities enhance their reading skills and higher level thinking skills. Some students who desire to do so, write dialogue for different scenes in the story using appropriate vocabulary. Others may read the story aloud and use puppets to enact it.

The mural painters, meanwhile, identify the scenes of the story, listing the adjectives for the time, place, and descriptions of each location. Small groups of students select scenes to paint and begin sketching the background with colored chalk on large pieces of butcher paper. The background is then painted or filled in with tissue paper collage.

The story's characters are next presented much in the same way as for the puppet group. The mural painters make paper cutouts of the characters for each scene and glue them to the prepared backgrounds. Once the preliminary murals are done, the story is reread to reveal additional details to be included in each scene. Students identify which details should be included and why, and these are then drawn, cut out, and glued onto the scenes. The scenes are joined together, and as the story is read, the students point out the main ideas and details in each scene. Storytelling is rehearsed and finally, other classes are invited to hear the storytelling and see the puppet shows and mural.

INTEGRATING ART AND MATH

An especially effective approach to integrating math and art is evident in the LEAP fractions quilt project. To introduce the concept of fractions, elementary students are provided with scissors, a pencil, and four squares of construction paper. Rather than being given pre-cut paper, students must cut the pieces themselves to comprehend the concept of fractions. The first fraction taught is one half. The students are directed to fold one piece of construction paper in half, cutting it down the middle. They next draw a line across the middle of each half of the paper as the teacher explains that this line indicates they are no longer dealing with a whole but now rather with a part. The students are asked to identify how many parts they have and write the number two as the denominator which indicates into how many pieces they have divided the paper. Holding one piece of paper, the students write one as the numerator on it to help them learn that numerators indicate the number of the whole they represent. To see how many halves make a whole, students place both halves on top of a whole piece of construction paper. This process of folding, cutting, writing, and placing parts onto wholes is repeated for quarters and eighths and sometimes extended into other fractions as well.

With a basic understanding of fractions, students are now ready to construct a quilt. On a large square of construction paper, they mount different-sized pieces of paper into various "quilt" patterns. All the fraction patterns are next mounted on a classroom wall to look like a quilt. Space is left between each of the fraction patterns so that students can write equations beneath each pattern. They then solve the equations, reducing them to the lowest common denominators.

In an article appearing in the *Phi Delta Kappan* journal evaluations of the LEAP projects reveal their academic and affective success with students and teachers alike. Over 93% of the students in the program gained a better understanding of the subject matter. Teachers reported that 95% of the students demonstrated enhanced problem-solving skills, 96% improved creative writing skills, 93% gained self-discipline, and 97% acquired a more positive attitude toward school. When asked if they would repeat the projects in the future, 97% of the teachers said they planned to teach the integrated units again. For teachers interested in learning more about the LEAP approach, contact them at Learning through an Expanded Arts Program (LEAP), 580 West End Avenue, New York, New York 10024.

INTEGRATING THE ARTS AT THE HIGH SCHOOL LEVEL

Another integrated arts approach effective with secondary students was implemented at the John F. Kennedy High School in the Bronx. Frustrated with declining reading scores, the school faculty determined that conventional instruction failed to yield improved student achievement. In the fall of 1975, the Reading Improvement through Art program was established to serve high school students whose reading scores had plateaued or declined for two or more years.

The RITA class meets once daily in a studio with an art teacher who works with a reading specialist to develop lessons. The RITA lessons, based on art experiences, address four specific reading skills: word identification, comprehension, study skills, and scanning. One comprehension unit includes making comparisons. Students read about Picasso and talk about the transformations in his artistic style. They make comparisons between figurative and non-figurative paintings in written form while painting an abstract still life themselves.

Daily class sessions in the art studio begin with vocabulary and written instructions posted on an easel. In their personal journals, students record the day's vocabulary lesson, write plans for their projects, and list books they select from the studio's reading corner (a permanent feature of any RITA classroom). Once a week, students write a paper based on their notes, plans, and

readings. These papers are maintained in a writing portfolio while an art portfolio contains records of their visual projects. To highlight reading improvement, each project culminates with two sets of records.

This blending of visual and language arts has resulted in significant achievement gains in reading scores. The Division of Educational Evaluation in New York City found that for every six months in the RITA program, the average student improved one year in reading as measured by standardized tests.

Encouraged with such success, a math teacher at the high school, Dr. Andrew Janovsky, has experimented with integrating math and art. During two-hour daily blocks, the students spend the first period learning about mathematical concepts that enable them to build models. During the second period, an art teacher supervises the construction of mathematical designs. In this approach, students learn about and then construct products that demonstrate their knowledge of prime numbers, modular arithmetic, geometric forms, and theorems. Learning is also collaborative and shared, with students turning to each other as resources for ideas and feedback. Throughout their construction activities, students are required to use and master basic computational and conceptual skills.

As the above examples demonstrate, stimulating, arts-based lessons result when content area teachers and arts specialists team teach or co-plan. Not only do students learn well; they also benefit from the fundamental artistic processes of problem-solving, self-expression, and invention. If, however, teachers are unable to team with arts specialists, opportunities for students to learn and demonstrate their knowledge through the visual arts might still be offered. Some suggestions follow:

Art Across the Curriculum

1. Each classroom can feature an art center complete with markers, paints, colored paper of varying sizes and textures, cloth, natural and man-made objects. Supplies should be frequently refurbished and students encouraged to use them.

2. Classroom projects that involve drawing, construction, photographic essays, videography, and model building enliven learning in any content area. At least one art option can be suggested for each unit of study.

3. Collages provide opportunities for visual interpretation of ideas and can illustrate classroom lessons. Old magazines and journals appropriate for diverse subject matter areas can be collected, stored, and made available for student use.

4. Timelines, maps, and charts embellished by students with color, imagery, and fanciful backgrounds, will spark attention and memory.

5. Classroom friezes can bring important facts to life. One junior high school teacher encircled her room with a frieze of Greek and Latin word parts. Each student contributed one or more visual images to represent the meaning of his or her words. Colorful friezes can be constructed and displayed for nearly any content area.

6. Wall size murals personalize a classroom and make it possible for students to see the concepts they are learning. Those students with artistic skills can draw the murals for their classmates to paint or label.

7. Large or small scrolls, made out of butcher paper and doweling, make excellent graphic displays of quantities of information. One seventh-grade class created the history of the universe on 200 feet of four-foot-wide butcher paper. Scenes focused on the origin of the universe, first life forms on earth, early civilizations, and significant cultural contributions. Students also wrote poems on the topics and included these on the scroll. Different roles emerged among the students as the project unfolded, including planners, sketchers, painters, writers, and even mechanics to design and construct the scroll.

8. Replicas of famous art, maps, or other visuals can be reproduced by students through jigsaw or grid techniques. For example, one class made two twelve-foot-square maps of the eastern and western hemispheres. After sketching the continents onto large paper, they drew jigsaw puzzle lines on the back, dividing each map into 25 pieces, the number of students in the class. After the pieces were cut out, each student took one. They next had to determine where the pieces fit onto the map, what constituted land, water, and continents, and how to coordinate adjacent pieces. In another school, a giant mural of Van Gogh's "Starry Night" was created as a school project. Filling one entire wall of the library, the mural was made from dozens of paper squares, each corresponding to a smaller one from a grid of the original painting. Each student painted an enlarged version of what appeared on the numbered square of her grid. Again, coordination was necessary, particularly when a star, house, or tree crossed from one square on the grid to another.

9. Prints, posters, and photographs that relate to the subject matter can decorate the classroom while providing springboards for discussions and inspiration for student art work. Holt, Reinhart and Winston, Inc. have a package called *Art Works* featuring a wide variety of gender-balanced art from many cultures. By writing art museums to request their catalogues, teachers will find a wealth of resources. From post cards to full-sized prints, artists and their works can be brought directly into the classroom. Local galleries and framing shops often have good selections of prints as well.

10. Computer software that facilitates drawing, timelines, and graphing can add a visual dimension to classroom assignments and displays.

11. At the secondary level, students who are particularly artistic may be able to design an arts-based classroom activity as well as teach it to their peers.

12. Teachers might create a list of local community artists or arts agencies who upon invitation are willing to share their expertise with schools.

13. Teachers can take advantage of numerous resource books available such as *Doing Art Together* by Muriel Silberstein-Storfer, *Art from Many Hands* by Jo Miles Schuman, *Making Things: The Handbook of Creative Discovery* by Anne Wiseman, and *Cultural Journeys: 84 Art and Social Science Activities from Around the World* by Margaret W. Ryan.

Of course, some teachers and students may want to develop their own visual skills. Mona Brookes, author of *Drawing with Children* and *Drawing with Adolescents* and founder of Monart Visual Arts Schools, believes everyone is an artist. Her own drawing method consists of five basic shapes easily learned and applied by anyone from pre-schoolers through senior citizens. Brookes recommends, however, that budding artists take advantage of diverse drawing methods. To nurture children's artistic skills, teachers might encourage early childhood symbolic stick and figure drawing. At around age four or with beginners of any age, instructors may want to use Brookes' books, *Drawing with Children*, for skill development or *Drawing with Adolescents*.

Enrichment activities at this time might consist of cartooning from Mark Kistlers' *Draw Squad*. For the development of art history awareness and art appreciation, educators may want to turn to the Los Angeles Getty Center for Education in the Arts' *Discipline-Based Art Education programs*. The DBAE programs are dedicated to improving the quality of arts education by including studio art, art history, criticism, and aesthetics in school programs. When older students are ready to tackle live model drawing and fine art styles, they may want to work with Betty Edwards' book, *Drawing on the Right Side of the Brain*. Additional methods for older students are also explained in art classics such as Nicholaides' *The Natural Way to Draw*.

TECHNOLOGY THAT ENHANCES VISUAL-SPATIAL INTELLIGENCE

Today's students have grown up watching television and are highly oriented to visual learning. Slides, overhead transparencies, film strips, and movies are important adjuncts to their learning. Copy-machines and computer-printers are also essential support-systems for any kind of academic work. When interactive systems are also part of the learning process, students move from passive observers to active thinkers.

For example the VCR, which is available to most teachers, lends itself to active learning in numbers of ways. Rather than running a program from beginning to end, teachers can take advantage of the opportunity to stop, rewind, and replay. Frequent opportunities to discuss what students have already seen and what they are about to see next make possible the anticipatory and participatory learning that are critical to the educational process.

In presenting dramatic productions, teachers may wish to preview a film to make note of the location of various segments that can be played out of context ahead of time for the purposes of comparison and contrast. Or the film may be stopped before the ending, allowing students to guess what occurs next. The VCR is a flexible and adaptable tool that can be utilized for innumerable educational purposes.

It is a logical next step to use a newer form of technology, the interactive videodisc (IVD). The IVD combines into one system all the different media and delivery options, including lectures, slides, films, video, and computer-based instruction. The disc can hold 54,000 frames or slides on each side, 30 minutes of video, and two 30-minute audiotracks. It can randomly access from a menu any video or audio segment in 3.5 seconds, when the user presses a button or "mouse" or moves a wand over a bar graph.

Operated through a videodisc player, a television monitor or two, and a personal computer, the system is easy to learn and operate. It is flexible enough to incorporate other emerging technologies such as compact disc-read only memory (CD-ROM), digital video interactive (DVI), compact disc interactive (CDI), and artificial intelligence.

In a 1986 study of a number of IVD classrooms, IBM reported a 30-to-50% increase in learning scores and a 300% increase in the number of students reaching mastery level.

Geographic Television (GTV) is currently one of the most recent developments in interactive video for the classroom. It has been developed by the National Geographic Society in association with Lucasfilm Ltd., and combines the interactive capabilities of the computer with instant access of the videodisc composed of National Geographic pictures. The subject of the first program is U.S. history with an emphasis on geography; other subjects in the proposed series are under way at this writing.

Another pioneering educational effort is The National Geographic Kids Network, a telecommunications system that links students throughout the world. Students share information with each other about geography and experiments in science using computer-generated maps and charts.

The availability of camcorders makes it possible for students to produce their own videos as an alternative to written reports. Teachers may also produce videos as lesson presentations—this is one way for teachers to clone themselves and reduce class size for portions of the day!

Students with special needs can also be helped in new ways through visual media. For example, those with speech difficulties can actually see their speaking patterns through IBM's SpeechViewer; from this visual feedback, they learn to make appropriate changes. Students who cannot move, may talk into the computer and it will print out what they say; others who can move but cannot speak may work with computers that say back what they have written on the screen. Children with delayed speech may be helped by using a "Wolf" board with overlays of pictures or words that "say" what they are when touched.

Computers allow visually-oriented students to learn through their strengths as they interact with the technology. They can take advantage of opportunities to see and manipulate the material they are accessing or creating in many different forms before they make final copies of a written project. Such publications as Stanley's *Exploring Graphic Design: A Short Course in Desktop Publishing* offer helpful information on the essential principles of design and how to apply them to the preparation of publications.

By using Hypercard or LinkWay software, students can create multimedia reports. Or, they may create a report totally in visual form, combining film clips, slides, photographs, and other illustrations. These multimedia productions make learning a fascinating process, as students work with knowledge in many forms. Scholastic "HyperScreen" is one example of a software program that contains built-in fonts, clip art, and drawing tools. Each screen can contain up to 15 "hotspots," or buttons, that make it possible for users to interact with the lesson or report.

Scholastic "Slide Shop" is a program for creating computerized slide shows, producing audiovisual aids for talks, video title and credit screens, or for creating illustrated pages in student-produced books. Students can design their own screens using clip art, backgrounds, borders, fonts, music, and sound effects from this program.

An increasing number of graphics programs, such as "IPAINT" or "SuperPaint," offer a wide range of experiences that can enhance artistic creativity and fluency by facilitating the technical processes involved in graphic design. Students can create their own works of art or modify existing ones as they explore such compositional devices such as perspective, balance, and color.

Interactive videodiscs are also becoming more available in the classroom as costs for equipment and software decrease. Valuable information for teachers using this technology is available through The International Society for Technology in Education Hyper/MultiMedia Special Interest Group and the *HyperNEXUS: Journal of HyperMedia and MultiMedia Studies* published by ISTE.

An interactive disc on Picasso's painting "Guernica" produced by EduQuest is one means for exploring art. In this random-access database, the viewer can learn about the technical creation of the painting, biographical information on Picasso, images drawn from the Spanish war, and historical and mythological sources of the subject-matter. The viewer can ask questions that are answered not only in visual images but also in text and voice.

Visual peripherals that reinforce topics and skills to be learned are an important part of accelerated learning classrooms, and needless to say the task of changing them frequently can be made easier through technological "teaching walls." In some newer schools, entire electronic walls may be available; in others, large screens or monitors perform this function. Teachers and students alike can be involved in creating the visuals for such displays, using material, for example, from documentary files of CNN or from live newscasts accessible through computer networks.

And on the horizon, is Virtual Reality technology—which will make all other simulations pale by comparison. Still in its infancy, this computer-generated world, offers memorable learning in new dimensions. A student dons a helmet or goggles which contain miniature television monitors, earphones, and an electronic glove. This equipment is linked to a computer that coordinates sensory input with physical movement. The computer monitors the location of the gloved hand, and will create "real" experiences. One of the first programs allowed the participant to "walk" down a street in Aspen, observe the surroundings, and even change seasons of the year. When the

participant reaches the corner by directing the electronic glove, he or she can turn right or left to continue the tour, and explore the inside of some buildings. It takes little imagination to project what such learning experiences might offer to students of physics, chemistry, biology, architecture, or medicine.

Although these visual-spatial tools are not essential for the learning process, they do offer exciting and motivating ways to engage the learner through exercising visual-spatial intelligence and make any subject more accessible to a variety of students. They will surely be of major value to students with physical disabilities or other special needs. They will, in fact, move what might otherwise, for many, remain meaningless abstractions into understandable, visible reality.

SUMMARY

●●

Visual-spatial thinking is a fundamental means of accessing, processing, and representing information. This chapter has surveyed a variety of strategies aimed at improving observation, visualization, and drawing skills. When such processes are used with increasing frequency and skill, it becomes evident that visual thinking encourages mental operations not usually performed in verbal modes. As Robert McKim notes in *Experiences in Visual Thinking*,

Creative thinkers do what computers cannot. They abandon language when occasion demands and enter into other modes of thought. Specifically, creative thinkers are ambidextrous...Learning to think visually is vital to this integrated kind of mental activity.

The visual-spatial techniques included in this chapter are listed below in order to summarize and identify ones that may be appropriate for individual classroom use.

APPLYING VISUAL/SPATIAL INTELLIGENCE

●●●

1. Important ideas or insights gleaned from this chapter: _____

_____

_____

_____

_____

_____

_____

2. Areas I'd like to learn more about: _____

_____

_____

_____

_____

_____

_____

3. Ways I can use this information in my teaching. Please note that all the strategies mentioned in this chapter are listed below with space provided to note how each strategy might be incorporated into classroom instruction:

VISUAL-SPATIAL STRATEGY   CLASSROOM APPLICATION

Establishing a Visual Learning Environment:
Visual Tools _____
Display Areas _____
Peripheral Stimuli _____
Changing Perspective through Rotating _____
Seating _____
Non-Verbal Communication _____

Pictorial Representation:
Flow Charts _____
Visual Outlines _____
Unit Charts _____
Visual Chart Starters _____

Visual Note-Taking and Brainstorming Tools
Concept mapping _____
Mindmapping _____
Clustering _____
Mindscaping _____

Visualization:
Classroom Imageries _____
Visual Memory Techniques _____

Visual Variety in Learning Materials:
Highlighting with Color _____
Varying Shapes _____
Visual Accompaniment for Lectures, _____
Discussions or Readings _____

Board and Card Games:
Guidelines for Making Board Games _____
Card Games _____

Architecture:
Learning to Think like an Architect _____
Getting Started with Architecture _____

The Visual Arts:
Art as an Instructional Tool _____
Blending the Visual and Language Arts _____
Integrating Art and Math _____
Integrating the Arts at the High School Level _____
Art Across the Curriculum _____

Technology that Enhances Visual-Spatial Intelligence: _____

VISUAL-SPATIAL REFERENCES:

Armstrong, T. (1987). *In Their Own Way.* Los Angeles: Tarcher.

Beardslee, E. and Davis, G. (1989). *Interactive Videodisc and the Teaching-Learning Process.* Phi Delta Kappan Educational Foundation. Bloomington, IN.

Beebe, R. (1979) "The Links Grow in the Bronx." *Dromenon: A Journal of New Ways of Being.* February, 1979, Vol. 1, No. 5-6.

Brookes, M. (1986). *Drawing with Children.* Los Angeles: Tarcher.

Brookes, M. (1992). *Drawing with Adolescents.* Los Angeles: Tarcher.

Buzan, T. (1984) . *Use Your Perfect Memory.* N.Y.: E.P. Dutton.

Buzan, T. (1974). *Use Both Sides of Your Brain.* N.Y.: E.P. Dutton.

Carlgren, F. (1972). *Education Towards Freedom.* Rudolphe Steiner Education. East Grinstead, England: Lanthorn Press.

Clark, J. (1990). *Patterns of Thinking: Integrating Learning Skills in Content Teaching.* Needham Heights, MA: Allyn & Bacon.

Dean, J. Gross, I.L. (April, 1992). "Teaching Basic Skills through Art and Music." *Phi Delta Kappan.*

Dhority, L. (1991). *The ACT Approach: The Artful Use of Suggestion for Integrative Learning.* Bremen, Germany: PLS Verlag.

Dunn, R. and Dunn, K. (1978). *Teaching Students through Their Individual Learning Styles.* Reston, VA: Reston Publishing Co.

Galyean, B. (1984). *Mind Sight: Learning through Imagery.* Tucson, AZ: Zephyr Press.

Getty Center for Education in the Arts. (1991). *Proceedings of Future Tense: Arts Education and Technology Conference.* Los Angeles: Getty Center.

Goldman, E. (January/February, 1992). "Learning through Architecture" in *The Harvard Education Letter.*

Held, C. Newsom, J. & Peiffer, M. (March, 1991). "The Integrated Technology Classroom: An Experiment in Restructuring Elementary School Instruction." *The Computing Teacher.*

Hollingsworth, P. and Hollingsworth, S. (1989). *Smart Art: Learning to Classify and Critique Art.* Tucson, AZ: Zephyr Press.

Jones, B. F. (1988). *Graphic Forms with Corresponding Text Frames.* Aurora, CO: North Central Regional Educational Laboratory.

Lorayne, H. and Lucas, J. (1974). *The Memory Book.* N.Y.: Ballantine Books.

Maddex, D. (1986). *Architects Make Zigzags: Looking at Architecture from A to Z.* Washington, D.C.: Preservation Press.

Margulies, N. (1990). *Mapping Inner Space.* Tucson, AZ: Zephyr Press.

McKim, R. (1980, second edition). *Experiences in Visual Thinking.* Monterey, CA: Brooks/ Cole Publishing.

Meister-Vitale, B. (1982). *Unicorns Are Real: A Right-Brained Approach to Learning.* Rolling Hills Estates, CA: Jalmar Press.

National Standards for Arts Education. (1994). *Dance, Music, Theatre, Visual Arts: What Every Young American Should Know and Be Able to Do in the Arts.* Reston, VA: Music Educators National Conference.

Novak, J. and Gowin, B. (1984). *Learning How to Learn.* Cambridge University Press.

Olson, L. (January 8,1992). "Profiles in Technology: Striving to Harness the Power of Technology to Improve the Nation's Schools." *Education Week.*

Rico, G. (1983). *Writing the Natural Way.* Los Angeles: Tarcher.

Stanley, M.L.G. (1989). *Exploring Graphic Design: A Short Course in Desktop Publishing.* International Society for Technology in Education.

Taylor, A. and Vlastos, G. *School Zone: Learning Environments for Children.* School of Architecture, University of New Mexico. Albuquerque, NM.

Verlee Williams, L. (1983). *Teaching for the Two-Sided Mind: A Guide to Right Brain/ Left Brain Education.* N.Y.: Simon & Schuster.

CHAPTER 5

TUNING IN:
MUSICAL INTELLIGENCE

Music is the manifestation of the human spirit, similar to language. Its greatest practitioners have conveyed to mankind things not possible to say in any other language. If we do not want these things to remain dead treasures, we must do our utmost to make the greatest possible number of people understand their idiom.

— *ZOLTAN KODALY*
A Zanei Iras-Olvasas Modszertana

DANNY'S SONG

The young American singer and composer Danny Deardorff was struck by polio when he was an infant. The disease left his body crooked and crippled, but from the earliest years, his strong spirit has revealed itself through song.

As a child, he made up songs about the mailman walking down the street, about the screen door keeping bugs out and letting cool air in. Whatever Danny saw inspired lyrics and music.

Today he is an internationally recognized composer, performer, producer, and inspirational speaker. He has received numerous national awards and believes that music is a powerful form of communication, one that reaches the mind through the heart. Danny's music teaches important social messages, some of which include learning to love more fully, caring for the environment, and appreciating the differences among individuals.

One song Danny recently wrote and recorded with Lorraine Bayes, is entitled "Everyone is Differently Abled." In this song, Danny has replaced the term "disabled" with "differently abled," which applies to everyone and emphasizes what we can do, instead of what we can't do.

Danny's Song ...continued

The song echoes Howard Gardner's Theory of Multiple Intelligences by affirming:

Everyone is Differently Abled.

Everyone has abilities.

Everyone is Differently Abled

Making their lives work differently.

You might use a chair with wheels to get around.

Or, you might use your hands to speak without a sound,

'Cause there are a million ways to do most anything.

Some people love to dance.

Some people prefer to sing.

Now you can use a working dog to help you see.

Or use your mouth or feet to paint and write poetry.

There are a million different ways that you can be.

It's true that all of us live interdependently.

I will not be defined by my limitations,

But rather by my possibilities.

We can respond to the needs of those around us.

The best ability is response-ability.

Everyone is Differently Abled.

Everyone has abilities.

Everyone is Differently Abled

Making their lives work differently.

This song is part of an album entitled, *Let's Be Friends*, by the award winning children's performing group, Tickle Tune Typhoon.

DEFINITION: UNDERSTANDING MUSICAL INTELLIGENCE

Music is undoubtedly one of the oldest art forms, utilizing the human voice and body as natural instruments and means of self-expression. It is an art that comes into the world with us. We live with our mother's heartbeat for nine months before we are born. We live with the rhythms of our own heartbeat and respiration and the more subtle rhythms of metabolic and brain wave activity. We are all inherently musical and can develop this capacity in ourselves and in others.

The early childhood years appear to be crucial to musical growth. There appears to be a critical period of sensitivity to sound and pitch between the ages of four and six. During that time, a rich musical environment can provide the basis for later musical ability. In Bloom's *Developing Talent in Young Children*, he points out that among the gifted pianists he studied, many were not from musical families. They all had parents, however, who were supportive of their children's musical interests. In addition, the musicians' first teachers were consistently warm, caring, and supportive. Task-masters came later in their careers.

In the Hungarian "singing schools," based on the work of Zoltan Kodaly, children sing every day. By the third grade, there are few children who cannot sing on pitch and make beautiful sounds. It has been noted that Hungarian students have also excelled in math and science as a result of their on-going musical training.

Musical intelligence involves its own rules and thinking structures, not necessarily linked to other kinds of intelligence. Stravinsky once commented that "Music expresses itself," underscoring the independence of this form of human competence. Music is an aural language which uses three basic components: pitch, rhythm, and timbre or the quality of a sound. It is often notated with unique symbol systems. The countless combinations of these three elements have given rise to the remarkable variety of music found throughout the world.

Howard Gardner asserts in *Frames of Mind* that any normal individual who has had frequent exposure to music can manipulate pitch, rhythm, and timbre to participate with some skill in musical activities, including composing, singing, or playing instruments. The foundations for such interests can be laid at an early age through the kinds of activities described in this chapter. Music in the home and early environment provides an important basis for these musical experiences which can later be integrated throughout a school's curriculum.

Because of the strong connection between music and the emotions, music in the classroom can help create a positive emotional environment conducive to learning. Music can also be used to heighten the suspense, sadness, tragedy, or joy of stories from great literature and history. Music can even be used or created to express humor. Musical puns such as those by "P.D.Q. Bach" are interesting tools for sharpening listening and concentration skills. Humorous songs can also add warmth and a welcoming atmosphere in the classroom.

✔ CHECKLIST OF MUSICAL QUALITIES

Many ancient philosophers included music as an important part of education. Plato claimed that "Rhythm and harmony sink deep into the recesses of the soul and take the strongest hold there, bringing the grace of body and mind which is only to be found in one brought up in the right way." Aristotle was also an early proponent of extensive music education believing that "We become of a certain quality in our characters on account of it."

Confucius thought music was influential both personally and politically: "The superior man tries to promote music as a means to the perfection of human culture. When such music prevails, and people are led toward ideals and aspirations, we may see the appearance of a great nation." During the Middle Ages and the Renaissance, music was considered one of the four pillars of learning, along with geometry, astronomy, and arithmetic.

In our time, however, music has suffered as one of the first subjects to be cut from school programs when budget reductions are made. Back-to-basics proponents have also eliminated music education in many schools in order to devote more time to reading, math, and science. Ironically, music may be one of the important means of developing those very skills so desired in American students. For example, a report compiled by the Music Educators National Conference found that in 1987-1989, students taking music courses scored an average of 20 to 40 points higher on both verbal and math portions of the Scholastic Achievement Tests than students who did not take such courses. Additionally, a College Entrance Examination Board study found that students who took four or more years of music and the other arts scored 34 points better on verbal SAT scores and 18 points better on math SAT scores than students who took music for only one year. It appears that music may positively affect general academic achievement.

Activities such as constructing and playing instruments, taking lessons to improve performance skills, playing or singing in ensembles, dancing, and attending concerts are perceived as positive challenges for students when it is a standard part of their education. At the St. Augustine School of the Arts in the Bronx, New York, all students have such opportunities. The children who attend this school are mostly from poor, under-educated families, yet the school ranks among the highest academically in the United States.

In a survey of ninth grade science achievement in 17 countries, the top three countries, Hungary, Japan, and the Netherlands have all incorporated intensive music and art training into their public school basic curriculum. Perhaps some day a direct correlation will be found between musical training and enhanced mathematical and scientific thinking.

There are those students who have greater musical ability than others, and their gift may appear early in life. As Howard Gardner notes, musical talent emerges inexplicably earlier than giftedness in other areas of human intelligence. These unique children are compelled to make music, and it is essential they have opportunities both to experience and create music. As noted earlier, however, virtually everyone including hard-of-hearing and deaf students, have the potential to develop their musical abilities.

Many, if not most children and adults, enjoy rhythm and melody and like to hear music or participate in musical activities. Individuals without any prior exposure often enjoy learning through musical methods or appreciate music in the learning environment as they work on non-verbal tasks.

It is a complex matter to attempt to identify students who have musical aptitude or well-developed musical intelligence. A broad range of musical abilities exists and it is unlikely any one individual embodies them all. For example, there are many well known cases of musicians who were successful at some musical endeavors and failed with others. It is rumored that Tchaikovsky nearly ruined the premiere of his Sixth Symphony because of his poor conducting. Chopin was a gifted composer for the piano but appeared uninterested in writing for any other instrument. Some individuals may fail music theory classes but demonstrate giftedness in singing. Others such as Louis Armstrong may have an outstanding ability to improvise in certain styles of music without the training to read musical notation. Thus, it is impossible to determine musical intelligence by using a checklist which captures only a few of the dimensions of this complex intelligence. However, a list, such as the following, may help to identify some of the characteristics of musically-endowed learners. It is likely that a person with well-developed musical intelligence:

1. **Listens and responds with interest to a variety of sounds including the human voice, environmental sounds, and music, and organizes such sounds into meaningful patterns.**

2. **Enjoys and seeks out opportunities to hear music or environmental sounds in the learning environment. Is eager to be around and learn from music and musicians.**

3. **Responds to music kinesthetically by conducting, performing, creating, or dancing; emotionally through responding to the moods and tempos of music; intellectually through discussing and analyzing music; and/or aesthetically by evaluating and exploring the content and meaning of music.**

4. **Recognizes and discusses different musical styles, genres, and cultural variations. Demonstrates interest in the role music has and continues to play in human lives.**

5. **Collects music and information about music in various forms, both recorded and printed, and may collect and play musical instruments including synthesizers.**

6. **Develops the ability to sing and/or play an instrument alone or with others.**

7. **Uses the vocabulary and notations of music.**

8. **Develops a personal frame of reference for listening to music.**

9. **Enjoys improvising and playing with sounds, and when given a phrase of music, can complete a musical statement in a way that makes sense.**

10. **May offer his or her own interpretation of what a composer is communicating through music. May also analyze and critique musical selections.**

11. **May express interest in careers involving music such as being a singer, instrumentalist, sound engineer, producer, critic, instrument maker, teacher, or conductor.**

12. **May create original compositions and/or musical instruments.**

MUSICAL LEARNING PROCESSES

The activities suggested in this chapter are not intended to provide a comprehensive or sequential course in music education or to substitute for such programs taught in the schools by trained music educators. Children and young people can develop their musical abilities through programs designed to achieve a balance of skills in performing, listening, and creating as well as reflecting on music. There are many fine music programs at all levels in schools throughout the nation. National standards for such programs are available from the Music Educators National Conference (MENC) in Reston, Virginia.

Instead, the following musical activities are meant to facilitate the learning of other academic content. Many educators shun musical teaching strategies because of their own lack of musical experience. No training, however, is necessary to incorporate these activities into lessons. The strategies offered here provide successful ways for students and teachers alike to foster positive attitudes towards music and to recognize its relationship to other kinds of learning. When teachers incorporate music in classroom lessons, an additional benefit may ultimately emerge: musical appreciation and skill may develop in formerly non-musical teachers and students!

The strategies described in this chapter include:

ESTABLISHING A MUSICAL LEARNING ENVIRONMENT

Music can become an important part of any educational setting. It provides a welcoming atmosphere as students enter; it offers a calming effect after periods of physical activity; it smoothes classroom transitions; it reawakens energy on gray days; and it reduces stress that commonly accompanies examinations or other academic pressures.

One principal, noticing the calming and quieting effect of background music in some teachers' classrooms, decided to play music in the school's hallways where numerous behavior problems frequently erupted. As an experiment, the principal played Steven Halpern's "Spectrum Suite" and other quiet selections in the school's passageways and lunchroom. Student behavior dramatically improved and music became an essential component of the total school environment.

When used softly in the background as students enter a classroom, music has the ability to focus student attention and to enhance physical energy levels. Students typically enter class with a variety of individual concerns, feelings, and preoccupations. Music can create a positive atmosphere that will help them focus to learn.

INTRODUCING MUSIC INTO THE CLASSROOM

Teachers interested in playing background music to enhance classroom ambiance may first want to increase student awareness of the ways music can enhance everyday living. We are surrounded with the sounds of radios, video games, cassettes, laser disks, television, and music as accompaniments to many of our daily activities. To heighten awareness of music and its influence in our lives, the teacher may want to engage the class in a discussion of how and when students listen to music. The teacher might suggest that since students often listen to rock and roll for entertainment purposes, they may want to expand their awareness of other kinds of music to discover how a variety of musical styles may enhance the quality of life.

There are several things a teacher might consider before making music a part of the classroom such as sound equipment, types of music to play, and times when it is appropriate to play music. For teachers who want to create a musical classroom environment, some guidelines follow:

Guidelines for Using Background Music in the Classroom:

1. Musical equipment, ideally of good quality, should be located and installed in the classroom. Music played through a stereo cassette or sound system with two separate speakers in different locations of the classroom provides the most effective sound. When speakers are placed at a distance from each other, it is easier for all students to hear well.

2. While high quality sound systems are rarely present in most schools, it is important to realize that the sound of poor quality cassette players can be distracting and frustrating. By identifying a school or household's available equipment, teachers may discover a variety of good quality cassette decks or other sound systems. One of the authors regularly "borrows" a teenage-son's portable equipment to use in his elementary classroom.

3. Since many homes do not have recordings of different kinds of music, teachers will want to share with their students a broad representation of selections including contemporary, romantic, baroque, and classical pieces played by orchestras, chamber groups, or soloists. Excellent recordings of world music should also be included. Some selections are suggested later in the chapter.

4. It is important to determine when and how background music is to be played in the classroom. Frequently, it is effective as students enter the room, during quiet reading, individual work sessions, study periods, tests, and transitions. Ultimately, teachers and students will want to experiment with timing such as at the beginning, middle, or end of a day or class period to determine what is most effective for each group. Selections may be chosen to quiet active or restless groups or energize students who are tired or sleepy.

5. Some research indicates that music may interfere with verbal tasks, and that some students may be distracted by music during any kind of academic work. In general, it is recommended that background music be played only occasionally. Just a few minutes of appropriate music can be useful in bridging between subjects or activities. Such a minimal amount of time allows students who enjoy a musical environment to have access to rhythmical stimulation without causing discomfort for those who find it distracting.

6. If the teacher plans to speak while the music is playing, the volume should be set at a level that does not compete with her voice.

7. Students often provide valuable feedback about their reactions to music in the classroom. Class discussions might address preferred selections, volume, and timing, as well as the type and the location of the sound system. Thus, students and teachers together can establish a positive musical learning environment.

Once students and teachers have experimented with a melodic background in the classroom, additional purposes for the use of music can be explored. The research of psychiatrist and educator Dr. Georgi Lozanov in Sophia, Bulgaria, suggests that music strongly influences our ability to relax, rejuvenate, and concentrate. Lozanov's work also suggests that music integrates the emotional, physical, and cognitive dimensions of the learner, as well as accelerates the quantity of information learned and retained.

In addition to creating a pleasant classroom ambiance, music can be used for specific purposes. Many teachers have intentionally used music in four ways: to relax, invigorate, focus student attention, or ease transitions. For example, when students appear overly stimulated, certain selections such as "Water Music Suite" by Handel or "Concerto for Three Violins and Orchestra" by Telemann often help them relax. After lunch when lethargy sets in, other pieces may prove invigorating such as "Divertimento" by Mozart or "Flight of the Bumble Bee" by Rimsky-Korsakov. When well-focused attention is necessary, some compositions such as "Four Seasons" by Vivaldi or "C Major Piano Concert" by Mozart may enhance student concentration. If teachers are interested in working with music for such purposes, they might want to review their personal collections, sorting their albums or cassettes into the four categories of relaxation, focusing attention, invigoration, and transitions, or locate music elsewhere that may be appropriate for such purposes.

Some suggestions are offered below that diversify classroom listening experiences with both contemporary and classical selections:

A Variety of Musical Selections:

For Relaxation:

"The Four Seasons"	Vivaldi
"Spectrum Suite"	Stephen Halpern
"Water Music"	Handel
"Afternoon of a Faun"	Debussey
"Deep Breakfast"	Ray Lynch
"Fantasia on Greensleeves"	Vaughn Williams

For Focusing Attention:

"Flute Concertos"	Vivaldi
"Concerto Grossi #4, 10-12"	Corelli
"Silver Cloud"	Kitaro
"Cosmic Classics"	Don Campbell
"C Major Piano Concerto"	Mozart
"Snowflakes Are Dancing"	Tomita

For Invigoration:

"Alexander's Feast"	Handel
"Dances for a Sleep Walker"	Don Campbell
"Well Tempered Klavier"	Bach
"Divertimento"	Mozart
"The Sting"	Movie Soundtrack
"Saving the Wildlife"	Mannheim Steamroller

For Transitions:

"Royal Fireworks"	Handel
"Apurimac"	Cusco
"The Norwegian Bridal Procession of Peer Gynt Suite"	Greig
"No Blue Thing"	Ray Lynch
"Nouveau Flamenco"	Ottmar Liebert

The compositions suggested above all rely on a musical theme and are structured with patterns and symmetry that are capable of influencing body rhythms and mental alertness. When well used, music can serve teachers and students as a powerful ally in the classroom.

LISTENING TO MUSIC

Sharing a variety of musical styles and compositions in the classroom can lay the groundwork for the development of musical taste and appreciation. It is important to offer opportunities for all children to hear, sing, and dance the folk songs of their own and other countries. They should also be exposed to fine music by soloists, and small and large ensembles, playing both classical and modern music. Students' musical interests may be piqued by studying the role of music in world cultures and the lives of various composers and performers. Teachers can create a composer-of-the-month learning center in which recordings, biographies, pictures, and literature are available for independent exploration and research.

For students to benefit from a musical learning environment, they must do more than listen passively to many musical selections. They must also learn to listen actively, focusing on the music itself. To shift from hearing background music to active, structured listening, the teacher may want to engage students in a discussion about a musical composition, its qualities, and the impact it has upon them as individuals. To assist students with structured listening, select a musical piece to play once or twice, and preview the following questions so that students can prepare for their listening experience:

Listening Discussion Questions

What did this music make you think of? Did it suggest colors, images, patterns or scenes?

What feelings did this selection evoke?

What instruments or singing did you hear?

Were there any repetitive sound patterns the composer used? Can you sing or tap them?

What portions of the music did you especially enjoy? What made them appealing?

Can you think of a situation when this music would be especially appropriate to play?

Does this music remind you of another selection? What is similar to it?

Can you imagine movement or dance to accompany this music? If so, can you move or dance in that way?

If you could, would you change this music in any way? How?

What do you think the composer was trying to communicate when he wrote this composition? Might the listener hear something quite different?

The questions listed above are not meant to develop a sophisticated understanding of music. They are intended, however, to help students listen actively and critically. Teachers can add other questions according to their interest and expertise. Students might also respond to music in non-verbal ways. While listening to a composition and using music as a source of inspiration, students might draw or paint, build with clay or wire, or move and dance.

Whenever possible, students should have opportunities to attend performances to listen to accomplished musicians. And perhaps, some students will perceive the powerful, inspirational quality of music as did 12-year-old Josef Knecht in Herman Hesse's *Magister Ludi*:

> "The boy looked at the player's clever white fingers, saw the course of the development faintly mirrored in his concentrated expression while his eyes remained quiet under half-closed lids. Josef's heart swelled with

veneration, with love for the master, his ear drank in the fugue. It seemed to him that he was hearing music for the first time in his life. Behind the music being created in his presence, he sensed the world of mind, the joy-giving harmony of law, and freedom of service and rule. He surrendered himself, and vowed to serve that world, and this master. In those few moments he saw himself and his life; saw the whole cosmos, guided, ordered and interpreted by the spirit of music."

SONGS IN THE CONTENT AREAS

Song lyrics containing curriculum information are invaluable instructional tools. Most students find it easy to memorize the lyrics to songs, and will find it just as easy to memorize academic content set to music. We recently met a trainer of European real estate sales people. He was challenged by the difficulty of his task, since each country had a different set of real estate laws and it was difficult to remember which laws were legislated by which country. The trainer tackled this problem by setting the laws of each country to representative music of that nation. For example, the laws of Spain were set to a Spanish tango, the laws of Italy to an Italian street song, the laws of Germany to a Lederhosen song, and the laws of France to a romantic ballad. He cut his training time in less than half and retention of key information was greatly enhanced.

Resources for Songs that Teach Curriculum

Singing songs not only helps many students remember important information, it also enlivens classroom learning. A challenge for educators is to locate tapes or records that include concepts to be taught. School supply catalogs list recordings, and music teachers are an additional resource. Music series texts with recordings are often available in schools or from textbook companies. Media centers of most school districts also lend cassettes, videos, and records that frequently contain curriculum-based songs. Students and colleagues may have other suggestions that could lead to the development of a library to share throughout the school.

Recorded Songs for a Variety of Curricular Areas

Some delightful resources are currently available to help teach common curricular topics. One book, entitled *Active Learning: Rappin' and Rhymin'* by Rosella Wallace features songs, raps and cheers that teach the names of continents, oceans, planets, months, and vocabulary words as well as math facts.

Another musical resource is *Learning Rock—Parts of Speech and More* by John and Gloria Wyatt, whose booklet and cassette contain songs that teach spelling and grammatical concepts such as "Rules for Adding Endings" and "Never Use a Double Negative."

Rise Up Singing is an outstanding resource book offering 1200 songs indexed according to curricular topics such as cities, freedom, food, war, physical disabilities, and humor.

An additional source of content-rich songs appropriate for elementary classrooms is available from the children's performing group, Tickle Tune Typhoon. Winner of six national awards for their highly professional, socially relevant, and always entertaining music, Tickle Tune has produced several cassettes and a videotape offering a wealth of songs to compliment many instructional units.

Songs for the Sciences

Excellent cassette tapes that address common curricular topics are also available. One is entitled, *Sing a Song of Science*, by Kathleen Carroll, and features 16 songs, raps, and stories about the physical and life sciences. One of the selections is called "Advantages and Disadvantages of Energy Sources." Its lyrics include:

> Wind,
> Wind can be a terrific source of energy.
> It's very, very cheap you know
> But then sometimes it doesn't blow.
>
> We need a source of energy,
> For heat, transportation, and electricity.
>
> Water,
> Water can be a terrific source of energy.
> It turns things here, it turns things there.
> But you can't find water everywhere.
>
> We need a source of energy,
> For heat, transportation, and electricity.
>
> Coal,
> Coal can be a terrific source of energy.
> It's easy as can be to store,
> But it pollutes our air that's for sure...

The songs on the cassette are catchy, enjoyable tunes sung by the students of the Duke Ellington School of the Arts. They effectively reinforce science concepts and may motivate students to write lyrics for their science lessons. Another source of science songs is written by teacher Leo Wood from Tempe High School in Tempe, Arizona. Wood uses a variety of techniques in teaching junior- and senior-level chemistry courses, some of which include playing background classical music while students conduct their lab work and teaching curricular information through songs he has written. One such song explains the chemical reactions of fusion, photosynthesis, combustion, respiration, and reactions of various types. Wood makes this and other songs available for classroom use through Tempe High School.

Songs for Math

The set of cassette tapes entitled *Rappin' Tappin' Time Tables* available from Toe Tappin' Teaching Aids teaches multiplication facts through music and rhyme. The tapes begin by stating a math fact such as 4 x 5. A rhyming phrase is given for the equation such as "good and plenty" and then the answer, 20, is provided. Each math fact is taught with its own rhymed association and melody. As students progress through the tape, they are eventually asked to reproduce the math facts and correct answers from recognizing the melodies provided for each. Many students with musical skills find such tasks to be delightful challenges. Nearly all students will appreciate replacing repetitive drill and practice with musically motivating learning. Rosella Wallace's *Active Learning: Rappin' and Rhymin'* mentioned above also features a song called "The Nine's Rap."

The resources listed above can delight, entertain, and educate both students and teachers alike. Some students may request that they listen to certain tunes repetitively. In such cases, teachers may want to have an individual cassette tape deck and set of headphones on hand.

MUSIC FOR SKILL BUILDING

Most people are aware of music's remarkably effective ability to enhance various physical skills such as typing, swimming, or aerobic exercises. The rhythm and flow of music can result in increased coordination, regularity, and speed of the activity in enjoyable ways. For young children, skipping, marching, running, or dancing to music develops rhythm and grace. For older children and adults, musical accompaniment can make tedious exercises and daily routines pleasurable. It is also useful in developing a sense of timing, whether it is getting ready to "1-2-3- go!" in sports, or learning how to deliver the punch-line of a story, as is the case in comic songs. However, music's influence with skill building extends beyond the kinesthetic realm into the academic.

MUSICAL SPELLING

Learning to spell new words to music is not only fun, it also accelerates learning. For example, two eighth grade girls who had difficulty spelling both enjoyed playing the piano. One of the authors asked the girls to label the piano keys with the letters of the alphabet, so that the girls could "play" the words on their keyboards. Later, on spelling tests, the students were asked to recall the tones and sounds of each word and write its corresponding letters. Not only did spelling scores improve, but the two pianists began thinking of other "sound" texts to set to music. Soon, they performed each classmate's name and transcribed entire sentences. Much to everyone's delight, the pianists and their classmates experienced the powerful bridging of language and music. Words can also be spelled by chanting in rhythm while accenting certain letters which are frequently missed or confused.

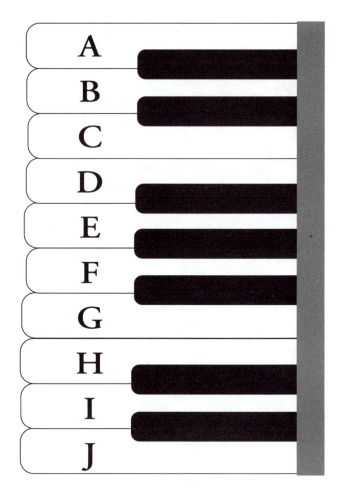

TEACHING READING MUSICALLY

Yamaha has sponsored studies in K-1 classrooms in the United States that associate music instruction with remarkable achievement in reading. One study in the Downey Unified School District in Downey, California, showed, for example, that the reading skills of first grade children who had a single year of music instruction were nearly one grade higher than those of their peers. Additionally, students with two years of music instruction scored at almost the third grade level and some even scored at the fourth and fifth grade levels.

Although many teachers are not musicians, there are easy ways to use music as instructional strategies. Sheila Fitzgerald at Michigan State University has developed a musical approach for teaching reading that does not require formal musical instruction. For teachers interested in developing reading skills through rhythm and music, Fitzgerald suggests the following procedures:

1. Encourage children to sing on a daily basis. Elementary classroom teachers might identify songs that children will enjoy and teach these as a part of each day's activities. Songs that are selected should ideally be a part of the children's experience or environment or ones that the students compose.

2. Once children are familiar with the words of a song, they are ready to see the lyrics in print. These can be transcribed onto the blackboard or a large chart. Usually, when reading the lyrics for the first time, there is great excitement among the students. Their musical familiarity with the words eases the transition to reading.

3. Students may next progress to reading individual words from a song chart. Students might volunteer to point out individual words written on the blackboard or they might locate words that appear more than once in the song. Additionally, teachers might provide students with words or phrases written on pieces of tagboard which are the same size as the words on the chart. The children might then match their cards with the chart by actually placing their piece of tagboard on the appropriate spots.

4. Students might be given a song booklet to help them learn the lyrics. To enhance sight reading skills, students can point to words they are singing, read (or sing) the lyrics with a friend, read (or sing) them to someone who doesn't know the song, or point out the words as they listen to someone else sing the song.

Using their song books as references, students might also become word detectives locating words in the song in other printed texts.

5. When children have sung and read a favorite song many times, they may be able to write from memory at least part of the lyrics. Nursery rhymes work well for this activity. Students should be encouraged to problem-solve, such as use invented spellings, and the teacher and classmates should accept and value all efforts at initial song writing without undue attention to correctness or completeness.

There are many excellent books of children's literature which illustrate songs and/or have musical themes. The added stimulation of the illustrations helps increase aesthetic richness and provides a context for understanding. An extensive listing of such books can be found in an article written by Linda Leonard Lamme in *The Reading Teacher* listed in the references.

Teaching beginning readers with a musically-based approach introduces children not only to reading skills but also to musical skills of pitch and melody and the more subtle nuances of rhythm and timing in language. Teachers who wish to receive further training in incorporating a range of musical activities using a language and movement approach may wish to attend workshops or courses in Orff-Schulwerk available throughout the country. An excellent resource for classroom integration using Orff principles is, *Teaching Creatively by Working the Word*, by Susan Katz and Judith Thomas.

MUSIC ACROSS THE CURRICULUM

Don Schiltz, a songwriter, provided testimony to the National Commission on Music Education in Nashville, Tennessee in 1990. He described how important music was for him as a secondary student:

> **"I'll tell you about a class I had…music appreciation. I didn't really think of it as a class. I thought of it as the period where we went and sang songs. We were learning that English precisely presents a writer's thoughts and feelings, that songs are a form of communication. We were learning history through the songs of the nation. It was better than any other history class in my life. We were learning math, discovering the relationships between parts, and that composition followed mathematical rules. And, we were learning to listen; if you don't listen you can't learn. This music appreciation connected my entire studies."**

As Don Schiltz explains above, music enhances learning throughout the curriculum. For example, since music is an integral component of any historical era, it provides an effective approach for identifying issues, attitudes, events, and values of a specific time period. Students might learn about political and social issues by listening to songs, operas, or musical comedies.

Since music is itself a language spoken in all cultures, it offers an important and stimulating way to learn about other countries. For example, listening to Japanese music provides a rich background for studying Japanese principles of simplicity, order, and balance. Haiku poems might be written to illustrate such principles in words. African drum beats, Balinese gamelon music, or Tibetan bells provide the accompaniment to rhythmical movements and offer further insight into the cultures that produced such musical forms. Students might also listen to the folk music of a selected culture noting its interpretation of human events, longings, and aspirations.

Mathematics can be taught through music, and for some students what would otherwise be a puzzling abstraction becomes clearly understood. For example, in learning to understand fractions, students can work with a simple song such as "Twinkle, Twinkle Little Star." While singing the song, one group claps on every syllable, in quarter notes. Another group claps on just the first beat of each measure, another on every other beat, and a fourth group claps eight times for each measure. Students can then compare whole, half, quarter, and eighth notes and relate them to cutting up a circle in the same proportions. To learn math facts, students can chant or sing addition, subtraction, multiplication, or division problems to familiar tunes. Older students may set geometric or algebraic formulas to music.

Science teachers at the Northwest School in Seattle teach chemistry through musical comedy. While playing music in the cafeteria, eleventh grade science students demonstrate their knowledge of protein synthesis by choreographing 100 unsuspecting parents and fellow students in a spontaneous dance of the polypeptides. Amidst much laughter and fun, order emerges out of chaos with both science students and audience members gaining insight into amino acids, polypeptide chains, and myoglobin, as well as the joy of learning through music and dance.

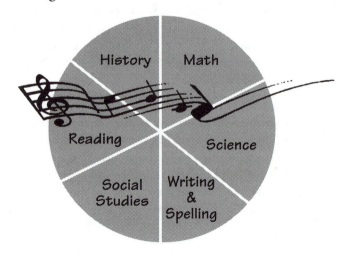

WARMING UP TO SINGING

Students and teachers are often shy about singing. When a teacher decides to introduce singing in the classroom, it should be emphasized that the goal is not to turn everyone into an accomplished singer but rather to enliven and enhance the learning process. At the same time, people learn to sing by singing. Teachers can increase singing accuracy by establishing the starting pitch of a song by singing or playing it (most children are comfortable singing in the range of middle C to the C above). The meter and flow of the song can be established by counting "1, 2, rea-dy sing" for a song in 2 or 4, and "1 rea-dy sing" for a song in 3. Students should be encouraged to sing with energy rather than to sing loudly and to blend with the voices of their classmates.

To alleviate concerns about the sound of one's voice, students and teachers might approach singing by initially chanting nonsense sounds. Such activities emphasize the playfulness of soundmaking and reduce fears about singing in perfect pitch or sounding accomplished like well known vocalists. Over time, the teacher can progress from chanting, to exaggerating the words in a sort of "heightened speech," and then into singing. It is important to encourage children to hear the differences between their "speaking voices" and their "singing voices."

NONSENSE SOUNDS

The following song incorporates nonsense sounds, and can be successfully used with students of varying ages.

Divide the class into four groups of equal size. Number the groups from one to four. The first group chants:

RAT-A-TAT-TAT RAT-A-TAT-TAT RAT-A-TAT-TAT...

Once the first group has its part going, the second group joins in with:

BOOM-DA BOOM-DA BOOM-DA BOOM-DA...

With the first two groups continuing, the third sings:

FIZZLE-WIZZLE FIZZLE-WIZZLE FIZZLE-WIZZLE...

The fourth group now begins singing the A-B-C song to the tune of "Twinkle, Twinkle, Little Star." After the students practice their four part songs two or three times, the teacher might want to record their singing. Frequently, this song sounds better than anyone would have anticipated, with the tape recording providing an important confidence boost.

Although at the outset this particular song involves singing the alphabet, once the technique is mastered, more sophisticated subject matter can be tackled, replacing the A, B, C's with the fifty states, the steps in conflict resolution processes, Spanish vocabulary words, or the periodic elements. Another nonsense syllable approach to singing consists of creating a refrain that reluctant singers might easily imitate. For example, adding sounds like oo-ee-oo-ah-ah-ting-tang-walla-walla-bing-bang provides interesting sound effects for passages read aloud. Young children can learn their addresses and telephone numbers to a tune. The music thus becomes a string to unify and memorize abstractions, much like beads strung into a necklace.

CHORAL READING

Once students have experienced success with nonsense syllable sound-making, they might progress to choral reading. Finding short poems, literary passages, or famous quotations that require vocal variations in rhythm, pitch, emotion, or dialect encourages students to use their voices in new ways while adding fluency, confidence, and expression in reading aloud. Poems such as de la Mare's "The Highwayman," Langston Hughes's "Homesick Blues," Poe's "The Raven" or Frost's "Mending Wall" are some examples of poetic selections that lend themselves to interesting choral interpretations. The book by Katz and Thomas, *Teaching Creatively by Working the Word*, includes many ideas for making these experiences musical as well as fun.

Original writing integrated with a lesson's content can be used for choral reading activities. The following excerpt was written by a teacher for a class studying the Stone Age:

Such a selection can be performed in a variety of ways. The choral reading might be staged with the class divided in parts, forming girls' and boys' parts, adding loud and quiet sections, and varying the pace. The important point in using either nonsense sounds or choral reading is to acquaint students with using their voices with greater expression, vocal range, and skill. Such preliminary warm-ups ready students for the joy of singing with confidence.

Get ready for a party
Time to set the stage
It happened long ago
In the Old Stone Age.

GATHER ROUND THE FIRE
GRAB A BIG STONE
BEAT IT TO THE RHYTHM
WITH AN OLD LEG BONE.

Here come the women
Bringing tasty roots
They gathered fresh berries
And other wild fruits.

GATHER ROUND THE FIRE
GRAB A BIG STONE
BEAT IT TO THE RHYTHM
WITH AN OLD LEG BONE.

MUSICAL NOTATION

"Music is… like mathematics,
very nearly a world by itself;
it contains a whole gamut of
experience, from sensuous elements
to ultimate intellectual harmonies."

— GEORGE SANTYANA

Unless students take formal music courses, they rarely learn to read musical notation. The abstract, musical, symbol system may remain an unfamiliar foreign language throughout their lives because of a lack of exposure. To decrease the mystery of musical notation, students can initially create their own symbol systems and then more readily grasp standardized musical notation. Research by Rena Upitis suggests that developing personal notational systems for music enhances the development of musical thinking. Her books, *This Too Is Music* and *Can I Play You My Song*, are useful tools for explaining personalized notation and give many practical ideas for classroom application.

INTRODUCING THE CONCEPT OF MUSICAL NOTATION

To introduce students to the concept that different shapes represent different sounds, Don Kaplan's book, *See with Your Ears*, suggests a variety of ways to draw the sound "Aah" to demonstrate the holding of a note. Teachers and students may want to experiment with pitch, timbre, volume, and duration with the following "aah's":

even and straight out:	aah ———————
wavy:	aah ∿∿∿∿∿
in a whisper:	aah - - - - - - - - -
sliding up:	aah ⟋
sliding down:	aah ⟍
softly:	*aah* ——————
loudly:	**AAHH**━━━━━
getting louder and softer:	aAh aAh ── ▬ ── ▬
on different pitches:	aah —————
	aah ———————
	aah —————————
short and fast, like a laugh:	ahahahahahahahahahahahahahahahahah
long and slow:	aah aah aah aah aah aah

Once students sing and learn these sounds and their corresponding "notations," they could each be given a notecard with one of the above "notations" drawn on the card. Divided into small groups of five or six, each group can "read" and practice their notations, composing a melody to perform for the rest of the class.

To move students to graphic representation of musical notation, the following approach is offered. The teacher may want to demonstrate to students that a simple bar system can represent the length of time each note is held in a song. For example,

"Mary had a little lamb"…
might look like this:

To extend this system to standard notation, the same bars can be put on a staff.

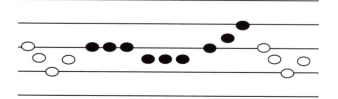

Students might then create their own graphic symbols to transcribe simple songs such as "Twinkle, Twinkle Little Star", "Row, Row Your Boat" or "Hickory, Dickory, Dock."

Another simple and enjoyable approach to musical notation combining music and art follows:

After selecting a provocative piece of instrumental music, explain to students that they will listen to a musical selection and while listening, they will be asked to draw simple symbols of what they hear. Blank paper and colored mark-

ers or crayons should be distributed to all students. As they prepare to listen, ask them to imagine lines, shapes, and colors suggested by the music itself. Inform them that they will listen to the music a second time and will then "draw" what they heard.

Students may want to pay particular attention to repeated musical patterns, using the same visual symbols for these portions of the composition. Or, they might focus on representing the beats, meters, or rhythmic patterns. If dynamic change (loud and soft) is particularly dominant, students may wish to draw those changes. Some works of music such as Pachelbel's "Canon" will suggest attention to melodic lines or layers of melodies. The unique features of each musical composition will be perceived by attentive students. To effectively notice and represent what is happening in the music, students may neeed to listen to the selection several times.

After they have listened to and drawn the music, engage students in brief discussions asking them to "translate" their drawings, noting which symbol or color represented which sound. Students may also volunteer to sing a portion of their musical notation. A sample sixth grader's musical notation drawing follows:

$$- -/\bullet\bullet/- -/\bullet\bullet/- - - - -/\bullet\bullet$$

Although student-generated musical systems may appear abstract and unreadable to others, they often provide valid ways for learners to begin reading music by introducing the concept of musical symbols.

Another approach to musical notation helps students learn keyboarding. By bringing a small synthesizer or keyboard into the classroom, the teacher can number the keys on a scale, one through eight. Many simple melodies can then be played. For example, the song "Mary Had a Little Lamb" would read:

3-2-1-2-3-3-3

2-2-2

3-5-5

3-2-1-2-3-3—3

3-2-2-3-2-1

One would represent middle C on the scale, two would be D, and so on. By using this simple number system, students can proficiently play a number of melodies as well as create their own number systems to accompany class songs.

Whether students are working with numbers, squiggly lines, or other symbols for musical notation, such approaches can ease the transition into reading standard notation. Students often gain confidence about working with abstract symbol systems when they have first created their own.

CREATING CURRICULUM SONGS

Since recorded songs are not always available for each curriculum unit, students and teachers can compose songs that are appropriate for any content area. Little musical talent is required to begin creating original songs by writing words to a simple, well-known melody. For example, one teacher wrote the following song about the water cycle to the tune of "Row, Row, Row Your Boat."

Drip, drip, drip from the sky
Into a little stream,
Down the mountains, through the plains,
And out into the sea.

Up, up, up it goes
Up into the sky,
Over the mountains it blows again,
Then watch the snowflakes fly.

Depending upon the age level and maturity of the students, longer songs can be written and memorized. Teachers and students may want to brainstorm familiar musical selections, using them to provide the rhythm and melody for the original, curricular-appropriate lyrics the students will add. Of course, original music can also be composed to accompany the words, adding yet another dimension to the project; however, teachers and students may want to use familiar tunes to provide the rhythm and melody for their lyrics. A few familiar selections are listed below:

Familiar Musical Selections:

> **You Are my Sunshine**
> **Twinkle Twinkle Little Star**
> **Jingle Bells**
> **Kumbaya**
> **When Johnny Comes Marching Home Again**
> **Oh, Susanna!**
> **Yankee Doodle**
> **She'll be Comin" around the Mountain**
> **The Battle Hymn of the Republic**
> **When the Saints Come Marching In**

One example of a curriculum song written by elementary students to the tune of "When Johnny Comes Marching Home" follows. The song represents the culmination of a social studies unit on multicultural art. Small groups each contributed a verse about the art of different cultures to create the song, "Art Around the World":

Sumeria, Egypt, China, Oo, Hooray, Hooray
Africa and America too, Hooray, Hooray
Japan and Greece have much to see
On and on through history
And they all had art that we have learned about.
(Refrain, repeat after each verse:)

In China they made paper and they printed on it too.
They also built pagodas and made kites that really flew.
They painted dragons in the air,
They played their music everywhere,
And they all had art that we have learned about.

In Africa, they kept the beat, Hooray, Hooray.
They played their drums and danced their feet,
Hooray, Hooray.
They dyed their cloth with patterns bright
And sculpted metal to catch the light.
And they all had art that we have learned about.

Long ago in America they worked with yarn, its true.
The Mayans and the Aztecs and the Inca people too.
With temples like the pyramids,
Big clay pots with perfect lids,
And they all had art that we have learned about.

In Japan they wrote Haiku, Hooray, Hooray.
They folded colored paper too, Hooray, Hooray.
Their gardens they made perfectly,
And did the same when they drank tea,
And they all had art that we have learned about.

Teachers may assign the content that curriculum songs are to cover. For example, if students have studied current world conflicts, or read literature that explores conflicts between individuals or groups, the teacher may want them to write a song about conflict resolution strategies. Students may be asked to create lyrics that would:

1. **Identify the actions taken by those involved in the conflict.**

2. **Provide reasons for the actions and feelings of those directly involved.**

3. **Suggest alternative solutions and brainstorm possible consequences.**

4. **Select the best solution.**

5. **Consider similar situations and what happened to resolve or exacerbate the conflict.**

6. **Determine if there are lessons to be learned from efforts to resolve previous conflicts.**

7. **Modify one's proposed solution if appropriate.**

8. **Generalize one's assumptions about conflict and how it might best be resolved.**

Students can work in groups to write their curriculum songs. In working with the above information, they may want to create a stanza for each step or two of the conflict resolution process. For example, in reflecting on the conflict over rights for all South Africans, one group of high school juniors began their song with:

"When all South Africans lacked rights and free expression,

The whites in power were accused of racial oppression.

The blacks rose up to gain self-determination.

The whites wanted to maintain their lofty position.

Most students enjoy this approach to singing and song writing. When an entire class sings curriculum songs, not only is subject matter learned and creativity released, but the affective atmosphere of the class also improves. An intangible bond is often created among those singing the same song for fun and learning. And not surprisingly many students claim at the end of the school year that they still remember the curricular songs written and sung from months earlier.

JUMPSTARTING CREATIVITY WITH MUSIC

"Schools are supposed to be able to help us express ourselves. Without knowledge of music, we are being deprived of a unique form of communication."

— *KENNY BYRD, Student who testified at the Nashville Commission on Music Education in 1990*

Frequently, when asked to write a story or poem, students complain they don't know where or how to begin. Music can serve as a source of inspiration, stimulating images and feelings and igniting storylines to pursue. When children are writing to music in the classroom, creative energies appear to be released so that they write more prolifically and with greater pleasure, ease, and depth.

The following sample activities are offered to spark creative writing in classrooms:

1. To introduce students to the potential flow of images and ideas generated by music, ask them to pretend they are film producers who must create a storyline appropriate to any portion of the following compositions: Prokofiev's "Peter and the Wolf," Moussorgsky's "Pictures at an Exhibition," Debussy's "Clouds," "Fireworks," or "Golliwog's Cakewalk," or more abstract selections such as a Chopin Prelude, a Strauss Waltz or a Bach Fugue. After listening, students might discuss the images and movie scripts they imagined and next generate poems or descriptive paragraphs based on this brainstorming process.

2. Short stories might also be developed from recordings played in a sequence. Beginning by playing either music or an environmental recording such as "Tropical Thunderstorm," "Dawn in an English Meadow," or "Slow Ocean," teachers may ask students to mindmap or write a description of the setting. Next, play a recording that suggests the first character. This could be any colorful selection, even a piece of popular music. Students then may mindmap or write a description of the character they "see" in the music. (Be careful to introduce the character without using "he" or "she" or even suggesting it is a person. Students might see animals, or wind, or imaginary objects in the music.)

Next, play a sharply contrasting piece of music and go through the same procedure for the second character. Finally, go back to the original "setting" sound or music as students "see" the plot unfolding around the characters they have created. Similar processes may be used to stimulate the writing of poetry to music. Such writing exercises will springboard most students into expressing themselves in remarkably creative ways.

3. Have students generate word banks of descriptive words in response to recorded music, then use such terms to write poetry describing the music. The poems might include the title of the music and the name of the composer.

In addition to writing activities, students may also explore other ways to shake off lethargy and ignite creativity with music. Music can be played while students are preparing class projects, doing silent reading, working in cooperative groups, taking tests, memorizing facts or scripts, or working on computers. By tuning into their own inner rhythms and needs, students can begin to identify the times when music might help optimize their learning.

MAKING MUSICAL INSTRUMENTS IN THE CLASSROOM

When students have the opportunity to make their own instruments, they not only enjoy the hands-on activity, they also increase their understanding of music itself. Simple instruments can be made from common everyday items. Pan lids, sandpaper, coffee cans, nails, boxes, fishing line, bamboo, conduit, hard wood, rawhide, and carpet tubes all have musical potential. If notified, parents often gladly contribute throwaways, white elephants, and junk drawer treasures, most of which can become important parts of musical instruments.

Some teachers approach instrument-making by appointing a day when collected items from home and school are made accessible to students with one stipulation —that each student invents an instrument capable of producing sound. Instruments can be made from directions found in one of many instrument construction books. Two excellent resources of simple-to-make instruments include *Make Mine Music* by Tom Walther and *Making Musical Things* by Anne Wiseman. Folk instruments can be constructed based on ideas from books such as *Musical Instruments of the World* by the Diagram Group. Folk instruments can be decorated to represent the designs of the cultures from which they come.

Once the instruments are made, they can be played individually, listened to, and discussed. Music terminology such as loud/soft, high/low, bright/dull, hollow, ringing, raspy, and rattling can be used to describe their sounds. Small ensembles or an entire classroom orchestra might emerge next.

Teachers might suggest that students make musical instruments representative of the four instrumental groups found in symphonic orchestras : string, woodwinds, brass, and percussion. Another possibility is to group instruments into categories commonly used by ethnomusicologists to describe instruments from around the world: membranophones (vibrating membrane); chordophones (vibrating strings); idiophones (vibrating surface); aerophones (vibrating column of air); and electranophone (vibrating electrical current).

USING INSTRUMENTS CREATIVELY

With access to instruments in the classroom, students and teachers might experiment with creating original compositions, adding musical accompaniment to songs, or performing instrumental works. Students might work in small groups to compose short, aural plans for musical pieces. They might work with solo instruments, then combine sounds. To begin the composition process, students can start with a favorite work of children's literature or a video they have recently watched at school. They might improvise their own opera for the dialogue and add instruments for color and rhythmic motion. Many other ideas for involving students in classroom musical composition can be found in *Sound and Silence* by Paynter and Aston, *Composition in the Classroom* by Wiggins, and *Creative Music Education* by Schafer.

Students can also work with familiar songs such as "She'll Be Coming around the Mountain." For example, one musical arrangement might consist of students adding different sounds to each verse. They could play some sounds with the beat or alternate beats and some with the rhythm of the words. The sounds should be carefully selected to fit the quality and character of the music and should not overwhelm the song itself. It is also not necessary that every student play constantly. Often the arrangement will be more musical if just a few instruments are added.

Orchestral arrangements can be explored. Teachers can divide the students into two groups to create echoes, omitting certain instruments and bringing them in later during the song or gradually omitting instruments until only one remains playing softly. Additionally, students' curiosity may be piqued about how an orchestra is physically structured: which instruments are placed where? A visit to a high school music classroom or a field trip to the nearest symphonic orchestra may be better appreciated after classroom hands-on experiences.

TECHNOLOGY THAT ENHANCES MUSICAL INTELLIGENCE

The development of musical intelligence can be enhanced by technology in the same way that verbal fluency is enhanced by word-processors. Fledgling composers can hum a tune into synthesizers such as the EPS16 from Ensoniq or the SZ-1 from Casio, for example, and have it sound like one of many instruments, fully accompanied by an electronic rhythm section. The Musical Instrument Digital Interface, or MIDI, makes it possible to compose for and orchestrate many different instruments through the computer. Pyware's "Music Writer" and Activision's "Music Studio" are examples of software programs that also make such magic possible.

Menulay's "Musicland" program has been used successfully with children as young as three. It enables children to compose music immediately by manipulating notes and graphic representations of musical concepts on the computer. A student can draw a shape on the staff on the computer screen, and see it translated into musical notation. The student then colors in the notes, with different colors for different instruments, and the computer plays back the composition in synthesized sounds.

"Band-in-a-Box" by PG Software lets students improvise backups to familiar jazz, pop, rock, and folk music. It also features editing capability so that students can create their own musical styles. Their improvisations and compositions can be saved on a MIDI file and sent to a music printing program such as "Nightingale" by Temporal Acuity Products which creates musical scores for other instruments.

One might wonder if such "artificial" music removes the need to understand and learn harmony, notation, scoring, and reading music. In fact, many students are so motivated by what they create through musical technology that they are stimulated to learn more about each of these areas. Their success becomes a driving force for further learning.

It is being discovered that digital technology, which combines digital audio with visual input, makes it possible for many students to learn about elements of music that are often too complicated for beginners to understand. One example is the Voyager Company's interactive multimedia compact disc of Beethoven's "Ninth Symphony," which enables the listener to understand the piece musically, historically, culturally, and politically. Stravinsky's "Rite of Spring" is even more extensive, progressing from simple to complex concepts; it can be accessed at any knowledge level. The few programs that currently exist are just the beginning of this exciting new way of learning about and creating music.

Warner's "Music Exploratorium" explores various aspects of the orchestra through Benjamin Britten's "Young Person's Guide to the Orchestra." It presents, in a random-access combination of video and audio, information about the composer and conductor, the players, the instruments, and the structure of the composition.

The University of Delaware Videodisc Music Series at this writing includes ten full-color video recordings. In each of the programs, the score scrolls across the screen as the music is played. The programs include color-coded musical analysis; supporting slides illustrate cultural highlights of the composers' life and historical period.

Such interactive videodiscs on music make it possible to "break out" and hear individual instruments, see the score while the music is playing, or identify the source of a particular theme or melody. The information on these discs is "random access," making it possible for the learner to follow a particular line of interest in a self-directed manner, at any ability level

The Association for Technology in Music Instruction (ATMI) annually publishes a directory which lists and summarizes all of the existing computer programs, videodiscs, films, CDROM discs, and music technology hardware on the market. It is available with membership in ATMI.

Such a technological support system for the learning of music and music-appreciation leads not only to proficiency, but to in-depth understanding. The development of musical thinking and creativity—musical intelligence itself—can thus be enriched and expanded.

SUMMARY

Most elementary music classes programs stimulate children's musical development in a variety of ways. However, such classes usually occur once or twice weekly, ending typically with the completion of fifth grade. Most music offerings at the secondary level focus on performance. Students not interested in performing frequently avoid such classes, foregoing opportunities to develop their musical intelligence and seldom experiencing the ability of music to enhance the quality of life.

In 1987, at the Music Educators National Conference a rationale for music education was provided. Why should music be included as part of the curriculum? It appears that there are many reasons:

1. **Music is worth knowing.**

2. **Music conveys our cultural heritage. It is as important to know about Beethoven and Louis Armstrong as it is to know about Newton and Einstein.**

3. **Music is an inherent intelligence in all people and deserves to be developed.**

4. **Music is creative and self-expressive, enabling the expression of our noblest thoughts and feelings.**

5. **Music teaches students about their relationships with others, in both their own and foreign cultures.**

6. **Music offers students avenues of success they may not experience elsewhere in the curriculum.**

7. **Music enhances learning throughout all subject areas.**

8. **Music helps students learn that not all of life is quantifiable.**

9. **Music exalts the human spirit.**

The activities in this chapter expand the concept of music education to include a variety of listening, singing, memory-enhancing, creativity-inspiring, and music-making techniques for reinforcing academics while introducing students and teachers alike to the joy of musical learning. In order to summarize, reflect and synthesize the content of this chapter, the following is offered:

APPLYING MUSICAL INTELLIGENCE

1. Important ideas or insights gleaned from this chapter: _____

_____

_____

_____

_____

2. Areas I'd like to learn more about: _____

_____

_____

_____

_____

3. Ways I can use this information in my teaching. Please note that all the strategies mentioned in this chapter are listed below with space provided to note how each strategy might be incorporated into classroom instruction:

MUSICAL STRATEGY	CLASSROOM APPLICATION

Establishing a Musical Learning Environment:
Introducing Music into the Classroom _____
Guidelines for Using Background Music _____
A Variety of Musical Selections _____

Listening to Music:
Listening Discussion Questions _____
Songs in the Content Areas _____
Resources for Songs that Teach Curriculum _____
Recorded Songs for a Variety of Curricular Areas _____

Music for Skill Building:
Spelling _____
Teaching Reading through Music _____
Music across the Curriculum _____

Warming up to Singing:
Nonsense Sounds _____
Choral Reading _____

Musical Notation:
Introducing the Concept of Musical Notation _____

Creating Curricular Songs:
Familiar Musical Selections _____

Jumpstarting Creativity with Music: _____

Making Musical Instruments in the Classroom:
Using Instruments Creatively in the Classroom _____

Technology that Enhances Musical Intelligence: _____

MUSICAL REFERENCES:

Ardley, N. (1984). *Sound and Music*. N.Y.: Franklin Watts.

Association for Technology in Music Instruction (ATMI). C/O Gary Karpinski, Department of Music, University of Massachusetts, Amherst, MA 01003.

Campbell, D. and Brewer, C. (1991). *Rhythms of Learning*. Tucson: Zephyr Press.

Carroll, K. (1990). *Sing a Song of Science*. Washington D.C.: Brain Friendly Teaching and Learning. 6801 6th St. NW Washington D.C. 20012.

Dhority, L. (1991). *The ACT Approach*. Bremen, Germany: PLS Verlag.

Gardner, H. (1983). *Frames of Mind: The Theory of Multiple Intelligences*. N.Y.: Basic Books.

Getty Center of the Arts. (1991). *Proceedings from Future Tense: Arts Education and Technology Conference*. Los Angeles: Getty Center for the Arts.

Kaplan, D. (1983). *See with Your Ears, The Creative Music Book*. PO Box 296 Lagunitas, CA: Lexicos.

Katz, S. and Thomas, J. (1992). *Teaching Creatively by Working the Word: Language, Music, and Movement*. Englewood Cliffs, N.J.: Prentice Hall.

Kline, P. (1988). *The Everyday Genius*. Arlington, VA: Great Ocean Publishers.

Lamme, L. L. (1990). "Exploring the World of Music through Picture Books." *The Reading Teacher*, Vol. 44 (4).

Lozanov, G. (1978). *Suggestology and Outlines of Suggestopedy*. London: Gordon and Breach Science Publishers.

Mandel, M. and Wood, R. (1978). *Make Your Own Musical Instruments*. N.Y.: Sterling Publishing Co.

National Commission on Music Education. (1991). *Growing Up Complete. The Imperative for Music Education*. Reston, VA: Music Educator's National Conference.

National Standards for Arts Education. (1994). *Dance, Music, Theatre, Visual Arts: What Every Young American Should Know and Be Able to Do in the Arts*. Reston, VA: Music Educators National Conference.

Patterson, Peter Blood. (1988). *Rise Up Singing*. Bethlehem, PA: The Sing Out Corp.

Rappin' Tappin' Times Tables. (1989). *Toe Tappin' Teaching Aids*. 49 S. Sunset Drive, Coldwater, MI 49036.

Rose, C. (1985). *Accelerated Learning*. N.Y.: Dell Publishing Co.

Schafer, R. M. (1976). *Creative Music Education*. N.Y.: Schirmer.

Schuster, D. (1985). *Suggestive Accelerative Learning and Teaching*. N.Y.: Gordon and Breach Publishing.

Tickle Tune Typhoon. (1989). *Let's Be Friends*. Seattle: Tickle Tune Typhoon Productions. PO Box 15153, Seattle, WA 98115.

Upitis, R. (1990). *This Too Is Music*. Portsmouth, N.H.: Heinemann.

Upitis, R. (1992). *Can I Play You My Song?* Portsmouth, N.H.: Heinemann.

Wallace, R. (1990). *Active Learning: Rappin' and Rhymin'—Raps, Songs and Cheers with Learning Lyrics*. Upbeat Publishing PO Box 70, Anchor Point, AK 99556.

Walther, T. (1981). *Make Mine Music*. Boston: Little Brown and Co.

Wiggins, J. (1990). *Composition in the Classroom: A Tool for Teaching*. Reston, VA.: Music Educators National Conference.

Wiseman, A. (1979). *Making Musical Things*. N.Y.: Charles Scribner's Sons.

Wyatt, J. and G. (1990). *Learning Rock - Parts of Speech and More*. Learning Rock, PO Box 566, Woodstock, GA 30188

CHAPTER 6

WORKING TOGETHER TO ACCOMPLISH THE IMPOSSIBLE

The Flying Karamazov Brothers are a world famous juggling/ comedy team of four individuals who believe that "people working together can accomplish the impossible."

UNDERSTANDING ONE ANOTHER: INTERPERSONAL INTELLIGENCE

If civilization is to survive, we must culminate the science of human relationships—the ability of all peoples, of all kinds, to live together, in the same world, at peace.

— *FRANKLIN DELANO ROOSEVELT*

In watching these skilled and humorous performers, one might assume that juggling and comedy come easily for this foursome. Part of their skill appears to derive from their years of working together. As they juggle in complex patterns while carrying on witty repartee, the Karamazov's seem connected to each other's thoughts and action. They say they concentrate "exactly enough and no more." According to these performers, it is this intense "non-concentration" that enables their seemingly impossible juggling feats.

Paul Magid and Howard Patterson met in college twenty years ago, and began juggling at college functions. A few years later Sam Williams and Timothy Furst joined them. The four believe that humor provides the "connecting wires" in their performances. The humor not only permeates each performance, it also inspires their work together. Each individual not only performs according to plan but also improvises in response to unanticipated comments from other performers or unexpected events. They refer to such improvisation as "surfing," while their

audiences respond with delight. In each performance, The Flying Karamazov Brothers always find ways to interact with the audience. They are adept at encouraging audience members to sing, make music, provide juggling objects, or to tell jokes. Their interpersonal skills also extend to other performers. Recently, the Karamazovs have identified several fledgling performing artists whom they invite to tour with them. This increases the visibility of the younger artists while also helping the Karamazov Brothers to create a 1990's vaudeville show with a diverse troupe of performers and active audience participation.

What do the Karamozovs say about the development of their inter personal intelligence? As children, the individual performers were loners, all of whom were bored with school routines. Their interpersonal skills flourished as they began working together. Perhaps they might have found school more interesting and challenging if they had had opportunities to exercise interpersonal intelligence through group projects of the kind described in this chapter.

DEFINITION: UNDERSTANDING INTERPERSONAL INTELLIGENCE

✔ CHECKLIST OF INTERPERSONAL QUALITIES

Interpersonal intelligence enables us to understand and communicate with others, noting differences in moods, temperaments, motivations, and skills. It includes the ability to form and maintain relationships and to assume various roles within groups such as group members or leaders. This intelligence is evident in those with polished social skills such as political or religious leaders, skilled parents, teachers, therapists, or counselors. Individuals who demonstrate a genuine commitment to and skill in bettering the lives of others exhibit positively developed interpersonal intelligence.

Interpersonally-skilled students enjoy interacting with others of similar or diverse ages. With a capacity to influence their peers, they often excel at group work, team efforts, and collaborative projects. Some are sensitive to the feelings of others, curious about multicultural variations in lifestyles, or interested in the social relevance of classroom studies. Some are able to entertain diverse perspectives on any social or political issue and can often help others appreciate differing values and opinions.

Interpersonal intelligence is also exhibited through humor whenever students make their friends and teachers laugh, when they create amusing skits, or analyze videos of old comedy teams such as the Marx Brothers or Laurel and Hardy which offer caricatures of different interpersonal skills.

One British psychologist, N.K. Humphrey, claims that social intelligence is the most important feature of the human intellect. Humphrey states that the greatest creative use of the human mind is to maintain human society effectively. Because of their social foresight and understanding, many people are able to consider the consequences of their own actions, anticipate the behavior of others, determine potential benefits and losses, and successfully cope with interpersonal issues locally and beyond. Successful living is often largely dependent on interpersonal intelligence.

It is likely that a person with well-developed interpersonal intelligence:

1. **Bonds with parents and interact with others.**

2. **Forms and maintains social relationships.**

3. **Recognizes and uses a variety of ways to relate to others.**

4. **Perceives the feelings, thoughts, motivations, behaviors, and lifestyles of others.**

5. **Participates in collaborative efforts and assumes various roles as appropriate from follower to leader in group endeavors.**

6. **Influences the opinions or actions of others.**

7. **Understands and communicates effectively in both verbal and nonverbal ways.**

8. **Adapts behavior to different environments or groups and from feedback from others.**

9. Perceives diverse perspectives in any social or political issue.

10. Develops skills in mediation, organizing others for a common cause, or working with others of diverse ages or backgrounds.

11. Expresses an interest in interpersonally-oriented careers such as teaching, social work, counseling, management, or politics.

12. Develops new social processes or models.

INTERPERSONAL LEARNING PROCESSES

Interpersonal intelligence is so closely connected to interaction with others that most educators claim they couldn't teach without pairing or grouping students. This chapter describes collaborative learning processes currently in use in many classrooms, as well as numerous other categories of interpersonal learning activities:

ESTABLISHING A POSITIVE INTERPERSONAL ENVIRONMENT
  Criteria for Effective Groups
  Determining Class Values and Rules
  Class Meetings

COLLABORATIVE LEARNING
  Collaborative Grouping Considerations
  Student Roles
  Social Skills
  Cooperative Learning Activities
  Student Collaboration in the Multilingual Classroom

CONFLICT MANAGEMENT
  Some Common Causes of Conflict
  Gordon's Conflict Management Process

LEARNING THROUGH SERVICE
  Integrating Service into a School Program
  Reflecting on Service
  Service Resources

APPRECIATING DIFFERENCES
  Teaching Students about Learning Styles

DEVELOPING MULTIPLE PERSPECTIVES
  Who Are We?
  Understanding Diverse Points of View
  Role Playing Current Events from Diverse Perspectives
  Global Perspectives in the Curriculum
  Systems Wheel

LOCAL AND GLOBAL PROBLEM-SOLVING

MULTICULTURAL EDUCATION
  Teaching with a Multicultural Perpsective
  Understanding Cultural Diversity through the Arts
  Culturgrams

TECHNOLOGY THAT ENHANCES INTERPERSONAL INTELLIGENCE

SUMMARY

ESTABLISHING A POSITIVE INTERPERSONAL ENVIRONMENT

In today's rapidly changing society, many students are deprived of close, stable relationships with caring adults. Without the support of cohesive families, some children bring unmet needs into the classroom. Besieged with numerous demands, schools might prefer to overlook students' social and emotional needs, yet ultimately, our educational institutions must compensate by evolving into supportive, caring communities.

Although students spend their school careers in groups, the potential benefits of group life are seldom realized. When the focus is primarily on achieving competitive and individualistic goals, students are isolated and their affective and social needs frequently neglected. Much recent research indicates, however, that learning is more productive and enjoyable when students feel a sense of belonging and the classroom functions as a caring community. How can such an environment be established? The starting point is to transform the numerous individuals in a classroom into an effective and cohesive group. Some suggestions follow:

CRITERIA FOR EFFECTIVE GROUPS

In researching effective groups, some consistent qualities have been identified. The following list is not exhaustive; teachers may want to add additional components from their experiences. The following criteria do, however, enable a teacher to assess their current classroom environments. In reviewing the list below, teachers may want to identify the qualities currently present in their classrooms and strive to include any missing components.

1. The classroom's environment is warm and accepting which provides the foundation for a supportive group. Extensive, positive interaction among students and teacher is evident and a sense of "school as family" is promoted.

2. Classroom rules, mutually established by students and teacher, define appropriate codes of conduct and are based on human values such as helpfulness and fairness. Together, the students and teacher develop solutions to behavior problems.

3. An emphasis on collaborative learning removes the win/lose pattern prevalent in many classrooms. Conventional, independent, competitive learning is frequently replaced with interdependent processes that require the participation and contribution of all students.

4. Learning is the well-articulated mission of the classroom. The teacher and students acknowledge that their chief purpose is to learn from the curriculum, one another, and life experiences.

5. Leadership functions are equally distributed. Responsibility for classroom and small group tasks are evenly shared so that students view themselves as valued members of the classroom community.

6. The learning activities are enjoyable. A variety of instructional and evaluation methods are used. Students occasionally make choices about what and how to learn and a sense of playfulness and humor are present in the classroom.

7. Opportunities are available for students to develop social, affective, and ethical skills in addition to academic ones.

An interesting perspective of an important group, that of the family, has been offered by Dr. Mihaly Czikszentmihaly, professor of behavioral sciences at the University of Chicago. Dr. Cziksentmihalyi has researched the family background of high achievers. He has found that the highest achieving and happiest students come from "complex" environments in which clear rules and high expectations are communicated, but which are warm, positive, and nurturing and offer much opportunity for choice. Since the classroom often substitutes for the home, every effort should be made to create "complex" environments in school as well.

The following activities suggest numerous ways to develop effective interpersonal and complex environments at school.

DETERMINING CLASS VALUES AND RULES

As mentioned above, it is important for each classroom to establish explicit codes of conduct based upon important human values. When students know what is expected of them and their peers, positive relationships can develop more easily. Often the most effective rules are those initiated by the students themselves. By using democratic processes to determine classroom values and appropriate conduct, students can assume responsibility for their behavior and for successful participation as members of their group.

Many teachers involve their students in determining classroom values and rules at the beginning of the school year or a new term. One simple approach consists of asking students to identify the behaviors that are conducive to learning. How should students behave so that a positive classroom environment is established and maintained? Which social values such as justice, compassion, or helpfulness are important to highlight?

Students can respond individually to such questions by writing their ideas for classroom values and conduct. Responses can then be discussed in small groups of three to five. Each small group might make a chart listing ideas for classroom values and behaviors. These charts, when shared with the whole class, serve to establish classroom management processes that every student helped plan. The teacher may want to emphasize that successful group life requires the balancing of one's individual needs with consideration for the needs of others. A list of rules and values, developed collaboratively, can be displayed prominently in the classroom.

Recently, one fifth grade classroom decided to guide their behavior with the following rules:

1. Everyone in this room has the right to learn.

2. Each student will be creative and original.

3. Each student will think and learn in many ways.

4. We will have fun while learning.

5. We will cooperate with group members.

6. We will be respectful of one another.

7. We will make friends with each other.

These fifth graders are not only committed to creative learning opportunities, but they also hope to have their social and emotional needs met in their classroom.

After rules are established and classroom activities undertaken, explicit discussions of group values and behavior can be initiated to reinforce important social skills. The students and teacher may want to meet periodically to develop solutions to discipline problems. In some classrooms, elected or appointed councils oversee classroom operations. Rotating councils of approximately five or six students make recommendations to the class and teacher about social concerns.

In such a governance system, each person in the class, including the teacher, has a single vote and the council implements the decisions voted on by class members. As the school year progresses, it is important that all students have the opportunity to serve as council members. Many teachers claim that such activities help students internalize classroom rules and assume responsibility for the successful operation of their class. By contributing to the well-being of the classroom, many students willingly abide by the norms and values their school community deems important.

CLASS MEETINGS

Once classroom rules and values are in place, student relationships can be strengthened. Often this can be accomplished by conducting class meetings once daily or weekly. Such meetings usually have an open-ended agenda for students to discuss differences, resolve personal or academic problems, and learn to listen to and support one another. Class meetings can foster affective, social, and ethical development of all students in the class.

At the elementary level, many teachers set aside a few minutes at the beginning of each day for students to greet one another, discuss important issues, and focus attention on the day's learning tasks. At the secondary level, some teachers devote 20 minutes during a class period once weekly for a "family" meeting. An agenda sheet is posted throughout the week and students are free to list issues they want to discuss.

To ensure successful and positive class meetings, it is important to establish ground rules: Some guidelines follow:

Guidelines for Conducting Class Meetings:

1. Identify a regular schedule for class meetings and the approximate length of the meetings.

2. Ask students to move chairs or desks in a circle so everyone is included equally.

3. Select a meeting facilitator. With younger children, this is most frequently the teacher or a parent. Older students, however, may assume the facilitator role.

4. Explain that the purpose of the meetings is to improve the atmosphere in the classroom and give students a chance to address their interests and concerns.

5. Provide everyone with an opportunity to talk. When one student is speaking, others cannot interrupt. Some teachers structure the taking of turns with a Native American tradition of the "talking stick," a decorated, small branch or piece of driftwood. The talking stick is handed to those who wish to speak. When a student has the talking stick, he must speak briefly, truthfully, and from the heart. He then passes it to the next person who desires a turn.

6. Explain that all students must feel free to express their feelings and opinions at the meetings, so negative comments about one another are not tolerated.

7. Request that everyone bring an open mind and heart to the meetings. Efforts should be made to consider the diverse perspectives shared by class members.

8. Bring closure to each meeting by thanking everyone for participating, reviewing the main issues discussed, or identifying unresolved concerns that should be raised at the next session.

Family meetings nurture a sense of interconnectedness and enable supportive relationships to flourish between children and teachers alike. A positive sense of group identity emerges from listening to and showing respect for one another. Such meetings can help transform classrooms into personal, humane, and caring communities.

COLLABORATIVE LEARNING

Collaborative learning is one of the most thoroughly researched instructional techniques in the United States. There are numerous models, theorists, and resources with various perspectives on cooperative learning. Some of the better known books include David and Roger Johnson's *Circles of Learning, Learning Together and Alone*; and *Cooperation in the Classroom*; Spencer Kagan's *Cooperative Learning: Resources for Teachers*; Elizabeth Cohen's *Designing*

Groupwork for the Heterogeneous Classroom; and Robert Slavin's *Cooperative Learning: Theory, Research and Practice*. In reviewing the research on cooperative learning, wide agreement exists that such methods enhance student achievement, accelerate learning, improve retention and recall, and result in positive attitudes toward learning. The Johnson brothers have identified two essential components of any successful collaborative learning approach which include:

Individual accountability: a group's success is based upon each member's ability to demonstrate that he or she has learned the required material. Student achievement has been shown to increase when group success depends on the combined score of all group members' quiz grades or when individual group members are assessed on contributions to a team project. It appears that achievement gains are less when a single worksheet or project is given to a group of students without assigning individual tasks and responsibilities.

Positive interdependence: the success of the group depends upon its ability to work together to achieve desired results such as recognition, grades, rewards, or free time. Merely asking students to collaborate does not insure that social skills will be learned. They must be taught intentionally.

COLLABORATIVE GROUPING CONSIDERATIONS

When students are beginning to learn collaborative skills, group sizes should remain small, ranging from two to four members. As social skills develop, students become capable of working in larger groups. It is also important to consider the length of time a group will work together. Groups meeting regularly over an extended period of time tend to be more successful than those who work together only occasionally.

Students can be grouped in different ways for different purposes. Some researchers distinguish between achievement groups and work groups. Achievement groups are homogeneous clusters formed according to achievement levels in order to organize instruction to match student needs. Work groups are more heterogeneous and are organized to promote social interaction as well as academic outcomes. Both rely upon cooperation.

Some teachers experiment with grouping according to gender, but mixed groups have proved to be more successful. Cross-age grouping can also be effective, as is mixed-ability grouping. It appears that low-achieving students increase their performance in heterogeneous groups; whereas gifted students benefit from working at least part of the time with other high achievers. Teachers may want to experiment with a variety of groups to determine which is most appropriate for their classrooms.

STUDENT ROLES

When students are assigned individual roles in their groups, they become active participants in the learning process and personally accountable for their tasks. Roles can take the form of specific jobs such as illustrator, recorder, resource person, facilitator, direction-giver, time-keeper, summarizer, and reporter. Sometimes, students can be assigned individual numbers so that a teacher can call upon a number "3" for example, who is accountable for information generated by the whole group. Roles can be assigned according to where students sit, by drawing task cards, by teacher assignment, or by group consensus.

SOCIAL SKILLS

It is essential that social skills be taught as part of any cooperative learning experience. Students do not have inherent interpersonal skills nor do such skills automatically emerge by placing students in groups. Therefore, students must learn and understand their importance. Common social skills include organizing effective groups, demonstrating appropriate behavior, using effective learning skills, and critiquing and evaluating ideas collaboratively. All require reflection, practice, and refinement and are appropriate for classroom use with pre-school through college-age students. Before any group task is undertaken, teachers might identify a social skill for groups to incorporate in their activities. Once social skills become internalized, they enable students to work effectively with others, while improving their academic achievement, and developing important lifelong skills.

COOPERATIVE LEARNING ACTIVITIES

A helpful classroom resource for cooperative learning is Roger and David Johnson's *Structuring Cooperative Learning: Lesson Plans for Teachers.* The three following activities that the Johnsons have found especially effective include The Jigsaw, Out Loud Problem-Solving, and Cooperative Discussions of Literature. They are described below:

The Jigsaw

The Jigsaw is an effective technique that nurtures positive interdependence among group members. It is appropriate for studying portions of textbooks or other written materials in any content area. The steps for a jigsaw activity are as follows:

1. Select a social skill students should practice (such as one listed above). Others might include management skills, paraphrasing, or summarizing one another's input. Provide the students with a rationale for practicing the specific skill.

2. Organize students into small groups of three to five.

3. Distribute a set of materials to each group. The set needs to be divisible into the number of members of the group. Give each member one part of the set of materials.

4. Assign students the task of meeting with someone else in the class who is a member of another learning group and who has the same set of materials. These pairs should then learn their material together and plan how to teach the material to the members of their original groups.

5. Send students back to their original groups where they take turns teaching their areas of expertise to group members.

6. Ask each group member to quiz the others until he or she is satisfied that everyone knows the information.

7. Evaluate each student's mastery of the information as well as the selected social skill in any appropriate manner.

Cooperative Out-Loud Problem-Solving

This activity is appropriate for use with worksheets or practice and drill materials.

1. Identify a social skill to develop as well as a rationale for doing so.

2. Assign small groups of approximately four students and provide each group with a worksheet. Instruct group members to divide the problems among themselves equally.

3. Model out-loud problem-solving with one problem from the worksheet. Determine that all groups understand the correct problem-solving procedures.

4. Instruct the groups to begin with each group member taking a turn to solve a problem out loud. The other students check for accuracy of thought as well as the correct answer and suggest any changes in the problem-solving strategy. Each group member should also make an effort to encourage the other students.

5. Additionally, advise the groups that in order for any individual to be successful, every other member of the group must know all information on the worksheet. Each group must determine that its members have mastered the material.

6. For accountability, the teacher might give students another worksheet with similar problems to solve. Individually, the students answer the questions and receive grades on the basis of their individual scores. Additionally, the teacher may want to reward groups whose members reach a pre-determined criteria of excellence. In assessing performance, attention should also be given to the social skill that was practiced.

Cooperative Group Discussion of Literature

At the secondary level, students can practice advanced social skills. In the following activity, students learn to participate in discussion while critiquing the ideas of others.

1. Assign a piece of literature for the students to read.

2. Prepare "talking" and "critiquing" chips. The talking chips should consist of enough red squares of paper or pieces of plastic so that each student has three chips. The critiquing chips can be made out of blue paper or plastic allowing five per student.

3. Prepare discussion questions that encourage individual interpretation of characters, themes, and events in the story. Divide students into small groups and provide each group with a set of discussion questions.

4. Explain to the groups that a red chip goes to the center of the table each time a student answers one of the questions. A blue chip is added for each critique. Emphasize that student critiques are to be based upon ideas shared and are not to be derogatory or directed at individuals. Each student must answer each question and every time someone talks he or she must put a chip on the table. Since

everyone is limited by the number of assigned chips, no one can dominate the conversation.

5. The teacher will most likely want to monitor the groups during their discussions to determine that ideas and not individuals are being critiqued and that all students are contributing equally.

6. Evaluation can be conducted of individuals, groups, or both.

The above activities merely hint at the countless possibilities for cooperative learning in the classroom. Because of the effectiveness of cooperative techniques in teaching social skills and improving academic achievement, some researchers recommend it as the dominant mode of instruction comprising 60% of classroom time. Whether or not educators devote a significant portion of their teaching efforts to this method, cooperative learning, whenever it is used, makes school pleasant and enhances success for students and teachers alike. As students readily and eagerly work with their peers, their enthusiasm for such activities makes teaching more enjoyable.

Student Collaboration in the Multilingual Classroom

Another approach to groupwork, developed by Elizabeth Cohen at Stanford University, addresses linguistic, ethnic, and skill differences in heterogeneous classrooms. Cohen's model called "Complex Instruction" fosters interracial and interethnic trust as students learn to use each other as linguistic and academic resources. The term "Complex Instruction" refers to different groups of children working at different learning stations in the classroom at the same time. Each center has an activity card for the group, plus individual work sheets. The group cannot move to another center until each member of the group is finished with the task. The tasks are multimodal in nature and emphasize learning by doing. The questions asked or the problems to be solved are open-ended, without a single right answer.

Each group member is assigned a role to ensure accountability. One person in each group serves as the facilitator who makes certain that everyone receives the help he or she requires. Roles are rotated to share leadership. Students are taught to use each other as resources, and classroom rules include the right to ask anyone in the group for help and to take the responsibility for assisting anyone who requests guidance.

Teachers introduce the daily tasks by describing the different intellectual abilities each requires. Students are informed that no one will be good at all tasks, but that each group member will probably excel in at least one. Teachers also make a special effort to acknowledge the skills of those children who typically lack status or prestige in the classroom. Once work begins at the centers, authority is delegated to the students, a situation that encourages reliance upon one's peers and not upon the teacher. Ten years of research at Stanford University indicates that Complex Instruction yields significant achievement gains and reduces status problems for culturally-different students. Linguistic, ethnic, and skill differences in the classroom need not be viewed as liabilities, but rather as assets that provide a rich environment in which students learn from each other.

CONFLICT MANAGEMENT

During early childhood, our sense of self emerges and our methods of coping with frustration and conflict are developed. Since schools are second only to families in shaping children's attitudes and values, they can play important roles in teaching ways to manage conflict. Conflict, as an inevitable part of life, can be viewed as a challenge that can teach positive and constructive ways to address disagreements.

One way to introduce conflict management is to identify the common causes of conflict. Teachers might ask their students to list as many underlying causes of conflict as they can find. Once the students have made their lists, they can be compared with the following:

SOME COMMON CAUSES OF CONFLICT

1. **Individual needs are not being met.**
2. **Power is inequitably distributed.**
3. **Communication is ineffective or non-existent.**
4. **Values or priorities differ.**
5. **Perception of a situation varies.**
6. **Learning approaches or personalities differ.**

After discussion, further causes may be added to the lists. Either personal, school, local, or world events might be analyzed for the underlying causes of conflict. By understanding and articulating the source of conflict, students find it easier to work towards positive resolutions.

Another interesting aspect of conflict is how individuals respond to it. There are various styles of handling conflict which people exhibit including the following:

Competing Collaborating

Avoiding   Accommodating

Compromising

After a discussion of the above responses, it may prove interesting for students to note which style they use most frequently in conflict situations. Discussions might also include alternative styles that students may want to intentionally develop.

There are many approaches to conflict management. Teaching students simple conflict resolution processes can empower them to resolve their disagreements peacefully and without adult intervention. The following six step process in Dr. Thomas Gordon's book, *Parent Effectiveness Training*, has been used extensively with children and adults alike. It is an effective model for classroom use when conflicts erupt.

Gordon's Conflict Management Process

Step 1: Identify and define the conflict.

Step 2: Brainstorm possible solutions.

Step 3: Discuss the potential solutions.

Step 4: Select the best solution.

Step 5: Develop a plan to implement the solution.

Step 6: Implement, then review and modify the solution.

To introduce students to the above conflict management process, the teacher might ask the class to suggest a problem frequently observed at school such as skipping class or interrupting others. Volunteers may role-play fictitious individuals such as a student who has skipped class and a teacher who is concerned with such absenteeism. The role-play should incorporate Gordon's six-step process with the class observing the procedure. Next, the teacher may want to divide students into small groups, instructing each to select a different source of conflict and resolve it with the six step procedure. Such practice with structured conflict management prepares students for disruptions that arise in and out of school. Students who have learned this process can be encouraged to apply it in a variety of situations; in fact, many students apply it spontaneously.

As a junior high teacher, one of the authors encountered two seventh graders who had chronic and serious differences of opinion. At least once weekly, their conflicts resulted in fighting. The teacher taught the above six-step process to the entire class, hoping but doubting it would be used to resolve the differences between the two boys. A couple of days later, the teacher overheard the boys arguing outside her classroom door. Assuming she would have to intervene once again, she was surprised as she heard the boys working through Gordon's six steps. Fighting was avoided and the teacher realized that the boys had not only learned a strategy but were able to apply it effectively.

Several resources exist for teaching students effective conflict management skills. An excellent book for older students is *Getting to Yes* by Roger Fisher and William Ury. A conflict management book geared for elementary students is entitled *Learning the Skills of Peacemaking* by Naomi Drew. Other resources for pre-school through six grade students is *I Can Problem*

Solve: An Interpersonal Cognitive Problem Solving Program by Myrna Shure. This award-winning program teaches children how to think, not what to think, in ways that help them resolve typical interpersonal problems. The ICPS (I can problem-solve) program teaches children ways to think about their own and others' feelings, the impact of their behavior upon others, and diverse approaches to solving problems. It significantly reduces impatient, aggressive, and social withdrawal behaviors which are high risk indicators for later problems such as violence, substance abuse, and dropping out of school. In its use with thousands of children in both low- and middle-income groups in cities around the country, ICPS has consistently enhanced positive peer relations, concern for others, ability and willingness to share, cooperation, and helping others in distress. This well-researched program documents long-term benefits that prevent adolescent social and emotional problems from occurring.

LEARNING THROUGH SERVICE

Youth Service America, a national clearinghouse for community service programs, estimates that high school volunteers donate 17 million hours of unpaid service annually at an estimated dollar value of almost $60 million. Yet, the real value of community service cannot be measured in dollar amounts. Although student service to communities is important, equally important is the effect of service on the students themselves. Students benefit by making significant contributions to their community, learning about responsible citizenship first hand, applying academic studies to real life situations, exercising individual initiative, and experiencing a positive transition into adulthood. Recent studies also suggest that service improves academic learning, increases social competence, and bolsters self-confidence.

INCORPORATING SERVICE INTO A SCHOOL PROGRAM

Many teachers and administrators are finding creative ways of incorporating service as part of their school programs. In some schools, community service is an integrated and required part of a school's curriculum. In others, it is offered as an option for student volunteerism. Teachers interested in service learning may want to implement one or more of the following models currently in practice:

Volunteer Information Center: Some schools approach service learning by establishing a central place in the school that identifies volunteer opportunities. When students find a suitable opportunity posted at the center, they call the agency, and if interested, sign a contract to carry out the service. Follow-up and review may be done by whomever operates the center—frequently teachers, community volunteers, or the students themselves.

Club or Co-curricular Activity: Frequently, students perform community service through after school clubs or co-curricular organizations. Some programs such as the Key Club identify volunteerism as its central mission, while others such as Honor Society frequently include service as one responsibility of all members. In this model, a teacher acts as an advisor and students receive neither credit nor release from school for their service efforts.

Community Service Credit: Many schools not only encourage learning through service, but they also offer credit to students who volunteer according to school guidelines. In some programs, students pursue a community service elective for a pre-established number of hours of work. In others, students are required to perform a specified number of hours of volunteer service in order to graduate. To earn the community service credit, students usually write a proposal specifying the activities, the timeframe, the purpose, and the product or goal to be achieved. A faculty adviser or program coordinator reviews student proposals and also evaluates the project at its completion. The students conduct their service projects outside of the school day as an independent activity.

Service as Authentic Applications of an Existing Course: In this model, students perform service as a way to gather, test, and apply the information for an existing school course. For example, students in a foreign language course might tutor immigrants who speak the language they are studying. Social studies students might work with homeless families to learn directly about this complex political and economic issue. Industrial arts students can design and build furniture for persons with special needs. Such volunteer efforts may be a one-time project or an on-going commitment and be treated either as extra credit or as a class requirement.

Community Service Class: Some schools offer a community service course, frequently a one-semester social studies class. Many service classes are two hours in length to enable students adequate time for their projects. These longer courses offer two credits and count as two classes for the teacher in charge. Frequently, four days a week are spent in the field, with one day back in class to reflect on the experiences, skills, information, and principles that make service activities successful.

Community Service as a School-Wide Commitment: In some schools and districts, community service is not an isolated activity but an integral part of the total school program. For example, each department in the school may identify ways to apply the knowledge and skills of its disciplines to improve the local community's quality of life. Thus computer students might provide services to non-profit organizations, English students could write letters for the elderly or disabled, science students could collect water samples from a nearby river for a governmental agency, and art students might design posters to advertise community events. Service right at the school site may be offered by integrating cross-age tutoring into the school program. Several ambitious schools such as Gig Harbor High School in Gig Harbor, and Washington Elementary School in Mount Vernon, both in Washington State as well as the entire district of Springfield, Massachusetts have the goal of involving all students at every grade level in learning through service.

REFLECTING ON SERVICE LEARNING

Teachers who implement some form of service learning will want to encourage students to reflect regularly on their experiences. Such reflection assists in real-life problem-solving, in articulating concerns students may have,

identifying positive approaches, and discerning the benefits of their experiences. Many students will readily practice their reading, writing, and speaking skills in the context of their service activities. Such reflection can be promoted in a variety of ways: through weekly class meetings, individual conferences with teachers and/or community members, and journal writing. Guidelines can help students structure their reflection and writing more carefully. Some possible questions include:

- **What is the most satisfying thing about your service project?**

- **What is the hardest thing about your service project?**

- **What personal qualities does it take to do your job successfully?**

- **What are you learning about yourself, the community, and others from your work?**

- **What is the most unexpected thing you've encountered in your project?**

- **Are you changing as a person from the work you have done? If so, in what ways?**

- **If you were in charge at your work, what would you change to improve the services or program?**

SERVICE RESOURCES

Several resources exist to assist educators in establishing effective learning through service in their classrooms or schools. Two books include Dan Conrad and Diane Hedin's *A Guidebook on Volunteer Service and Youth*, and Kate McPherson's *Enriching Learning through Service*. There are also organizations to turn to for information on service learning which include:

Jobs for the Future
1815 Massachusetts Avenue
Cambridge, Massachusetts 02140
(617) 661-3411

National Youth Leadership Council
1910 West County Road B
Roseville, Minnesota 55113
(800) 366-6952

Project Service Leadership
Kate McPherson, Director
12703 NW 20th Avenue
Vancouver, WA 98685

Youth Community Service
Council of Chief State School Officers
369 Hall of the States
400 North Capitol, NW
Washington D.C. 20001
(202) 393-8159

Youth Service America
Roger Landrum and Frank Slobig,
    Co-Directors
810 18th Street NW, Suite 705
Washington D.C. 20006
(202) 783-8855

Learning through service fosters an ethic of caring and community within a school. It also establishes positive partnerships between schools and their communities. Students learn that education is more than assimilation of information: it is a means to improving the lives of others. Many students also gain profound insights from their service experiences. This is perhaps best reflected in excerpts from their written reflections. One student who worked at a homeless shelter claimed:

"For me, this experience was eye-opening, stereotype-breaking, and attitude changing. I really grew attached to some of the kids at the shelter, and found myself wanting to return to see them again. I am a person who was initially opposed to the whole service learning thing... but I changed my attitude almost completely (which is not something I do very often.) You can be told about poverty until you think you've heard all there is to know about it. Until, you witness poverty and homelessness first hand, however, it will not have an impact. It does not take much exposure to a human need to get personally involved and begin to care about a situation. I am convinced that just a little time required in community service will yield a lifetime of dedication to help."

Another student who worked in a teen runaway shelter wrote:

"The way in which I personally benefited the most was by what I realized by the end of that Saturday night. I was feeling good about myself and was, in fact, on a small ego trip. After all, just look at what I had done—I must have spent thirteen hours collecting clothes and five hours slaving over an oven baking and eating peanut butter cookies. I essentially gave up my whole Saturday to feed the hungry. But after watching these teenagers, who had so little material wealth compared to myself and who could be satisfied with what I considered garbage, I began to see the truth. A very uncomfortable notion crept into my mind – the idea that these kids were, if anything, superior to myself. Not in what they had, but in who they were."

APPRECIATING DIFFERENCES

Henry David Thoreau once said, "If a man does not keep pace with his companions, perhaps it is because he hears a different drummer. Let him step to the music which he hears, however measured or far away." The diversity that Thoreau refers to has fascinated psychologists for centuries. Hippocrates delineated melancholic, sanguine, choleric, and phlegmatic personality types. At the beginning of the twentieth century, the psychologist Carl Jung described varying preferences among individuals for perceiving the world through "sensing" or "intuiting" and making decisions based upon "feeling" or "thinking."

Terms for understanding human differences in learning have been variously described as psychological types, personality types, cognitive styles, and learning styles. Since the 1970s, educators have been interested in the classroom applications of learning styles. Learning styles refers to individual differences in the way information is perceived, processed, and communicated.

To help students develop the ability to appreciate differences, it is important both to model the behaviors and to use strategies that articulate learning style concepts. While discerning individual differences, it is also crucial to emphasize to students the neutrality of variations in style. One's habits or traits are not better than anyone else's; they are simply different. Some ideas follow about introducing students to style concepts:

TEACHING STUDENTS ABOUT LEARNING STYLES

- There are a variety of perceptual activities and puzzles that help students understand differences in style. One is a simple word association. The teacher says words like "orange," "shell," "play," or "table." Students jot down a word or phrase that comes to mind, and then compare their responses with those around them. Students quickly notice the differences, and a discussion can ensue about individual perceptions.

- There are many optical illusions and visual perception tasks that illustrate the same point, such as the familiar design with the vases and the faces which can be found in many books of optical illusions. There are also sentences written with an extra word, such as "Paris in the the springtime." When this is read quickly, the extra "the" is usually ignored.

- Students can be offered a puzzle to solve or a logic problem that is brief and developmentally appropriate. Ask students to observe the process they use to problem-solve rather than focusing on a single correct response. By comparing their problem-solving strategies, students can recognize significant differences in how people address the same task.

- Students might discuss issues that are pertinent to their own lives such as favorite music, learning to ride a bicycle, playing video games, or other pastimes. When asked to tell why certain activities are enjoyable, students come to realize that individual preferences are unique, rather than right or wrong.

- When students finish a project, it is useful to discuss how they went about doing the assignment. Questions might include "How did you begin?" "How did you make that decision?" "What did you do when you ran into the challenge?" "If you were doing this again, would you do anything differently?" "Which parts were hard?" "Which were easy?" Discussing such questions in small groups can emphasize that people learn in different ways.

- There are also opportunities to capture the "teachable moment" when a child describes how he accomplishes a task. For example, one student may learn to ride a bicycle with training wheels, raising them gradually until he is no longer dependent on the wheels. Another might learn to ride a bike by spending all day Saturday practicing on the street in front of her home, with many falls and scrapes on her knees, until success is achieved. Students who play musical instruments will find, when they discuss how they practice, a variety of individual differences and yet, the final quality of their work may not vary significantly.

- Many teachers administer inventories and tests so that students can identify patterns in their own learning as well as formal activities which describe the applications of those patterns.

Perhaps, most importantly, teachers must model an appreciation for individual differences in their behaviors throughout the school day. Every student can be expected to develop the same skills and gain the same competence—learning to read, for example, knowing how to multiply fractions, spelling words correctly, or understanding the historical significance of events, yet teachers must be responsive to the fact that not all students learn and develop competencies in the same way. Educators who model that distinction, who maintain high expectations for all students while appreciating and celebrating the diversity of ways students learn, will teach more through their behavior than through strategies.

DEVELOPING MULTIPLE PERSPECTIVES

Our perceptions of others and of different situations stem from our life experiences, value systems, assumptions, and expectations. While it is easy enough to state that everyone perceives the world differently, such a concept is difficult to internalize. Repeated and ongoing effort is needed to see the world through the eyes of others and to understand situations from diverse points of view. In an increasingly complex world, students may need to develop what Steven Lamy, a foremost American global educator, calls "intellectual pluralism." Intellectual pluralism is the capacity to analyze or evaluate different or opposing perspectives.

The preceding section, Appreciating Differences, introduces students to the concept that people approach learning differently. The following activities ask students to consider multiple perspectives in their interactions with others. The strategies include acknowledging perceptions of others, understanding diverse points of view, reflecting on current events from several perspectives, considering global implications, and learning to think systemically by considering the impact of human action on natural and human-made systems. The first strategy focuses on students and their perceptions of each other.

WHO ARE WE?

Students are usually surprised to learn that others often perceive us differently from the way we perceive ourselves. The following activity introduces children to the concept of multiple perspectives by exploring the discrepancies between self-perception and the perceptions of fellow classmates.

Collage Portraits

Students can be asked to create "Collage Portraits" at home omitting any identifying name or picture. When these are brought to class and displayed, classmates guess which collage belongs to whom. A discussion then follows about how well students know each other.

To initiate the activity, ask students to collect items at home for their collages. The teacher should provide poster boards and discarded magazines for those who would like to use such materials. Once supplies are gathered, each tudent should make a collage at home that features favorite pastimes, baby or early childhood photos, travel experiences, heroes or heroines, or personal opinions on important issues. The collages must be anonymous and not reveal names, pictures, or identifying symbols in the art work.

On an assigned day, students bring their collages to class hidden in a grocery bag or other cover. While students are out of the room, the teacher displays the collages and places an envelope directly underneath each. On their return to the classroom, students observe the "portraits" and attempt to guess the artists. The guesses are written on a slip of paper and placed in the appropriate envelope. When everyone has viewed all collages, debriefing begins. Possible group discussion questions include:

- **Was it easy or difficult to identify classmates by their collages?**
- **Which students were easily identified as the artists of their collages? Why?**
- **What did you learn about others that was new or surprising?**
- **How well do you think you know your classmates?**
- **Is it possible to find one unique thing about each collage?**
- **Can you now perceive each student in a new light? If so, how?**

Students might end the discussion by reflecting on the problems that arise when one makes assumptions about another without truly knowing that individual.

UNDERSTANDING DIVERSE POINTS OF VIEW

One way to introduce elementary students to the concept of multiple perspectives is to study stories from diverse points of view. One delightful resource is *The True Story of the Three Little Pigs* by Jon Scieszka. This book explains the wolf's perspective in the story "The Three Little Pigs." Rather than being the mean, meat-eating wolf as portrayed in the original version of the story, Mr. A. Wolf explains he was merely suffering from allergies, causing him to huff and puff. Young children enjoy reading both stories and discussing the opposing perspectives. Older students may want to compare and contrast the account of historical events from their social studies textbooks such as the arrival of Columbus in the Americas with portions of Howard Zinn's *A People's History of the United States*.

Another way to help students explore points of view is to encourage them to share their reactions to a variety of situations. It will first be necessary to develop a list of events such as attending a football game or being assigned a mystery to read as homework. Read each event one at a time to the class with students volunteering their reactions to the situations. Encourage the sharing of a variety of opinions. After several students have reacted to the events, select one student to read silently and form an opinion about the next event on the list. The class then attempts to guess the selected student's reaction. Continue this process as long as the students enjoy comparing and contrasting one another's reactions.

List of Events

1. You win a trip to Egypt.

2. You are invited to a basketball game.

3. You are selected to write a feature story for the school newspaper.

4. Your mother buys you a piano.

5. A relative suggests that you study to become a doctor.

6. You are asked to take a lead role in a school play.

7. Your teacher assigns a book of your choice to read outside of class.

8. A birthday gift you wish you could receive is. . . .

To bring this activity to closure, ask students to discuss whether the predictions of their classmates' responses were accurate. If not, why not? It is also important to discuss whether students acknowledge the validity of others' perspectives.

After grasping the concept of points of view, students might be asked to reflect on events from their own lives. For example, what might a school bus driver think about children who are talking loudly on a school bus? How might the students perceive their actions? What would be their reasons for talking loudly? Why would the bus driver want them to talk softly?

ROLE-PLAYING CURRENT EVENTS FROM DIVERSE PERSPECTIVES

Older students can develop an appreciation for multiple perspectives through role-playing current local or world events. One simple activity is to ask students to bring newspaper articles to class that address controversial or conflict-ridden issues. Assign students to groups with each person briefly describing an article. The groups then select one article to pursue in greater depth by working through the following steps:

1. One student volunteers to read the article to the group.

2. The group identifies the conflict in the article and the diverse perspectives of the conflict.

3. Students determine potential roles represented by those involved in the conflict.

4. Each member of the group assumes a role.

5. The group role-plays the diverse perspectives.

6. Each group discusses the role-play, reflecting on the roles assumed, the validity of the diverse perspectives expressed, and any insights they gained.

7. The groups next consider how the conflict might be resolved by using win/win approaches.

8. The small groups share their experiences with the whole class.

GLOBAL PERSPECTIVES IN THE CURRICULUM

Another approach to seeing through the eyes, minds, and hearts of others is to infuse global perspectives into all curriculum areas, including the arts and sciences, literature, and extracurricular activities. As the world becomes more interdependent and students have increased opportunities to communicate with those from other cultures, it is important that cultural differences not be judged as right or wrong.

Educators can reflect on whether they encourage their students to entertain more than one perspective on cultural differences and issues. To determine if global perspectives are infused throughout their curriculum, teachers might want to consider the following questions:

- **Do students appreciate numerous world views?**

- **Are students knowledgeable about global issues and events?**

- **Do students understand that humans are diverse in terms of attributes, cultures, and experiences and yet share common human needs and goals?**

- Can students identify and understand the inter-dependence of numerous world systems?

- Are students learning strategies for participating in local, national, and international issues and settings?

- Are students acquiring the skills of decision-making, information-analysis, and citizenship participation?

By using resources available in most communities, students can explore cultural differences and similarities through the literature, music, games, or arts of diverse countries. Artists, guest lecturers, exchange students, discussion leaders, and resource materials can enrich any subject matter. One excellent reading series that offers short stories written by living authors from around the world is called *Short Story International*. Stories are appropriate for three reading levels: grades four through seven, grades eight through twelve, and advanced high school through adult students. Published every two months, each series contains 12 to 15 stories by celebrated authors including Gabriel Garica Marquez, Aleksandr Solzhenitsyn, and Kurt Vonnegut. Teachers' guides are also available.

SYSTEMS WHEEL

Another dimension of gaining perspective is to consider the consequences of one's actions. The last few years have witnessed increasing concerns about the long-term impact of human behavior on natural and human-made systems. Many contemporary issues reveal the interconnectedness of cultural, ecological, economic, political, and technological systems. To extend students' thinking beyond short-term solutions they can be asked to identify multiple factors and potential consequences involved in any one issue. The following five-step exercise called a "systems wheel" is a helpful tool for forecasting the consequences.

1. Ask students to identify an issue or make a forecast that is pertinent to class content. When one issue or forecast is selected, ask students to draw a circle in the center of a blank piece of paper and write the name of the issue in the circle. For example, assume that students in a science class identify increasing air pollution as the issue they want to address.

2. Next, students should brainstorm the global systems that will be affected by increased air pollution. Examples might include the natural environment, international relations, technology, world economies, or political systems. Once global systems are identified, students draw the appropriate number of spokes from the first circle and at the end of each spoke draw another circle. Inside each new circle, a global system affected by air pollution is noted:

3. A third set of spokes and circles are drawn from the second to indicate potential consequences of air pollution. The third ring of circles forecasts the likely impact of air pollution upon the global systems identified in the second ring.

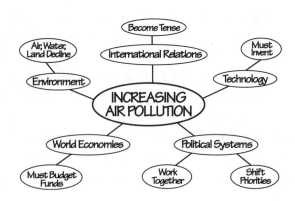

4. Students continue extending their rings of consequences as far as they can forecast. They may also want to predict the number of years before such effects are noted.

5. Students next identify circles that have relationships to each other by coloring all related circles in the same color or by drawing interconnecting lines.

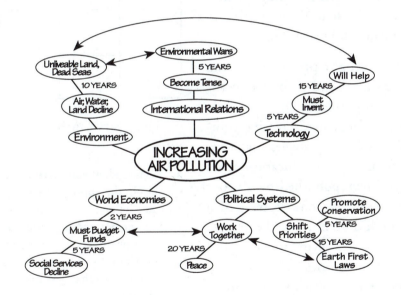

To bring closure to the activity, students might share their "systems wheels" in small groups, noting similarities and differences with classmates' forecasts. A class discussion can follow, with students synthesizing and revising their forecasts as well as identifying appropriate courses of action.

LOCAL AND GLOBAL PROBLEM-SOLVING

Students are usually eager to tackle real-life problems. When provided with information about current local or global problems and when taught problem-solving processes, children often surprise adults with their ingenuous approaches for addressing pressing needs. For example, during the 1980s a group of Russian and American students worked together to advocate limiting the proliferation of nuclear arms. To publicize their cause, they created jewelry made from dismantled rockets to sell as world peace jewelry. They also created a flag with powerful visual symbolism: half of the flag was the former Soviet Union's and half was the American flag. The two halves were blended together with a large heart framing the borders. The students' visual imagery and jewelry grabbed the attention of local citizenry as well as national radio and television.

Students can be taught problem-solving processes to address local and global concerns and perhaps, most importantly, they can take action to implement their own creative solutions. The problem-solving strategies suggested below are taken from a global education series entitled *Our Only Earth*, published by Zephyr Press. These strategies, which are part of a process called a Youth Summit, have been used in individual classrooms, entire schools, and with students in nine countries to address real life problems. The process begins with individual students or small groups researching a local or global issue. After the students have conducted their research, the following problem-solving steps can be initiated:

Step 1: In small groups, encourage students to share their thoughts, feelings, and ideas about the problem they have researched. Such discussions provide opportunities for the group members to get to know each other as well as share affective reactions to the problem at hand.

Step 2: Next, group members can review what they know about the issue and categorize key ideas generated by the group. Students may want to make a copy of the data retrieval chart below on a large sheet of butcher paper to synthesize the groups' knowledge.

DATA RETRIEVAL CHART

Name	Who	When	Where	Why

The chart can be completed in one of two ways:

a. **Each student summarizes and inserts information in the appropriate categories by placing one's name in the name column and completing one horizontal section of the chart. After group members have individually made their contributions, the completed chart displays information that is readily available for easy reference.**

b. **Another use of the data retrieval chart is to consider the issue from diverse perspectives. Students brainstorm individuals, organizations, or countries involved in the problem and look at it from diverse perspectives. Each student writes the name of the group or nation under the name column and then completes the horizontal questions from that perspective. Discussion follows focusing on the diverse perspectives represented on the chart.**

Once the chart is completed, the following problem-solving steps can be undertaken:

Step 3: Students must identify the specific problem they want to tackle. Frequently, topics are too vague or unwieldy for students to address. For example, students might state they want to help resolve the problem of air pollution, but the topic is too large to be manageable. If students narrow their focus to air pollution's connection to human respiratory ailments, or industrial pollutants crossing national borders the greater specificity will make their projects more successful.

To narrow their topics, students can consider the problem from several angles. How do people, animals, plants, businesses, or nations, view this problem? What sub-problems become evident when the issue is considered from many points of view? Students should brainstorm the sub-problems related to the original issue. Next, they should review their lists to identify which of the sub-problems appear most interesting to pursue as a group.

Once a sub-problem has been selected, students need to state their problem carefully. This is often best done in the form of a question rather than a statement. For example, if students are addressing the topic of air pollution, they might state their question as "How can we cut down on our families' use of cars?" Or, "How can we inform our community about the dangers of CFC's?" Ask students to experiment with the use of different verbs as they generate their questions.

Once students have created their questions to pursue, they may discover the need for additional research. If so, groups should plan a strategy for information gathering and allot time to do the work.

Step 4: In their small groups, students brainstorm possible solutions to the questions generated in Step 3.

Step 5: From their solution lists, students should select the top two they could actually implement. Using the chart below, each group evaluates the pros and cons of their solutions. Such analysis demonstrates that well-intentioned ideas frequently yield some negative consequences. It is important to consider short- and long-term consequences of any solutions before they are implemented.

YOUTH SUMMIT SOLUTION EVALUATION PROCESS						
SOLUTIONS: Rank in order your top 2 solutions and list	**POSITIVE OUTCOMES:** List 3 positive outcomes for each solution	**NEGATIVE OUTCOMES:** List 3 negative outcomes for each solution	**POSSIBLE SHORT- & LONG-TERM CONSEQUENCES:** List the consequences that might result from the implementatin of your solutions in a 1-, 5-, 10- and 20-year timeframe. Put a + or - by each consequence to signify whether it is positive or egative.			
			1 YEAR	**5 YEARS**	**10 YEARS**	**20 YEARS**
SOLUTION #1:						
SOLUTION #2:						

Once groups have completed their analysis, they select the best solution in terms of any positive and negative outcomes as well as short and long-term consequences. Each group then discusses their final solution and makes any modifications necessary at this point to minimize negative effects.

Step 6: Students plan how to carry out their solution. This step, while requiring much forethought, empowers students to take action by implementing their solutions in the broader community. To organize their action planning, students may want to use the group action plan form and individual commitment forms below:

Step 7: Each group prepares a presentation for the class and/or school, parents, and community members on the selected problems and plans of action.

Step 8: Projects are carried out and a celebration planned to acknowledge student efforts.

Student participants in the Youth Summit

YOUTH SUMMIT GROUP ACTION PLAN FORM

Group Topic: _____

_____

Group Members: (Please list first and last names.)

_____

_____

_____

_____

_____

_____

Describe the specific problem your group decided to solve:

_____

_____

_____

_____

Describe your best solution:

_____

_____

_____

_____

List the specific steps your group will take to carry out the solution, beginning with what you will do first, second, third, and so on. Also list the name of the group member who will be responsible for doing each step:

_____

_____

_____

_____

_____

Create a timeline stating dates of completion for the steps listed above:

_____

_____

_____

_____

_____

Describe the end result of your efforts. What exactly will you have accomplished?

_____

_____

_____

_____

YOUTH SUMMIT STATEMENT OF INDIVIDUAL COMMITMENT
TO WORK ON AN AREA OF GLOBAL CONCERN

Name: _____

Area of Global Concern: _____
_____
_____
_____
_____

List the commitments you made to your group at the Summit: _____
_____
_____
_____
_____

Please describe below any additional commitments you would like to pursue
independently: _____
_____
_____
_____

Signature: _____ Date _____

Thank you for your efforts to make the world a better place!

problem-solving process have generated numerous approaches to local and global issues. Some of their action plans have included a game about the effects of plastics on the environment, presentations to the United Nations, schools, community groups, and churches about the importance of international youth exchanges to promote world peace, booths at local fairs to educate others about ocean pollution, the implementation of school-wide self-esteem programs to combat drug abuse, and the creation of a film about wildlife's struggle to survive. Such projects help students acquire skills to address complex, real life issues. As Jason Schmidt, age 9, noted after participating in a Youth Summit,

— *I learned to be more caring for the world.*
I see that we can be world changers.

MULTICULTURAL EDUCATION

The changing nature of demographics is one of the strongest rationales for multicultural education in the United States. The Census Bureau has predicted that while the Caucasian population will increase by 25% between 1990 and 2030, the African-American population will increase by 68%, the Asian-American, Pacific Island- American, and American Indian populations by 79%, and the Hispanic-American population by 187%. The Population Reference Bureau forecasts that by the year 2080, 24% of U.S. citizens will be Hispanic, 15% African-American, 12% Asian-American and a little over 50% Caucasian. As the former University of Chicago President, Robert Maynard Hutchins, once said, "The best education for the best is the best education for all." It appears imperative then that the best education requires the inclusion of multicultural education for every student of all racial, ethnic, and social groups, since each will participate in an increasingly multiethnic future.

Many teachers view multicultural education as content limited to ethnic, racial, or cultural groups and irrelevant to many academic disciplines; however, just the opposite is true. Ideally, multicultural education should be an on-going, integrated, multidisciplinary process for all students. James Banks, one of the country's foremost experts in the field, and author of *Multiethnic Education: Theory and Practice* says that multicultural education requires changes in teaching approaches and school environments. Before educators can adequately infuse diverse cultural perspectives into their teaching, Banks recommends adjusting the content one teaches, helping students identify biases in how knowledge is constructed, ensuring the academic achievement of all students, and creating a total school climate that respects and values

diversity. Bank's suggestions for infusing multicultural education throughout the curriculum follow.

TEACHING WITH A MULTICULTURAL PERSPECTIVE

Integrating multicultural information into content areas: To successfully integrate multicultural education throughout the curriculum, teachers will find it necessary to use examples and content from a variety of cultures in all discipline areas. Before it is possible to do so, educators must first become informed about multicultural contributions and ask their students to provide additional examples from their cultural/ethnic heritages. Numerous resources exist for teachers in language arts, social studies, art, and home economic classes.

Reflecting on the construction of knowledge: Teachers can help students identify how cultural assumptions and biases influence the way knowledge is constructed within a discipline. Concepts, events, and issues taught in the classroom should be viewed from the perspectives and experiences of a range of racial, ethnic, and cultural groups. For example, during a unit on the discovery of America, students might read portions of Fred Olson's *On the Trail of the Arawacks* and parts of Christopher Columbus's diary to discern how European and Indian views of this event differed. Through such comparisons, students develop critical thinking skills and actively construct their knowledge instead of passively consuming textbooks.

Offering an equity pedagogy: An equity pedagogy refers to adjusting teaching methods to insure the academic achievement of all students from diverse racial, cultural, gender, and social class groups. By using cooperative learning, multimodal instruction, and personalized, self-directed options, students have more opportunities for success. Research shows that the academic achievement of African-American and Mexican-American students is increased when collaborative rather than competitive models of instruction are used. Cooperative learning helps all students including white middle-class ones to develop more positive racial attitudes. It is important, however, that teachers insure equal status of all students in intergroup interactions.

Creating an empowering school culture: Teachers can help create a positive school climate by preventing or discontinuing unfair tracking, labeling, or disproportionality in special programs, while encouraging the positive interaction of staff and students across ethnic and racial lines.

While individual teachers reflect on their integration of multiculturalism in instruction, Banks also offers guidelines for multiethnic education in total school programs. In order for schools to assess how well they incorporate ethnic pluralism, Banks has developed an *i*nventory available in his book, *Multiethnic Education*. This inventory assesses teacher in-service on multi-ethnic perspectives, school organization and grouping practices, curricular offerings, special education programs and other issues pertinent to effective multicultural practices. By taking Banks' inventory, school and community personnel can identify ways to improve local school programs.

An important goal of multicultural education is to help students acquire the knowledge and commitments needed to make reflective decisions and to take personal, social, and civic action to promote democracy and democratic living. When students learn content about their country and world from the diverse perspectives of those who have shaped local and international cultures, they will be better able to participate as citizens in a pluralistic nation and world.

UNDERSTANDING CULTURAL DIVERSITY THROUGH THE ARTS

Many sociologists and anthropologists claim that art emerges from a cultural context. A culture's customs, tastes, ideologies, and philosophies have profound influences upon artistic expression. When examining cultural artifacts, it is necessary to consider the social forces affecting their creation. Conversely, by analyzing a culture's art, one can gain insight into the mores that helped shape the art.

A Canadian educator, E. Margaret Andrews, intrigued with the cultural impact on art, has developed a multicultural education program that introduces children to ethnic diversity through the arts. By becoming "anthropologists" or "cultural detectives," students are introduced to another culture through its art. The procedures for this culturally-based program consist of six steps described below:

1. Students are asked to become "anthropologists" or "cultural detectives" with the task of investigating another culture through the collection, organization, and interpretation of artistic data. To begin, the teacher and students identify a theme such as Chinese Culture and Art to explore. Once the theme is agreed upon, individual learning goals are specified for each student.

2. Students begin the unit by collecting visual samples such as photographs, posters, magazine pictures, book pictures, and objects. Stories, legends, songs, and dances can also be gathered and shared.

3. Once the artifacts are brought into the classroom, the students examine and discuss the collection. They are asked to observe,

describe, analyze, and interpret the meanings of the collected data. Discussions and further investigations might focus on the:

- types of art represented, such as fine art, folk art, utilitarian art, tourist art, or indigenous art

- functions of art in any culture such as for apparel or personal adornment, everyday purposes (furniture, containers), play and leisure, ritual and celebration, promotion of political, or economic, and commercial pursuits

- history associated with the cultural art forms, the motivation behind the creation of such art, and the values and beliefs reflected in the art

- cross-cultural comparisons that analyze the similarities and differences in styles, symbols, or materials

- the materials and techniques used in the artifacts

4. During discussion of the artifacts and their cultural implications, teachers identify and organize production projects. Students learn about the materials and process of a culture's craftsmanship as they continue their studies. Classroom visitors who have special artistic expertise are invaluable resources at this stage.

5. For evaluation, students engage in group discussions and maintain logs to identify the most significant things they have learned. The log can reflect on personal insights, cultural meanings, and the attainment of individual goals.

6. Periodic sharing of cultural themes through school presentations such as puppet shows or culture-related events is an important part of students' learning. They may want to offer a multicultural arts festival for other classes, parents, and/or community members in order to exhibit the results of their cultural investigations.

Andrews' inquiry-based approach to multicultural education familiarizes students with diverse cultural perspectives and practices. Children also gain important learning skills as they begin to recognize and celebrate cultural diversity.

CULTURGRAMS

Another approach to exploring cultural diversity is offered by Brigham Young University's David M. Kennedy Center for International Studies. Their research process called Culturgrams develops profiles of diverse cultural groups with the goal of fostering intercultural understanding. The Center has noted that there are approximately 20,000 cultures in the world, and it has created Culturgrams for over 100 countries which are updated annually. Since the task of understanding such an array of human cultures is immense, the Culturgram was developed as one means of organizing and understanding different cultures and their characteristics.

A Culturgram is a research effort to gather information on many dimensions of a single culture. After the research is conducted and compiled, it is validated through personal experience and/or interviews with individuals of the culture under study. Since one person's interpretation of cultural behavior can differ from another's, updating and validation is an important part of the research process.

There are 24 broad areas of study in a Culturgram. Teachers who are interested in having their students begin work on such cultural profiles may ask students to select one or more of the research areas rather than attempting to compile an entire Culturgram. Research can be gleaned from library materials, embassies, foreign service, cultural support organizations, and interviews. The 24 categories of Culturgrams are included below with permission from

Brigham Young University's David Kennedy Center for International Studies:

1. Greetings
2. Visiting
3. Talks or speeches
4. Meetings
5. Role relationships
6. Gestures
7. Personal appearance
8. Expressions of general attitudes by age, sex, position
9. Languages
10. Religion and philosophy
11. Special holidays and Holy Days
12. Family
13. Dating, courtship, and marriage
14. Social and economic levels
15. Group distribution
16. Work
17. Diet and food customs
18. Recreation, leisure, sports, arts
19. History and government
20. Education
21. Transportation and communication systems
22. Health, sanitation and medical facilities
23. Land and climate
24. Other distinctive customs, courtesies, conditions

After students have collected their data, they may want to identify a native of that culture to verify their research. The information should then be compiled and shared in a written or visual format and saved for others who may want to learn about that culture as well. Researching any or all of the components of a Culturgram introduces students to many key aspects of a culture. Culturgrams, especially when validated by natives of the culture being studied, promote increased understanding of and communication with others.

Culturgrams are available as a full set or individually by country of choice. For information on how to order Culturgrams write Brigham Young University, Kennedy Center Publications, 280 HRCB, Provo, UT 84602, or call them at (800) 528-6279.

TECHNOLOGY THAT ENHANCES INTERPERSONAL INTELLIGENCE

Students frequently use technology alone, and for purposes such as remediation or personal exploration, this is often preferable. Current research indicates, however, that when students use computers in pairs or small groups, comprehension and learning are facilitated and accelerated. Positive learning experiences can result as students share discoveries, support each other in solving problems, and work collaboratively on projects. In today's workplace, such skills are increasingly important.

There are many ways that technology can be used in the classroom to enhance interpersonal skills. For example, students can be videotaped as they give a presentation or performance. They can then observe their facial expressions and body movements to see whether these enhance or detract from what they wish to communicate. Groups of students can discuss their observations of each other, understanding that they should begin and end with a positive observation and that criticism is only to be offered in a constructive manner.

Interpersonal skills can be enhanced through small technology groups in the classroom, as well as through computer networking with students in other classrooms, schools, or countries. Even more dramatic is the increasing frequency of teleconferencing through satellite transmission. The face-to-face contact with children who can see and hear each other via technology is a highly motivating way to develop communication skills as students in different parts of the country or the world join together in problem-solving environmental, economical, or political issues.

The Copen Family Fund in New York has been instrumental in fostering the development of school-based computer networks: l*EARN links five centers in the United States with projects in fifteen foreign countries. The Global Education Model in Yorktown Heights, New York, links 42,000 students in grades K-12 with students in the Netherlands, Spain, and Indonesia. The Albuquerque Public Schools links 600 users in the district's 120 schools through a district-wide electronic mail network. And the Pacific Northwest Center links Washington State's 34 Schools for the 21st Century. The Copen Fund is piloting on-line, low-cost, computer-teleconferencing for such projects.

Among the large numbers of other networks are National Geographic's Kidsnet, ATT's Learning Network, and Peacenet. The Internet, which is a network of computer networks, includes thousands of networks used by millions of people of all ages. For educators, telecommunications networks offer an important resource and support system. Growing numbers of networks such as America Tomorrow, have been created to link educators with each other, and offer up-to-the minute educational news and resources on educational innovations and restructuring.

Distance Learning facilitates communication between teachers and students in different parts of the community, state, or world. This interactive technology develops expanded and enhanced interpersonal skills and breaks through cultural barriers as students and teachers learn to communicate in new ways appropriate to this medium.

SUMMARY

As Howard Gardner has noted, the positive development of the personal intelligences determines whether an individual will lead a successful and fulfilling adult life. Interpersonal intelligence is called upon to live and work with others in our immediate environments, in our communities, nations, and world. Learning to live collaboratively and learning to manage conflict effectively are necessary skills for both individuals and nations.

Albert Einstein once said,

*The general level of world information
is high but usually biased,
influenced by national prejudices
serving to make us citizens of our nation
but not of our world.*

Student perspectives of local and global issues can be broadened so that they may assume citizenship not only of one country but also of the world. While anchored firmly in one's cultural roots, it is possible to stretch beyond national borders to collaborate with others in resolving the complex issues facing humankind.

This chapter has surveyed numerous interpersonal approaches important for living in an increasingly interdependent world. These processes include: 1) establishing effective groups 2) collaborative learning 3) conflict management 4) learning through service 5) appreciating differences by learning about learning styles 6) developing multiple perspectives 7) local and global problem-solving 8) multicultural education, and 9) interpersonal uses of technology. In order to summarize, reflect upon, and synthesize the content of this chapter, the following is offered:

APPLYING INTERPERSONAL INTELLIGENCE

1. Important ideas or insights gleaned from this chapter: _____

_____

_____

_____

_____

2. Areas I'd like to learn more about: _____

_____

_____

_____

_____

3. Ways I can use this information in my teaching. Please note that all of the strategies mentioned in this chapter are listed below with space provided to note how each strategy might be incorporated into classroom instruction:

INTERPERSONAL STRATEGY	CLASSROOM APPLICATION

Establishing a Positive Interpersonal Environment:
Criteria for Effective Groups
Determining Class Values & Rules
Class Meetings

Collaborative Learning:
Collaborative Grouping Considerations
Student Roles
Social Skills
Cooperative Learning Activities
Cooperative Out Loud Problem-Solving
Cooperative Group Discussion of Literature
Collaboration in the Multilingual Classroom

Conflict Management:
Causes of Conflict
Gordon's Conflict Management Process

Learning through Service:
Incorporating Service into School Programs
Reflecting on Service Learning
Service Resources

Mentoring, Aprenticeships, and Tutoring:
Sample Programs

Appreciating Differences:
Teaching Students about Learning Styles

Developing Multiple Perspectives:
Who Are We?
Understanding Diverse Points of View:
List of Events
Role Playing Current Events
Global Perspectives
Systems Wheels

Local and Global Problem-Solving:

Multicultural Education:
Teaching with an Multicultural Perspective
Understanding Cultural Diversity through the Arts
Culturgrams

Technology that Enhances Interpersonal Intelligence:

INTERPERSONAL REFERENCES:

Andrews, E.M. (1983). "The Innovation Process of Culturally-Based Art Education: A Qualitative Analysis of the In-Service Programming and Implementation Processes of an Innovative Multicultural Art Curriculum in Canada." Unpublished doctoral dissertation. University of Bradford, Yorkshire, England.

Andrews, E.M. (1981). "The Study of Art in Cultural Context." *The Annual Journal*, Canadian Society for Education through Art.

Banks, J. A. (1991) "The Need for a Broad Definition of Multicultural Education." *Multicultural Leader*, Vol. 4, No. 1 Winter/ Spring. Educational Materials and Services Center, 144 Railroad Ave. Suite 107, Edmonds, WA 98020.

Banks, J. A. (1994). *Multiethnic Education: Theory and Practice.* Boston, MA: Allyn and Bacon, Inc.

Barrett, J. P., Daniels, C.G., Hutton, L., and Kasanaw, P. (1981). *Teaching Global Awareness: An Approach for Grades 1-6.* Denver: Center for Teaching International Relations.

Bird, J. and Peterson, K. (1988). *Cooperative Computers: Lesson Plans for Teachers.* Denver, CO: Cherry Creek Schools.

Campbell, L. and McKisson M. (1990). *Our Only Earth: A Global Problem Solving Series.* Tucson, AZ: Zephyr Press.

Cohen, E. G. (1986). *Designing Group Work for the Heterogeneous Classroom.* N.Y.: Teachers College Press, Columbia University.

Conrad, D. and Hedin, D. (1982). *Youth Participation and Experiential Education.* N.Y.: Haworth Press.

Drew, N. (1987). *Learning the Skills of Peacemaking: An Activity Guide for Elementary-Age Children on Communicating, Cooperating, and Resolving Conflict.* Rolling Hills Estates, CA: Jalmar Press.

Fisher, Rand and Ury, W. (1981) *Getting to Yes: Negotiating Agreement Without Giving In.* N.Y.: Houghton Mifflin.

Flaxman, E. et al. (1989). *Youth Mentoring Programs and Practices.* N.Y.: ERIC Clearinghouse.

Gevirtz, G. and Kelman, P. (1990). *Educational Computer Networks.* N.Y.: Scholastic.

Gordon, T. (1970). *Parent Effectiveness Training.* N.Y.: Peter Weyden.

Hamilton, S. (1991). "Is There Life after High School: Developing Apprenticeship in America" *The Best of the Harvard Education Letter*, Sept., 1988 to October, 1990. Cambridge, MA.

Humphrey, N.K., (1976). "The Social Function of the Intellect" in P.G. Bateson and R.A. Hinde, eds. *Growing Points in Ethology.* Cambridge, England: Cambridge University Press.

Independent Sector, *A Guidebook for Developing and Operating Effective Programs.* 1828 L Street NW, Washington D.C. 20036.

Johnson, D. W. & Johnson, R. T. (1984). *Circles of Learning: Cooperation in the Classroom.* Alexandria, VA: Association for Supervision and Curriculum Development.

Johnson, D. W.& Johnson, R. T. (1987). *Learning Together and Alone: Cooperative, Competitive and Individualistic Learning.* Englewood Cliffs, N.J.: Prentice Hall.

Johnson, D. W. & Johnson R. T. (1987). *Structuring Cooperative Learning: Lesson Plans for Teachers.* New Brighton, Minnesota: Interaction Book Company.

Kagan, S. (1988). *Cooperative Learning; Resources for Teachers.* Riverside, CA: University of California.

McPherson, K. *Enriching Learning through Service. Project Service Leadership*, 12703 NW 20th Avenue, Vancouver, WA 98685.

Muller, R. "World Core Curriculum" available from the Robert Muller School, 6005 Royal Oak Drive, Arlington, TX 76016.

Portland Public Schools, "Multiethnic Historical Timeline for Mathematics and Science." (1984). Portland, OR.

Short Story International, P.O. Box 405, Great Neck, N.Y. 11022. (516) 466-4166.

Shure, M.B. (1992a). *I Can Problem Solve (ICPS): An Interpersonal Cognitive Problem-Solving Program (pre-school).* Champagne, IL. Research Press.

Shure, M.B. (1992b). *I Can Problem Solve (ICPS): An Interpersonal Cognitive Problem-Solving Program (kinder-garten/ primary grades).* Champagne, IL. Research Press.

Shure, M.B. (1992c). *I Can Problem Solve (ICPS): An Interpersonal Cognitive Problem-Solving Program (interme-diate grades).* Champagne, IL. Research Press.

Slavin, R. E. (1986). *Student Team Learning: An Overview and Practical Guide.* Washington D.C.: National Education Association.

Tiedt, P.L. & Tiedt, I.M. (1990). *Multicultural Teaching: A Handbook of Activities, Information, and Resources.* Needham, Heights, MA: Allyn and Bacon.

Tye, K. (1990). *Global Education: From Thought to Action.* Alexandria, VA: Association for Supervision and Curriculum Development.

CHAPTER 7

THE WORLD WITHIN: INTRAPERSONAL INTELLIGENCE

What lies behind us and what lies before us are tiny matters compared to what lies within us.

— *OLIVER WENDELL HOLMES*

BILL'S INNER WORLD

When Bill was a young child, his mother found him difficult to handle. He was slow to learn, had frequent seizures, and suffered from behavior disorders.

With two babies at home, a broken marriage, and the necessity of returning to work, Bill's mother felt overwhelmed with the care her son required. Immediately after his ninth birthday, Bill was sent to live in a state institution for the mentally retarded, where he spent the next twelve years of his life.

After entering the institution, Bill ceased to share in the usual experiences of childhood. He was isolated from his family, friends, and the small town he lived in. Bill's isolation also included illiteracy. Considered "ineducable" with an IQ under 50, Bill was never taught to read or write. His days in the institution were spent doing menial chores.

Upon release from the state facility, Bill lived with the support of a community agency dedicated to assisting formerly institutionalized adults to achieve fuller and

more independent lives. The agency required Bill to identify and meet yearly personal goals to help him more fully integrate into his local community. When Bill turned 31, he identified a new goal to pursue: learning to read and write.

His service-provider located a reading teacher who used a multi-modal approach to teach reading. Bill immediately expressed his desire to write a letter to his estranged mother, and he carefully dictated his thoughts to his tutor, and then practiced reading portions of the letter. Bill and his teacher also worked with a reading series called *Ball, Stick, Bird* by Renee Fuller. Together, they read cigarette packs, cereal boxes, road signs, food and medicine labels, and newspaper headings. Bill practiced writing words and sentences first with colored markers and next with a typewriter given to him by his teacher.

BILL'S INNER WORLD ...continued

Bill worked avidly on his own, filling notebooks with sentences to proudly show his tutor during their next session. Writing about reading material of his own choice and setting and achieving personal goals were yielding positive results. Both Bill's skills and confidence increased greatly. After a month of learning to read and write, Bill set another goal: to write a book.

When Bill informed his teacher of this new goal, she hesitated, wondering if Bill's idea was realistic. As if to respond to these unspoken doubts, Bill told the tutor he knew the title of the book. It would be called *The Inside World* and would recount his life in the institution. Six months later, Bill completed his book. The following excerpts are taken from Bill Knake's *The Inside World*:

I would like to be able to teach other people to learn to read. I'd be a good teacher. I could teach them what I know, and help them find the words they want to know. I am good at working with people. I do understand people and their problems. I'd like to see if I can help or not. I know a lot of people who do not know how to read. I would like to start a school to teach them how. Reading is fun. You're never too old to read. I'd like to take people who are illiterate and turn them around so they can read.

Since I learned to read I feel better about myself. I always wanted to read. I feel proud of myself. I want to keep getting better at reading and writing, and I want to write some more books. I'm done with the institution for now. I want to write about other things, good things like how we can get along much better. I feel good about myself and I feel good about my life.

Bill Knake's perseverance and compassion, two aspects of intrapersonal intelligence, have served to inspire countless others to set and achieve goals formerly assumed impossible. Today, Bill lives and works in Mt. Vernon, Washington.

DEFINITION: UNDERSTANDING INTRAPERSONAL INTELLIGENCE

At the heart of our inner world are the strengths that we rely on to understand ourselves and other people, to imagine, plan, and solve problems. There as well lie qualities such as motivation, determination, ethics, integrity, empathy, and altruism. Without these inner resources, it is difficult to live a productive life in the fullest sense.

Most researchers believe that as soon as we come into the world, the personal intelligences are already developing from a combination of heredity, environment, and experience. The infant's bonding with the mother or care-giver establishes emotional security, and continued nurturing leads to a growing sense of personal identity and forms the basis for other positive, social relationships. Thus, from the beginning, intrapersonal and interpersonal intelligence are interdependent.

Parents or other care-givers and teachers serve critical functions in modeling these intelligences for the developing child, and the positive, nurturing, stimulating environments they create help to lay the foundations for the healthy development of the human being, intellectually, emotionally, and physically.

Intrapersonal intelligence includes our thoughts and feelings. The more we can bring them into consciousness, the better we can relate our inner world to the outer world of experience. Occasionally, when we find ourselves doing something automatically, it is useful to interrupt this pattern and begin again what we were doing, carefully and thoughtfully observing our own behavior. Such critical self-observation is one way to become more conscious of our inner world, an awareness as important for teachers as it is for students.

In this chapter, we explore ways to better understand ourselves, our desires and goals, and our emotional natures, so that ultimately we may effectively plan our experiences based upon an accurate working model of the self. Such intrapersonal skills are crucially important to the development of successful learners who will become increasingly ethical, productive, and creative human beings who are both independent and collaborative.

Intrapersonal intelligence need not be a solemn quality. In fact, the ability to understand ourselves better by being able to laugh at our foibles or mistakes is a non-threatening way to greater self-understanding. Students will be well-served by realizing that making an honest mistake should not automatically lead to self-depreciation or shame or anger. When we are able to laugh at ourselves, we are much better able to start over again. When teachers model this ability in front of students, they model a basic survival skill.

CHECKLIST OF INTRAPERSONAL QUALITIES

Young children are often curious about their inner experiences and can benefit from a variety of intrapersonal activities. Such activities include self-directed, independent learning approaches, opportunities to imagine, and quiet times and private places to work and reflect. In addition, students can benefit by learning ways to process their feelings, set and achieve goals, and gain self-knowledge and self-esteem. Posing questions about life and personal ambition, and then finding answers to such mysteries is rewarding for children and adults alike.

When attempting to describe characteristics of those with developed intrapersonal intelligence, it is important to note that individuals may not demonstrate all aspects of this intelligence. For example, a person may have an accurate inner image of himself without having high self-esteem. Another may exhibit self-contentment and not strive for self-actualization. The following list suggests some indicators of this complex intelligence. It is likely that a person with well-developed intrapersonal intelligence may be one who:

1. **Is aware of his range of emotions.**

2. **Finds approaches and outlets to express his feelings and thoughts.**

3. **Develops an accurate model of self.**

4. **Is motivated to identify and pursue goals.**

5. **Establishes and lives by an ethical value system.**

6. **Works independently.**

7. **Is curious about the "big questions" in life: meaning, relevance, and purpose.**

8. **Manages ongoing learning and personal growth.**

9. **Attempts to seek out and understand inner experiences.**

10. **Gains insights into the complexities of self and the human condition.**

11. **Strives for self-actualization.**

12. **Empowers others.**

INTRAPERSONAL LEARNING PROCESSES

The learning activities in this chapter fit into the following broad categories: self-esteem, goal-setting, emotional processing skills, journal-writing, clarification of values and purpose, the curricular model of self-directed learning, and intrapersonal forms of technology. These instructional approaches offer a variety of ways to begin nurturing intrapersonal intelligence. The educator is cautioned, however, against

expecting immediate changes within students, since deep self-knowledge requires a lifetime of living and learning to develop. The specific strategies described in this chapter include:

ESTABLISHING AN ENVIRONMENT TO NURTURE THE SENSE OF SELF
Characteristics of Schools that Nurture Self-Esteem
SELF-ESTEEM ENHANCERS
Compliment Circles
Individual Acknowledgment
Peer Support
Guidelines for Enhancing Self-Esteem
SETTING AND ACHIEVING GOALS
Student Interest Survey
Individual Student Goal Sheet
Challenging Students to Learn
Olympian Goal-Setting
THINKING SKILLS
Metacognition
Assignment Planning and Reflecting Form
EMOTIONALLY INTELLIGENT EDUCATION IN THE CLASSROOM
Establishing an Environment that Permits Emotional Expression
Identifying Feelings
Feelings Inventory
Expressing Feelings through the Arts
Resources for Personal Support
Educating for Human Values
JOURNAL WRITING
Suggestions for Classroom Journal Writing
Keeping a Journal for Personal Insight
GETTING TO KNOW ONESELF THROUGH OTHERS
Gaining Intrapersonal Insights through Interpersonal Feedback
REFLECTING ON THE WONDER AND PURPOSE OF LIFE
Classroom Activities to Nurture a Sense of Wonder
Finding Purpose in School and Life
SELF-DIRECTED LEARNING: AN INTRAPERSONAL EDUCATIONAL APPROACH
Self-Directed Learning Contact
Suggestions for Implementing Self-Directed Learning
TECHNOLOGY THAT ENHANCES INTRAPERSONAL INTELLIGENCE
SUMMARY

ESTABLISHING AN ENVIRONMENT TO NURTURE THE SENSE OF SELF

Many educational programs have been developed to enhance student self-esteem. While there is no single agreed-upon definition of self-esteem, it is generally viewed as the sum of one's feelings about oneself, including one's sense of self-respect and self-worth. To have high self-esteem, a person must feel worthwhile, lovable, competent in one's environment, and capable of contributing to others in meaningful ways. Students with high self-esteem believe in themselves and their abilities. They participate in school and other activities, are able to learn from their mistakes, and are comfortable with not being "perfect."

School environments can be organized to enhance the self-esteem of all students. By creating a warm and caring atmosphere, adhering to democratic procedures, nurturing human dignity, and promoting cultural diversity, schools can assist students in feeling welcome and accepted. There appear to be five essential qualities which characterize schools that successfully nurture self-esteem. Educators may want to review these qualities to determine which ones their schools exhibit and which might be strengthened.

CHARACTERISTICS OF SCHOOLS THAT NURTURE SELF-ESTEEM

Equity: A school-wide belief system is in place that acknowledges that all students can learn and all are offered high quality educational opportunities.

Community: Students, school personnel, parents, and community members share a common purpose to make school positive, relevant, and meaningful.

Participation: Students are actively involved in school governance, curriculum planning, and evaluation.

Collaborative grouping: Students are grouped heterogeneously and are taught to value interdependence and cultural diversity.

Active learning processes: Hands-on, problem-centered or project-based curriculums emphasize the personal and social relevance of what is being learned.

School conditions that undermine self-esteem include the rejection of students, ambiguity about academic and behavioral expectations, disrespect, excessively high levels of competition, and negative expectations. Common practices such as student tracking, authoritarian procedures, competition, and a mono-cultural curriculum can limit self-worth. Enhancing the self-image of teachers so that they feel positive, affirmed, and encouraged is also an important aspect of any school-wide effort. Teachers who respect and care for themselves find it easier to offer care, respect, and acceptance to others, thus modeling and encouraging greater self-acceptance among students.

The Apollo High School in Simi Valley, California is dedicated to enhancing the self-esteem of its 400 at-risk students has succeeded at motivating most students to achieve by offering alternatives for students who have not succeeded in traditional secondary environments.

To nurture students' sense of self-worth, the Apollo teachers base their programs on the four A's: Attention, Acceptance, Appreciation, and Affection.

Apollo students help establish and enforce school rules and have input into their learning experiences. At teacher-student meetings, which are held frequently, students discuss their opinions and feelings about school. The staff, valuing and respecting their ideas and suggestions, often make curricular adjustments to incorporate student suggestions.

The Apollo model is based upon William Glasser's Control Theory which suggests that human behavior is motivated by five needs: survival, belonging, power, freedom, and fun. Brad Greene the former principal of Apollo High School, and now educational consultant, helped teachers and administrators structure the school's environment to meet these five needs. Discipline is not handled in traditional ways at Apollo but rather through problem-solving approaches with students input. A number of common high school problems have been resolved with the following procedures:

- **Graffiti on school walls disappeared after students painted murals.**

- **Alcohol and drug abusers are not suspended but receive credit for attending support groups that help them discontinue drug use.**

- **Nonproductive students are motivated by lessons geared to their learning styles and interests.**

The Apollo approach is effective. After students enter the school, dramatic decreases in drug use, absenteeism, and criminal activity are evident, and 86% of the students graduate. For these reasons William Glasser dedicated his book *The Quality School* to Apollo High School.

SELF-ESTEEM ENHANCERS: LEARNING TO LOVE ONESELF

In addition to school-wide endeavors, there is much that individual teachers can do to enhance the self-concept of their students. This section highlights a variety of classroom approaches to bolster student self-esteem. It is important to recognize, however, that because of individual as well as cultural differences, some students thrive with group acknowledgment while others prefer individual feedback and interaction. All students benefit, however, from peer support and feedback.

COMPLIMENT CIRCLES

One of the authors first participated in this activity at a faculty meeting. The principal placed the teachers in small groups of six to eight, carefully including those who seldom interacted with each other in this large suburban high school. The teachers were instructed to take turns giving and receiving compliments from everyone in the small group. Some of the heartfelt comments are still remembered and appreciated to this day!

Before conducting a compliment circle with a classroom of students, important ground rules must be considered. Each student should be the compliment recipient at least once during the school year. With a class of 25 to 30 students, a circle will require approximately a half hour, so time factors must be considered. Some teachers hold a "circle" for birthdays to spread them out over the year. Others plan them towards the end of the school year, while some teachers prefer to organize them on an "as needed" basis such as times when a student could use a psychological boost.

To begin, arrange chairs in a circle and identify the compliment receiver to sit in the center.

The students should understand the following procedures: As the compliments are given, the receiver can only smile or say, "Thank you." Those who are sitting in the circle must each think of something to say that is honest and sincere. No "passes" or duplications are allowed. Some teachers like to create a written record of the compliments by assigning two students to copy what is said. The written version is then presented to the recipient. Such documents usually become lifelong, cherished items.

Another approach to conducting compliment circles is to tape-record classmates' messages. A tape recorder can be set up in a corner of the room and students are free to record compliments for an individual throughout the school day. At the end of the day, the teacher can send the tape home with the recipient of the compliments.

For some students, compliment circles can serve as tremendous morale boosters as well as self-image transformers. An eighth-grade boy named Dave had been in several fights and had few friends at school. One of his instructors planned a compliment circle with Dave as the recipient which resulted in his being visibly shaken by listening to the 28 compliments from his peers. He later commented to the teacher that "I didn't know anybody thought of me like this!" Dave's behavior and demeanor softened after seeing himself through the eyes of his classmates and discovering new qualities to appreciate within himself.

INDIVIDUAL ACKNOWLEDGMENT

Some students prefer not to receive public acclaim, while others desire recognition both publicly and privately. A teacher can boost a student's self-esteem by individually communicating concern and support. Spending an occasional few extra moments with a student provides important opportunities for the teacher to recognize and affirm the value of the student. The child's success in an academic, social, or real-world event can be mentioned and assistance given in transferring appropriate skills and qualities to classroom use.

In one-to-one encounters, active listening can reveal student concerns and issues. Often attempting to understand the feelings behind the words, a teacher can rephrase the student's conversation to verify the message. It is important for teachers to avoid adding their own messages including advice, opinions, judgments, questions, or solutions. In active listening, the teacher expresses as accurately as possible what the student says and often a positive, personal relationship may be created. As a result, many students may decide to participate more actively in school.

During individual or whole-group discussions, it is important to communicate high expectations for student achievement. Even though some students may face difficult personal or academic challenges, teachers can emphasize their confidence that students can succeed in accomplishing learning goals. The skills required to complete a specific task may need to be explained or taught.

When students have participated effectively in class activities, private and authentic recognition often encourage continued involvement; on the other hand, inappropriate amounts or kinds of praise and concern should be avoided. Some students interpret such responses as indicators of low expectations. Praise, when given, should be sincere, appropriate for the task accomplished, and specifically descriptive of what the child did. As with many other aspects of teaching, self-esteem enhancement is complex, and teachers must proceed with sensitivity to the individual qualities and needs of their students.

PEER SUPPORT

Some students, who have difficulty with their academic work, often find success tutoring younger children. Many schools have formalized cross-age tutoring programs between high school and elementary school students or between various grade levels within the same school. Typically, leadership opportunities are reserved for high-achieving students, making it difficult for those with low self-esteem to participate in a variety of student relationships. Cross-age tutoring multiplies the opportunities for a student to experience the satisfaction of helping others while boosting one's self-esteem in the process.

Some teachers have experimented with establishing peer support networks consisting of students who lack self-confidence as well as others who enjoy social interaction. Such networks offer a cohesive group approach to improving self-esteem, academic achievement, and the opportunity to develop more friendships. Some guidelines for establishing positive youth networks follow:

Peer Networks

1. Identify an even-numbered group of students who agree to meet once a week after school, during lunch, or before school for peer support purposes. The students also must be willing to make one phone call to their partner each evening. Participation should extend for at least one month.

2. At the first session, students list what they consider their academic and social strengths on sheets of paper that are then distributed as a resource to other group members. Students can freely call any person in the resource pool for assistance.

3. At the first session, each student reflects on academic and/or social challenges and creates an action plan to improve school experiences.

4. Each student is then assigned a peer partner to work with for a month or longer. Partners make lists of all assignments and/or social efforts they will undertake. The partners are responsible for phoning one another each evening to troubleshoot problems and to determine whether progress is being made with their action plans.

5. At weekly meetings attended by both peer networkers and the classroom teacher, students discuss and refine their support network. Evidence of progress is celebrated and as action plans and goals are achieved, students may leave the network if they wish.

Support networks can assist students in acknowledging and using skills that are valuable to others. Through positive interdependence, students not only enhance self-esteem but may improve their academic and social skills as well.

GUIDELINES FOR ENHANCING SELF-ESTEEM

Since classroom approaches to enhancing self-esteem are limitless, some brief guidelines follow to assist teachers in their efforts to address this important part of classroom learning:

1. **Each day, acknowledge every student in the classroom either verbally or non-verbally.**

2. **Maintain high expectations for each child.**

3. **Seek student input on ways to make classroom learning relevant and meaningful.**

4. **Involve students in establishing classroom rules, lessons, and assessment approaches.**

5. **Provide hands-on, multimodal learning experiences.**

6. **Use a variety of group processes including pairs, and both small and large group options.**

7. **Assist students in identifying their strengths both in and outside of the classroom.**

8. **Acknowledge each student's positive qualities and contributions in ways that are appropriate for each child.**

9. **Help students understand that setbacks are a part of the learning process and yield important feedback on ways to proceed more effectively in the future.**

10. **Model positive self-esteem for oneself.**

Many educators' efforts to enhance student self-worth reach far beyond the classroom. In some elementary and secondary schools, children who require extra time and attention are identified. Teachers elect to mentor one or more of the students on an on-going basis. Mentoring responsibilities include any or all of the following: meeting with the students during the teacher's regularly scheduled preparation time, occasional phone calls or visits home, attending extra-curricular activities the student might be involved in, providing tutoring assistance, serving as an advocate for the student at school, connecting the student and/or her family with appropriate community agencies, taking the student out for an occasional lunch, and other activities that evolve as appropriate. With this gift of time, attention, and love, many teachers are helping students discover that they are worthy and lovable. The forging of a positive identity will benefit the students in all aspects of their lives.

SETTING AND ACHIEVING GOALS

Students can discover aspects of their inner selves by intentionally articulating individual interests, strengths, and preferred ways of gaining recognition. Identifying such information is beneficial not only in what it reveals to students but also in providing teachers with information that help them individualize instruction. The following survey asks students to reflect on their desires, anxieties, and preferred forms of praise. The survey can be used in numerous ways: as an ice breaker when new groups have formed, as a data-gathering source of confidential information between teacher and student, or as a small group discussion tool. Before administering the survey, it is advisable to ask students to note items that they want to keep confidential.

STUDENT INTEREST SURVEY

Student Name: _____

1. Three words that describe me are _____

   _____

2. Things I like to do when I'm not at school are _____

   _____

3. The subject I do best at in school is _____

4. I would like to learn more about _____

5. Someday I would like to _____

6. Learning is fun when _____

7. If I could do anything I wanted at school, it would be _____

8. I like to get praise for _____

9. At school, when I've done something well, I like to be acknowledged by _____

10. I wonder a lot about _____

11. I like people who _____

12. Sometimes I worry about _____

13. I learn best when _____

14. One thing that really bothers me is _____

15. Something that really challenges me is _____

16. One thing I know about myself is _____

Once students have completed the survey, they might discuss items they are willing to share with one other person, with a small group, or with the teacher. Ask students to reflect on what they learned about themselves from the activity, what they learned about others, what similarities and differences between themselves and others they discovered, and what might account for the contrasts. The information gathered from the student interest survey might also assist the teacher in planning curriculum and personalized projects that appeal to individual students.

Once interests and challenges are identified, students can more readily identify goals they may wish to pursue. Goal-setting is an important process for students since goals offer concrete and tangible standards for identifying and monitoring progress. When students are able to determine individual goals, their attitude towards learning is frequently enhanced resulting in improved academic performance.

For student-determined goals to be effective, they must meet several criteria: they should be specific rather than general, short-term rather than long-term, harder rather than easier, realistic and not idealistic, and action-oriented rather than passive. The following form can be used to help students identify and meet their personal goals:

INDIVIDUAL STUDENT GOAL SHEET

Student Name: _____ Date: _____

Describe your specific goal for today (this week) (this project): _____
_____
_____

The skills I need to accomplish this goal are: _____
_____
_____

The reason I think I can attain this goal is: _____
_____
_____

Possible challenges I might encounter are: _____
_____
_____

Resources and people I can go to for help are: _____
_____
_____

(Please respond to the following at the end of the activity)

I met or did not meet my goal because _____
_____

From this experience, I learned _____
_____

My level of satisfaction with what I accomplished is _____
_____

What I feel about this project is _____

Goal-setting can be used at any grade level with any content. In addition to academic topics, goals can be identified for social skills such as courtesy, sharing, or collaborative problem-solving, or for behavior issues such as raising hands before speaking, completing assignments on time, or attending class regularly.

When students have set and then met their goals, it is important to point out that any successful outcome resulted from personal effort or ability. It is also helpful to identify the techniques students used that led to their success. Conversely, when students are unsuccessful, explain that the failure was due to a lack of appropriate strategies rather than any lack of intelligence or potential. Since many students do not understand why they failed, it is vital for them to gain insight into how to improve their performance in the future.

CHALLENGING STUDENTS TO LEARN

Occasionally, students may pursue goals at an inappropriate challenge level. When students succeed at easy classroom activities, they often attribute their success to the ease of the task. When they succeed at extremely difficult endeavors, they often credit luck. Neither type of success enhances a student's self-worth. Feelings of pride and accomplishment result from succeeding at activities that are at the edge of one's ability level or in the Soviet psychologist's Lev Vygotsky's terminology "in the zone of proximal development." Students need opportunities to learn what is just beyond their grasp.

When developing challenging classroom procedures, the teacher may discuss with students how to set stimulating goals. Students can reflect on their individual goals to determine whether they are just beyond reach. By asking students the following questions, they can learn to identify appropriate challenges that will result in more stimulating learning:

1. **What ability level is challenging for me?**

2. **How might games, simulations, or practice sessions help me learn?**

3. **What would I pursue in depth if I had the opportunity?**

4. **What kinds of learning opportunities are most meaningful to me?**

5. **What motivates me to do my best?**

6. **What learning processes am I using?**

7. **Are there other learning processes that might be more effective?**

8. **How can I learn from my mistakes?**

9. **What kind of feedback is helpful? From whom?**

10. **How do I want to be assessed?**

Teachers who are successful at challenging their students offer feedback on students' efforts without threatening self-confidence and empower them to take control of their learning. They nurture risk-taking and celebrate success. Such teacher behaviors work to instill a love of learning in their students that encourages them to face the world with confidence and curiosity in years to come.

STRATEGIES

FEEDBACK

CHALLENGE

INSIGHT

SUCCESS

OLYMPIAN GOAL-SETTING

Marilyn King, a former Olympic athlete, has investigated what gives peak performers their competitive edge. Marilyn herself was a member of the U.S. Olympics team in 1972 and 1976 and competed in the Pentathlon. While preparing for the 1980 Olympics, Marilyn suffered a back injury that resulted in her being bed-ridden for four months. During that time, while unable to practice physically, she watched films of successful pentathletes, visualizing and mentally rehearsing herself doing the same events. Despite her lack of physical preparation, Marilyn placed second in the trials, and believes her success was the result of her well-prepared psychological state.

After her years of training and competing in the Olympics, Marilyn began wondering why she was able to accomplish so much physically when her athletic skills were, in reality, only slightly above average. To answer this question, she decided to interview other Olympians about their experiences with superior performance. Marilyn hoped to identify any commonalties the peak performers shared.

During their discussions, three consistent elements were identified by the athletes. Peak performance appeared to be based upon passion, vision, and action. Passion was defined as "knowing what really matters on a gut level." The Olympians claimed that what appeared to be willpower and discipline to others was actually inner passion and emotional commitment. Being passionate about something, they claimed, unlocked the energy and creativity necessary to achieve one's goal.

The second component of peak performance was identified as vision. This referred to envisioning one's achievement in detail as well as the "how to" images of attaining the goal. The athletes stated that it was important to understand the influence of self-fulfilling prophecies and to learn how to control one's inner imagery.

The third component, action, emphasized the necessity of taking action on a daily basis according to a plan that brings one closer to one's goal. Action plans included short, intermediate, and long-term goals as well as a daily challenge. While physical skills were important to the Olympian athletes, they determined that superior physical skills were not the primary factor in peak performance. Far more important were passion, vision, and the dedication to daily work at attaining one's goal.

Another interesting aspect of peak performance consists of social support. The Olympic athletes stated that their families did not push them into their activities, but rather helped them believe in their ability to succeed at their goals. Sometimes instead of their families, it was a coach, or a friend who believed in the individual and was there to cheer him on. The Olympians concluded that high performers are not gifted with unique talents. Instead, they have innate abilities common to all of us if we choose to develop them.

Marilyn King now teaches others how to apply the skills of peak performance in any endeavor. She has worked with numerous schools and districts helping students excel aca-

demically. Uniting body, mind, and spirit to achieve a common goal, Marilyn recommends that students and others proceed as follows to push the upper limits of their ability in any endeavor:

Peak Performance Guidelines

1. Identify what one truly cares about, wants to do, or be.

2. Determine the skills, traits, and characteristics needed to achieve the desired goal.

3. Identify the qualities one already possesses and those that need to be developed.

4. Select the traits one wants to acquire.

5. Identify a person knowledgeable in this area who would be willing to serve as a mentor while new traits are developed.

6. Find another person who is also reaching for success and wants to be one's training partner.

7. Identify the major obstacles that must be overcome, and develop action plans to address such obstacles.

8. Create some form of measuring stick or award to acknowledge success along the way.

9. Make a short-term contract to achieve one's goal.

10. Affirm on a daily basis that one already is what one wants to be.

This process for achieving peak performance has been used successfully with Olympic athletes, astronauts, and corporate executives. It has also been successful with inner-city youth who, against numerous odds, have succeeded in earning their high school diplomas. Successful people share the qualities of passion, vision, and action in common. Ordinary people are capable of extraordinary accomplishments when they incorporate the same three qualities into their behavior. Marilyn King's program *Dare to Imagine* is currently being implemented in elementary, junior, and senior high schools to help students increase their performance in and outside of school.

THINKING SKILLS

Many educators, philosophers, and psychologists agree that an important goal of education is the teaching of thinking. Today's society demands creative, critical thinkers. Yet educational systems that focus on single right or wrong answers do not produce this kind of thinking. Students must be prepared to face a world of rapid change, seemingly unanswerable questions, and complex personal decisions.

The teaching of thinking can assist in meeting individual and societal needs and benefit both. The success of our institutions, private enterprise, and the democratic system are all based upon a population's ability to analyze problems, make thoughtful decisions, and create workable solutions. Ethical, altruistic, creative, and long-range thinking are desirable and needed attributes of an educated person at the dawn of the 21st century. By acquiring effective thinking processes, students can probe their own inner natures, learn to self-monitor and adjust, and to discern who and what they are and can be, both in their personal and professional lives.

Thinking skills programs have been developed and implemented in schools around the country. Arthur Costa's book *Developing Minds* contains an overview of 30 such programs. Costa and others caution against teaching thinking as a separate topic recommending instead that thinking skills be taught in conjunction with regular classroom content. They suggest that educators teach not only rich and interesting content, but also an array of cognitive skills so that students can meaningfully use information, not only academically, but also socially and personally. It is helpful if teachers model the ongoing development of their own thinking skills such as intellectual curiosity, flexibility, goal-setting, and problem-solving to encourage similar efforts in their students.

There are many types of thinking skills. Some of the terms commonly used include higher order thinking skills, learning-to-learn skills, questioning strategies, decision-making, problem-solving, and metacognition. Although it is beyond the scope of this book to explore the whole spectrum of thinking skills, the next section introduces classroom activities that engage metacognitive processes.

METACOGNITION

One way that human beings are distinct from other forms of life is our ability to reflect upon our own thinking. The term metacognition literally means "thinking about one's thinking." Through reflecting on how they learn at school, students can gain metacognitive insight about their individual thinking processes. There are several aspects to metacognition. Some include awareness of one's preferred mode of learning, commitment to and persistence in tasks, goal-setting, attitude towards learning, risk-taking, and paying attention. To assist students in gaining metacognitive awareness, teachers may want to plan class discussions or create questionnaires in which students reflect on their self-knowledge as learners. Such processes provide insight into students' individual characteristics and into attitudes that are beneficial or detrimental to their thinking.

Through self-observation, students begin to perceive the personal control they possess in academic and non-academic situations. They can learn that the ultimate responsibility for commitment, attitude, attention, and persistence rests with them. Such metacognitive awareness can encourage students to make successful choices for effectively refining their behavior.

Gaining Control of the Learning Process

Another aspect of metacognition entails giving students the tools to control their own learning experiences. At the outset of an assignment, students benefit from gaining an overview of what is expected of them and how best to proceed. Ideally, students should be informed of what facts and concepts are required, and which strategies or procedures are necessary for success. Frequently, asking students to consider what should happen before, during, and after a task provides them with information for effectively managing their learning. For example, if students were asked to illustrate the process of photosynthesis, they might initially ask if they knew enough to complete the task, if they should seek additional information, and if so, where and how? During the drawing of the photosynthesis model, students might decide whether they had adequate information, whether the model was accurate, and if not, how to revise it. After the drawing is complete, they might then reflect on what was learned and what else they might like to know.

In order to teach students to manage their assignments effectively, the following form asks questions to help them organize their learning:

How should I start this project?

ASSIGNMENT PLANNING & REFLECTING FORM

Student Name: _____

Before you begin this assignment, answer the following:

Brief description of the assignment: _____

_____

What I already know about this topic: _____

_____

Facts or concepts I must know or learn to complete this assignment: _____

_____

Resources I have to turn to for assistance: _____

_____

Activities that will help me succeed at this assignment include: _____

_____

What I should do before beginning this assignment: _____

_____

After you have completed this assignment, aswer the following:

What I did during the middle of this assignment: _____

_____

On completing this assignment, I found I learned the following facts and concepts:

_____

On completing this assignment, I realized I learned the following about the processes I used:

_____

I am now curious about _____

_____

My feelings about this task are: _____

_____

Until recently there has been little recognition that thinking skills can be taught and learned. The above information begins to identify key components of thinking that may be integrated into instruction. When applied to classroom activities, such information helps students learn more effectively, enhances their intellectual processes, and provides them with valuable insight into their nature as learners and as individuals.

EMOTIONALLY INTELLIGENT EDUCATION

Research in the neurosciences is revealing that emotions and cognition, long considered separate and distinct from each other, are clearly linked. The research of Dr. Paul MacLean at the National Institute of Mental Health suggests that information is processed not only by the neocortex, which controls higher order thinking processes, but also by the limbic system, which is the emotional center of the brain.

MacLean suggests that positive emotions such as love and humor can facilitate the neocortex's higher order thought processes, whereas negative emotions such as tension, fear, anger, or distrust inhibit learning and higher order thinking. Whether or not a student learns may be dependent upon emotions that affect all thought processes and are a key component of intrapersonal intelligence. Teachers can assist students in gaining awareness of as well as finding positive ways to express their emotions. In so doing, teachers will be enhancing the learning process.

ENGAGING FEELINGS IN THE CLASSROOM

While emotional issues are overlooked in some classrooms, it is frequently this aspect of intrapersonal intelligence that determines whether we will get along with our peers and ourselves. With the current changes in family structures, many children bring to school needs that are not necessarily met at home. In order to succeed academically, some children require positive emotional outlets. For teachers interested in assisting the development of this aspect of intrapersonal intelligence, there are ways to engage and develop healthy emotional expression in educational settings. Some approaches include establishing a positive classroom environment, recognizing the range of feelings students experience, teaching appropriate methods of emotional expression, and offering feedback on emotional behavior. Some suggestions follow for addressing the affective domain of human experience in the classroom:

ESTABLISHING AN ENVIRONMENT THAT PERMITS EMOTIONAL EXPRESSION

The classroom environment can facilitate emotional expression of both students and teacher. To determine whether a classroom adequately encompasses the affective domain, it may be helpful for teachers to reflect on their own receptivity to emotions. The following questions can facilitate such reflection.

Are lessons taught with emotional expression?

What kinds of feelings are encouraged in the classroom? From whom?

What behaviors or feelings are discouraged? Why?

How are emotions expressed—verbally, physically, or visually?

What tools do students possess to express their feelings? What tools might they need?

When are feelings expressed—at lunch or recess, during math?

How might appropriate expression of emotion be encouraged in the classroom?

By reflecting on such questions, teachers may gain insight into their classrooms' emotional ambiance as well as their own comfort with emotional expression in the school setting.

If they are interested in creating an enhanced affective atmosphere in their classrooms, teachers might intentionally increase the emotional impact of their instruction. Students respond both to content that is taught and how it is taught. When planning lessons, teachers may want to highlight the potential feelings associated with different subjects or topics. Is there humor, pathos, courage, or intrigue to emphasize so that the minds and hearts of students become engaged in their learning?

One high school algebra teacher wearied of the negative reaction his students had whenever story problems were assigned. Deciding to relieve student anxiety, the teacher donned a monster mask one day during math class and announced that he was the story problem monster. In a fearsome, booming voice he stomped around the room, bemoaning the ghoulish nature of story problems, and howling the students' typical complaints about such assignments. Delighted with their teacher's display of humor and fun, the students eagerly attacked the day's assignment and laughed through similar assignments in the weeks that followed.

In addition to teaching with feeling, educators can teach students about emotional expression through appropriate role-modeling. By identifying and expressing their own feelings, students learn that the classroom can accommodate this dimension of human experience. A teacher might want to reflect on current emotional issues or events that are relevant for the students and then risk speaking from his heart. Chances are the students will respond in kind.

Asking students to share their emotional reactions to coursework involves them in expressing feelings in a low risk way. Such discussions often reveal unsuspected insights about class lessons and give students the opportunity to reflect on their affective experience of school work. By encouraging honest answers, teachers can monitor and adjust assignments to reduce anxiety or boredom. Conversations might follow about the importance of positive emotion for enhancing learning, and teachers and students could work together to make the classroom and its activities as positive as possible.

Time might also be set aside on a weekly, monthly, or as-needed basis for class meetings when students, teachers, and/or guest speakers openly discuss emotional issues of concern to the group. By allotting time for emotionally-charged topics, the teacher demonstrates that such discussions are valuable learning opportunities. Spontaneous emotional events that erupt in the classroom also provide rich opportunities for reflection.

By modeling appropriate emotional expression and initiating conversations about affective issues, teachers can create classrooms that nurture students wholistically. When students tap their emotional nature, they connect with a wellspring of energy to apply to learning and remembering.

IDENTIFYING FEELINGS

By acknowledging and experiencing a variety of feelings, students develop a strong emotional foundation that enriches their lives. Frequently, however, many children lack the vocabulary to identify their emotions and can only indicate a limited number of feelings such as "happy" or "sad" that they have experienced. Creating a emotional vocabulary helps students name and begin to understand inner experiences. Some ideas follow to expand affective vocabulary.

Students might be asked to name diverse feelings. One way is to identify one or more emotions for each letter of the alphabet. Another is to create six broad categories of feelings such as happy, sad, mad, confused, strong, weak, and fearful. To work with feeling categories, students brainstorm at least ten words synonymous with each category. For example, under "confused," students might add "addled, anxious, baffled, bewildered, bothered, confounded, disoriented, embarrassed, foggy, flustered, mixed-up, muddled, panicky, and uncertain."

After diverse emotions have been identified, students might reflect on how many of the listed feelings they have personally experienced, how the feelings affected them physically and intellectually, when they experienced them, and how and why their feelings changed.

Teachers may want to display the emotions alphabet or categories of feelings in the classroom so that they are available to include in dis-

cussions or in student writing. Such displays also serve to remind students of the range of emotional experiences commonly encountered within.

EXPRESSING EMOTIONS

Students need opportunities to express their feelings and to channel them into constructive outlets. As MacLean's research demonstrates, emotions inhibit or facilitate learning. Once students identify their affective experiences, it may be appropriate to provide them with a variety of options for self-expression. To assess current emotional behaviors, teachers may ask students to respond to the following inventory:

FEELINGS INVENTORY

Most people experience and express feelings in a variety of ways. Suggest to students that they consider how they typically respond to different emotions and to answer the following:

1. When I am happy, I often _____

2. When I am worried, I _____

3. When I am confident, I _____

4. When I am nervous, I often _____

5. When I am bored, I often _____

6. When I am excited, I _____

7. When I am scared, I might _____

8. When I am confused, I _____

9. When I am upset, I sometimes _____

10. When I am feeling content I _____

Once students have completed the inventory, they may want to review it and add the name of someone with whom they can be happy, worried, or excited. Next, arrange students into small groups for a discussion of how they currently express emotions, sharing two or more feelings they are willing to discuss with their classmates. (They should not be expected to share the names of individuals they have listed.) Also, students might analyze how their emotional reactions affect others. Next, the groups might generate alternative responses to each of the inventory items. Once completed, everyone's responses can be shared so that multiple options are identified for expressing common feelings. One group of eighth-grade students who had been discussing their responses to different life events created the following list to display in their classroom:

When you Feel Upset, You Can...

1. **Have a discussion with someone you trust.**

2. **Go for a walk, run, or do some kind of physical activity.**

3. **Listen to music that you enjoy.**

4. **Do some art work of your choice.**

5. **Write in a journal.**

6. **Take a shower.**

7. **Cry!**

8. **Go shopping.**

9. **Brainstorm all the possible ways to react to the situation and choose one.**

10. **Play an instrument.**

11. **Talk it out with a pet.**

12. **Play a game.**

13. **Seek advice.**

14. **Watch a video or go to a movie.**

15. **Know that your feelings will shift and change, so be patient with yourself.**

Expressing Feelings through the Arts

Intentional instruction in emotional behavior can encourage important intrapersonal development. There are numerous creative approaches to educating the emotions in the classroom. The arts, including the visual arts, drama, movement, or music let students access their feelings while relieving stress, hurt, or excessive excitement. As powerful tools for channeling feelings into positive and creative expression, the arts can be integrated into classroom activities at appropriate times. When a teacher senses that emotional issues raised in the classroom should be processed, they may want to review the following suggestions to identify which might be useful in any given situation:

Visual art: Suggest that students draw their feelings, using color, abstract shapes, or images to represent the issues they are addressing. Students might also watch a film or video that addresses some of the concerns.

Music: To relax, students might listen to background music played for the entire class or individually through headsets. They could also compose music or write lyrics as a way to express feelings. Some may want to choreograph a dance to familiar or original music. Certain musical selections can be played to evoke specific feelings such as Tchaikovsky's "Nutcracker Suite" for happiness, Dvorak's "Symphony No. 5 in E Minor" for sadness, and Edvard Grieg's "Peer Gynt Suite" for fear.

Role play: Hypothetical, impromptu situations generated by students or teacher can be performed to address emotional issues. Mini-dramas might deal with fictitious characters but real events. (Refer to the kinesthetic chapter for additional ideas.)

Creative writing: Students might create clusters or mindmaps, beginning with their feelings as central concepts. Their associations can be synthesized into a poem or paragraph. Stream-of-consciousness journal writing or story writing may also serve as appropriate outlets for some.

Sculpting: Students may want to use clay to sculpt in abstract or representative forms the emotions they are experiencing such as "angry" or "happy" shapes.

While the arts offer a language for feelings, some students require other forms of emotional response. For those who become especially aggressive or angry, time-out options such as running laps or hitting a punching bag in the gym may release excessive tension. (It is especially important with such students to teach the conflict management techniques described in the interpersonal chapter.) Some students need to process their feelings by talking with one another in a quiet part of the classroom or out in the hallway. Fantasy, guided imagery, and relaxation techniques are soothing de-stressers in or outside of the classroom.

Literature, containing emotionally-charged issues, in fiction or non-fiction stories, books, or articles, offers a springboard for discussing and expressing feelings. Once a selection for sharing is identified, prepare the students for the context of the material, read it, and then begin a class discussion. Some excellent resources that address the feeling life of students through literature include *Helping Children Cope: Mastering Stress through Books and Stories* by Joan Fassler, *Books to Help Children Cope with Separation and Loss* by Joan Bernstein and *The New Read-Aloud Handbook* by Jim Trelease.

Occasionally, a student's emotional needs may require the help of a school counselor, intervention or at-risk specialist, psychologist, or psychiatrist. Both teachers and students should know whom to turn to for help including available community resources. Teachers can also ask students to identify individuals they can trust in times of need. The following form may prove helpful for identifying such resources:

RESOURCES FOR PERSONAL SUPPORT

Consider those whom you trust, and list their phone numbers:

Friend: _____

No. _____

Teacher: _____

No. _____

Neighbor: _____

No. _____

Relative: _____

No. _____

Counselor: _____

No. _____

Identify by name and phone the following community resources should you or a friend need their services:

Emergency (911) _____

Crisis Line _____

Children's Protective Services _____

Youth Suicide Prevention _____

Mental Health Center_____

Runaway Hot Line _____

Hospital _____

Alcohol/ Drug Help Line _____

Youth Services_____

Family Services _____

Community Information Line _____

Public Health _____

Other _____

In order to better meet special needs, some schools are integrating human services into their programs cutting across the traditional boundaries of education, mental health, and welfare. For example, at Ashland High School in Ashland, Oregon, an on-site health clinic features mental health programs, drug and alcohol dependency services, career counseling, and juvenile department representatives.

Classrooms, with their emphasis upon academic material and cognitive development, frequently overlook affective development. When educational programs offer opportunities to bring emotional knowledge and assumptions to awareness, students may experience healthier emotional growth. The above activities create a classroom environment that invites emotional expression, enhances students' affective awareness, provides opportunities for children to seek ideas about emotional expression from others, and offers numerous options for self-expression. There are, however, other aspects of affective education that have not yet been addressed. Students also need opportunities to understand values and ultimately develop their own value systems. The next section begins to address these needs.

EDUCATING FOR HUMAN VALUES

The word value is derived from the Latin word, *valere*, meaning to be worth, to be strong. Values refer to the ideals that are significant in our lives. They are established by family, school, society, religion, and our personal belief systems. Some values may be maintained throughout one's entire life, while others may change as a result of experience and/or maturity.

While debate exists about whether schools should teach values, students are confronted with a variety of temptations and distractions. It appears that willingly or not, schools must address some form of ethical education. One approach is to teach commonly accepted values that underlie both traditional religious and secular principles such as integrity, altruism, justice, honesty, human dignity, and diligence. All students need opportunities to identify their ethical perspectives, to find inner purpose and direction from their value systems, and then translate that commitment into their daily behavior.

Many traditional school subjects already contain numerous ethical issues. Teachers might enlist students in thought-provoking discussions in literature, for example, by asking students to reflect on the ethical dilemmas of characters. In science and technology, students can discuss the implications and possible future consequences of technological advances as well as social and political priorities in practice today. In history, contrasting historical accounts of the same event might be shared and the underlying ethical perspective of each account probed.

More directly, schools can assist students in discerning personally-held values by identifying and defining such concepts. Students may be given the following list and in small groups come up with definitions as well as examples of how such values are expressed in daily life.

Some Common Values

Altruism	Honesty	Compassion
Humility	Consideration	Integrity
Courage	Interdependence	Courtesy
Justice	Creativity	Kindness
Determination	Love	Dignity
Loyalty	Diligence	Mercy
Empathy	Patience	Enthusiasm
Peace	Excellence	Respect
Faithfulness	Responsibility	Forgiveness
Self-discipline	Friendliness	Tolerance
Generosity	Trust	Helpfulness
	Truthfulness	

By individually reflecting on the list, students can identify which values they currently hold and which ones they might like to develop. By using the goal-setting processes mentioned earlier, students can select a new value to integrate into their behavior. Needless to say, the models that teachers and parents present are far more powerful than any list of terms. School-wide conversations with parents can also be initiated to identify the most important values to be inculcated within the school community. It may also be necessary to point out to students that if they want to establish and live by a value system, it is necessary to act upon their belief system. Speaking up for one's beliefs, acting upon them, and maintaining them over time is indicative of a person whose life is founded upon personal integrity.

As students clarify and express values they hold, they will also confront and interact with the value systems of others. Learning to defend one's values without diminishing those who maintain different perspectives will become an important skill. Perhaps our classrooms can begin to demonstrate the respectful free speech that democracy requires. Through opportunities to interact with different value systems, students may find that they can strengthen their interpersonal and intrapersonal intelligences:

Have you learned lessons only of those
who admired you, and were tender with you
and stood aside for you? Have you not
learned great lessons from those who
braced themselves against you
and disputed the passage with you?

—*WALT WHITMAN, 1860*

JOURNAL WRITING

Some years ago, a study of high-achieving students in the Yale University graduating class was undertaken to determine whether there were common denominators in their success. It was discovered that the top ten percent of those students kept clearly in mind their goals and ambitions. Of those, the top one percent were distinguished by the fact that they took time to write out their goals and ambitions. A follow-up study of the students in that class over the next ten years revealed that those who clearly articulated their vision for the future were among the most successful in their chosen work, and the most successful of those were still writing down their goals and ambitions.

Some of the greatest thinkers, inventors, and creative geniuses throughout history have kept journals. Leonardo da Vinci's notebooks are filled with ideas, observations and insights, sketches, and plans for his works of art and inventions. Samuel Pepys is still remembered for the diary he kept in the 17th Century. Einstein and Schweitzer both maintained journals.

It seems that the simple act of writing can often move abstractions into reality. Gabriele Rico, author of *Writing the Natural Way*, noted in a recent interview that "writing is always there for us to use for the kind of exploration that leads to discovery, recognition, and new learning about ourselves, our feelings, and the world in general."

When students are encouraged to keep journals in any subject-matter area, they often make those discoveries about themselves. These insights, springing from the boundless resources of intrapersonal intelligence, are thus brought into consciousness and into reality.

SUGGESTIONS FOR CLASSROOM JOURNAL WRITING

For those who wish to incorporate journal writing into classroom activities some suggestions follow:

Ideally, students should be allowed to keep their journals private even though they may use class time to write. Needless to say, much of the value of personal writing lies in the student's confidence that their journals will be free from grading and public sharing. Once a week, students may be asked, however, to read over their writing from previous days and make observations about their progress, or to quote particular comments they would like to share with the teacher or the class. Once again, no grades!

Student journal writing can easily complement the goals of the teacher and help the student maintain a record of his progress. Journals can be used to explore one's thinking on any subject. Sometimes when we read what we have written we may be surprised to learn what we think.

Asking students to write what they know about a subject before beginning to learn about it can establish an anticipatory set which is essential to learning. Just five minutes of such writing at the beginning of learning something new can pay high dividends in terms of student involvement.

At the end of class, five minutes of journal writing can also be rewarding in terms of consolidating prior learning and reviewing at a time when it is most effective. At the outset, the teacher may wish to suggest a few questions to "prime the pump." For example, "What did you learn today that was new to you?" "How did you feel about the learning experience?" "How do you think you can apply what you learned to other subjects or in other areas of your life?" "In the light of what you learned today, what do you anticipate you will be learning about next?"

"What are five good questions to ask tomorrow?" "What can you add to the subject from your personal experience?"

Later on, once students have become used to journal writing, the teacher may wish to ask them to do a five or ten minute "fastwrite." A "fastwrite" consists of writing as quickly as possible everything they can remember about what they just learned. Or students may be asked to make a mindmap or cluster before they write. For many students, as discussed previously, this process can springboard them into accessing feelings, insights, and connections that may not yet have reached their conscious mind. It may be useful to create a format for journals such as using the left page for mindmaps, and the right page for writing. Some people combine the two on the same page, as does prolific journal-keeper Bob Samples, author of *The Metaphoric Mind* and numerous other books.

Many teachers and students have found that journal writing yields significant improvement in understanding and retention which often results in increased scores on both objective tests and essay tests. In addition, students identify their own emotional reactions to and personal insights into classroom learning.

JOURNALS FOR PERSONAL INSIGHT

Keeping a journal may also be suggested for an in-depth probing of intrapersonal intelligence. Students may explore their own identities through writing that accesses self-awareness, self-acceptance, self-actualization, and self-disclosure. Teachers could assign journal sessions for older students that include responses to the following:

1. **Students might be asked to write ten "I am" sentences that reveal their understanding of themselves. In preparing to write, students may want to consider the self-awareness they have gained from life experiences, interactions**

with others, from their world views, and from images of how they would like to be as people compared to how they currently are.

2. To enlist self-acceptance, students might reflect on positive qualities they already possess and ones they might like to change. After the ten "I am" sentences are written, ask students to classify the sentences according to several categories 1) their physical attributes, 2) emotional attributes, 3) mental qualities, 4) roles in relationship to others such as sister, son, or friend. Students can evaluate their responses in terms of what is or is not growth-promoting. Then additional statements might be written that state "I lack......," then the ideal correlate "I will.......," onto "I want to....... ," and finally "I am."

3. Students might also reflect on other important aspects of self-acceptance such as the image they are attempting to live up to, the constant change they must cope with, and the answers to some of life's questions they must live without. They might also evaluate their own level of self-esteem and identify how it could be improved.

4. Students might reflect on their internally motivated growth. Explain to students that self-actualization consists of capitalizing on one's strengths and abilities, making decisions that serve one's own and others' best interests, and remaining flexible and open to life's possibilities and events. As students ponder their ability to self-actualize, they may want to articulate their potential, how they plan to actualize it, and how such actualization may ultimately benefit others. To help students work towards such possibilities, ask them to record their goals and list actions they might take to achieve them.

5. After the above activities have been completed, students might next consider what they would be willing to share or disclose to a small group of classmates. In their small groups, students might intentionally commit themselves to personal growth, to emotional expression, to trust, to clarification of their thoughts, and to risk-taking. In their small groups, students can share, discuss, and receive feedback on their journal entries.

GETTING TO KNOW ONESELF THROUGH OTHERS

Gardner maintains that the personal intelligences are inextricably linked and that under ordinary circumstances, neither can develop without the other. It is through relationship with others that one gains knowledge of the self. Observing how others think about and respond to an individual reveals much information that shapes one's sense of self. When intrapersonal intelligence is well-developed, the purpose of self-knowledge might be to forego one's personal agenda in efforts to insure the smoother functioning of the broader community. Through interacting with others we gain a deeper appreciation for our personal identities and by knowing who we are, we can contribute to the betterment of others. Ultimately, our sense of self, as Gardner suggests, results from a fusion of one's interpersonal and intrapersonal knowledge.

Many of the strategies suggested elsewhere in this book yield intrapersonal insights. Whenever students interact with others, their intrapersonal knowledge can be enhanced by reflecting on what they learned. What feedback did they receive from others? How did they respond to it? Was the feedback accurate? Why or why not? What did the students learn about themselves from their own reactions to the activity? Which of these reactions do they feel good about? What is one thing they might wish to improve?

Teachers may also want to develop activities in which, working with partners or small groups, students are encouraged to ask thoughtful questions that shed light on their growing sense of self. Some suggestions follow:

GAINING INTRAPERSONAL INSIGHTS FROM INTERPERSONAL FEEDBACK

1. As a group ice breaker, students might conduct interviews of each other. The information gained from the interviews might then be used to introduce one another to the class. Interview questions might consist of:

   What would your life motto be?

   What are three wishes you would like granted?

   What is the most important value that guides your life?

   Who is your hero/ heroine?

   What is one of your fears?

   If you could change anything about yourself, what would it be?

   If you could change anything about the world, what would it be?

   When the introductions are being made, classmates should feel free to ask additional questions of the student being introduced.

2. In pairs, students might explore personal perceptions of themselves and their partners. Topics that can guide such conversations might include:

   Who I think I am

   Who you think I am

   Who I think you think I am

   Who you think you are

   Who I think you are

   Who you think I think you are

   When the conversations are complete, students might reflect in their journals how their self-perceptions compare with the perceptions of others.

3. Students might be asked to give a brief speech on an object that has deep, personal meaning in their lives. Perhaps the object has affected their personal development, perhaps it has sentimental value, or perhaps it indicates a symbol of their futures. For the brief speech, the student should bring the object to the class, describe how it works or what it means, and tell a story of the role it represents in their lives. Again, classmates should be able to pose questions at the end of the speeches.

4. For an assignment, students might write a character sketch of themselves. Since these will be shared with the rest of the class, fictitious names are necessary to keep the writings anonymous at first. In their character descriptions, students should include multisensory details about themselves, their behaviors and the reasons for them, their desires and goals, and their impact upon others. On an agreed-upon date, the anonymous descriptions should be brought to class with the students' real names written and concealed on the backs of their papers. The teacher can then organize students into small groups, hand out character descriptions of those in the group, and have the students read and discuss the writings. Each group should then determine whose descriptions they are reading and explain the reasons for their matches or mismatches.

REFLECTING ON THE WONDER AND PURPOSE OF LIFE

Life for all of us is a Great Mystery.
The big questions like, 'What is the universe?'
'Where does it come from?'
'Who am I?' 'What is my purpose?'
- are the questions we all come
face to face with eventually.

—HERBERT MARTIN, *Professor,*
Department of Teacher Education,
California State University, Sacramento

The word education evolved from the Latin *educare*, which means to draw out or lead forth. The original definition of the word, then, suggests that schooling can facilitate the expression of what is contained within one's mind, heart, and the deepest recesses of being. Both children and adults seek meaning in their experiences and answers to humankind's ageless questions. While each individual arrives at personal explanations to life's mysteries, it is possible for classrooms to create the conditions for wonder and awe to flourish. Encouraging the expression of children's wisdom and helping them grapple with meaning-making educates in personal, relevant, and profound ways.

How can we cultivate a sense of wonder in children? How can we assist them in articulating their insights and posing their questions? One answer is to expose them to a curriculum enriched with all seven intelligences. Language can be used to reflect and discuss feelings, thoughts, and ideals significant to each student; math reveals numerical principles in operation throughout nature and on a universal scale; games evoke challenge and delight, while relaxation and visualization ready our bodies and minds for contemplation; dance, the visual arts, and music all express insights through the symbol systems of the arts; and the personal intelligences provide opportunities for interaction which enable us to know and understand others and ourselves better. Teaching and learning through all the intelligences lets us perceive through multiple lenses the wholeness within. Such wholistic teaching also enables children to discover an inherent area of personal interest and fascination that may spark a lifetime of personal or professional pursuit.

Some teachers desire to encourage their students to wonder, to question, and to forge meaning in their lives. We offer some suggestions below that enable students to use their imaginations in pondering life's possibilities:

CLASSROOM ACTIVITIES TO NURTURE A SENSE OF WONDER:

1. **By creating original poems, myths, legends and tall tales, students may reflect on the mysteries of life while seeking their own answers and explanations.**

2. **Children may write, draw, or compose a song about an event that changed their lives and what they learned from that experience.**

3. **Teachers might create a visualization exercise in which students travel into time to view themselves and personal concerns from a distant perspective, imagining themselves in a safe and beautiful place in which to do problem-solving, and seeing a future newspaper with headings that refer to their achievements.**

4. **Classroom discussions may be initiated about what is important and of value in life.**

5. **Students may be asked to react to the qualities, values, and actions of those featured in stories or poems.**

6. **Students may be asked to respond to works of art in verbal or non-verbal ways.**

7. **Students may write a letter to an unknown person introducing themselves by including descriptions of their appearance, activities, interests, significant people in their lives, as well as their hopes and dreams for the future. This letter may be to a prospective pen-pal, employer, or someone they would like to meet.**

8. Students may create a self-portrait by drawing a diamond shape, a circle, or a crest, and dividing it into a number of parts to include any of the following: the physical attributes they possess, intellectual qualities, artistic skills, emotional characteristics, social qualities, fears they have, wishes and dreams they hold, major turning points, and essential values. Students may then draw or write in each section of their self-portrait what is most descriptive of them and share it with their classmates if desired. This same activity may also be done in the future tense by drawing the attributes and qualities they hope to acquire a year from now, or five years from now.

9. Students might be encouraged to pay attention to their intuitive hunches while using reason to check the accuracy of their intuitions.

FINDING PURPOSE IN SCHOOL AND LIFE

When planning lessons to teach any topic or concept, educators must reflect upon an important question: "So what?" Students want and deserve to know the relevance of what they are learning to their lives. They wonder, "What can I do with this information?" "Can it be used in the real world?" "How will it benefit others?" When beginning a new lesson or unit, the teacher may want to engage the class in a discussion of the larger purpose underlying coursework. In addition to the instructor's perspective, students can share their perceptions of the meaningfulness of classroom assignments. Ideally, each student should be able to identify one valid reason for investing time, energy, and effort in their school work.

Some teachers are interested in addressing one of the greatest questions of all—the purpose of life—with their students. To begin such discussions, it is first necessary to define purpose as something we are compelled to do and as a process that continues to unfold throughout our lives. Purpose provides a sense of direction and a means of contributing to the betterment of others.

One way that students may access their own inner sense of purpose is through writing activities that address a topic such as the one following.

To prepare, ask students to get paper and pencil ready and then sit quietly in their seats. Explain that you will ask them a series of questions that help reveal one's inner sense of direction. They need only to write down key words and phrases or make note of any fleeting image that appears. Explain that you will ask the questions slowly, giving them time to seek their answers from within themselves:

- **What are you good at?**
- **What have you always loved?**
- **What do you care for the most?**
- **What have you always known?**
- **What do you feel compelled to do?**

Ask students to continue to sit for a moment or two in silence, making note of ideas or images present, then discuss in pairs or small groups any insights they choose to volunteer. For those who may not have glimpsed images or insights during the exercise, suggest that they make up answers to the questions that seem most appropriate for them. Students may also discuss what aspects of their schooling contribute to their perceived life purpose.

While it may appear that it is adolescents and teenagers who would benefit most from reflecting on life purpose, young children often possess a very strong sense of direction also. At the age of four, one of the authors of this book informed family members that she was going to be a teacher, and she has never once swerved from that childhood certainty. Frequently, young children love to fantasize about what they will be, enjoy discussing their interests, and value acknowledgment from adults who make them believe their childhood dreams will come true. Educators can open the doors to wonder.

SELF-DIRECTED LEARNING: AN INTRAPERSONAL LEARNING APPROACH

Self-directed learning is an outstanding example of intrapersonal education since it is founded upon student choice and autonomy. Conventional educational approaches are based on autocratic principles that require teachers to serve as authority figures with infrequent opportunities for student choice or participation in decision-making. In self-directed classrooms, however, the student rather than the teacher is the central decision-maker, and self-motivation and self-discipline are the keys to success. With guidance from teachers, students select and manage their own learning processes, including the topic to be studied, the goals to pursue, the learning strategies and activities to apply, and the resources to utilize. They may also have some choice in how to demonstrate and assess their accomplishments. The teacher's role expands from teaching content to teaching learning processes so that students can experience success in designing and managing independent learning.

Some teachers use self-directed learning as a primary mode of instruction while others use it less frequently such as once or twice during an academic term. Most self-directed learning programs are organized with a learning contract. Frequently, the contracts are negotiated with the student, parents, and teacher. One such sample contract follows:

SELF-DIRECTED LEARNING CONTRACT

Name: _____

Project Topic: _____

Goals: (What do you want to leran?) _____
_____
_____

Learning Strategies: (Howare you going to learn about it?) _____
_____
_____

Resources: (Who and what will provide information?) _____
_____
_____

Tasks and Timeline: (What will you accomplish when?) _____
_____
_____

Demonstration: (How will you demonstrate what you have learned?) _____
_____
_____

Evaluation: (How would you like to be evaluated?) _____
_____

As is evident from the contract, students determine what and how to learn, a timeframe, ways to demonstrate their newly acquired competence, and persons to verify their skills. The teacher's role consists of working with individuals and small groups, diagnosing student abilities, negotiating contracts, arranging contacts for the students to pursue, and helping students problem-solve around planning, managing time, and utilizing resources.

Since motivation to learn springs primarily from the needs, interests, and aspirations of students, teachers who use self-directed learning do not need to rely on material rewards or competitive activities. When students have a choice about what they want to study, they typically pursue their interests in greater depth.

Classrooms, teachers, and students need to make gradual adjustments as they move into self-directed formats. Many students are unfamiliar with exercising choice and control over their learning, and many teachers find it difficult to let students decide what they will study and to take responsibility for the results. Most classrooms are not prepared for the extensive networking and incorporation of community resources required for independent learning. For these those teachers interested in working with this intrapersonal aproach, some practical suggestions follow:

SUGGESTIONS FOR IMPLEMENTING SELF-DIRECTED LEARNING:

1. Encourage students of all ages, from kindergarten through high school, to suggest topics of personal interest to study throughout the school year.

2. Teach independent learning skills which include decision-making, problem-solving, goal-setting, time management, and self-evaluation.

3. Enlist both school and community resources for students to access.

4. For primary-age children, teachers might want to establish learning centers in the classroom, each devoted to a different intelligence area, and let students select one to work at daily during "choice time."

5. For elementary through high school-aged students, independent projects can be assigned every other month or so. The projects can be organized with learning contracts.

6. For elementary through secondary level students, the school schedule might be reorganized so that one portion of the day is dedicated to traditional academics and the other to self-directed learning.

7. Some schools attempt to create a complete self-directed learning program with support from parents and the administration. The traditional subjects, grading systems, and learning activities are replaced with those designed by the students, the teacher, and parents together. If possible, children of mixed-ages, or even children and adults have opportunities to study together. Students can be free to move about at will using the school's playground, library, laboratories, classroom, and community resources, within democratically-determined guidelines.

In such programs, long-term concentration, focused interest, enjoyment, and imagination are encouraged. Frequently, tutorials or apprenticeship options are established based upon student interests. For assessment, teachers and others meet frequently with students who exhibit what they have learned and identify what they next wish to pursue.

8. When establishing self-directed learning options, it is important to be aware of the difficulties in adopting such approaches. At the beginning, when students assume responsibility for their learning, they often experience great enthusiasm. Yet when they confront the enormity of the task, they typically feel incompetent or overwhelmed and need assistance with planning and problem-solving. Teachers, too, often have difficulty shifting from dispensing information to facilitating and monitoring their students' efforts.

While an ultimate goal of any educational experience is to produce capable, independent learners, it is ironic that many students never exert choice or control over their learning while in school. All educational programs will benefit from implementing self-directed learning procedures that lead to the development of autonomous learners, ones who are able to nurture their personal and professional growth throughout their lifespans.

TECHNOLOGY THAT ENHANCES INTRAPERSONAL INTELLIGENCE

The development of intrapersonal intelligence can be facilitated through the use of technology to explore and expand the human mind. Technology offers the means to pursue a line of thought in great depth as well as to have random access to divergent ideas. The opportunity for students to make such choices is at the heart of giving them control over their own learning and intellectual development.

Although the most common use of technology in the classroom today is still for drill and practice, many teachers are finding successful applications of computer technology to develop higher-order thinking skills. Classrooms that use computer technology in this way become centers for inquiry. Students learn not only to use databases, but to create their own. Technology can be used to explore and expand intelligence, as students build "mental models" with which they can visualize connections between ideas on any topic.

Bob Olson, senior Associate of the Institute for Alternative Futures in Alexandria, VA., notes that "hypermedia may thus expand the ability to think holistically—to be able to jump back and forth from detail to overview and to see the 'big picture.'" Hypermedia presents multimedia material in a way that is similar to how the human brain works—making connections between ideas and images—just as hypertext does with words.

Computer programs such as Ceres' "Inspiration" are thought processors that make it possible to capture ideas and visualize the relationships between them by combining graphics with text. The programs facilitate individual brainstorming, and as ideas are generated, they can be clustered into mindmaps or into traditional outlines. Mainstay's "Think'n'Time" uses visual outlining to help structure and develop ideas at the same time as other applications are being used. Such programs allow students to manipulate ideas in whatever form best suits their thinking, and they encourage personal ownership of the educational enterprise as students become more active in developing their own learning and understanding.

Individual student learning or personal growth plans, developed collaboratively by student and teacher, encourage the development of intrapersonal intelligence. They can be well facilitated through computer programs that make possible on-going modifications or revisions, as well as the recording of accomplishments in the form of electronic or multimedia portfolios of student work. Research by Allen Tough at the Ontario Institute for Studies in Education indicates that individual learning projects account for around 80 percent of all learning during a lifetime. Thus, learning-to-learn is an essential part of preparation for lifelong learning.

Intelligent tutoring systems are very different from earlier models of computer-assisted learning in that they offer students choices in how to learn any topic, keep track of the students' preferred ways of learning, and eventually offer information in forms that make it possible for students to learn through their strengths as well as to exercise and improve less well-developed skills.

John Sculley, Chief Executive Officer of Apple, suggests that "within a few decades people will look back and wonder how anyone in the past could keep up with knowledge without the assistance of such 'knowbots' or 'knowledge navigators.'" These are powerful tools that can become an extension of the human brain and facilitate the exploration and expansion of intrapersonal intelligence when used in appropriate, interactive ways that are sensitive to the needs of the student.

SUMMARY

In his book *On Becoming a Person* Carl Rogers describes one aspect of intrapersonal intelligence as it develops throughout life. He writes,

> "Becoming a person means that the individual moves toward being, knowingly and acceptingly, the process which he inwardly and actually is. He moves away from what he is not, from being a facade. He is not trying to be more than he is, with the attendant feelings of insecurity or bombastic defensiveness. He is not trying to be less than he is, with the attendant feelings of guilt or self-deprecation. He is increasingly listening to the deepest recesses of his psychological and emotional being, and finds himself increasingly willing to be, with greater accuracy and depth, that self which he most truly is."

To gain deep inner knowing of oneself and to gain peace with that knowledge requires considerable life experience. Intrapersonal intelligence develops gradually over time, and in the classroom, intrapersonal processes require time in planning and teaching as well as time to unfold within the learner. Yet teaching to nurture knowledge of oneself is critically important since such knowing underlies success and fulfillment in life. This chapter has addressed numerous aspects of intrapersonal intelligence including 1) establishing an environment to nurture the sense of self 2) self-esteem enhancers 3) setting and achieving goals 4) thinking skills 5) emotional skills 6) journal-writing 7) getting to know oneself through others 8) reflecting on the wonder and purpose of life 9) self-directed learning, and 10) intrapersonal forms of technology. In order for the reader to summarize, reflect, and synthesize the content of this chapter, we offer the following opportunity for reflection:

APPLYING INTRAPERSONAL INTELLIGENCE

1. Important ideas or insights gleaned from this chapter: _____

_____

_____

_____

2. Areas I'd like to learn more about: _____

_____

_____

_____

3. Ways I can use this information in my teaching. Please note that all of the strategies mentioned in this chapter are listed below with space provided to note how each strategy might be incorporated into classroom instruction:

INTRAPERSONAL STRATEGY	CLASSROOM APPLICATION

Establishing an Environment to Nurture the Sense of Self:
Characteristics of Schools that Nurture Self-Esteem _____

Self-Esteem Enhancers:
Compliment Circles _____
Individual Acknowledgment _____
Peer Support _____
Guidelines for Enhancing Self-Esteem _____

Setting and Achieving Goals:
Student Interest Survey _____
Individual Student Goal Sheet _____
Challenging Students to Learn _____
Olympian Goal-Setting _____

Thinking Skills:
Metacognition _____
Assignment Planning Form _____

Emotionally Intelligent Education in the Classroom:
Establishing an Environment that Permits
Emotional Expression _____
Identifying Feelings _____
Feelings Inventory _____
Expressing Feelings through the Arts _____
Resources for Personal Support _____
Educating for Human Values _____

Journal Writing:
Suggestions for Classroom Journal Writing _____
Keeping a Journal for Personal Insight _____

Getting to Know Oneself Through Others:
Gaining Intrapersonal Insights
through Interpersonal Feedback _____

Reflecting on the Wonder and Purpose of Life:
Classroom Activities to Nurture
a Sense of Wonder _____
Finding Purpose in School and Life _____

Self-Directed Learning: An Intrapersonal Educational Approach:
Self-Directed Learning Contact _____
Suggestions for Implementing
Self-Directed Learning _____

Technology that Enhances Intrapersonal Intelligence: _____

INTRAPERSONAL REFERENCES

Alderman, K. M. (September, 1990). "Motivation for At-Risk Students." in *Educational Leadership*, Volume 48, No. 1.

Batey, A. & Cowell, R. (1986). *Distance Education: An Overview.* Portland, OR: Northwest Regional Educational Laboratory.

Bernstein, J. E. (1977). *Books to Help Children Cope with Separation and Loss.* N.Y.: Bowker.

Bloom, B.S. ed. (1956). *Taxonomy of Educational Objectives: The Classification of Educational Goals. Handbook 1: Cognitive Domain.* N.Y.: David MacKay.

Carkhuff, R., Berenson, D., and Pierce, R. (1977). *The Skills of Teaching: Interpersonal Skills.* Amherst, MA: Human Resource Development Press.

Clifford, Mt. (September,1990). "Students Need Challenge, Not Easy Success." in *Educational Leadership.* Vol. 48 No. 1.

Csikszentmihalyi, M. (1990). *Flow: The Psychology of Optimal Experience.* N.Y.: Harper and Row.

Csikszentmihalyi, M. (1991). "Thoughts about Education" in *Creating the Future: Perspectives on Educational Change.* Ed. Dee Dickinson. Aston Clinton, Bucks., United Kingdom: Accelerated Learning Systems.

Evans, T.D., Corsini, R.J., Gazda, G. M. (September,1990). "Individual Education and the 4Rs" *Educational Leadership.* Vol. 48 No. 1.

Fassler, J. (1978). *Helping Children Cope: Mastering Stress through Books and Stories.* N.Y.: Free Press.

Feuerstein, R. (1980). *Instrumental Enrichment.* Baltimore: University Park Press.

Feuerstein, R., Rand, Y., and Rynders, J.E. (1988). *Don't Accept Me as I am: Helping "Retarded" People to Excel.* N.Y.: Plenum.

Glasser, W. (1986). *Control Theory in the Classroom.* N.Y.: Harper and Rowe.

Gray, P. and Chanoff, D. (May, 1984). "When Play is Learning: A School Designed for Self-Directed Education." *Phi Delta Kappan.*

Greene, B., and Uroff, S. (February, 1989). "Apollo High School: Achievement through Self-Esteem" in *Educational Leadership*, Vol. 46, No. 5.

King, M. (1988). *Dare to Imagine Program: An Olympian's Technology.* Aurora, CO: Mid-Continent Regional Education Laboratory.

Knake, B. (1989). *The Inside World,* May be ordered by sending $10 to Bill Knake at 1802 North 40th Place, Mt. Vernon, WA 98273.

Krathwohl, D., Bloom, B. Masia, B. (1969). *Taxonomy of Educational Objectives: Handbook 2: Affective Domain.* N.Y.: David MacKay.

LePage, A. (1987). *Transforming Education: The New Three R's.* Oakland, CA: Oakmore Press.

Marks, L. (1989). *Living with Vision: Reclaiming the Power of the Heart.* Indianapolis, Indiana: Knowledge Systems.

Marzano, R.J., Brandt, R.S., Hughes C.S. , Jones, B.F., Presseisen, B.Z., Rankin, S.C., and Suhor, C. (1988). *Dimensions of Thinking: A Framework for Curriculum and Instruction.* Alexandria, VA: Association for Supervision and Curriculum Development.

Resnick, L. (1987). *Education and Learning to Think.* National Academy Press: Washington, D.C.

"Restructuring and Technology." (1988). *Radius.* AFT Center for Restructuring. Vol. 1, Nos. 3 and 4.

Rogers, C. (1961). *On Becoming a Person.* Boston: Houghton Mifflin.

Trelease, J. (1989). *The New Read-Aloud Handbook.* N.Y.: Penguin Books.

CHAPTER 8

CURRICULUM DEVELOPMENT
THROUGH THE MULTIPLE INTELLIGENCES

*Ultimately, a full understanding of any concept
of any complexity cannot be restricted to a
single model of knowing or way of representation.*

— *HOWARD GARDNER, The Unschooled Mind*

THE ART IN SCIENCE

"…four hundred
conference-goers
jumped to their feet
in a standing ovation
for the science
students-turned-
actors."

A junior high science class undertook a study of geologic eras and the evolution of plant and animal life. The teacher organized the curriculum thematically, calling the unit Origins, intending to spark student interest in the beginnings and transformations of the planet as well as its life forms. At one point in the unit, students were required to participate in individual or small group projects. To initiate their research, students posed questions to organize and focus their efforts. Numerous resources both inside and outside of the class were pursued in search of answers. At the end of two weeks, the projects were shared with classmates; it was then that the real work began. Appreciative of the quality and content of one another's work, the students objected to bringing their work to closure. Deciding that their material was interesting and well-presented, the class wondered how best to share their learnings with others.

The idea of a play, of combining the projects into a single cohesive drama to be shared with other classes and parents, was suggested and readily embraced. The reports were reformatted into small improvised scenes. Each scene began with the questions that initiated student research and the small vignettes were sequentially arranged according to a geologic timeline. The set consisted of a large, unfolding scroll, 100 feet in length, featuring scenes of plant and animal life, odes to prehistoric events, and geologic graffiti. A choreographer from the local community assisted in the creation of a dance entitled "In the Beginning" and a musician parent working with a group of volunteers composed a song called "Backwards and Forwards in Time."

The resulting play, entitled *Life and Everything You Wanted to Know about It,* was performed for other classes and parents and eventually, for an international educational conference where four hundred conference-goers jumped to their feet in a standing ovation for the science students-turned-actors.

There were numerous ingredients that made the Origins unit a success. Students learned and interacted with their material in numerous modes. They told stories and drew timelines; they painted, sang, and danced the content. They were mentored by others more skilled than themselves, and they received feedback from parents and community members on their efforts.

When provided with open-ended learning experiences, students are capable of perceiving concepts through numerous lenses and applying what they learn in fresh contexts, rather than simply imitating what has been taught. In addition, when the Multiple Intelligences are incorporated into curricular units, it is likely that at least one mode will facilitate learning for each student.

Previous chapters surveyed environmental factors and teaching strategies to expand instructional repertoires while providing students with options to increase the likelihood of their learning. This information would be incomplete without reflecting on an additional aspect of professional practice: curriculum development. Just as Gardner's theory has profound implications for pedagogy, it offers equally provocative options for lessons, units, and school programs.

Backwards and Forwards in Time

THE IMPLICATIONS OF THE THEORY OF MULTIPLE INTELLIGENCES FOR CURRICULUM

Many educators interpret Gardner's work as suggesting numerous entry points into traditional curriculum. The Multiple Intelligences are perceived as instructional processes capable of enhancing student learning in any discipline. Such a perspective in practice often encourages teachers to team with others who possess different professional skills or to include diverse media and technology in a course's curriculum.

Some teachers perceive the Theory of Multiple Intelligences as promoting early specialization with efforts being made to develop each student's area of promise as early as possible. Others maintain that the Theory of Multiple Intelligences is a justification for broadening the curriculum to include a wider variety of courses. Many promote increased time for the visual and performing arts arguing that the arts deserve equal time in the curriculum. For example, at the Key School, the nation's first MI school, the curriculum broadened to feature visual arts, music, creative dramatics, and dance for every student beginning in kindergarten. In addition to the elementary teachers who serve as generalists, the Key School also employs teachers licensed in specialized arts areas to insure that students receive quality arts instruction.

After exposure to Gardner's work, some teachers grapple with fundamental questions such as, "What are schools for if not to engage the greater capacity of each student?" Gardner himself sketches an "individual-centered curriculum" where schools ideally provide educational options responsive to each student. Teachers who desire to identify and nurture the intelligence strengths of each child often attempt to establish apprenticeship and mentoring options for their students.

TEACHING & LEARNING THROUGH THE MULTIPLE INTELLIGENCES

Still others perceive Gardner's work as emphasizing the importance of student understanding, not rote memorizing, of essential curriculum. Insuring that students truly understand academic content so that they can apply their knowledge in new situations is not an easy educational goal to achieve. Reducing the pressure for coverage, project-based teaching, and providing multiple entry points into content are some of the methods educators employ to improve student understanding.

As Howard Gardner has stated, in terms of curricular approaches, the Theory of Multiple Intelligences is like a Rorschach test. Individual teachers and entire schools may go about applying MI curricular ideas in diverse and often conflicting ways. Gardner asserts that one application of his theory is not necessarily "right" and another "wrong." Typically, both approaches can be justified and prove appropriate for their settings.

This chapter explores numerous Multiple Intelligences curricular models. Educators who are considering adopting MI theory may want to reflect on which approaches might be most beneficial for their students and school communities. The specific curricular issues addressed in this chapter include:

LESSON PLANNING THROUGH THE MULTIPLE INTELLIGENCES

The Theory of Multiple Intelligences helps teachers transform existing lessons or units into multimodal learning opportunities for students. Since most teachers are comfortable working with two or three intelligences, attempting to integrate additional capacities involves risk-taking and flexibility. The rewards for such efforts are tangible, however. It is gratifying to observe students' enthusiasm, engagement, and achievement increase while experiencing the expansion of one's own intellectual capacities.

Numerous strategies have been suggested in previous chapters for planning daily or weekly lessons. Many teachers, however, find it daunting to create lessons that incorporate all seven areas. The authors recommend that at least four intelligences serve as entry points into any content. Such efforts provide students with four opportunities to access information while challenging teachers to work in new ways. Teachers often report that thinking in multiple modes for lesson planning becomes second nature during or soon after the first year of teaching through the seven intelligences.

To begin lesson planning, educators might reflect on a concept they want to teach and identify the intelligences that seem most appropriate for communicating such content. Teachers may also seek input from students about ways they would most like to learn. To quickly infuse variety into classroom lessons, the following "Instructional Menus" provide teachers with ready options to expand their pedagogical repertoires:

INSTRUCTIONAL MENUS

LINGUISTIC MENU:

Use storytelling to explain…

Conduct a debate on…

Write a poem, myth, legend, short play, or news article about…

Relate a short story or novel to…

Give a presentation on…

Lead a class discussion on…

Create a talk show radio program about…

Write a newsletter, booklet, or dictionary about…

Invent slogans for…

Make an audiotape of…

Conduct an interview of… on…

Write a letter to…about…

Use technology to write…

Others of your choice….

LOGICAL-MATHEMATICAL MENU:

Create story problems for …

Translate…into a mathematical formula…

Create a timeline of…

Design and conduct an experiment on…

Make a strategy game that…

Use a Venn Diagram to explain …

Make up syllogisms to demonstrate…

Make up analogies to explain…

Use…thinking skills to …

Design a code for …

Categorize facts about …

Describe patterns or symmetry in…

Select and use technology to…

Others of your choice…

KINESTHETIC MENU:

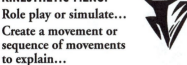

Role play or simulate…

Create a movement or sequence of movements to explain…

Choreograph a dance of…

Invent a board or floor game of…

Make task or puzzle cards for…

Build or construct a…

Plan and attend a field trip that will…

Use the qualities of a physically-educated person to demonstrate…

Devise a scavenger hunt to…

Make a model of…

Use hands-on materials to demonstrate…

Design a product for…

Select and use technology to…

Others of your choice

VISUAL MENU:

Chart, map, cluster, or graph…

Create a slide show, videotape, or photo album of…

Design a poster, bulletin board, or mural of…

Use a memory system to learn…

Create artwork that …

Develop architectural drawings that…

Make advertisements for…

Vary the size and shape of …

Color code the process of…

Invent a board or card game to demonstrate…

Illustrate, draw, paint, sketch, sculpt or construct…

Use the overhead projector to teach…

Use technology to…

Others of your choice…

MUSICAL MENU:

Give a presentation with appropriate musical accompaniment on…

Write song lyrics for…

Sing a rap or song that explains…

Indicate the rhythmical patterns in…

Explain how the lyrics of a song relate to…

Explain how the music of a song is similar to…

Present a short class musical on…

Make an instrument and use it to demonstrate…

Use music to enhance the learning of …

Collect and present songs about…

Write a new ending to a song or musical composition so that it explains…

Create a musical collage to depict…

Use musical technology to…

Others of your own…

INTERPERSONAL MENU:

Conduct a meeting to address…

With a partner, use "out loud problem solving" to…

Role play multiple perspectives on …

Organize or participate in a group to…

Intentionally use…social skills to learn about…

Participate in a service project to…

Teach someone else about…

With a small group, collaboratively plan rules or procedures to accomplish…

Help resolve a local or global problem by…

Practice giving and receiving feedback on…

Using one of your strengths, assume a role in a group to accomplish…

Create a culturgram or systems wheel *(see interpersonal chapter)* of…

Use a telecommunication program to reach…to…

Others of your choice…

INTRAPERSONAL MENU:

Describe qualities you possess that will help you successfully complete

Create a personal analogy for…

Set and pursue a goal to…

Describe how you feel about…

Explain your personal philosophy about…

Describe one of your personal values about…

Use self-directed learning to…

Write a journal entry on…

Explain the purpose you perceive in studying…

Conduct a project of your choice on…

Receive feedback from another person on your efforts to…

Self-assess your work in…

Use technology to…

Others of your choice…

While these lists provide several instructional options, teachers have found other uses for the menus. Some give students copies of the menus and ask them to select their own ways to proceed in learning classroom content. This removes some of the responsibility for multimodal teaching from the instructor and places it on, in many cases, the "eager" shoulders of the students.

Other teachers use the menus for homework. Sometimes, a teacher will distribute a single menu such as the musical list and ask that students do their homework musically for a week. Typically on Fridays, students will review or share their musical homework with classmates. At the beginning of the following week, students might receive a different menu and again be directed to study according to the listed options. By rotating through the seven intelligences during the course of seven weeks, all students are challenged to address their weaknesses and to enjoy working through their strengths. Some teachers encourage students to identify their favorite homework strategies for the eighth

week. Teachers then have opportunities to observe student preferences and to glimpse inherent strengths or areas in which students are motivated to take risks. Parents frequently report that they have seldom seen their children so engaged with homework. The multimodal requirements create new challenges that many students enjoy undertaking.

Teachers have also used the menus for assessment options. After reviewing the menus to students, students select how they will demonstrate their learning. As long as the criteria are clearly specified for quality work, knowledge, and skills, students can communicate their achievement through charts, movement sequences, role plays, or original songs.

Whether used as instructional, assessment, or homework tools, the menus and the learning activities described earlier in this book teach students that the seven intelligences are effective problem-solving strategies for educational and real-life challenges.

A LESSON PLANNING MATRIX

There is no single, preferred model of Multiple Intelligences-based lesson design. Teachers are highly adept at creating approaches that best suit their teaching styles as well as the needs of their students. When beginning to approach MI as an instructional framework, realistic expectations must be set. For secondary level educators working within the confines of 50 minute class periods, it is unlikely that all seven areas will be addressed within a single period. Rather, including one strategy from each intelligence in one to two week's time may prove manageable. Elementary school teachers may find that over the course of two days the seven intelligences can be easily integrated into classroom activities. Other teachers have eased into MI-based instruction by identifying one intelligence to highlight each day. After seven days, their students have worked in all seven modes. Some teachers let students continue work in an intelligence of their choice on the eighth day of class.

It is important to note that while the Multiple Intelligences provide an effective framework, it is not desirable to turn Gardner's theory into a rigid pedagogical formula. One teacher who wanted to teach all content through seven modes admitted that he occasionally "tacked on" activities to complete his daily lessons. This practice ceased when students complained that some lesson components were "really stretching it." What is most important in MI instruction is that the tools of instruction are appropriate for the content. This is not to say, however, that a teacher should consistently avoid an intelligence because it is "out of his comfort zone." Instead, teaming with a colleague can enhance the learning options of both students and teachers alike.

A few educators prefer to develop a latent capacity within themselves before applying it to classroom instruction. Some teachers have identified drawing, movement, or musical activities, for example, to study formally or informally. Once confidence is gained, the educators teach students what they have learned or infuse their new knowledge and skills into classroom lessons.

One of the authors directs a mid-career teacher preparation program in which students are required to select a latent intelligence to develop over a year's time. Additionally, the pre-service candidates must incorporate their budding capacities into classroom instruction during their student teaching practicum. It has been interesting to observe the choices adults make about which intelligences to develop. One year, out of the 40 students in the program, two chose to improve linguistic skills through speech lessons and a survey of children's literature. Eleven dived into logical-mathematical intelligence through attending math phobia classes, reviewing math curriculums, and studying problem-solving models. Ten pursued art courses. Six experimented with kinesthetic intelligence through participating in physical education programs. Eight took vocal or instrumental lessons. Two studied collaborative learning processes, and one engaged in extensive journal-writing. Educators who are willing to continue to enhance their human capacities become important role models for students as they embody the practices they seek to nurture in others.

A sample matrix is suggested below as one option for organizing Multiple Intelligences instruction. The reader will note that two sample lessons are also provided. The first on photosynthesis incorporates all seven intelligences while the second lesson suggests the use of five.

LESSON/UNIT PLANNING WITH THE MULTIPLE INTELLIGENCES

LESSON/UNIT TITLE: _____

LESSON/UNIT OBJECTIVE(S): _____

_____

ANTICIPATED LEARNER OUTCOME(S): _____

_____

CLASSROOM RESOURCES OR MATERIALS: _____

_____

LEARNING ACTIVITIES:

LINGUISTIC:	MATHEMATICAL-LOGICAL:
VISUAL-SPATIAL:	BODILY-KINESTHETIC:
MUSICAL:	INTERPERSONAL:
INTRAPERSONAL:	

LESSON/UNIT SEQUENCE: _____

_____

ASSESSMENT PROCEDURES: _____

_____

SAMPLE ONE: LESSON/UNIT PLANNING WITH THE MULTIPLE INTELLIGENCES

LESSON/UNIT TITLE: Photosynthesis: Converting Sunlight to Food

LESSON/UNIT OBJECTIVE(S): For students to learn the process of photosynthesis through seven modes

ANTICIPATED LEARNER OUTCOME(S): Students will be able to explain the process of photosynthesis visually, logically, linguistically, or musically, and to relate the concept of transformation and change to their own lives

CLASSROOM RESOURCES OR MATERIALS: Displayed posters or charts of the process of photosynthesis, a variety of musical tapes or compact disks and player, water color supplies, science textbooks

LEARNING ACTIVITIES:

LINGUISTIC:
Read textbook section describing photosynthesis and appropriate vocabulary.

LOGICAL-MATHEMATICAL:
Create a timeline of the steps of photosynthesis.

VISUAL-SPATIAL:
With watercolors, paint the process of photosynthesis.

BODILY-KINESTHETIC:
Role play the "characters" involved in the process of photosynthesis.

MUSICAL:
Create a musical collage with different musical selections that represent the sequence of steps involved in photosynthesis

INTERPERSONAL:
In small groups, discuss the transformative role of chloroplasts in photosynthesis and draw parallels to students' lives.

INTRAPERSONAL:
Write a journal entry that reflects on a personally transformative experience and compare it to photosynthesis.

LESSON/UNIT SEQUENCE: 1. Linguistic activity 2. Logical-mathematical activity 3. Bodily-kinesthetic activity 4. Visual-spatial activity 5. Musical activity 6. Interpersonal activity 7. Intrapersonal activity

ASSESSMENT PROCEDURES: 1. Grade mathematical timeline and/or painting

2. Ask students to evaluate one another's role plays and/or songs

SAMPLE TWO: LESSON/UNIT PLANNING WITH THE MULTIPLE INTELLIGENCES

LESSON/UNIT TITLE: Solving Algebraic Equations

LESSON/UNIT OBJECTIVE(S): For students to learn how to solve equations through five intelligences

ANTICIPATED LEARNER OUTCOME(S): Students will be able to explain and apply the concepts and processes of solving equations

CLASSROOM RESOURCES OR MATERIALS: Textbooks, colored markers, tape and casssette player for "When Johnny Comes Marching Home"

LEARNING ACTIVITIES:

LINGUISTIC:
Read and discuss textbook information.

MATHEMATICAL-LOGICAL:
Solve equations for unknown using a sequential flow chart.

VISUAL-SPATIAL:
Color code the various steps in solving algebraic equations.

BODILY-KINESTHETIC:
N/A

MUSICAL:
Create song lyrics to the tune of "When Johnny Comes Marching Home" that explain commutative, associative, and distributive laws.

INTERPERSONAL:
Students create song lyrics in small groups and teach their songs to others in the class.

INTRAPERSONAL:
N/A

LESSON/UNIT SEQUENCE: 1. Visual-spatial activity 2. Logical-mathematical activity 3. Linguistic activity 4. Musical activity 5. Interpersonal

ASSESSMENT PROCEDURES: 1. Assess sequential flow charts. 2. Provide students with algebraic equations and suggest they use their song lyrics to solve the problems.

As is evident in the sample lessons, the same concept is taught in several ways. This avoids a common problem in MI-based teaching. Teachers often enjoy brainstorming numerous multimodal experiences and soon find themselves far afield of the originally desired objectives and outcomes. Students can get lost in engaging, but fragmented experiences. As with any instructional method, it is essential that educators determine what is of greatest value for students to know and then pursue the teaching of those concepts in a cohesive manner.

INTERDISCIPLINARY UNITS

Traditionally, the academic disciplines have been taught without meaningful connections to one another or to students' lives. When teaching to the Multiple Intelligences, discrete subject matter distinctions begin to dissolve, enabling an individual or team of teachers to plan interdisciplinary units if desired. Math, reading, music, art, movement, and both cooperative and independent work can be woven into the teaching of any topic.

A group of middle school teachers in the Seattle School District expressed a desire for an all-purpose matrix for lesson planning as their schools embraced interdisciplinary instruction. In addition to the Multiple Intelligences, the teachers wanted to emphasize critical and creative thinking skills, parent involvement, student choice, and real-world connections in their units. The matrix they use to organize curriculum planning follows:

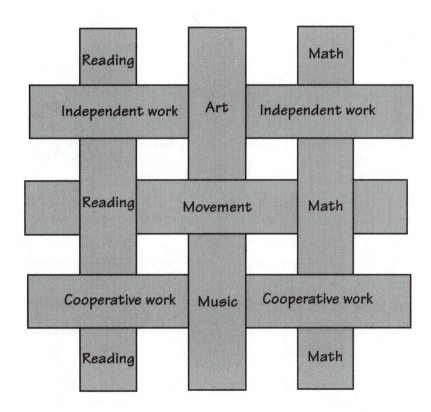

INTERDISCIPLINARY PLANNING THROUGH

Theme: _____ Resources and Materials_____

OBJECTIVES:	LINGUISTIC ACTIVITIES:	MATHEMATICAL ACTIVITIES:	VISUAL ACTIVITIES:	KINESTHETIC ACTIVITIES:	MUSICAL ACTIVITIES:	INTERPERSONAL ACTIVITIES:	INTRAPERSONAL ACTIVITIES:
STUDENT OUTCOMES:							

THE MULTIPLE INTELLIGENCES

UNIT SEQUENCE:

HIGHER LEVEL THINKING SKILLS: • Analysis • Synthesis • Evaluation	CREATIVE THINKING SKILLS: • Fluency • Flexibility • Elaboration • Originality	REAL WORLD CONNECTION ACTIVITIES:	PARENT/ COMMUNITY ACTIVITIES:	STUDENT CHOICE ACTIVITIES:	ASSESSMENT ACTIVITIES:	RESOURCES NEEDED:

UNIT CLOSURE:

INTERDISCIPLINARY PLANNING WITH DEVELOPMENTAL SEQUENCES

The preceding interdisciplinary matrix provides students with numerous enriched learning opportunities. At times, however, teachers may want to focus on in-depth sequential knowledge and skill development in one or more intelligences. To plan such a unit, teachers identify what the student should be able to do by the end of the unit, what the developmental tasks are in the targeted intelligence(s) and the specific activities to be undertaken. A sample follows:

INTERDISCIPLINARY UNIT PLAN
WITH DEVELOPMENTAL SEQUENCES

Theme: _____ Resources and Materials _____

	LINGUISTIC SKILLS	MATHEMATICAL SKILLS	VISUAL SKILLS	KINESTHETIC SKILLS	MUSICAL SKILLS	INTERPERSONAL SKILLS	INTRAPERSONAL SKILLS
Student Outcomes:							
Developmental Tasks:							
Assessment Measures:							

Unit Sequence: _____

Unit Closure: _____

INTERDISCIPLINARY UNIT PLAN
WITH DEVELOPMENTAL SEQUENCES

Theme: Colonial Life in America   **Resources and Materials** Quilt and music supplies, cleared space for dance' research project format

	LINGUISTIC SKILLS	MATHEMATICAL SKILLS	KINESTHETIC SKILLS	VISUAL SKILLS	MUSICAL SKILLS	INTERPERSONAL SKILLS	INTRAPERSONAL SKILLS
Student Outcomes:	Write a biographical character sketch	Apply geometric shapes to quilting	Dance a reel or traditional square dance	Make a quilt or wall hanging	Provide musical accompaniment	Gain diverse perspectives on land use	Conduct research project of one's choice
Developmental Tasks:	1. Choose an individual from colonial America 2. Gather information from three sources 3. Write draft according to teacher criteria 4. Solicit teacher and peer feedback 5. Rewrite draft	1. Using colored construction paper, cut out squares, rectangles, trapezoids, right, isosceles, and scalene triangles 2. Arrange in quilt patterns 3. Identify geometric parts, congruent angles, and symmetry	1. Walk through steps of Virginia Reel 2. Perform steps with music 3. Practice dance 4. Perform dance for another class	1. Transfer construction paper quilt designs to fabric 2. Learn piecing and quilting techniques 3. Sew a quilt or wall hanging together	1. Listen to music of colonial America 2. Select an instrument to make 3. Make the instrument 4. Practice playing the instrument 5. Play accompaniment for colonial song	1. In pairs, role-play a European Colonist and an American Indian 2. Discuss land use rights 3. Join another pair 4. Identify diverse points of view	1. Identify an interest sparked in colonial unit 2. Follow research format provided by teacher 3. Identify a product or form for sharing research 4. Share research with class
Assessment Measures:	Submit final copy of character sketch	Submit a quilt pattern with identified geometric shapes	Perform dance for others	Submit sewn quilt or wall hanging	Accompany a recorded song with one's own instrument	Explain diverse perspectives of land use	Present independent research project

Unit Sequence: Concurrent through centers

Unit Closure: Colonial fair for another class

When extensive planning is undertaken as the above interdisciplinary units require, it is useful to share such work with other colleagues. In fact, some teachers and schools create portable lessons that are boxed with all the necessary resources, a brief teacher's guide, and an inventory list for refurbishing supplies. Many schools and districts catalogue such portable lessons, making them available to interested colleagues, and preventing the proverbial, time-consuming re-invention of the wheel.

INTERDISCIPLINARY SCHOOLWIDE APPROACHES AT THE SECONDARY LEVEL

Most of the Multiple Intelligence pilot programs around the country are housed in elementary schools; yet, Gardner's theory can be easily applied at the secondary level since all of the intelligence experts in a junior or senior high school are readily identified by the subjects they teach. In order to achieve greater depth of content knowledge and to decrease students' fragmented curricular experience, teachers can plan schoolwide interdisciplinary units.

At the New City School in St. Louis, middle school teachers have 90 minute blocks for their basic skills subject areas. The teachers split their block time in three equal ways: 30 minutes of direct instruction, 30 minutes of cooperative learning, and 30 minutes of independent learning. When planning the blocks, teachers review the seven intelligences to see if they are incorporated into all lessons if not daily at least weekly. Without making major curricular changes, the time blocks are becoming much more interdisciplinary in nature.

Teachers at any middle, junior, or senior school might meet to identify the major units each covers during the year. The topics can be charted month-by-month on a large calendar enabling everyone to see what is taught when. By learning about one another's curriculum, it becomes easier to align topics that are mutually supportive. Plans can be made to teach such topics concurrently. For example, the history department in a high school might teach a consumerism unit each spring. The math department notes that it covers percentages, ratios and probability each fall. By shifting such math topics to the spring and by adding lessons on stocks and bonds, the two departments can enrich one another's content. Similarly, the art department might choose to have students study commercials and create packaging for consumer prod-

ucts. In language arts, student journals could reflect on their purchases and what such products reveal about their value systems. English teachers might also oversee independent learning projects of students' choice. P.E. classes could study the claims and actual results of diverse fitness programs. In science, small groups of students might study consumerism and its environmental effects. In music classes, songs could be analyzed for the societal values they promote and students might write songs addressing consumerism issues. In Industrial Arts, display cases could be built for the school's student store, and in Home Economics, students might compare natural versus synthetic products. By tapping the inherent resources of a high school staff, Multiple Intelligence-based, interdisciplinary units naturally emerge.

One Seattle high school with a diverse population decided to pilot a schoolwide MI week on the topic of international awareness. The literature teachers introduced short stories from the cultures represented among their students. Business education teachers addressed international trade issues. Math teachers taught lessons on foreign currency. P.E. teachers taught games from around the world, and in science classes, students studied local and global environmental issues. Social science teachers addressed diverse forms of government and civil rights issues. Health teachers covered a unit on infectious diseases rampant in many countries. Art and music teachers engaged students in diverse visual media and ethnomusicology. During the planning stages for their MI week, the teachers grew so excited with the possibilities for their units, that they decided to invite parents to the event as well. Realizing that many parents would not be able to attend school during the day, they changed the week's schedule beginning each day at 3:00 p.m. and ending at 9:00 p.m. Not only was the event a huge success with the students, the school had literally hundreds of parents attending classes with their children. It was the first time in the school's recent experience that so many parents, and especially immigrant parents, came to school.

Short-term pilot efforts such as the above introduce a faculty to interdisciplinary collaboration avoiding the typical caution that surrounds year-long commitments. In this way, secondary teachers continue to work in their specialized areas and need not spend extensive time planning for new lessons. Yet students benefit from the opportunity to view a topic or theme through numerous perspectives while experiencing connections among their formerly separate subject areas. After such units are taught and assessed, many teachers express their appreciation for the in-depth learning students experienced. They claim that the interdisciplinary units improve instruction and learning, and some decide to discard the traditional artificial barriers among subject areas.

INTELLIGENCE TEAMS

Rather than teaming based on content areas, some schools feature "intelligence teams" where each member of the team identifies his or her intelligence expertise. Such teams typically consist of two to four educators, each of whom assumes responsibility for one or more intelligences in lesson planning or daily instruction. Working with theme-based or traditional curricula, such teachers serve as resources for one another.

There are countless ways teacher teams self-organize to incorporate the intelligences into school programs. In some schools such as Seven Oaks Elementary, in Lacey, Washington, and the Key School in Indianapolis, Indiana, specialists in the seven intelligences work directly with teachers to infuse each capacity into daily instruction. At Wheeler Elementary in Louisville, Kentucky, teachers form grade-level teams, each assuming responsibility for one or more intelligences. Students rotate among classrooms, working with teachers who assume responsibility for providing all students at the same grade level with opportunities for full spectrum learning. Another option includes teachers who co-plan Multiple Intelligence-based lessons while maintaining responsibility for instruction in their self-contained classrooms. In some cases, teams of four divide instructional tasks by having three teachers assume responsibility for two intelligences each while one oversees student choice activities for intrapersonal intelligence:

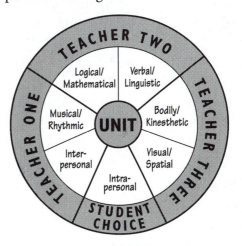

THE BENEFITS OF TEAMING

Such teaming provides numerous benefits. When working together, coordinating lessons, sharing successes, and addressing challenges, the aggregate accomplishments of the teams far outweigh solitary efforts at improving instruction. When teachers collaborate, they avoid the problem of being shunned by colleagues for teaching differently, and they reap the benefits of collective practice. Increased dialogue about teaching, education, and one's own personal and professional strengths ensues, and resources are pooled. When planning lessons together, teachers have opportunities to reflect on and refine what, why, and how they are teaching. The students in their classrooms have much to gain from this professional dialogue. More students in more classes benefit from the combined expertise of the intelligence teams, and teachers begin assuming responsibility for promoting the growth of their colleagues just as they do for their students.

Many teams find that lessons including all seven intelligences not only provide greater depth in content, they also require more time to teach. Important implications for curricular programs emerge. Questions commonly asked include, "What are the truly essential concepts my students should acquire?" "What should be omitted from the curriculum; what should be retained or added?" "What should a student be able to do by the end of grade level?" "How can student choice be worked into the classroom?" "How many themes can be taught in a school year?" In addressing such questions, teacher teams begin rethinking their school's curriculum. Over time, program-wide changes may come about, addressing what to keep in the current curriculum, what to change, how to assess student work, and what connections to make among subject areas. Multiple Intelligences teaching often becomes a driving force for major curricular reform within a school.

CURRICULUM DEVELOPMENT FOR INTELLIGENCE DEVELOPMENT

While most teachers apply MI theory to enhance student learning, a few endeavor to develop the individual intelligences themselves. This is no small undertaking since each intelligence contains a complex cluster of knowledge and skills and most curriculums are so overcrowded they preclude additional goals. Nevertheless, some teachers are forging ahead with efforts to develop one or more of their students' intelligences in a variety of ways.

Some teachers identify one or more intelligences to emphasize throughout their semester or year-long courses. For example, one middle school teacher sought to infuse one aspect of kinesthetic and musical intelligences, dance, throughout her classes. She selected the following core movement elements and skills to apply to the regular curriculum:

1. **basic locomotive movements such as walking, running, sliding, skipping, moving forward, backward, diagonally, and turning.**

2. **steps, positions, and patterns from different dance styles or traditions**

3. **the cultural and historical context of selected dances**

These three core "intelligence" components, regularly appeared in lessons. For example, when students were learning about platonic solids in geometry, they improvised "dances" using basic locomative movements. In social studies, students learned folk dances of Germany and Scandinavia and the social context for such dances. Classroom exercise breaks or transitions often featured movement skills.

Multiple-Intelligence Outcomes:

One of the authors developed seven, year-long intelligence outcomes that he wove throughout the curriculum for his multi-age classroom of third through fifth grade students. These goals included:

Linguistic Intelligence:
  The writing process

Logical-Mathematical Intelligence:
  Pattern identification in mathematical processes

Visual-Spatial Intelligence:
  The use of color, shape, and design

Kinesthetic Intelligence:
  Eye, hand, body coordination through juggling

Musical Intelligence:
  Two-part rhythms

Interpersonal Intelligence:
  Conflict mediation

Intrapersonal Intelligence:
  Personal goal-setting

Some schools have identified Multiple Intelligence outcomes around which they mold their entire programs. Such schools have determined the essential tasks, achievements, and habits of mind all students should exhibit. Curriculum and assessment are driven by the MI outcomes. For example, the Key School states that upon graduation each student will demonstrate the following core abilities:

- **Communicates clearly in written form**
- **Is verbally articulate in two languages**
- **Sings or plays a musical instrument proficiently**
- **Uses math and logic in applied areas**
- **Uses technology as a tool for inquiry and communication**
- **Recreates the three-dimensional world through the visual or practical arts**
- **Is physically fit**
- **Selects applied area for inquiry, reflection, and apprenticeship**
- **Participates in stewardship activities demonstrating a shared relationship with nature**
- **Expresses capacity to care about global issues**
- **Participates in groups and organizations in the larger community**
- **If 18, is an active registered voter**

When attempting to teach to develop intelligence, educators find it necessary to identify both core curriculum and core aspects of the selected intelligence. In so doing, they are no longer teaching *through* the intelligences. They are teaching *for* intelligence.

A LEARNING CENTERS INSTRUCTIONAL FORMAT

One of the authors has developed and implemented a successful public school classroom model featuring seven learning centers for mixed-age elementary students. Initially, the centers were named after Gardner's intelligences; more recently, however, they feature the names of individuals who typify a particular intelligence. The names of the centers rotate on a yearly basis. The beginning of the school year is dedicated, in part, to studying the "intelligence experts," and how they developed and used their intelligences. In this way, seven geniuses become mentors in absentia to the students in the classroom. The accompanying chart describes the names of the centers:

SEVEN LEARNING CENTERS BASED ON THE THEORY OF MULTIPLE INTELLIGENCES

WILLIAM SHAKESPEARE CENTER
(other individuals include Maya Angelou, Li Po) Linguistic Intelligence

ALBERT EINSTEIN CENTER
(other individuals include Marie Curie, Stephen Hawking) Logical-Mathematical Intelligence

PABLO PICASSO CENTER
(other individuals include Diego Rivera, Frank Lloyd Wright) Visual-Spatial Intelligence

MARTHA GRAHAM CENTER
(other individuals include Jim Thorpe, Wilma Rudolph) Kinesthetic Intelligence

RAY CHARLES CENTER
(other individuals include Kitaro, Carmen McRae) Musical Intelligence

MOTHER TERESA CENTER
(other individuals include Mahatma Ghandi, Florence Nightingale) Interpersonal Intelligence

EMILY DICKINSON CENTER
(other individuals include Anne Frank, Sigmund Freud)Intrapersonal Intelligence

---

The curriculum is thematically organized through the learning centers. At the beginning of the school year, students list topics they want to study. The teacher reviews the district's learning objectives and textbooks. Themes are selected which integrate district requirements and resources with student interests. The thematic units typically span four to six weeks and cover such topics as "Art from around the World," "Things in Space," "Our Planet's Problems," and "Life in Ancient Civilizations." Student learning objectives are deliberately taught in the thematic units without being tied to textbook sequences.

Once a theme has been identified, it is divided into a series of specific lessons. For example, a unit on outer space might include lessons on galaxies, the solar system, comets, planets, and satellites. Each day the instructor presents one aspect of the unit, beginning with a morning "main lesson" which gives an overview of the topic for that day. Students then divide into small groups to work at the centers where they learn about the topic in seven ways. They read, write, listen, sing, build, act, collaborate, invent, make books and models, conduct research, solve problems, and do art projects. Some students prefer to move through the seven centers in an orderly, structured way. Others enjoy traveling more randomly. All students are expected to complete certain tasks during the day but each does so in his or her own way.

The lesson which follows is an example of how the theme of space, can be narrowed down to one topic, comets, and presented in multiple ways:

A SAMPLE LESSON USING SEVEN CENTERS

Main Lesson: "Comets."

The teacher gives a short lecture with pictures and diagrams describing comets, their size, composition, and orbits. Included is a kinesthetic activity where some students portray the sun and others assume the different parts of the comet and "walk" through the comet's orbit around the sun.

Centers:

Martha Graham Center: Students make their own comets with sticks, marshmallows, and ribbons for comet tails. Then, as comets, they walk through an elliptical orbit, keeping their tails pointed away from the sun.

Diego Rivera Center: Using glue and glitter, students make comets on colored paper, correctly labeling all the parts.

William Shakespeare Center: Students read about comets from science textbooks, library books on astronomy, or encyclopedias, and answer questions about their reading.

Kitaro Center: Using the melody to "Twinkle, Twinkle Little Star," small groups compose songs about comets which must contain several facts.

Emily Dickinson Center: Individually, students write about how they are alike or different from comets.

Albert Einstein Center: Using graph paper and rulers, students draw a series of comets to different scales: with the tail 10X as long as the head, 50X as long, 100X as long, and 500X as long.

Mother Teresa Center: In their groups, students create a game show about outer space that includes visuals and fact cards. Questions presented to the "contestants" must call upon higher level thinking skills.

Because of the daily variety of student activities, drill and practice are no longer monotonous repetitive tasks. Skills are learned and applied in numerous modes. The work at the centers enables children to make informative, multimodal presentations of their studies to classmates or others. It is the norm rather than the exception for students to sing, dance, draw, role play, calculate, and write what they have learned. It also is the norm for each child to experience some form of daily academic success, since there are numerous opportunities to learn through one's strengths. In the seven years since this program has been implemented, not a single student has failed to find at least one area in which to excel.

The main lesson and the center time consume the first half of the school day. At the end of the center experiences, time is set aside for sharing of individual and group center work. On a voluntary basis, students sing or play songs, read poems, display artwork, or explain games they have made. Classmates critique each other's products, and discussions ensue about the topic, what constitutes quality work, and what next students might address.

The remainder of the school day is dedicated to independent projects with students pursuing their own interests. The combination of centers in the morning and independent projects in the afternoon provides students with both structure and flexibility in their daily routine. Additionally, it enables the teacher to guide both the academic and personal growth of the students.

Because of their afternoon project work, students acquire important self-directed learning skills. They learn to ask researchable questions, to identify numerous resources, to create realistic timelines, and to initiate, implement, and bring closure to a learning activity. Students are responsible for initiating, completing and presenting one project per month. Time is set aside for project presentations the last week of the month. The topics are numerous as are the modes in which students present their ideas to classmates and others. The academic as well as diverse communication skills developed during centers emerge in highly personal ways through the independent projects.

For their projects, students frequently select classroom topics to explore in greater depth. Since they are also free, however, to work on non-curricular topics, some study a single area of personal interest for months at a time. For example, one girl was fascinated with mechanical processes, and did her monthly projects on how things work. Such freedom of choice enables students to deepen their understanding of school curriculum or to enhance an intelligence of the students' choice.

Numerous challenges confront a teacher who attempts to engage the seven intelligences in daily classroom centers. Although planning is initially a challenge, teachers report the task gradually becomes easier through ongoing practice and through developing a repertoire of instructional approaches. Teachers also learn shortcuts to daily planning, such as providing long-term projects at one or two of the centers or asking students to take charge of planning certain centers.

Whenever possible, it appears helpful to create plans for a week at a time, freeing the instructor to focus on the daily topics and projects at hand. A sample weekly planning grid is shown below:

WEEKLY PLANNING GRID

DATE _____

	Monday ____ lesson	Tuesday ____ lesson	Wednesday ____ lesson	Thursday ____ lesson	Friday ____ lesson
Picasso Center (Spatial Intelligence)					
Martha Graham Center (Kinesthetic Intelligence)					
Ray Charles Center (Musical Intelligence)					
Mother Teresa Center (Interpersonal Intelligence)					
Shakespeare Center (Linguistic Intelligence)					
Einstein Center (Logical-Mathematical Intelligence)					
Emily Dickinson Center (Intrapersonal Intelligence)					

While the majority of students work at the centers and on projects, teacher time is spent with individuals or small groups. Time becomes available to confer with individual students, evaluate their work, suggest opportunities for improvement, tutor those with reading or math difficulties, assist gifted students with challenging pursuits, and work with small groups to design structures, create dances, and plan projects. In summary then, the four main components of this classroom model are as follows:

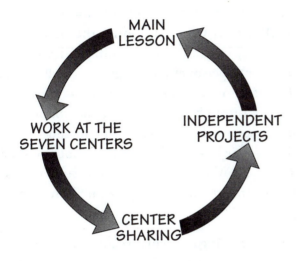

While most classrooms featuring centers are elementary ones, some teachers at Lincoln High School in Stockton, California, also use centers based upon the seven intelligences. Fewer centers are set up on a daily basis due to limited classroom space. Students select which centers to work at each day and then regroup to discuss their experiences. These teachers and others working at the secondary level find that the use of centers decentralizse the classroom and adds the flexibility that many students require for effective learning.

The role of classroom teacher in such a model shifts from that of a director to that of a facilitator, guide, and resource provider. In addition, new teaching competencies frequently develop. Skills emerge enabling one to observe students through seven lenses. Planning for diverse modes of learning often results in enhanced creative capacities within oneself. One teacher experiencing new capacities develop within himself after working with the Multiple Intelligences asked, "Who is changing the most, the students or myself?"

PROJECT SPECTRUM

Another approach to center-based teaching is used at Project Spectrum, an early childhood pilot effort at Harvard and Tufts Universities. In a Spectrum classroom, children interact with a variety of materials and numerous centers on a daily basis. Rather than attempting to access each of the seven intelligences directly, centers are established to reflect respected social roles, or in Gardner's terminology, "adult end states." "End states" are skills not only useful in school programs, but also in assuming rewarding adult roles. By working at centers complete with "end state" activities, many intelligences are combined. For example, at the science center, termed the "naturalist's corner," various plant and animal specimens are available for observation and comparison. This center engages sensory and logical-mathematical capacities as well as the skills and activities in which naturalists typically engage.

There are eight centers in a Spectrum classroom. These centers and the key abilities they enlist are described below:

Art Center: Visual arts perception, production, and composition

Language: Storytelling, reporting, and wordplay

Math: Numerical reasoning, spatial reasoning, and problem-solving

Mechanical: Fine motor skills, visual-spatial abilities, problem-solving with mechanical objects, and understanding of causal relationships

Movement: Body control, sensitivity to rhythm, expression, generating movement ideas, responsiveness to music

Music: Music perception, production, and composition

Science: Observations, identifying similarities and differences, hypothesis formation and experimentation, interest in knowledge of natural environment or scientific phenomena.

Social: Understanding of self, others, assumption of various social roles: leader, facilitator, caregiver, friend

Adult end states shift to match the focus of center activities. For example, at the language center, the skills of a storyteller, novelist, reporter, lawyer, playwright, and poet are profiled at different times. To further elucidate adult roles, Spectrum features Connections, a community mentoring program for young children. Students work with adults from their neighborhoods who are employed in the various professions under consideration in the classroom. In this way, children gain insight into the materials and skills they encounter at school.

The curriculum at Project Spectrum is presented in theme kits that draw on the full range of intelligences. Some themes include "Night and Day" or "About Me" that easily access each of the seven intelligences. The thematic format enables children to perceive relationships among the disciplines and to examine a topic from multiple perspectives. In an attempt to create a wider learning sphere for children, curriculum linkages are made between home, school, and community. Suggested activities that complement classroom lessons are given to parents as well as to local museums to make museum exhibits more accessible to children. Through integrating the resources of home, school, and community, Project Spectrum students may ultimately internalize deep understandings of their learnings.

DISCOVERING CURRICULUM BIAS

Over the years, numerous curriculum trends have proliferated, each with its own philosophic assumptions, goals, and teaching and learning processes. With the advent of Gardner's theory, educators are now able to scrutinize any curricular model through seven lenses to see if it includes the full range of human capacities. When one does so, it becomes readily apparent that many programs actually have a strong bias. They appear to be founded upon one or two intelligences while excluding the others. For example, collaborative learning relies heavily upon interpersonal and linguistic intelligences. To ensure that students gain access to subject matter through other modes, the cooperative processes might be adapted to include kinesthetic, visual, musical, logical, and intrapersonal activities. With such adaptation, students can learn through their strongest intellectual entry points.

In surveying curricular trends such as writing across the curriculum, integrated technology, and others, it is evident that biases are inherent in their formats. In fact, one may ask whether curriculum theorists generate models that reflect their individual intelligence strengths! When a teacher, school, or district is considering curriculum adoption, it may be wise to pose several questions before embracing a new program. The following questions reveal a model's strengths and weaknesses:

- **What is the philosophical perspective promoted by the curriculum?**

- **What are its assumptions?**

- **What are the main components of the curriculum (i.e.: procedures, assessment, and materials)?**

- **Which intelligences does the program emphasize?**

- **Which intelligences must students possess in order to succeed?**

- **Which intelligences does it require of the teacher?**

- **Which intelligences are overlooked?**

- **How might the curriculum be adapted to include all seven intelligences?**

When integrating Gardner's theory into school programs, it is unnecessary to discard current or new programs. Just as teachers adapt individual lessons and units, major curricular programs can also be enhanced. In fact, it is inadvisable to discard what is working well or has the potential to do so. Rather, maintain curriculum that is successful and endeavor to enhance its success.

PROJECT-BASED CURRICULUMS

Noting that most productive human work occurs in the form of meaningful and complex projects, Gardner recommends that curriculums feature projects to prepare students for their adult lives. Students readily gain knowledge and skills when they are acquired in realistic contexts through active exploration of their environments and through participation in real-world experiences. Whether community service programs, school trips, or laboratory experiments, projects involve students in efforts that are personally relevant and of value for others. Open-ended in nature, a project poses multiple solutions and engages students in a "whole" situation, one that encourages discovery of its parts, relationships, meaning, and resolution.

John Dewey claimed that schooling should ideally consist of a total and continuous experience rather than a series of abstract, fragmented courses taught by several educators. Dewey

objected to curriculums that were organized for the convenience of adults, and stressed the value of real world experiences that engaged children's multi-faceted natures. In *School and Society*, Dewey wrote,

> **"No number of object lessons, got up as object lessons for the sake of giving information, can afford even the shadow of a substitute for acquaintance with plants and animals of the farm and garden acquired through actual living among them and caring for them. No training of the sense organs in school, introduced for the sake of training, can begin to compete with the alertness and fullness of life that comes from daily intimacy and interest in familiar occupations. Verbal memory can be trained in committing tasks, a certain discipline of the reasoning powers can be acquired through lessons in science and mathematics; but after all, this is somewhat remote and shadowy compared with the training of attention and of judgment that is acquired in having to do things with a real motive behind and a real outcome ahead."**

While most schools are not organized around what Dewey would call a continuous, total experience, many teachers include projects that blend the classroom with real life experiences. For example, one fifth-grade class wanted to travel to Washington D.C. to see the government at work. To achieve their goal, the students developed a business plan for a recycling project for fundraising. They had to determine how many residents lived in their town, how many cans were used in the average household per week, how many people would participate in recycling, and how much the projected collection of cans would weigh to estimate their revenues. Expenses also had to be deducted from their proceeds. By planning and implementing this complex, real-world project, the students achieved their goal of a class trip to Washington, D.C.

Primary students at Project Spectrum study local birds and their nesting habits for one classroom project. They design and build bird houses and then observe whether their designs successfully meet the needs of the birds or whether modifications are required.

Middle school students in Lakewood, Washington, learn biology concepts through a project that involves solving a mock crime. Students conduct investigations, gather evidence, and attempt to solve the crime. Once the crime has been solved, students analyze the problem-solving approaches that led to the correct answer.

High school students in Palo Alto, California, wanted to determine the use of a piece of property in a redevelopment section of their city. The students prepared videotape documentaries to present to the city council as a way to propose their land use recommendations.

Other high school students in Ithaca, New York, became concerned about cancer therapies after a classmate was diagnosed with leukemia. The students undertook research projects, conducted interviews of medical personnel, and made hospital visits to understand the disease and identify traditional and non-traditional healing approaches.

Such projects typically span from two weeks to two months in length. Some teachers include three or more projects in a year's curriculum claiming that projects enable students to cover more information than possible with conventional classroom approaches. Additionally, projects are frequently interdisciplinary in nature, drawing on a wide range of intelligences in their execution. For teachers interested in implementing projects into their curriculum, some guidelines follow:

GUIDELINES FOR EFFECTIVE PROJECTS

1. **Identify important concepts or practices and determine an open-ended project that encompasses such knowledge.**

2. **Involve students in planning the various aspects of a project. At times, students should also determine their own projects.**

3. **Identify needed materials and resources such as knowledgeable community members, parents, or older students.**

4. **Guide students through the various stages of project initiation, implementation, refinement, presentation, reflection, assessment, and plans for new and subsequent pursuits.**

5. **Select student drafts and final work to submit for documentation during and upon completion of the project.**

6. **Ask students to think back over their learning processes and personal growth achieved as a result of a project.**

7. **Have students present their projects to an audience of classmates, parents, community members, or others who will support as well as offer constructive criticism of student efforts.**

8. **Assess the project from numerous perspectives. Gardner recommends the following:**

    how well the project was planned, presented, and executed

    accuracy

    challenge level

    creativity and originality

    use of resources

    feedback from knowledgeable individuals about its achievements

    the amount of student learning

    the quality of student reflection

9. **When students have completed their projects, reflect on what their work reveals about them—their interests, strengths, challenges, whether they are independent or collaborative workers, and what interests emerged that might be addressed in future projects.**

Project-based learning skills must be explicitly taught. Students seldom have opportunities to manage their own learning at school, and they usually require guidance in how to proceed. In Bruce Campbell's book, *The Multiple Intelligences Handbook, Lesson Plans and More,* he outlines the following eight steps for teaching students how to carry out projects:

EIGHT STEPS FOR DOING PROJECTS

1. **STATE YOUR GOAL.**
   "I want to understand how visual illusions work."

2. **PUT YOUR GOAL INTO THE FORM OF A QUESTION.**
   "What are visual illusions and why do they fool our eyes?"

3. **LIST AT LEAST THREE SOURCES OF INFORMATION YOU WILL USE.**
   Library books on visual illusions
   Eye doctors or university professors
   Prints of M.C. Escher's work
   The art teacher

4. **DESCRIBE THE STEPS YOU WILL USE TO ACHIEVE YOUR GOAL.**
   Ask the librarian to find books on visual illusions.
   Read those books.
   Look up visual illusion in the encyclopedia and read what it says.
   Talk to the art teacher and maybe others about visual illusions.
   Look at Escher's work.

5. **LIST AT LEAST FIVE MAIN CONCEPTS OR IDEAS YOU WANT TO RESEARCH.**
   What are visual illusions?
   How is the human eye tricked?
   How are they made?
   Who are some artists who have made visual illusion art?
   Can I learn to make some visual illusions?

6. **LIST AT LEAST THREE METHODS YOU WILL USE TO PRESENT YOUR PROJECT.**
   Explain what optical illusions are.
   Make a diagram of how the human eye works.
   Make posters with famous optical illusions.
   Try to make optical illusions of my own.
   Hand out a sheet of optical illusions for class members to keep.
   Have the class try to make some.

7. **ORGANIZE THE PROJECT INTO A TIMELINE.**
   Week 1: Read sources of information.
   Week 1: Interview adults.
   Week 2: Look at a variety of optical illusions.
   Week 2: Try to make my own optical illusions.
   Week 2: Make diagram of eye.
   Week 2: Make handouts for class.
   Week 3: Practice presentation.
   Week 3: Present to class.

8. **DECIDE HOW YOU WILL EVALUATE YOUR PROJECT.**
   Practice in front of my parents and get their feedback.
   Practice in front of Matt and John and get their feedback.
   Ask class for feedback on my presentation and visuals.
   Fill out self-evaluation form.
   Read teacher's evaluation.
   Analyze videotape.

Project-based classrooms vary greatly from conventional ones. Students become the active initiators of their own learning, making school more relevant. For most students, projects naturally foster their academic and personal strengths, and provide insight into how to manage the numerous real-life projects they will undertake during their adult years.

APPRENTICESHIPS

Some teachers and schools who desire to nurture individual student talent establish mentoring or apprenticeship programs. Apprenticeships offer students powerful opportunities to work with older students or adults who have achieved competence in a discipline or craft. Students begin to perceive where their efforts are headed when immersed in the real world tasks that apprenticeships offer. Such programs usually occur in one of two formats—as part of the regular school curriculum or as extracurricular enrichment opportunities. Some examples follow:

SAMPLE PROGRAMS THAT ARE PART OF THE REGULAR SCHOOL DAY

Community members in the rural town of Concrete, Washington, volunteer to serve as master teachers in an apprenticeship program geared for fifth through seventh graders. Students spend one day a month "on-the-job" with transportation to and from school provided by community volunteers. All students are eligible to participate in apprenticeships of their choice.

Many schools have implemented cross-age tutoring programs where older students assist younger ones with school assignments. Not only do positive relationships develop among the students but academic skills are reinforced for both, and the older students usually appreciate

contributing to their school in such a tangible way.

The Key School in Indianapolis features 17 pods where students are mentored by teachers, parents, or community members in crafts or disciplines of their choice. Each student attends a pod four times weekly to work on material related to one or more intelligences with the goal of gaining real-world skills. Since the pods are open to any student in the school, they consist of children of varying ages. Pod topics include architecture, cooking, gardening, as well as the Sing and Song Pod, Logowriter, Imagine Indianapolis (a city planning pod), and Young Astronauts. In addition to the in-school apprenticeships, a local museum offers Key students apprenticeships in shipbuilding, journalism, animation, or weather monitoring.

EXTRACURRICULAR APPRENTICESHIPS

Through Jobs for the Future in Cambridge, Massachusetts, youth apprenticeships are established nationwide by linking employers with high schools to enhance student academic achievement and to create better pathways for transitions from school to work. JFF is a multi-year effort to establish a national system of apprenticeships especially geared for the 75% of students who do not earn a four year baccalaureate degree.

The PTA of an elementary school in Kent, Washington organized a once weekly after-school enrichment program offered by parents throughout the school year.

Similarly, to address their student latchkey problem, elementary teachers at another school created seven after-school clubs each dedicated to one of the seven intelligences. Most of the clubs meet weekly and provide an engaging alternative to being at home alone for young students.

The award-winning "Breakout" program at Skyview Junior High in Bothell, Washington encourages each student to pursue a personal interest and to become an expert on that topic. The main goal of "Breakout" is for students to make a difference in their community. Some choose to work in local hospitals, nursing homes, or schools. Others fundraise for causes of their choice, hold debates, make presentations, create a piece of art that communicates their interest in a topic, write short stories, make videos, or design computer software. A mentor is assigned to each student to help track her progress and to evaluate the project upon completion. While students pick the content of their community project, the teachers select the skills they must address. These cut across all disciplines and include interviewing, note-taking, statistical analysis, goal-setting, and performance techniques in the arts.

When contemplating how to establish apprenticeships, teachers might first identify the partnerships, resources, and allies already present at their schools. Many individuals, if asked, are willing to give of their time and expertise. Such programs require imagination and coordination to initiate and sustain. Apprenticeships need not become an additional teacher responsibility. At some schools, parent groups organize such efforts while at others, part-time coordinators are hired to implement and oversee the programs.

Some enterprising elementary teachers who were working with a centers-based MI classroom model decided that they would seek local community members to mentor their students. In recruiting local citizens, the teachers explained they would name their classroom centers after those who agreed to work the students. The school received numerous offers and the students benefited from real life mentors who shared their expertise on a bi-monthly basis in the classroom.

APPRENTICESHIP POSSIBILITIES

Gardner suggests that schools personalize their programs for students by offering apprenticeships during the elementary and middle school years. The apprenticeships he recommends would not track students into careers at an early age. Instead, they would contribute to a well-rounded liberal arts education and consume approximately one third of the students' schooling experience. Ideally, each student would participate in three apprenticeships:

one in an art form or craft,

one in an academic area, and

a third in a physical discipline such as dance or sports.

Students would have input into which apprenticeships they pursued. Through their apprenticeships, students would learn something frequently lost in today's fast-paced society: that one gains mastery of a valued skill gradually, with effort and discipline over time. Once students had achieved competence in the disciplines they are studying, they should experiment with their own approaches and creative extensions. Mentors and teachers should encourage and nurture the self-expression and creativity of each student. If apprenticeships became part of the norm of schooling, they would not only immerse students in context-rich learning, they would also dissolve the artificial walls between the real world and educational institutions, and graduate students who have amassed significant skills and knowledge during their years of education.

TEACHING FOR UNDERSTANDING

In nearly every student there is a five year old "unschooled" mind struggling to get out and express itself.

—HOWARD GARDNER,
*The Unschooled Mind:
How Children Think and
How Schools Should Teach*

In the first five years of life, the young child amasses a wealth of information—and misinformation. The young "intuitive learner" as Gardner refers to children of this age, develops comprehensive, "homespun" theories to make sense of the world. In *The Unschooled Mind*, Gardner suggests that such early notions later supersede instruction encountered in schools. When confronted with rote learning and uninspiring educational experiences, a student's early theories, scripts, and stereotypes hold sway; they do not readily dissolve with instruction. While education should endeavor to preserve the positive attributes of the youthful mind, it is also the responsibility of schools to revise the misconceptions students harbor. This can happen only when educators teach for understanding.

What is understanding? David Perkins, Co-Director with Howard Gardner of Project Zero at Harvard University, addresses the enigmatic nature of human insight. Perkins contrasts the concept of understanding with knowledge. When a person knows something the statement usually means he or she has mentally stored information and can readily retrieve it. By contrast, when a student understands something, it is assumed her skills surpass stored information. Perkins maintains that understanding refers to what individuals can do with information,

rather than what they have memorized. Insight involves action more than possession. When students understand something, they can explain concepts in their own words, use information appropriately in new contexts, make fresh analogies, and generalizations. Memorization and recitation are not indicative of understanding.

How can we approach teaching and learning for understanding? While interdisciplinary instruction is popular, Gardner is careful to remind educators that the core disciplines offer humanity the most sophisticated knowledge accrued throughout centuries. In fact, before we can think interdisciplinarily, we must first possess disciplinary knowledge. In order to move beyond the possession of information to truly understanding it, there are several approaches we can undertake as educators. There appear to be six important aspects of teaching for understanding. These are explained below.

PRINCIPLES FOR TEACHING FOR UNDERSTANDING:

1. **Educators can identify essential skills, knowledge, and outcomes for students to tackle.** We can ask, "What core ideas and issues are most crucial for students to know?" Instead of trying to cover a breadth of content, we can strive for depth. Some topics have more possibilities for offering depth of knowledge than others. For example, in social studies, students might focus on core concepts such as democracy, and in the sciences on change and evolution. In math and music, they might address patterns and transformation, and personal identity and values in literature. Once teachers have identified essential concepts, they can then plan to teach them through diverse modes and media.

2. Once timeworthy topics and essential goals or outcomes are determined, teachers next might address how best to help their students achieve understanding. **Curricular sequences and activities must next be mapped out.** Some teachers begin by organizing curriculum around broad themes. Yet the question may be asked, "If we want to teach thematically, where do themes come from?" The Key School suggests identifying themes through conversations with diverse groups: teachers, scholars, experts, business and government leaders, those working in cultural institutions, parents and students. By identifying themes with community involvement, it is often easier to gain greater acceptance of an innovative curriculum while also encouraging community members to participate. Sample themes from the Key School include:

Changes in Time and Space

The Renaissance Past and Present

Working in Harmony Here and Now

Working in Harmony In Other Cultures

Working in Harmony in Nature

Let's Make a Difference

Some teachers prefer organizing curriculum around open-ended questions for students to answer by the end of a unit. For example, the Montana Office of Public Instruction's new program, *Framework for Aesthetic Literacy*, suggests that K-12 English and language arts be taught through the visual and performing arts. Each unit begins with a focus question that provides the cohesive glue for the students' work. A sampling of the some of the *Framework for Aesthetic Literacy* questions include:

What is beauty? Who determines the standards for what is beautiful?

What does the past tell us about the present?

How do the arts reflect their cultures?

What can we learn from misfortune?

Why do authors write what they do? How do they do it?

By working with such open-ended questions, students learn basic skills, and in the process they deepen their understanding of the content through generating and defending their answers to some of life's most interesting questions.

Having identified their essential learnings and guiding questions, the Montana teachers involved in the pilot program teach curriculum through a three stage model. To introduce units, teachers provide students with a real world aesthetic encounter such as going to a museum, seeing a film, or interviewing a guest author. Next, students study English and language arts concepts while also practicing diverse thinking and communication skills. The final curricular phase asks students to generate their own products and their own answers to the unit's focus question.

3. **In addition to teacher-directed curriculum, students benefit from occasionally determining their own curriculum.** If a goal of K-12 education is to nurture lifelong learners, students need opportunities during their elementary and secondary years to acquire and apply self-directed learning skills. This can be accomplished through projects or through personal academic goals students identify and pursue. Through self-initiated academic experiences, students not only deepen their understanding of content knowledge, they also learn to be autonomous learners, thinkers, and creators.

4. **Another strategy for educating for understanding is to offer students apprenticeship opportunities where they can observe and interact with experts who embody the knowledge and practices of the individual disciplines.** By spending time with such individuals, students can grow in skills more readily than they might by filling out work sheets or questions at the end of the chapter.

5. **Instead of short-answer, fill-in-the-blank demonstrations of learning, all students should be expected to use higher level thinking skills in their studies.** They should be able to generalize what they learn, to provide examples, to connect the content to their personal experiences, and to apply their knowledge to new situations. For example, in a study of the criteria of life, students could be introduced to a bacteria or virus and be asked to determine whether the organism is alive or not. Students could explain the organism's potential impact on their or others' health, compare and contrast it with similar entities, and apply their knowledge of the organism and criteria of life to similar issues.

6. **Assessment can be naturally integrated throughout all learning activities.** Students should help establish the criteria by which their work will be evaluated before they begin their studies. Such public criteria will guide their efforts, as do samples of high quality work generated by others. Additionally, student work should be assessed through multiple perspectives: with the teacher assessing the student, students assessing each other, and students assessing themselves. In addition, it is important for students to give their teachers feedback on each major curriculum unit, suggesting ways to improve the learning experience for future classes.

A RUBRIC FOR EDUCATION FOR UNDERSTANDING

While the above principles of education for understanding may be interesting in theory, what might they look like in practice? To implement such principles in classroom teaching, the authors have developed the following rubric. Some teachers use the rubric as a guide for their curriculum development efforts or as a tool for peer feedback when reviewing one another's lessons or when observing in a colleague's classroom.

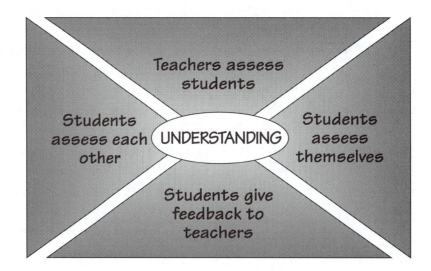

EDUCATION FOR UNDERSTANDING CRITERIA FOR CURRICULUM DEVELOPMENT AND TEACHER FEEDBACK

Criterion:	Evident:	Not Evident:	Comment:
THEME/GUIDING QUESTIONS: Is the theme and/or guiding question timeworthy? In what ways?			
OUTCOMES: Are student knowledge and skill outcomes identified, relevant, and developmentally appropriate? How might you explain to children and others that the outcomes are valuable?			
ESSENTIAL CONTENT: Are essential concepts of the major disciplines included? If so, which concepts?			
THINKING SKILLS: Are higher order thinking skills included? Which ones?			
PROJECTS: Do students pursue projects based on their interests?			
DIVERSE ENTRY POINTS: Do students learn through the seven intelligences?			
REAL WORLD APPLICATIONS: Are students asked to apply learning beyond the classroom?			
IN-DEPTH DEVELOPMENT OF INTELLIGENCE: Are student strengths developed through mentoring? How?			
ASSESSMENT: Are three dimensions of assessment (inter- and intrapersonal, and content and skills) included? How does the teacher receive feedback?			

CURRICULUM DEVELOPMENT MATRICES FOR STUDENT UNDERSTANDING

Two sample matrices follow. The first outlines an elementary unit on the theme of cooperation. This unit is currently being piloted by three elementary schools in Yakima, Washington. The second blank matrix is provided to assist those teachers interested in planning units that incorporate the principles of education for understanding.

CURRICULUM DEVELOPMENT MATRIX
FOR STUDENT UNDERSTANDING (SAMPLE)

THEME OR FOCUS QUESTION: Cooperation - What does our community offer?

RATIONALE: Human beings interact in communities

OUTCOMES:	ESSENTIAL CONTENT:	THINKING SKILLS:	PROJECTS:	M.I.-BASED LESSONS:
Students will explain reasons for immigration	Immigration	Cause & effect	Interview immigrants	One community with much diversity
Students will create map of local community	Population	Compare & contrast	Map one's block or neighborhood	Neighborhood Local resources
Students will actively particiate in their community	Interaction	Sequencing	Community service at food bank	Participation

DEVELOPMENT OF STUDENTS' STRENGTHS: Small group mentoring provided by local community members

UNIT ASSESSMENT: Small group discussions with suggestions for changes

CURRICULUM DEVELOPMENT MATRIX
FOR STUDENT UNDERSTANDING

THEME OR FOCUS QUESTION: _____

RATIONALE: _____

_____

OUTCOMES:	ESSENTIAL CONTENT:	THINKING SKILLS:	PROJECTS:	M.I.-BASED LESSONS:

DEVELOPMENT OF STUDENTS' STRENGTHS: _____

_____

UNIT ASSESSMENT: _____

_____

SUMMARY

Educators who are considering adopting a Multiple Intelligences curriculum should plan to discuss with their colleagues what such an approach might look like in their building. As stated at the outset of this chapter, there is no single preferred approach to lesson or unit design suggested by the Theory of Multiple Intelligences. Instead, Gardner's theory presents educators with numerous curricular challenges.

Some of these include how to design multimodal lessons, how to identify what is most essential to teach, how to team with other colleagues, how to encourage self-directed learning through projects, how to nurture individual student talent, and finally, how to acknowledge and more effectively teach the "five year old mind" so that education results in genuine understanding.

APPLYING THE MULTIPLE INTELLIGENCES IN YOUR CLASSROOM

1. Important ideas or insights gleaned from this chapter: _____

_____

_____

_____

_____

_____

_____

2. Areas I'd like to learn more about: _____

_____

_____

_____

_____

_____

_____

3. Ways I can use this information in my teaching. Please note that all of the strategies mentioned in this chapter are listed below with space provided to note how each strategy might be incorporated into classroom instruction:

CURRICULUM STRATEGY	CLASSROOM APPLICATION

Lesson Planning through the Multiple Intelligences:

Instructional Menus _____

A Lesson Planning Matrix _____

Sample Lessons _____

Interdisciplinary Units _____

Interdisciplinary Planning through the
Multiple Intelligences _____

Interdisciplinary Planning with
Developmental Sequences _____

Interdisciplinary Schoolwide Approaches
at the Secondary Level _____

Intelligence Teams _____

Benefits of Teaming _____

Curriculum Development for Intelligence
Development _____

A Learning Centers Instructional Format
Project Spectrum _____

Discovering Curriculum Bias: _____

Project-Based Curriculums:

Guidelines for Effective Projects _____

Eight Steps for Doing Projects _____

Apprenticeships:

Sample Programs that Are Part of the
Regular School Day _____

Extracurricular Apprenticeships _____

Apprenticeship Possibilities _____

Teaching for Understanding:

Principles for Teaching for Understanding _____

A Rubric for Education for Understanding _____

Curriculum Development Matrices for
Student Understanding _____

CURRICULUM DEVELOPMENT REFERENCES

Campbell, B. (1994). *The Multiple Intelligences Handbook: Lesson Plans and More.* Stanwood, WA: Campbell and Associates.

Dewey, J. (1899). *School and Society.* Chicago: University of Chicago Press.

Educational Testing Service and Harvard Project Zero. (1991). *Arts Propel: An Introductory Handbook.* Available from Harvard Graduate School of Education. Cambridge, MA 02138.

Framework for Aesthetic Literacy: Montana Arts and English Curriculum. (1994). Helena, MT: Montana Office of Public Instruction.

Gardner, H. (1989). *To Open Minds: Chinese Clues to the Dilemma of Contemporary Education.* N.Y.: Basic Books.

Gardner, H. (1991). *The Unschooled Mind: How Children Think and How Schools Should Teach.* N.Y.: Basic Books.

Krechevsky, M. (1991). "Project Spectrum: An Innovative Assessment Alternative." *Educational Leadership.* Vol. 48 No. 5 Feb. 199.

Krechevsky, M. (1992). "Multiple Intelligences: Theory into Practice." A presentation for the State Department of Education of Kentucky in Frankfurt, KY: February 3, 1992.

Perkins, D. (1991). "Educating for Insight." *Educational Leadership.* Volume 49 No. 2 October, 1991.

CHAPTER 9

DISSOLVING THE BOUNDARIES: ASSESSMENT THAT ENHANCES LEARNING

" Unless assessment is placed in the context of authentic domains and social environments, we doubt it can adequately represent human intellectual performance."

— Howard Gardner, Multiple Intelligences:
The Theory in Practice

ASSESSING SUCCESS:

Gabriel experienced little success throughout his elementary and middle school years. Labeled by teachers as a poor student with a bad attitude, Gabriel readily accepted his instructors' appraisals.

His low expectations of any future academic accomplishments were evident in his statement to his math teacher on the first day of high school when Gabriel blatantly suggested, "Give up on me." Knowing that first impressions mattered, the teacher quickly responded, "I'm not intending to give up on you!" Gabriel retorted cynically, "It's just a matter of time."

The teacher already knew that Gabriel scored at the third or fourth grade level on standardized math tests. What he didn't know, however, was how he might work with this recalcitrant student. To learn more about Gabriel, the teacher informally observed him both inside and outside of class. In the hallways, the boy was animated, often talking with several students

and jocularly swatting and slapping his friends. Noting whom Gabriel spent time with, the teacher later approached the boys, asking them to tell him about Gabriel. The teacher learned that Gabriel held a job at a local grocery store, and that he enjoyed skateboarding. This information inspired ideas about how to engage him in math.

The next day, the teacher suggested to his ninth grade math class that they had the option of replacing some textbook work with math projects. When the class unanimously voted in favor the real-world projects, the teacher explained that students must research information about products or concepts they found interesting, and identify mathematical principles that were represented in their topics. The students spent the rest of their math class brainstorming criteria for assessing their projects. Since Gabriel spent the hour with his head down, looking bored and disengaged as usual, the teacher approached him individually just as the bell rang. "Gabriel, I know you're good at skateboarding. Your friends tell me so. Why don't you do a project on skateboards? You could even bring one or two skateboards to school to do a demonstration for the class." In response to the teacher's well-meant suggestion, Gabriel shrugged and walked out of the room.

Since the projects weren't due for two weeks, the teacher did not know that Gabriel was working on one until another student in the class blurted out, "Wait until you see what Gabriel's doing!" The teacher's spirits rose—perhaps, after all, he was choosing to participate.

As the appointed project day drew closer, students began signing up to present their work. When Gabriel stated he wanted to do his first, he quickly remarked to the teacher that he "just wanted to get it over with."

Students created score sheets for assessing each other's projects. The teacher explained he would use the same form. On project day, Gabriel was the first to share his work. He displayed one chart that compared

several brands of skateboards in relation to performance, cost, and design; another diagram that gave a statistical analysis of top ranking skateboarders and their abilities; and a third that revealed the results of a survey he conducted of fellow classmates and their attitudes towards skateboarding. Without using appropriate math terminology, Gabriel also explained that skateboarding involved several mathematical principles including those of physics, symmetry, probability, and mathematical thinking and problem-solving skills. When students and teacher handed Gabriel their assessment sheets evaluating his project, his slight smile went unnoticed by most except the math instructor.

The project assignment was the first time Gabriel chose to participate in his math class. His involvement not only enhanced his self-image, but also revealed an effective mathematical thinker. By the end of the semester, on a standardized test, Gabriel's math scores improved significantly. Though his participation in class remained somewhat inconsistent, neither Gabriel nor his teacher talked again about giving up.

A NATION ASSESSES

According to the National Center for Fair and Open Testing, over 100 million standardized tests are administered annually in the United States. On the average, American children take three standardized tests each school year. At some grade levels, children are required to sit for as many as seven to twelve standardized tests in a year's time. Scores from such tests determine what courses students will take, with whom, and what kind of academic gains they are expected to achieve. Standardized test performance dictates student promotion from one grade level to the next, placement in remedial or gifted programs, and graduation from high school. While powerfully affecting individual students, standardized tests also influence broad educational goals and programmatic funding. They provide a standard against which policymakers can measure student and educator performance, identifying programs that should receive rewards or sanctions.

In recent decades, reliance on standardized testing has increased, as have concerns about its impact on educational resources, curricular, and instructional practices. In 1990, the National Commission on Testing and Public Policy released a report entitled *From Gatekeeper to Gateway: Transforming Testing in America* that highlights many of the growing concerns with standardized testing of both children and adults. Most standardized tests tend to overassess rote knowledge while underassessing what students can do with their knowledge. The Commission recommended that the United States:

- **revise how it develops and uses human talent by restructuring educational testing.**

- **limit reliance upon multiple choice testing since it lacks accountability, leads to unfairness in the allocation of opportunity, and undermines vital social policies.**

- **cease using test scores as the single measure in**

making important decisions about individuals and their competencies.

- **promote greater development of all Americans with alternative forms of assessment so that testing opens gates of opportunity rather than closing them off.**

While norm-referenced, multiple choice tests are quick and efficient to administer, policymakers are nevertheless reconsidering their value. Rhode Island, Vermont, California, Kentucky, and Connecticut have pioneered approaches that yield more genuine pictures of student learning than possible with paper and pencil, short-answer evaluations. In 1991, the Council of Chief State School Officers identified 40 states currently planning or implementing some form of alternative assessment. Numerous teachers and districts are also working with portfolios and performance-based tasks. Admittedly still in the developmental phase, new forms of assessment are fraught with questions about time, reliability, and manageability. Yet many educators, acutely aware of the deficiencies and limitations of standardized measures, believe that new approaches to assessment will capture more of what students know and can do both within and outside of school.

Through Project Zero, Howard Gardner and others studied classroom assessment and determined that effective monitoring of student work cannot exist in a vacuum. The classroom itself must be transformed before meaningful assessment is possible. It is not enough to change current evaluation procedures. Instructional practices must be altered so that an effective assessment culture emerges in our schools. Currently, assessment comes at the end of a unit of study and emphasizes grading and accountability. While such evaluation practices serve important roles at times, they do not necessarily improve students' learning. In an assessment culture, the focus is upon understanding of content which necessitates providing students with criteria, feedback, and opportunities for reflection and self-assessment throughout any course of study. This chapter, then, describes numerous facets of an assessment culture including:

The intention of this chapter is to provide tools to expand the assessment repertoires of classroom teachers. The authors do not suggest that these techniques appropriately apply across schools, districts, or the nation for high-stakes policy decisions about schools and those who study in them. Rather, our intention is to encourage teachers to create classroom assessment measures that require students to use rather than merely recall their knowledge.

PRINCIPLES TO GUIDE CLASSROOM ASSESSMENT

Between 1986 and 1991, Arts PROPEL, a pilot approach to teaching and assessing in the arts and humanities, was field-tested by Harvard Project Zero, by Educational Testing Service, and by teachers, administrators, and students in Pittsburgh, Cambridge, and Boston. The two main goals of Arts PROPEL included observing how students learn in the arts at the middle and high school levels, and devising evaluation methods to enhance student learning and assess their progress. While Arts PROPEL initially assumed its work had relevance for secondary level arts instruction, its implications appear appropriate for elementary grades as well as other academic subjects.

Important principles, included below, guided Arts PROPEL assessment efforts. The name PROPEL is an acronym for the three roles students should play in assessment: PRO is for *production*, which includes an R for *reflection*, PE for *perception*, and L for the *learning* that results. PROPEL principles may serve as guidelines for teachers interested in changing their assessment procedures. Also provided are sample assessment tools and examples that bring each principle to life.

I. ASSESSMENT CAPTURES GROWTH OVER TIME:

Frequently, student work is assessed in an isolated, snapshot manner, eclipsing a long-term perspective of academic growth. The portfolio is one tool that effectively offers longitudinal perspectives of student work while encouraging ongoing reflection of classroom learning. Depending on their use, portfolios provide evidence to students, teachers, parents, and others of both academic and intrapersonal growth.

Students, when given the opportunity, often enjoy assuming an active role in evaluation by determining their own longitudinal, academic gains. This can be achieved by asking students to contrast their former knowledge with their current skills and comprehension. Students can actively reflect on their growth in each subject matter area by reviewing the contents of their portfolios, journals, or several samples of their work. To aid such reflection, teachers might pose the following questions for students to consider:

STUDENT REFLECTION OF ACADEMIC GROWTH

In reviewing samples of your work during the last few months,
please respond to the following questions:

- What samples of your work did you review? When were the assignments completed?

- How has your work changed? What is different about it now from before? What evidence do you have of such change?

- What did you learn that you didn't know previously? When and how did you learn this new information?

- How have you used your new knowledge both in this class, in other classes, and outside of school?

- Do the changes in your work affect how you see yourself as a mathematician, writer, artist, etc.?

- Have you achieved an adequate knowledge and skill level? If not, how might you gain additional information in the future?

- What other comments might you make about your work over the last few months?

Even second or third grade students can begin to respond to similar questions when asked to reflect on their progress. The important issue to remember is that teachers need to ask reflective questions to help children perceive their own growth. Parents, teachers, and others can also assess student work using the same questions suggested above. In fact, it is often beneficial for student, teacher, and parent to compare and contrast their responses to the same questions.

2. ASSESSMENT IS MULTIDIMENSIONAL

Single grades or scores provide the student, teacher, and others with insufficient information about achievement. Traditional measures such as letter grades or numerical percentages merely state whether a student is low, average, or high in a subject matter area. This unidimensional view does not convey what the student accomplished and what she found challenging. For example, in a math class, a student might receive a C grade. This single score does not indicate that the student performed at a superior level in mathematical thinking and problem-solving, above average on daily assignments, yet tended to fail most tests and quizzes due to severe test anxiety. If the "C" grade was replaced with additional dimensions of assessment, meaningful and relevant interventions might be possible. One alternative math assessment might appear as follows:

MATHEMATICS QUARTERLY ASSESSMENT

Student name: _____ Date: _____

Major concepts studied: _____

_____

Student Performance Checklist:

	Strong	Adequate	Poor
Comprehension of math processes e.g. quadratic equations			
Interpretation of problems			
Problem-solving of text problems			
Problem-solving of open-ended, real world problems			
Performance on assignments			
Performance on tests			

Narrative comments: _____

_____

_____

Identified student strengths to build upon: _____

_____

_____

Recommendations for strengthening skills: _____

_____

_____

In contrast to most reporting measures, this assessment tool identifies student strengths and weaknesses, and recommends options for ongoing learning.

Another approach to multidimensional assessment is to gain feedback on student performance from numerous sources. In fact, Arts PROPEL recommends that assessment include three perspectives: 1) assessment of content and skills, 2) interpersonal assessment from peers, parents, or knowledgeable community members, and 3) intrapersonal assessment where the student is responsible for assessing his or her own achievement.

One of the authors developed the following report card for elementary students that incorporates all three perspectives. This report augments the school's traditional trimester evaluation of student progress.

DIFFERENT PERSPECTIVES REPORT CARD

NAME _____ DATE _____

How are you doing in the following categories?

Write one sentence in the box under self describing your progress in each area.

Then, ask a classmate to evaluate your performance in the second column.

Next, take it home and ask a parent or other adult to assess your work in the third column.

Compare and contrast everyone's opinion of your progress. Do you agree or disagree with their comments? Write your reactions to this feedback on the back of the card, and place the card in your portfolio when completed.

	SELF	CLASSMATE	PARENT
LANGUAGE ARTS: reading writing speaking listening			
VISUAL & PERFORMING ARTS: music movement drawing			
MATH: computation problem-solving			
CENTERS WORK: completing tasks working with others			
INDIVIDUAL PROJECTS: research planning presenting			

3. ASSESSMENT INFORMS INSTRUCTION

A frequent criticism of standardized or traditional assessment is that it focuses instruction on memorization and recall. When assessment addresses even more essential and important aspects of learning, it can influence and improve instruction in positive ways. For example, a recent survey of language arts teachers involved in the California Assessment Program (CAP) revealed that over 90% made changes for the better in their teaching of writing when using the performance-based assessment tools. The teachers claimed that CAP increased their expectations for student writing achievement, and that the new performance measures served to strengthen their schools' English curricula.

As most educators would agree, one of the greatest obstacles to effective learning is the pressure to cover content. Frequently, we can do little more than survey a smorgasbord of topics with our students. Many teachers, when teaching through the Multiple Intelligences, claim that learning slows down, that less content is covered but that what is studied is addressed in greater depth with resultant increases in student understanding. Instead of despairing over pressure for coverage, teachers might take solace in the fact that our entire culture is fully immersed in the information age. Since more information is available than we will ever access or use in each discipline, it becomes imperative for teachers and others to identify what is most essential for students to know, and what behaviors will benefit them most as adults. It appears likely that teachers, schools, districts, states, federal agencies, and national associations will ultimately determine essential curriculum.

In some cases, classroom teachers are deciding what is most important to teach, following the principle, "If it is important enough to teach, it is important enough to assess." For example, teachers in Northglenn, Colorado, have identified the five following essential components of writing: organization, sentence structure, usage, mechanics, and format. Their assessment consists of a five point scale ranging from a low skill level of one to a high of five that scores each essential element of writing in student work. The writing curriculum integrates what students are to learn and how they will be assessed. Students know in advance not only what their task is, but the standards for their writing.

Just as essential classroom curriculum can be identified, schoolwide outcomes can also be specified to guide curriculum development and assessment in each subject area. For example, a middle school might select the following outcomes as integral to all subject areas: identifying a problem, accessing information and resources, learning disciplinary content, considering diverse perspectives, collaborating on projects, reflecting on one's growth, and effectively managing one's behavior. To help students achieve these outcomes, each classroom, as part of its curriculum, might feature open-ended problems, group and independent projects, access to technology, multicultural issues, portfolios, and positive discipline strategies. Each teacher in each discipline would then teach to and assess the same outcomes.

Another way assessment informs instruction is through specifying the standards by which students will be assessed. Grading criteria are most meaningful when democratically determined by teachers and students together. Students gain insight into both assessment and learning when they engage in discussions about what constitutes good work. Ideally, high standards in any classroom should address both the knowledge of content and the processes of learning. Typical tests tend to overemphasize factual knowledge with little focus upon the thinking and learning processes. The following example shows how grading criteria can include both content and process:

```
┌────────────────────────────────────────────────────────────────────┐
│                        SCIENCE ASSESSMENT                            │
│                                                                      │
│    Name: _____  Date: _____     │
│                                                                      │
│         PROCEDURES:                    COMMENTS:                      │
│    ────────────────────────────────────────────────────────────     │
│    Understands target concept     _____    │
│    Makes a meaningful prediction  _____    │
│    Selects an effective approach  _____    │
│    Uses correct equipment         _____    │
│    Analyzes data                  _____    │
│    Measures accurately            _____    │
│    Graphs data appropriately      _____    │
│    Seeks peer help if needed      _____    │
│    Records observations           _____    │
│    Considers next steps           _____    │
│    Cleans up after experiment     _____    │
│    Other:                         _____    │
└────────────────────────────────────────────────────────────────────┘
```

Traditionally, assessment has provided information about student comprehension and performance. It also indicates, however, the quality of instruction, providing insight into how effectively students were taught in the first place and what kinds of additional instruction they might need. Teachers should hold discussion sessions or seek written feedback from their students at the end of each major curriculum unit to learn what was effective and what was lacking in the instruction. Teachers should observe when students struggle with concepts and plan to reteach the topics through the seven intelligences to increase understanding. It is also just as necessary to evaluate students multimodally so they can demonstrate what they have learned in numerous modes.

Rather than being concerned that all students master all concepts at the same rate, or that some need more help than others, teachers and schools can create support structures to insure greater student success at varying times. At the beginning of any term, teachers might specify what concepts are to be learned and how and what assignments are required. Students can be free to work at their own pace, completing curriculum projects in a timely manner. Other resources in addition to the classroom teacher should be made available. By having binders or notebooks of student assignments from previous years, students can perceive how their predecessors approached similar topics, how they problem-solved, and how they brought their projects to fruition. Cross-age tutoring with older students or community volunteers often increases achievement. In Washington State, students from Sedro Wooley High School tutor children from Concrete Elementary School, some 35 miles away, by fax. Homework halls, phone hotlines, or centers in community agencies can also provide important support.

Teachers can also begin to rethink instruction and assessment by reflecting on valued social roles that adults assume. What are the projects or tasks performed by accountants, historians, journalists, naturalists, artists, musicians, or social workers? What content knowledge and abilities do they each possess? Are there implications for classroom instruction and assessment? Typically, vocational education programs have addressed this issue well by identifying a few important performance tasks that effectively cover essential content while providing students with increasingly complex tasks to be mastered such as building a usable structure in carpentry. Debate and arts programs are often structured similarly.

Even with pre-school and primary-age students, assessment can focus on abilities relevant to achieving rewarding adult roles or endstates. For example, at Project Spectrum in language arts, a child's ability to tell stories or provide descriptive accounts of experiences (the skills pertinent to journalists or novelists) are assessed rather than the repetition of a series of sentences. When grounded in real world activities, assessment is more meaningful to the child, teacher, and the child's family.

4. INFORMAL ASSESSMENT IS IMPORTANT

Both formal and informal assessment is valuable. Teachers know much more about their students than is typically recorded with traditional paper and pencil measures. Students are informally assessed daily by teachers who observe their participation in regular classroom activities and interactions. At times, such informal knowledge can be made explicit through simple observation checklists such as the one provided below:

OBSERVATION CHECKLIST

Teacher: _____ Class: _____ Date: _____

TARGET SKILLS

Ratings: + = Frequently
          ✓ = Sometimes
          o = Not yet

Names of Students						Comments
1.						
2.						
3.						
4.						
5.						
6.						
7.						
8.						
9.						
10.						
11.						
12.						
13.						
14.						
15.						

In addition to observation, teachers can hold small or whole group discussion sessions where students critique good or low quality work as well as comment on the quality of instruction. Such critiques do not leave a paper trail, but instead provide the teacher with insight into student perceptions of their work, their classroom experiences, and their accomplishments and frustrations.

5. STUDENTS ARE ACTIVE SELF-ASSESSORS

If a goal of K-12 education is to develop autonomous, lifelong learners, students need opportunities to manage their own learning and to critique their achievement. Students are capable of evaluating their strengths and weaknesses, of articulating what they have learned, and recognizing how they have applied appropriate thinking and learning processes. They can actively document their learning in journals, peer assessment sessions, checklists, exhibitions, informal student/teacher discussions, or portfolios. One example of active student reflection is evident in the following portfolio reflection sheet:

PORTFOLIO ITEM REFLECTION

Name: _____ Date: _____

Description of the portfolio selection:

Why did you select this sample from your portfolio for reflection?

What content knowledge did you learn from your work on this piece?

What did you learn about yourself as a historian, biologist, etc.?

If you were to continue working on this selection, what would you add, delete, or change? Why?

What problems did you encounter working on this piece? How did you resolve them?

In what ways does your selection meet the specified grading criteria for this assignment? In what ways does it not meet such criteria? Identify any ways it may have surpassed such criteria.

What would you like to research further because of what you learned from this piece?

When students are asked to reflect on their own work, they assume an active, not passive, role in the learning process. They construct their own understanding of a subject matter. They perceive and begin to internalize standards that are relevant and meaningful. They realize the choices they made in their work and the options they rejected. They also acquire the skills for ongoing growth outside of school wherever self-initiated and open-ended activities occur.

By extending these five principles of assessment into classroom procedures, the line between assessment and learning naturally blurs and dissolves. Information about students is valuable when it is gained over time while students are actively engaged in learning. Assessment levied when students have completed their work is often too late to be helpful. "Intelligence fair" measures tap student abilities directly through the seven intelligences without an exclusive reliance upon linguistic, logical-mathematical, standardized measures. Assessment becomes less threatening, less decontextualized, and assumes its rightful place as a partner in learning. In such an environment, student work is not done once and thrown away. Students continue to refine their learning by resubmitting their work for suggestions and critique, and by reviewing it for evidence of what they have learned and have yet to learn. Assessment ceases merely to reflect learning—it enhances learning.

ASSESSMENT OF THE INTELLIGENCES

Project Spectrum, a laboratory pre-school at Harvard based on the work of Howard Gardner and David Feldman, is dedicated, in part, to exploring the development of the Multiple Intelligences in young children. Originally, Gardner intended to create seven instruments at Project Spectrum to assess his identified intelligences. He quickly realized, however, that since intelligence does not exist in a vacuum any attempt at gauging human capacities would necessarily have to measure prior life experiences and other influences. Prior learnings, the environment, heredity, and cultural values, all shape and mold the capacities an individual develops. Because of the interplay among biological, environmental, and cultural potentials, it makes little sense to consider intelligence in the abstract.

MEASURING INTELLIGENCE AT PROJECT SPECTRUM

In order to measure the Multiple Intelligences of students at Project Spectrum, Gardner and his colleagues decided first to immerse children in a year-long, enriched environment and then to assess the capacities they demonstrated in a natural context. Mara Krechevsky, Director of Project Spectrum, works extensively with a comprehensive approach to assessing individual intelligences of Spectrum students. Children's unique cognitive profiles are determined in part through a variety of processes:

- **the classroom environment features engaging materials, games, and learning opportunities for each of the seven intelligences;**

- **several forms of documentation are used consisting of score sheets, observation checklists, portfolios, and tape recordings;**

- **information is gathered over time in the child's environment;**

- intelligences are tapped directly through each particular medium rather than assessing abilities through conventional linguistic and mathematical means;

- children's strengths are emphasized;

- assessment is embedded in real-world activities useful both in and outside of the school setting.

One sample assessment activity used in a Spectrum classroom is the bus game. This game identifies a child's ability to use a notational system, perform mental calculations, and organize number information for one or more variables. Using props, the game features a cardboard bus, a game board with bus stops, adult and child figures who get on and off the bus, and sets of colored chips. The adult supervising the activity assumes the role of the bus driver, while the student being assessed serves as the conductor. To play the game, the child must keep track of how many people get on and off the bus at each stop. The bus trips become increasingly more challenging. At the first stop, for example, people can only get on the bus. At the second, they may get on or off. The student is also asked to count the number of adults and children on the bus. For some trips, the chips may be used to keep track of the numbers while on others, the child must count in his head.

In this game, students are assessed on their ability to organize numerical information efficiently in a real-world situation, but quantitative skills are only one aspect of logical intelligence measured. Students are also assessed on their abilities to create a notational system and code different kinds of information. As the child assumes the role of a conductor, he practices the skills needed by an adult in such a job. Such assessment procedures have meaning for the child, the teacher, the child's family, and the community at large.

Numerous other games and activities totaling some 15 measures in all have been devel-oped at Project Spectrum. All of the measures are "intelligence fair" by avoiding hypothetical situations and abstractions and providing children with challenging concrete tools to manipulate in each intelligence area. For example, physical skill is measured, in part, with an obstacle course; mathematical intelligence is assessed through the bus, treasure hunt, and dinosaur games. Other Spectrum tasks include: storytelling and reporting for linguistic intelligence, using portfolios for art, analyzing interpersonal interactions and intrapersonal awareness with a classroom model and events, singing, playing and learning new songs for musical intelligence, participating in creative movement curriculum for kinesthetic intelligence, and completing assembly tasks and observations for additional logical-mathematical activities.

WORKING STYLES:

In assessing individual intelligences, Project Spectrum researchers discovered the importance of considering the "working styles" of children as they interacted with materials or tasks of a specific kind of intelligence. Some students demonstrated the same working style across several intelligences, while the styles of others appear influenced, in part, by the task at hand. Some children, for example, were focused and reflective when working in their areas of strength, and distractible and impulsive when working in areas that proved more challenging. Working styles refer to processes of learning and may provide insight into approaches to tasks that may help or hinder learning. Student working style characteristics noted at Spectrum include:

Easily engaged..........Reluctant to engage
Confident.................Tentative
Playful.....................Serious
Focused....................Distractible

Persistent................Frustrated by task

Reflective................Impulsive

Apt to work slowly...Apt to work quickly

Conversational........Quiet

Responds to visual, kinesthetic or auditory stimuli

Demonstrates planned approach

Brings personal agenda or strength to task

Finds humor

Uses materials in unexpected ways

Has pride in accomplishment

Pays attention to detail

Is curious about materials

Is concerned with correct answer

Focuses on interaction with adult

Transforms the task or material

When Spectrum teachers observe a student in action, they identify the distinctive styles he or she exhibits. It should be noted that there are no negative or positive connotations attached to the working style descriptions. Of course, not all characteristics are evident in a single student's learning processes. The concept of working styles may provide additional information about each intelligence and may reveal important implications for educational interventions.

SPECTRUM REPORTS:

Spectrum tasks are implemented over the course of a year. During this time, the working styles of each child are also observed. At the end of the year, a Spectrum Report summarizes all information gathered about a child. The document describes the child's personal profile of strengths and weaknesses and suggests what might be done at home, at school, or in the community to further enhance strengths and bolster weakness. Such informal recommendations are offered in an effort to help students and families make informed choices about future options. A sample Spectrum Report follows:

Spectrum Report
June 1998

Greg

Greg has shown a strong ability and interest in many of the Spectrum activities presented to the class this year. He has distinguished himself in the areas of visual arts and numbers.

Greg's efforts in the area of visual arts are impressive for a child his age. What is most striking is his comfort and effectiveness in using a wide variety of media. These include paint, markers, collage, wood and styrofoam. In drawings, Greg has shown an unusual sensitivity to color, composition and detail. His drawings consist of both complex representations and designs. In one drawing, Greg drew an extremely detailed underwater scene including a half dozen distinctively different fish, an underwater vehicle, a whale spouting water, and flecks of "super red fish food". In another drawing, he drew a Native American with his donkey after carefully looking at a similar picture on the wall of the classroom. He added stripes of face paint in alternating colors and a large headdress complete with dozens of feathers. Greg's use of space is also very effective. He uses the whole page for his compositions, relating individual parts to one another and to the page as a whole. Greg's 3-D sculptures are outstanding as well. He exhibits an understanding and awareness of design and

composition "all the way around" his creations. Informal observations of Greg in the classroom have shown that he can spend a long time working on a single painting or drawing and that he enjoys reworking many of them over and over again.

Greg has revealed a strong competence with numbers and number concepts. When playing the Dinosaur Game, a Spectrum activity centered on numbers and number concepts, his counting was a bit inconsistent, but he understood the strategy component of the game. When given the choice of a die that had five out of six signs meaning that he could move his gamepiece forward, or five out of six signs meaning he could move backward, he chose the die that would help him to win and articulated the reason for the choice. He also correctly chose the move that would be most beneficial to him and the move that would be least beneficial to the adult, his opponent in the game.

Whereas earlier in the year Greg appeared to have some difficulty counting accurately while playing the Bus Game, in the spring he exhibited an outstanding facility with numbers for a child his age. He devised a successful method of using different colored chips to help him keep a running tally of figures entering and exiting a toy bus at a series of station stops. Later in the activity, he was able to calculate in his head the number of figures entering and exiting the bus at the various stops.

Greg has also demonstrated a strong interest in the Discovery Area of the classroom. At the very beginning of the year, Greg helped to dig up animal bones in the playground. He spent a lot of time looking at the bones and trying to figure out how the pieces fit together. This interest has persisted throughout the entire year. Greg oftens brings in an assortment of his pets from home to put in the discovery area and tell the children about during "Show and Tell". In addition, he made a remarkably accurate sculpture of a bone out of clay. Based on these observations, we feel that Greg might enjoy additional opportunities to explore the natural world. The Children's Museum and the Museum of Science both have excellent displays and resources in this area.

In an activity which involved taking apart and reassembling two small food grinders, Greg showed a competence with and understanding of mechanical objects. He approached the task in a straightforward, serious and focused manner and completed it with very little help from the adult. Greg was attentive to detail and demonstrated an understanding of the causal connection between the various parts of the objects.

One activity in which Greg was not initially eager to participate was creative movement. He had some difficulty with the structure of the movement sessions earlier in the year. He would usually choose to be in the "audience" rather than participate and would sometimes disrupt

the group and exress his disdain for the movement activities. As the year progressed, Greg became an active member of the creative movement sessions. He generated some inventive movement ideas for the group and participated willingly in most of the group's activities.

Greg revealed strengths in many areas throughout the course of the year. He was enthusiastic and energetic in his approach to many of the Spectrum activities. He showed that he was capable of extremely focused work in areas of particular interest to him such as the visual arts and natural science. There were, however, some activities in which Greg chose not to engage. For example, he chose not to participate in the two music activities and the storyboard activity. He expressed an interest in the materials themselves, asking how things were made and where things came from, but did not always show an interest in the structured activities related to the materials.

As the year progressed, Greg became comfortable with the one-to-one format of the Spectrum activities. This enabled him to share his ideas more freely and make apparent the strengths and interests he had in a variety of areas.

Over the last few years, Harvard's Spectrum program has been adapted in several ways. Teachers and researchers from around the country have used the program at their schools with average, gifted, and at-risk children from four to eight years old for research, enrichment, or as the foundation for compensatory programs. Harvard's Spectrum is also creating wider spheres of learning for children by forging links among, school, museum, home, and local communities. For example, Spectrum has developed a curriculum for pre-schoolers to be used at The Children's Museum in Boston to make museum exhibits more accessible to young children. Its program "Connections" is a community mentor program that enables young children to work with professional adults who exhibit blends of different intelligences in their jobs. Spectrum hopes that its approaches may prove to increase academic achievement, enhance self-esteem and school adjustment, and for those children at risk of school failure, improve their attitudes and make educational success possible.

PERCEIVING STUDENT STRENGTHS

One of the most fundamental implications of Gardner's work is how we perceive our students. Educators want to identify student strengths. This has proved challenging to accomplish for several reasons. We can appreciate, at least theoretically, that students possess individual cognitive profiles with varying strengths. And, yet when trying to put such knowledge into practice it is difficult to observe each child through a Multiple Intelligence lens. The initial challenge educators face is to look beyond our own inherent strengths to perceive those that may be unfamiliar to us. Additionally, when we discuss how students are doing in school, we continue to think in traditional ways such as how well students perform in basic skill areas. These issues are exasaerbated by the fact that most teacher development efforts at both the pre-service and in-service levels emphasize how to educate for traditional literacies. There is very little work being done in teaching teachers how to perceive student strengths across content areas. We need new tools to expand our observation skills, to assist us in identifying and documenting diverse student gifts.

Many educators wish there were simple checklists that could readily indicate the intelligence strengths of their students. In fact, several such Multiple Intelligence checklists have appeared. Educators should use them with caution, if at all, since they do not adequately reflect the numerous facets of each intelligence, nor do they use "intelligence fair" measures to assess student strengths.

Even when teachers have embraced the belief that all students possess strengths, it remains all too easy to limit the perception of talent to linguistic and logical-mathematical skills. One school's experience makes this issue clear.

Montgomery Knolls Elementary School in Maryland County, Maryland has made a strong commitment to MI theory and practice in curriculum and pedagogy. Yet, teachers there have learned that perceiving student strengths in non-traditional areas such as in kinesthetic or visual domains is not easy. A study at that school has shown that students even though gifted in dance, mechanical ability, or in collaborating with others will not be perceived as gifted unless they are also highly verbal. As educators, we rely on the traditional measures of academic success even when confronted with diverse gifts.

How can we go about counteracting our basic skill bias? How can we broaden our perception of student strengths? Some suggestions follow:

Approaches to Perceiving Student Strengths:

1. Enrich your classroom environment with manipulatives, art supplies, musical instruments, hands-on math activities, books and book-making materials, and other items to engage all seven intelligences. Provide students with free time and observe the choices they make or what they enjoy doing the most.

2. Survey parents to determine student interests and strengths. Learn what students like to do outside of school as one way to identify interests and talents.

3. Interview teacher specialists such as P.E., art, music, librarians, and technology personnel to learn if they have identified students with great interest or evident strengths in their programs.

4. Provide students with self-directed learning opportunities and independent project work so that they may pursue their interests. Observe their choices.

5. Determine how to enhance your classroom lessons with movement, music, the visual arts, cooperative learning, and self-reflection. Observe student reactions and engagement.

6. Offer students in-school or out-of-school mentoring or apprenticeship opportunities to deepen their knowledge and skills.

7. Videotape students in action in the classroom. Later observe the tape either alone or with another colleague to learn about diverse students' strengths.

Some teachers choose to educate themselves about selected intelligences they have not previously used. Several teachers in the Kent School District in Washington State, for example, read the document entitled, *Dance, Music, Theatre, Visual Arts: What Every Young American Should Know and Be Able to Do in the Arts* published in 1994 by the National Standards for Art Education. This document provided them with insight into the content and skills of artistic aspects of several intelligences, and inspired them with ways to infuse such instructional and intelligence strategies into classroom lessons.

One teacher after reading the dance standard for choreographic principles that states—"Create a sequence with a beginning, middle, and end both with and without a rhythmic accompaniment. Identify each of these parts of the sequence"—asked small groups of students to create a movement sequence or "dance" of formulas for volume in her math course. She could offer this window into math with some degree of confidence even though she herself had never studied dance. She also had an opportunity to observe which students greeted this activity with enthusiasm and skill.

Once teachers have identified student strengths, it is important to encourage them to pursue their strengths while also using their talents to ameliorate weaknesses. For example, if a student is strong mechanically, but weak linguistically, she might be asked to write a book explaining how to put together a clock or other object of her choice.

To reinforce basic skills at Montgomery Knolls Elementary School, the teachers commonly incorporate significant language activities into projects the students purse. Students are asked to explain or write what they are doing while working in their areas of strength. And at the closure of each project or curriculum unit, students must give oral and/or written presentations to accompany their multimodal work. This blends student strengths with literacy skills.

ASSESSMENT THROUGH THE MULTIPLE INTELLIGENCES

Just as students benefit from learning in numerous modes, they also benefit from demonstrating their knowledge in diverse ways. The Theory of Multiple Intelligences offers a framework both for classroom teaching and assessing. Some students find it easier to share what they have learned through charts, role plays, songs, journals, models, or cartoons

rather than through paper and pencil means. All students may find multiple assessment options motivating and interesting.

When providing students with multimodal assessment options, it is critical that the criteria for quality work be clarified before students begin their studies and that the same criteria be evident in their assessment activities. Suggestions for assessing through each of the seven intelligences are summarized in the chart below. In the descriptions of sample assessment tools that follow, job roles or endstates, as referred to at Project Spectrum, are also listed. These roles can serve as templates for performance-based assessments in each intelligence area.

Assessment through the Intelligences

Culminating Essay · Analytic Scoring Guide · Pictorials · Peer Review · Reflective Journal · Exhibitions · Song-writing

SAMPLE VERBAL-LINGUISTIC ASSESSMENT APPROACHES:

Culminating essay: A culminating essay reviews what students have accomplished with a project or curriculum unit or what they have learned by the middle or end of a grading period. Essays in any content area ask students to construct meaning from their coursework, to interpret their experiences, and to reveal their mastery of content and process knowledge. When assigning a culminating essay, students should be familiar with proper essay formats, the concepts or processes they need to address, and the criteria by which they will be assessed. A sample planning form follows:

CULMINATING ESSAY PLANNING FORM

Student Name: _____

Date: _____   Class: _____

Concepts: What was (were) the main principle(s) or concept(s) you learned during this unit (i.e. platonic solids, causes of pollution, the legislative process)?

_____

_____

_____

Learning processes: In reviewing your work, what learning or thinking skills did you use to complete this unit (i.e. expresses ideas clearly, interprets and synthesizes information, considers multiple perspectives)?

_____

_____

_____

Essay format: Use standard essay format: an introductory paragraph, three to five paragraphs for the body of the essay, and a concluding paragraph.

CRITERIA FOR ASSESSMENT:	SCORES:		
	Not evident	Evident	Well done
Are the essential concepts well described?			
Are diverse perspectives explored?			
How well is the information synthesized and interpreted?			
How well is the essay format followed?			
Is the essay well-written in terms of mechanics and style?			

Other linguistic assessment approaches include: journals, logs, portfolios of written work, word-processor products, newspaper articles, magazines, brochures, advertisements, discussions and debates, and storytelling.

Linguistic job role: Students might be asked to assume the role of newspaper editor and writer and write feature articles and letters of the topic under study.

SAMPLE LOGICAL-MATHEMATICAL ASSESSMENT APPROACHES:

Scoring sheets: Numerical scoring sheets provide feedback on student work in the form of number scales that range from one to three or five per criterion. The teacher (or the teacher and students together) determines the qualities expected in academic work. A numerical point spread can be assigned to each criterion indicat-

ing exceptional work, above average work, average work, and incomplete work. It is often helpful to work with a four point spread since four does not easily correlate with the five of traditional grades of A, B, C, D, and E.

Such score sheets can be used to evaluate portfolios, products, essays, content skills, and process skills such as problem-solving, collaborative learning, and goal-setting. Since these measures are criterion-based, student work is not compared with that of others, but rather scored on the basis of given guidelines or established criteria. Students might be given the option to revise their work to attain higher scores.

A sample numerical scoring tool is shown below. This one was jointly developed by a teacher and high school students in a creative writing course. The class identified the poetry components as criteria for assessment.

POETRY ASSIGNMENT NUMERICAL SCORE SHEET

Name: _____ Date: _____

Class: _____ Period: _____

Ranking system:

- 0 = skill not evident
- 1 = minimal skill evidence
- 2 = effective demonstration of skills
- 3 = highly effective skills demonstrated

POETRY COMPONENTS:					STUDENT SCORE:	TEACHER SCORE:
Craftsmanship	0	1	2	3		
Sensory imagery	0	1	2	3		
Word or language play	0	1	2	3		
Provocative ideas	0	1	2	3		
Cohesive theme	0	1	2	3		
Overall effect of poem	0	1	2	3		
Total score:						

As is evident in the above score sheet, both teacher and student assign the scores that each deems appropriate for the submitted poetry. Once it has been scored, students might later reflect on any discrepant criteria.

Other logical-mathematical assessments include: Out-loud problem-solving, staging a trial, doing surveys, outlining or charting what's been learned, playing puzzles or games, making timelines, and interpreting data.

Logical-Mathematical job role: Students might be asked to bid on a job that is related to their studies such as surveying a geographic region, buying or selling of goods, or performing statistical analyses.

SAMPLE VISUAL-SPATIAL ASSESSMENT APPROACHES:

Concept maps or mindmaps: Concept maps or mindmaps (please see visual chapter) can reveal what students know before a study begins, during a unit, or at the end of a unit. The maps begin with a major concept, key words are identified and attached, and a clustering of related ideas follow. One example of an evaluation mindmap is included below:

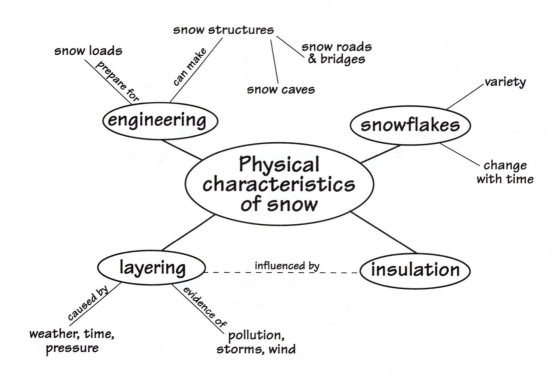

Sample assessment criteria for visual concept maps or mindmaps might consist of the following:

a clear, central focus

adequate number of key concepts, ideas

appropriate detail

pertinent examples

accurate relationships among data

neatness, clarity, and legibility

Other visual-spatial assessment approaches include: flow charts, three-dimensional models, photographic essays, videotapes, collages, scrapbooks, mobiles, or art work.

Visual job role: Students might assume the roles of artists to create public art that communicates an aspect of their studies.

SAMPLE BODILY-KINESTHETIC ASSESSMENT APPROACHES:

Exhibitions: Academic progress can be assessed through exhibitions where students demonstrate their knowledge of a subject matter area. Exhibitions typically involve students in developing products or giving presentations. While some schools such as Ted Sizer's Coalition of Essential High Schools use exhibitions as comprehensive, interdisciplinary activities seniors must complete to graduate, others use them as performance assessments of what students have learned and whether they are able to apply their knowledge. Such exhibitions consist of group projects, dramatic skits, presentations, portfolios, integrated art and writing products, or constructed models. Evaluation of exhibitions frequently involves the teacher, students, a family member or guardian, and in some cases, experts from the community. Some exhibitions are presented at parents' nights, or for school board members and administrators, other classrooms, or general community members. Exhibitions often diminish the importance of standardized test scores as indicators of student success. When community members actually see what students have accomplished, they find such presentations more meaningful and relevant than unidimensional scores on a computer printout.

Two sample classroom exhibitions and one interdisciplinary, end-of-the-year senior exhibition follow. In many cases, students must develop their own formats for their exhibitions, and they can choose to work independently or with a partner. Some classroom time is provided so that the teacher and adult volunteers may serve as resources for students, but most of the work is completed outside of school to encourage students to manage their learning and time effectively. Typically, such assessments require anywhere from one week to two months of preparation time.

Sample classroom exhibitions:

1) **Students are asked to compose a portrait of themselves as able learners for a specific subject matter area. They must identify, select, and present evidence that they have learned and can apply the content, skills, and appropriate behaviors of the discipline both in and outside of school.**

2) **Based on their study of Contemporary World Problems, students must identify a current issue of crucial importance and provide a rationale for their selection. Additionally, they must demonstrate knowledge of how others have attempted to resolve the issue, the reasons for success or failure of previous efforts, and specify what contributions the students have made or will make to ameliorate the problem. To fulfill the above requirements, students are required to submit a videotape or other visuals, one shoe box diorama, one skit, and one written paper.**

Sample interdisciplinary senior exhibition required for graduation:

Students must identify and explain a particular behavior pattern evident in the insect world, in animals, in humans, and in literature. They are to draw on their knowledge from coursework in science, social studies, literature, and health as well as their own observations and reflections about behavior. Students may select a format of their choice, written, artistic, graphed, etc. to explain the selected behavior. References must be made, however, to learnings gleaned from science, social studies, literature, health, personal observations, and reflections.

Criteria for evaluation of the exhibitions might include:

Knowledge of the discipline(s)

Provision of supporting evidence from diverse subjects

Provision of supporting evidence for student opinions

Appropriateness of format

Ability to narrow a broad topic into a workable one

Execution of the project

Ability to apply content knowledge outside of school

Resourcefulness

Inventiveness

Time management

Other bodily-kinesthetic assessment approaches include: model building with manipulatives, making a product or game, doing a simulation, role play, pantomime, or dance.

Bodily-Kinesthetic job role: Students might assume the role of product or model designers and submit samples of their work to a panel.

SAMPLE MUSICAL ASSESSMENT APPROACHES:

Musical contracts: Working independently or in small groups, students can select a musical approach to demonstrating their content knowledge. The teacher must specify what students are to address such as the theoretical concepts of democracy or evolution, or writing procedures such as rules for comma or semi-colon usage. In the sample assessment tool that follows, the options offer student choice in an area that is challenging to some and highly motivating to others. Assessment criteria are also included.

Other musical assessment approaches include: Dances that illustrate concepts, songs, sound scripts, musical mnemonics, and advertisements.

Musical job role: students might serve as composers or producers who are responsible for creating appropriate musical scores to accompany coursework.

MUSICAL ASSESSMENT CONTRACT

Name (s): _____ Date: _____

Your assignment is to demonstrate your knowledge of the following concepts:

_____

_____

Through one type of musical activity (Please check one):

_____ Make a musical collage using diverse musical selections that reveal
        your knowledge of the concepts studied
_____ Choreograph a dance that addresses the concepts
_____ Perform a dance
_____ Create and perform on a keyboard an original song or rap about the concepts
_____ Create and perform a song with percussion
_____ Create and perform a song with an instrument of your choice
_____ Create a song to sing without accompaniment
_____ Write lyrics to the melody of a song you already know
_____ Find pre-recorded songs or compositions that address the concepts.
        Identify what ideas the recordings addressed and didn't address.

Prepare to turn in on (date) _____

With one of the following products (Check one):   _____ live performance
                                                        _____ audio tape
                                                        _____ music video

You will be assessed on the following:	Low		High	STUDENT SCORE	TEACHER SCORE
Demonstrated knowledge of concepts Included at least 10 important facts	1	2	3		
Included at least three examples to enrich concepts	1	2	3		
Demonstrated the ability to use the concepts beyond this class	1	2	3		
Well-presented performance	1	2	3		
Other:					

SAMPLE INTERPERSONAL ASSESSMENT APPROACHES:

Peer problem-solving: In pairs, students work on content area problems provided by the teacher. One student attempts to solve the problem out loud while the other student observes, listens, and asks questions about the problem-solving strategies. Roles are then reversed using the same problem or a new one. Students provide feedback to one another on their problem-solving strategies.

The emphasis in peer problem-solving is on thinking through a problem, not just providing the right answer. By receiving feedback on their thinking processes, students learn how to problem-solve and increase their ability to use appropriate strategies in the future on similar problems. As students prepare to work in pairs, they need to be reminded to be supportive of one another. After all, most great discoveries involved much trial and error.

There are numerous benefits to this interpersonal activity. Students not only learn subject matter, they develop good listening and questioning skills, they learn to refine their thinking and problem-solving, and they gain effective interpersonal communication techniques. Student responsibilities and feedback criteria are provided below. Teachers may find it helpful to conduct a trial run with the class so that the steps of the process are clear before students work with their partners.

Other interpersonal assessment approaches include: collaborative learning, interviews, service projects, teaching others, and leadership opportunities.

Interpersonal job role: Students might role play being job interviewees who are attempting to get hired for jobs related to course content.

PEER PROBLEM-SOLVING ACTIVITY

For this activity, you will work in pairs. Your goal is to learn how you and your partner problem-solve, not just whether either of you provides the correct answer. After the teacher provides the problem and organizes the pairs, follow these steps:

1. For the first round, one of you assumes the role of the "problem-solver" while the other is the "listener."

2. The problem-solver begins the activity by working on the problem by thinking out loud so the listener can learn how the problem is being solved. In addition to words, the problem-solver may also graph, chart, walk through, or draw his or her thinking methods while explaining to the listener what he or she is doing.

3. While the problem-solver is working, the listener asks questions about the problem-solver's thinking strategies. The listener does not offer suggestions or advice about ways to proceed.

4. If the problem-solver gets stuck, the listener summarizes his or her thinking methods so far. This sometimes helps to jumpstart thinking. If the problem-solver wants, he can change the problem in a way that suits him better.

5. When the problem-solver solves the problem or stops working on it, the listener describes what he or she observed about the other's problem-solving methods.

6. For the second round, the roles should be reversed and the same procedure followed.

7. When the second round is completed, both students should complete the chart below. The written feedback should be shared with one another. The teacher will explain whether the written information should be turned in.

_____

Partner's name: Your name: _____

1. I noticed this person solved problems by _____

   _____

   _____

2. This person seemed to get stuck when _____

   _____

   _____

3. This person got unstuck when _____

   _____

   _____

4. My feedback was (check one) _____ somewhat helpful or _____ very helpful.

5. My feedback would be more helpful if I _____

   _____

SAMPLE INTRAPERSONAL ASSESSMENT APPROACHES:

Reflective Journal: Students can maintain journals to track both the content they are learning and their attitudes towards the content. Teachers should be sensitive to the fact that there are many ways to reflect in addition to writing. For example, the only words in Picasso's journals were laundry lists, Jung filled his journals with mandalas, and Einstein computed abstract equations. Sometimes students resist maintaining journals because they lack ideas about what to write, draw, or equate in them. To alleviate this concern, teachers can suggest prompts to guide student reflection. Some prompt statements include:

Key ideas I've learned about this topic

Questions I have are

One thing I discovered is

What frustrates me is

If this topic had a sound it would be _____ because

What I feel good about is

I could use some help with

If I could change one thing about this topic it would be

One thing I would like to master is

When I work with others in this class, I

My attitude toward this class, when drawn, would look like:

This topic connects to other subjects at school because

The best part about class today was

What I feel most confident with is

At first I thought _____, but now I think _____

My personal goal for today, this week, this unit, is

Rather than establishing criteria to assess journal reflections, students might select entries for comment by the teacher or a classmate. This reflective dialogue provides students with important intrapersonal feedback on what they are learning, struggling with, succeeding at, and enjoying. The dialogue journals also offer valuable information for teachers about classroom learning and assessing.

Other intrapersonal assessment approaches include: participating in entry and exit interviews, writing editorials, awards, autobiographical sketches, memoirs, setting and achieving goals, and managing self-directed projects.

Intrapersonal job role: Students might serve as expert witnesses in a mock trial where they must testify on behalf of or against a current ethical issue involved in their studies.

When using a variety of assessment tools, students have a number of ways to express their knowledge. Such multimodal tools can be implemented in the course of students' involvement in regular classroom experiences rather than appearing as unnatural, sporadic events at the end of a unit. Additionally, the above suggestions demonstrate how instruction and assessment naturally integrate, as well as how schooling and real life might more effectively integrate. Instead of making students anxious about evaluation, such strategies serve to heighten motivation and enjoyment in learning.

PROCESSFOLIOS

While the portfolio is gaining increasing popularity as an assessment strategy, Gardner recommends the use of processfolios. Noting that portfolios typically contain completed work, processfolios, by contrast, provide insight into both the processes and products of student learning. They document initial goals, drafts, and revisions; they include early as well as later works, and may also contain student journals as well as articles or photographs that influenced student work.

Rather than serving as storage containers, processfolios provide the means for students and teachers to dialogue about learning and personal development. Used throughout a term, they serve as assessment tools that naturally integrate with academic work. Ongoing dialogue about the contents of processfolios between student and teacher, student and student, student and parent, and student and outside expert, transforms classrooms into learning laboratories that support the acquisition of new information and skills, and that reflect upon the meaning of such course content in a student's life.

To fit their classroom needs, teachers must establish guidelines for processfolios. Arts PROPEL teachers and researchers identified several procedures which are suggested below:

PROCESSFOLIO GUIDELINES

1. To begin their processfolios, students should be provided with folders. They can be asked to provide background information about their attitude and knowledge of the subject matter at the outset of the course and to maintain an annotated table of contents.

2. Teachers should identify lessons and units that reflect their instructional objectives. During the course of their studies, both students and teachers can select items for inclusion in processfolios such as drafts, final works, jour-

nal, and multimedia entries. To guide the selection of processfolio entries, teachers might request pieces that:

> reveal accomplishment
> reflect change or growth
> reveal student risk-taking
> reveal satisfying and unsatisfying
>   learning experiences
> indicate student working styles

3. Student journal entries might also accompany each selection in the processfolio. The reflections might consist of written or taped justifications for selected work, what has been most beneficial and challenging in their studies, and how students apply subject matter content outside of school. Such journal entries can provide rich opportunities for dialogue.

4. When students and teachers review processfolios together, both accomplishments and next steps can be discussed. During the review, student strengths, weaknesses, goals, and learning strategies should be identified so that students perceive their overall accomplishments, their challenges, and next steps to pursue.

5. It may be necessary to adjust how processfolios are reviewed according to the size of the class. In a small classroom, individual conferences between students and teacher can be easily arranged, whereas in larger classrooms, peer group feedback may be more practical. A limited number of issues should be pursued in any session so that students are not overwhelmed with too much feedback.

6. If desired, several people can be involved in the evaluation of processfolios including the teacher, the student, classmates, parents, and community experts. The evaluation must be closely linked with the original instructional goals. The emphasis on what and how a processfolio is assessed will vary from teacher to teacher and from classroom project to project. The staff at Arts PROPEL have suggested the following topics to consider in assessment:

> Craftsmanship revealing skill and
>   principle use

Ability to set goals
Pursuit of learning over time
Risk-taking and problem-solving
Use of the tools of the content area
Care and interest evident in work
Ability to assess own work
Ability to grow from constructive feedback
Ability to work independently
Ability to work collaboratively
Ability to access resources

The criteria teachers establish to assess processfolios can consist of quantitative scores and qualitative comments. There should ideally be a reference group against whom students are being assessed. For example, the reference group might consist of 1) other students of the same grade level, 2) past performances of the students, or 3) expectations of community members who have expertise in the area being assessed.

Processfolios contribute numerous benefits to a classroom. Not only do they serve as ongoing, natural forms of assessment, they also encourage students to be active learners who are aware of their own academic and personal development. By assuming responsibility for self- assessment of

both the products and processes of learning, students may be encouraged to initiate change and growth not from external rewards or pressures, but from within themselves.

AN ASSESSMENT SCHEDULE

So far in this chapter we have reviewed numerous principles and forms of assessment. Teachers typically spend a great deal of time planning their curriculum and multimodal lessons. The authors suggest that the same kind of effort might go into planning a comprehensive assessment system. Assessment should be as varied and well-thought out as any major unit of study. Teachers rarely have the opportunity to step back and reflect on the timing and types of assessment tools they use. To aid in such reflection, one kind of grading period assessment calendar is suggested below. It emphasizes the importance of the personal intelligences in evaluation by placing increased responsibility on the student as the assessor of her personal and academic gains. The following schedule is suggested as only one possible model, but hopefully, it will provoke reflection about assessment approaches for individual classrooms:

An Assessment Calendar

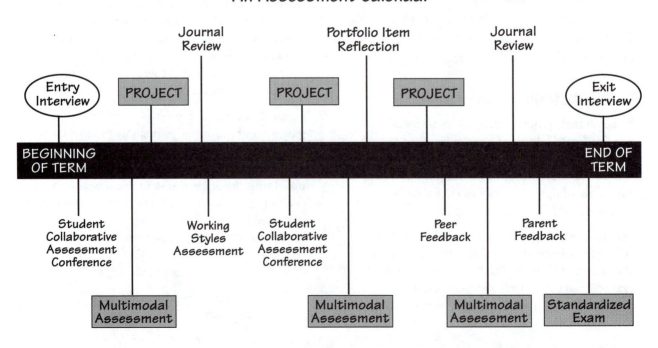

As the above schedule suggests, to begin a marking period, whether a quarter, trimester, or semester timeframe, the teacher might want to establish baseline data about each student. Such information serves to inform future curricular decisions as well as provides a reference point to later gauge student growth at the end of the term. Entry interviews provide one means for getting to know students' knowledge, attitude, and skill levels at the outset of a marking period. Such interviews may be conducted by the teacher, instructional assistants, parent volunteers, or the students themselves. A sample is provided below:

ENTRY INTERVIEW

Name: _____ Date: _____

Class: _____ Period: _____

Interviewer's Name: _____

1. Have you had a class that dealt with similar subject matter before? If yes, what was it? (Or, if the student is in an elementary grade, mention some things he is likely to learn this new term and ask what he has learned at home or elsewhere.)

2. What did you learn before that will be helpful to you in this class?

3. What did you learn about studying, thinking, or learning itself that might be helpful to you in this class?

4. How do you use what you learned previously inside and outside of school?

5. What interests you about this subject matter or grade level?

6. What do you hope to learn?

7. What would you like to be able to do with your learnings from this class or grade level?

8. Is there something you would like your classmates to know about you?

9. Is there something you would like your teacher to know about you?

10. Is there any other comment you would like to make?

To conduct entry interviews, students can write their own responses, be queried by peers or classroom volunteers, and, in the case of young children, dictate their answers to older students or adults. Entry interviews provide valuable additions to student processfolios.

Before any kind of assessment is undertaken, the authors recommend that students and teachers conduct "Collaborative Assessment Conferences" to identify the criteria and processes of assessment for each major assignment. It is also effective for teachers to show samples of previous work from former classmates so that students have concrete images of the standards they are to meet.

The ongoing curriculum will provide numerous opportunities for assessment. Over the course of the marking period, the instructor might assess students through each of the seven intelligences using the assessment tools suggested earlier in this chapter or other tools better suited for classroom activities.

In addition to multimodal assessment, the "working styles" of students, such as those observed at Project Spectrum, might also be identified. During informal conferences with students, teachers can share their observations, and discuss whether such approaches to learning are beneficial or whether other behaviors might be more appropriate.

As mentioned in the curriculum development chapter, projects provide students with opportunities to develop the skills they will rely on as adults. The authors recommend that two or three projects be pursued and evaluated during a marking period or over the course of a year. Student presentation of projects is one form of assessment used effectively at The Key School. Three times yearly, students complete projects that are videotaped and become part of their permanent school record. These videotapes provide ready evidence of student knowledge, skills, and growth over time. Whether or not teachers decide to create video archives of student projects as done at the Key School, the following evaluation form may prove useful in assessing student projects:

Entry Interviews

Working Styles

Collaborative Assessment Conferences

Student Presentation of Projects

Parent Feedback

PROJECT EVALUATION

Name _____ **Project** _____

Research question _____

TEACHER AND PEER ASSESSMENT

Research:

	Excellent	Satisfactory	Needs Work
Used at least three sources	3	2	1
Documented sources of information	3	2	1
Gathered interesting and new information	3	2	1
Identified new topics to pursue	3	2	1

Presentation Skills:

Was well-prepared and organized	3	2	1
Demonstrated good delivery skills	3	2	1
Used multiple modes	3	2	1

STUDENT SELF-ASSESSMENT

1. Please explain what you learned about doing a project: _____

_____

_____

2. Please explain what you learned about doing a presentation: _____

_____

_____

3. Please explain what was the most difficult part of this project: _____

_____

_____

4. Please explain what was the most enjoyable part of this project: _____

_____

_____

5. If you did this project over, what would you do differently? _____

_____

_____

Another intrapersonal form of assessment is the class journal, notebook, or learning log. If students maintain such documents, teachers periodically might request that students review their contents to identify significant learnings. Such reflection, occurring once or twice a term, actively engages students in summarizing and synthesizing both the process and content of their studies.

As the marking period draws to a close, students might benefit by receiving feedback on their coursework from adults other than their teachers. Students can gather samples of their work or prepare their processfolios to take home to discuss with a parent, relative, or neighbor. To shape and guide the feedback students will receive, teachers might create questionnaires to accompany student work home such as the one provided below:

STUDENT FOLDER REVIEW AND REFLECTION

Student: _____ Date: _____

Class or subject matter area: _____

Adult reader: _____

Enclosed, you will find samples of this student's work from _____(class or subject area). We believe that it is important for students to receive feedback on their academic efforts from numerous sources, and we invite you to become part of our assessment team. Please review the work included in this folder, and consider constructive, encouraging comments to make to the student. The following questions may serve as a guide for your discussion. We also ask that you jot down your responses to these questions so that the student can later include your feedback in his or her work folder.

1. **What piece or pieces of work tell you the most about this student's knowledge?**

2. **What strengths do you see in this student's work?**

3. **What areas of improvement might be addressed?**

4. **Have you noticed the student applying his or her knowledge from this class outside of school? If so, how?**

5. **Do you have suggestions that might aid the class's growth?**

6. **Do you have other comments you would like to make?**

Thank you for your time and effort to contribute in meaningful ways to this student's academic progress!

After discussing their work with a parent or another adult, students typically experience positive or negative reactions to such feedback. Teachers have found it helpful to provide opportunities for students to reflect on and respond to their discussions. To debrief their feelings, the following questionnaire or another of the teacher's choice may prove useful.

STUDENT RESPONSE TO ADULT FEEDBACK

Student Name: _____ Date: _____

Please take a few minutes to reflect on the feedback you received from a parent or another adult about your academic work. The following questions may guide your response:

1. What was your general reaction to sharing your work with an adult outside of school?

2. Do you think that this sharing provided you with relevant feedback on your progress? Why or why not?

3. What do you think the adult learned about you as a student?

4. What did the adult not observe or understand about your work that you would have liked him or her to know?

5. What did you learn about yourself as a student?

6. What surprised you most about the conversation?

7. What might have made the conversation better?

8. Would you like to share your work again in this manner? Why or why not?

SCHOOLWIDE ASSESSMENT PROCESSES:

In addition to the assessment calendar suggested above, one MI school, Eleanor Roosevelt Elementary School in Vancouver, Washisngton, has identified the alternative assessment strategies in use at their school. The school values engaging the personal intelligences in assessment. This effort is evident in numerous forms of student and parent evaluation. A chart of Eleanor Roosevelt's assessment strategies follows:

ELEANOR ROOSEVELT ELEMENTARY SCHOOL'S
COMPREHENSIVE ASESSMENT APPROACH

At Eleanor Roosevelt Elementary School in Vancouver, Washington, teachers, parents, and students are all actively involved in assessment as the sample chart indicates:

TEACHER EVALUATION	STUDENT EVALUATION	PARENT EVALUATION
Portfolios	Portfolio	Portfolio
Anecdotal reports	Anecdotal self-assessment	Observations made while in classroom
Interviews	Self-reflection	Goal-setting with child
Multi-media performance assessments with specified criteria	Evaluation of one's own and peer projects	Review videotapes of projects
Mental notes from "kid watching"	Interest inventories	Formal and informal conferences
Checklists	Peer evaluation	Participation in classroom and schoolwide meetings
Teacher-made tests	Evaluation of teacher	Program surveys
Relevant published tests	Self-reflection	Phone contacts
Trimester report cards	Evaluation of course	Written comments

Ultimately, each teacher must decide how best to assess student learning in his classroom. Realistically, both standardized as well as alternative forms of evaluation will co-exist in most classrooms, and yet, by expanding the assessment repertoire, students discover enhanced opportunities for demonstrating what they know. They also may feel a keener sense of ownership in their learning if they collaborate with their peers and teacher about what constitutes good work in the first place.

MULTIPLE INTELLIGENCE REPORT CARDS:

Some educators working intentionally with the Multiple Intelligences have found that traditional report cards do not adequately reflect what their students are learning. Some have devised new kinds of report cards. Using such reporting measures, however, typically requires the education of parents, administrators, and others so that they understand the rationale for such changes. One of the authors writes a brief parent newsletter each month explaining his academic goals, philosophy, and some of the learning experiences of students in his class. When he subsequently experimented with a new report card reflecting the Multiple Intelligence nature of his classroom, parents willingly considered the alternative since they already understood this teacher's classroom procedures. While not yet perfected, the report card looks like this:

MULTIPLE INTELLIGENCES REPORT CARD WITH DEVELOPMENTAL INDICATORS

Name: _____

	Novice	Apprentice	Practitioner	Scholar
READING (Linguistic Intelligence)				
WRITING & SPELLING (Linguistic Inteligence)				
MATH & SCIENCE (Logical-Mathematical Intelligence)				
VISUAL ARTS (Visual-Spatial Intelligence)				
MOVEMENT ACTIVITIES (Kinesthetic Intelligence)				
BUILDING ACTIVITIES (Bodily-Kinesthetic Intelligence)				
MUSIC SKILLS (Musical Intelligence)				
GROUP WORK (Interpersonal Intelligence)				
REFLECTIVE THINKING (Intrapersonal Intelligence)				
RESEARCH (Project Preparation Skills)				
PRESENTATIONS (Project Demonstration Skills)				

Novice: *recognizes concepts, begins to develop skills*
Apprentice: *acquires increasingly complex skills through guided practice*
Practitioner: *works independently and accurately with knowledge and skills*
Scholar: *demonstrates mastery of concepts and practices, applies in new settings*

Colored bars demonstrate beginning points in each area as well as level of progress to this point in time. The longer the line, the greater the improvement.

The goal of this report card is to show the developmental progression of children's skills in several intelligence areas. Each quarter, the bar graphs are filled in with one color up to the level at which the child is performing. The next quarter, the bar graphs are completed in a different color to represent growth during the second term. If little or no growth occurs during a term, a vertical line is drawn to represent the static nature of work in that area. If a student's skills were to slip backwards an arrow would be drawn to represent the regression.

Another example of a Multiple Intelligences report card is in use at the Key School. Each quarter, teachers assess student accomplishments in all seven intelligences while also recording intrapersonal progress in project presentation, POD choices (student or small group mentoring activities), and in Flow activities. Flow at The Key School consists of a classroom that students visit four times weekly to pursue activities and games of their choice. Teachers observe and record what activities students select. Such observations result in a profile of each child that shows what she chooses to do when given free choice.

Another unique area assessed at the Key School is POD participation. Four times weekly, each student attends a POD of her choice to work on material related to one or more intelligences. On the Key School report card PODS are assessed by the primary intelligences they elicit.

SUMMARY:

Effective assessment cultures develop in classrooms in which assessment is considered as part of the learning process. When the usual secrecy surrounding tests is removed, students can engage in public discussions about what constitutes good work and use assessment criteria they generated to inform their ongoing work. Students can also play active assessment roles by contrasting earlier and recent efforts. Assessment naturally integrates with learning when students demonstrate what they know through project presentations, exhibitions, or other multimodal means. Additionally, accurate information about a student's capacities is readily perceived without taking additional time from teaching and learning.

It is not realistic to assume that alternative approaches to assessment will totally supplant standardized measures. Foregoing the machine-scored, efficient, low-cost, single-snapshot testing sessions will not occur while numerous questions remain about the value of assessment alternatives. And yet, teachers in their own classrooms can begin to augment traditional testing procedures with authentic assessments. Standardized measures can be supplemented with alternative ones, with both teachers and students benefiting from the potential rewards of such changes.

For teachers, the strategies proposed in this chapter ask them to rely extensively on their clinical judgments, acknowledging the quantity and quality of professional knowledge they possess about the students with whom they work. Through reliance on such informal as well as formal and diverse means of assessment, teachers can teach students how to evaluate themselves. Fostering the ability to direct and redirect their own educational efforts, students and teachers together can achieve a major goal of education—learning how to learn and how to improve one's learning.

APPLYING ASSESSMENT INFORMATION

1. Important ideas or insights gleaned from this chapter: _____

_____

_____

_____

2. Areas I'd like to learn more about: _____

_____

_____

_____

3. Ways I can use this information in my teachng. Please note that the strategies mentioned in this chapter are listed below with space provided to note how each strategy might be incorporated into classroom assessment:

ASSESSMENT STRATEGY	CLASSROOM APPLICATION
Principles to Guide Classroom Assessment:	
Assessment Captures Growth over Time	_____
Assessment is Multidimensional	_____
Asssessment Iforms Instruction	_____
Informal Assessment is Important	_____
Students are Active self-assessors	_____
Assessment of the Intelligences:	
Project Spectrum	_____
Working Styles	_____
Spectrum Reports	_____
Perceiving Student Strengths	_____
Assessment Through the Intelligences:	
Verbal-Linguistic Assessmen Approaches	_____
Logical-Mathematical Assessment Approaches	_____
Bodily-Kinesthetic Assessment Approaches	_____
Visual-Spatial Assessment Approaches	_____
Musical Assessment Approaches	_____
Interpersonal Assessment Approaches	_____
Intrapersonal Assessment Approaches	_____
Processfolios:	_____
An Assessment Schedule:	
Entry Interview	_____
Project Evaluation	_____
Exit Interview	_____
An Assessment Calendar	_____
Multiple Intelligence Report Cards	_____

ASSESSMENT REFERENCES:

Bamburg, J. (1992). *Assessment: How Do We Know What They Know?* Union, WA: Washington State Association for Supervision and Curriculum Development.

Harvard Project Zero and Educational Testing Service. (1991). *Arts PROPEL: An Introductory Handbook.* Available from Harvard Graduate School of Education. Cambridge, MA: 02138.

Madaus, G. F. and Tan, A.G. (1993). "The Growth of Assessment" in Cawalti, G. (ed.) *Challenges and Achievements of American Education.* Alexandria, VA: Association for Supervision and Curriculum Development.

Medina, N. and Neill, D.M. (1990). *Fallout from the Testing Explosion: How 100 Million Standardized Exams Undermine Equity and Excellence in America's Public Schools.* Cambridge, MA: National Center for Fair and Open Testing.

Maeroff, G. L. (1991). "Assessing Alternative Assessment." in *Phi Delta Kappan.* Dec. 1991.

National Standards for Arts Education. (1994). *Dance, Music, Theatre, Visual Arts: What Every Young American Should Know and Be Able to Do in the Arts.* Reston, VA: Music Educators National Conference.

Report of the National Commission on Testing and Public Policy. (1990). *From Gatekeeper to Gateway: Transforming Testing in America.* Chesterhill, MA: Boston College Press.

Perrone, V. (Ed.) (1991). *Expanding Student Assessment.* Alexandria, VA: Association for Supervision and Curriculum Development.

Wiggins, G. (May, 1992). "Creating Tests Worth Taking" in *Educational Leadership.* Alexandria, VA: Association for Supervision and Curriculum Development.

Wiggins, G. (May, 1992). "On Performance Assessment: A Conversation with Grant Wiggins" in *Educational Leadership.* Alexandria, VA: Association for Supervision and Curriculum Development.

Wolf, D.P. (1992). *Assessment as An Episode of Learning.* Cambridge, MA: Harvard Graduate School of Education.

Zessoules, R. & Gardner, H. (1991). "Authentic Assessment: Beyond the Buzzword." In *Expanding Student Assessment.* Alexandria, VA: Association for Supervision and Curriculum Development.

CHAPTER 10

EDUCATING FOR INTELLIGENCE

LESSONS LEARNED

"Do not then train youths to learning by force and harshness, but direct them to it by what amuses their minds so that you may be better able to discover with accuracy the peculiar bent of the genius of each."

— *Plato*

Since Howard Gardner first published *Frames of Mind: The Theory of Multiple Intelligences* in 1983, educators have readily perceived implications of his work for their professional practice. These implications include the very topics this book addresses: how to perceive and nurture diverse student strengths, how to teach to reach all students, how to develop Multiple Intelligences-based curriculum, and how to better assess student learning.

Since the mid 1980's numerous schools throughout the country have pioneered Multiple Intelligence programs. While distinct from one another, these model sites share many of the same characteristics and all have learned much about transforming their programs. This final chapter surveys both the common components of MI schools and the lessons they have learned about translating Gardner's work from psychological theory into educational practice in rural, suburban, and inner city classrooms.

LINKING STUDENTS AND THEIR TALENTS

One of the most provocative implications of the Theory of Multiple Intelligences is the responsibility of educational institutions to engage each child's talents. Somewhere in his or her schooling, it is vital that every student discover at least one area of strength. In so doing, students may avidly pursue their inherent interests. Such pursuits not only nurture joy in learning—they also fuel the required persistence and effort necessary for disciplinary mastery and inventiveness. Conversely, if students do not discover an area or areas of interest, they may never develop a love for learning and may instead travel aimlessly through school or abandon formal education altogether.

How can schools nurture these critical linkages between students and their talents and interests? As stated throughout this book, no formula exists for adopting an MI approach, however, there are certain steps schools might take to initiate such efforts. Educators might first identify elements of the Multiple Intelligences in their current curricular and extracurricular programs. They can work to insure the widespread availability of these offerings for all students. For example, when, as is all too often the case, the visual arts and music are offered as separate subjects for only a few students, efforts can be undertaken to infuse the arts throughout the curriculum. The school's technology systems and software programs might be surveyed for the intelligences they engage and for those overlooked. Plans can be made expand the technological options. Teachers might reflect on their own strengths and volunteer to team plan with other colleagues. Project-based and hands-on learning might become preferred instructional methods. Discussions with parents and local community members might uncover apprentice-

ship opportunities for students. By taking stock of their existing programs and determining what to enhance or add, schools can offer Multiple Intelligences options to their students.

LESSONS LEARNED FROM PILOT EFFORTS

During the last ten years of Multiple Intelligences implementation efforts, pioneering schools have experienced successes, encountered challenges, and identified important issues to consider when working with Gardner's ideas. The lessons these schools have learned fall into five broad areas: 1) how we perceive students, 2) how we teach, 3) how we organize curriculum, 4) how we assess, and 5) how we develop as educators when working with MI. The pilot schools' experiences may be instructive for others and are summarized below:

LESSON #1
Our Perception of Students Must Change

One of the most fundamental implications of Gardner's work is how students are perceived. In contrast to IQ scores and labels such as smart, average, or dumb, the Theory of Multiple Intelligences enables educators to look at the diverse ways children problem solve and apply what they have learned. We can appreciate, at least theoretically, that students possess individual cognitive profiles with varying strengths. And, yet when trying to put such knowledge into practice, many teachers find it challenging to observe each child through a seven-faceted lens. Teachers must provide enriched learning opportunities, sharpen their observation skills, solicit information about talents and passions from students and others who know them, and take time to learn about unfamiliar intelligences.

Otherwise, our estimation of our students' potentials may continue to be unnecessarily limited by the perpetuation of a basic skills bias.

LESSON #2:
Teachers Need Support and Time to Expand Their Instructional Repertoires

A second implication of The Theory of Multiple Intelligences concerns changing how we teach. Each of the chapters on the seven intelligences in this book describes ways to enhance our instructional repertoires. While the Theory of Multiple Intelligences affirms that any content can be taught in numerous ways, educators ultimately develop instructional methods that are the most appropriate for their students and their settings Whatever pedagogical approach a teacher assumes, the Multiple Intelligences provide a mental checklist for assessing the multimodal nature of instruction. For example, at the New City School in St. Louis, middle school teachers have 90 minute blocks for language arts. Some teachers split their block time into three equal parts: 30 minutes of direct instruction, 30 minutes of cooperative learning and 30 minutes of independent learning. When planning their 90 minute sessions, teachers review the seven intelligences to see if they are incorporated in their lessons if not daily at least weekly. The seven intelligences become an organizing tool for educators to determine how many windows exist into the content they teach.

Providing Support to Alter Practice

Many teachers, however, find it daunting to incorporate all seven intelligences in instruction. Pilot efforts have revealed that changing pedagogy requires ongoing dialogue among colleagues, opportunities for teachers to grow, and enlarging the circle of those responsible for educating students. Ultimately, teachers need support to alter their professional practice. Some forms of support that have evolved at pilot MI schools include the following:

- Organize schoolwide study groups to read *Frames of Mind* or any other of Gardner's works. For example, the staff at New City School in St. Louis conducted study groups for a year or more before creating an MI program.

- Ask staff members who are highly skilled in an intelligence to provide experiential workshops for their colleagues.

- Better integrate building specialists who have strengths in PE, the arts, or reading, by seeking their input into curriculum development or providing in-class services and instruction to students.

- Enlist experts such as professional artists to mentor teachers or students.

- Visit other MI sites to see how educators from around the country are working with Gardner's ideas in their school programs.

Creating Time for Multiple Intelligence Programs

The demands of daily teaching are such that it is difficult to find time to transform classroom or schoolwide practices. Rather than finding time, however, some MI programs are *creating* time for teachers to secure the support they need, to work independently, and to collaborate with their peers. Some time management strategies that have proven effective include:

- Providing full day releases: Substitutes can be hired to release teachers, or teachers can be paid for working during vacation.

- Altering the school's schedule: Each school day can be lengthened by a few minutes to accrue a partial day of teacher planning once or twice monthly. Or, in team teaching situations, team members might alternate between teaching and planning. Scheduling can be changed so that several teachers share the same planning time. The school's calendar can be reworked to provide more teacher planning days.

- **Inventing time:** Student teachers, parents, community members, volunteers, or administrators might assume teacher tasks or classes to free teachers to work together during the school day.

- **Using faculty meetings differently:** One or more faculty meetings a month can be dedicated to co-planning or problem-solving issues of pedagogy, curriculum, and assessment.

- **Providing credit for time:** Teachers can be compensated with in-service credit for their efforts. University faculty can develop courses that include practicums for educators to reflect upon and apply new instructional approaches.

Meeting the challenges of teaching in multi-modal ways appears worth the effort since many teachers claim benefits from their MI work. Some appreciate the intellectual framework and common language the theory provides. Some state it validates their professional practice by giving them permission to teach in ways they always have or have wanted to teach. Some like the mental checklist of the seven intelligences saying it reveals instructional gaps. Nearly all appreciate the enhanced ability they have to acknowledge diverse strengths within their students. Some enjoy developing their own latent intelligences as well as teaching students in ways that motivate and engage them.

LESSON # 3:
MI School Curriculums Differ

Another implication of Gardner's work for education is a reshaping of school curriculum. It is evident that in most cases, rather then being totally reworked, curriculum is adapted by teachers to incorporate various intelligences. In general, these curricular changes are perceived as enhancements rather than major overhauls. One school, Concrete Elementary in Concrete, Washington explains their MI adaptations as simply enriching their curriculum.

When reviewing pilot efforts across the country, it is evident that all MI schools are committed to nurturing the multi-faceted minds of their students. The ways in which they approach this goal, however, vary greatly. The authors have noted that there appear to be four curricular approaches emerging at the pilot programs. These are briefly described below:

1. Multimodal Curriculum Design:

This currently appears to be the single, most common approach to MI classroom or school-wide efforts. The Multiple Intelligences are used as tools of instruction providing seven entry points into disciplinary content. Many individual teachers are applying Gardner's theory in their daily work with students. Some use learning centers occasionally, weekly, or daily. Others employ direct instruction through multimodal means. Others team with colleagues including building specialists to round out their students' educational experience.

Some schools make a building-wide commitment to teach through the seven intelligences. In this case, several, if not all of the teachers in a building attempt MI-based instruction. This might occur on a daily basis or, in some cases, on a special events basis. An example of an MI special event occurs at Fairview Elementary School in Port Angeles, Washington. Each May, the entire school participates in an MI week. The week is thematically structured and typically highlights a culture represented among the school's student body. Teachers specify what and how they will contribute to the theme according to their strengths and interests. Students rotate in multi-age groups throughout the building with obvious enthusiasm for the event.

A K-12 school, Hart-Ransom in Modesto, California, provides another example of multimodal curriculum design. While the schoolwide commitment to the Multiple Intelligences is evident in instruction, the teachers maintain, however, that the school's mission is to provide education. The school does not perceive the Multiple Intelligences as exit outcomes. Instead, they focus on the basic skills, critical and creative thinking, and effective communication. Hart-Ransom is clear that at their school, as at many others around the country, the Multiple Intelligences serve as instructional delivery tools.

2. Developmentally-Based MI Curriculum

In this curricular model, the focus is upon in-depth knowledge and skill development. Teachers attempt to put restructuring proponent Ted Sizer's suggestion of "Less is more" into classroom practice. By streamlining their curriculum to emphasize essential concepts, teachers forego survey-mode learning in favor of in-depth student understanding. The Multiple Intelligences continue to serve as tools of instruction in a narrowed and deepened curriculum. Additionally, some schools promote project-based learning so that students acquire self-directed learning skills, and some identify performance-based standards for students to achieve.

Lincoln High School in Stockton, California, offers one developmentally-based MI model. There, students work on projects that reflect the standards determined by the State of California. The California curricular frameworks stress that what teachers teach, they must teach in depth. The standards discourage the practice of exposing students to vast amounts of information that they typically don't retain or understand. At Lincoln, teachers make the essential concepts of their courses explicit. Students know what it is they are to learn as well as how they should demonstrate and apply their knowledge. In addition, teachers focus on the processes by which students

learn. Students often work cooperatively at centers as well as pursue projects of their choice that deepen their understanding of core concepts.

Not only do Lincoln students learn and apply core curriculum, they also identify their intellectual strengths and weaknesses. Students are taught that intelligence is modifiable and capable of change throughout life. Teachers emphasize that with intentional effort and guidance any underdeveloped areas of intelligence may be enhanced. With this developmental focus, Lincoln students come to respect the intellectual diversity of their peers and others as well as perceive new possibilities for themselves.

3. Arts-Based MI Curriculum

Some schools interpret the Theory of Multiple Intelligences as providing a strong rationale for arts-based programs. With Gardner's claim that visual, musical, kinesthetic, and interpersonal competencies are actually forms of intelligence, arts proponents recommend that dance, music, theatre, film, visual arts, and creative writing be allotted equal status and time in the school curriculum. They claim that the arts provide important symbol systems that represent, interpret, and convey the world. Mathematics, science, and language communicate only part of our human experiences. The arts are necessary to explain other aspects of life. Students who learn the basic skills and artistic symbol systems gain a more comprehensive picture of the world, while also developing more of their intelligences. MI schools such as Ashley River Elementary School in Charleston, South Carolina, The New City School in St. Louis, Missouri, the Expo for Excellence School in St. Paul, Minnesota, and Seven Oaks Elementary School in Lacey, Washington all infuse the "artistic intelligences" throughout the curriculum and teach the arts as core subjects in their own right. All students at these schools on a daily or near-daily basis study the visual and performing arts to better understand the world and to better develop the spectrum of intelligence.

4. Intelligence-Based Curriculum:

Perhaps the least common MI curricular approach is the one that strives to develop each student's intelligence strengths. At such model sites, the schools' missions, goals, and programs are significantly reorganized to accommodate individual student interests. Instead of emphasizing teaching through the intelligences, the schools emphasize teaching *for* intelligence.

The Key School in Indianapolis is committed to enhancing each student's intellectual strengths. While all Key students learn academic content through the seven intelligences, they also identify their strengths and reflect on how these skills might guide their life choices. At this K-8 school, students have numerous opportunities to enhance their preferred intelligences. For example, students select their electives in Pods which meet daily. The Pods provide additional instruction in areas where students demonstrate interest and promise. Students also attend the Flow Room several times weekly to immerse themselves in self-selected activities that are personally motivating, challenging, and gratifying. Because of the extensive curricular time dedicated to student choice at the Key School, teachers have less time to teach the traditional basic skills. They capitalize on the time for basic skill instruction by seeking highly effective ways to teach the traditional literacies. This dedication, however, to an intelligence-based model rather than a basic skills model appears successful academically since all but a handful of students at the Key School score at or above grade level on standardized test scores.

Another approach to educating for intelligence is evident at Clara Barton K-8 School in

Minneapolis. In 1991, the staff decided to individualize Gardner's theory for each student through goal-setting meetings with students, teachers, and parents. During September, teachers conduct goal-setting conferences with each student and a parent. The teacher begins the meeting by asking what goals the student wants to achieve, what is important to the parent, and what the teacher recommends as well. During the three-way discussion, one or more goals for each of the seven intelligences are identified. Some goals encourage student interests while others focus on challenges. The first intelligence considered at the conference is intrapersonal intelligence. Some of the intrapersonal goals students have identified include completing assignments on time, asking questions when teacher directions are unclear, and feeling proud of one's work. The conference continues until the teacher, parent, and student identify goals for all seven intelligences.

Throughout the school year, students are encouraged to intentionally meet their goals. They identify the steps to take for success, they reflect on their efforts in their journals, and they discuss their progress or frustrations with teachers and others.

In February of each year, a second round of teacher, parent, and student conferences reviews student progress with their goals. These conferences reaffirm, refocus, revise, and celebrate student efforts. At the end of the school year, parents are invited to attend Achievement Days to review student portfolios and to learn how goal-setting has affected their children's educational experiences. While, admittedly, the goal-setting process requires precious teacher time, the school community at Clara Barton is supportive of this program component. The staff claims that individual goals encourage students to enhance each intelligence in personally relevant ways and teaches them how to manage independent learning. Additionally, parents demonstrate an increased respect for their children's abilities since their competencies have been raised to the status of "intelligences." Clara Barton teachers also appreciate that the school is concerned with all areas of human growth and that diverse forms of excellence are celebrated.

LESSON #4:
New Approaches to Assessment are Necessary

There are at least four implications of Gardner's work for assessment which include 1) how to assess student intelligence 2) how to improve assessment in general 3) how to involve students in assessment processes and 4) how to assess MI programs and their effectiveness.

Culturally-Fair Intelligence Testing

While it is unlikely that most teachers will be interested in formal intelligence testing of their students, there was, nevertheless, fascinating work with intelligence testing in Arizona. A three year, 1990-1993, Project Step Up Grant through the United States Department of Education funded efforts to identify minority, economically disadvantaged, students as gifted. June Maker, a researcher from the University of Arizona, selected Navaho children to work with at three different sites for the grant. Maker's premise was that Navaho children do exhibit giftedness even though they are routinely assessed below the 50th percentile on school records for ability and achievement. Maker devised problem-solving tasks according to Gardner's model of the seven intelligences. Before she began such work, there had never been a single American Indian child identified as gifted from the Chinle Boarding School, one of the Arizona pilot sites. After she assessed the students with tools such as tangrams and storytelling, Dr. Maker identified 85 students at the boarding school with high potential.

The researcher says she learned many things about working with Navaho children. Maker observed that Navaho students perform far better when tested in small groups than when tested individually. Her small group evaluation is in stark contrast to the individualized intelligence testing conducted at Project Spectrum. Her approach raises the question of whether intelligence testing or perhaps any form of standardized testing should be administered in *culturally-fair* ways. In addition, Maker learned to begin her work with the Navaho students with three-dimensional tasks such as bead work or sculpting before proceeding onto evaluation activities. By initially working in their areas of strength the students were motivated to tackle additional tasks both in and out of their comfort zones. Maker also states that Gardner's model of intelligence does not appear to be biased against or for any cultural, ethnic, or linguistic group. This work in Arizona as well as elsewhere around the country reveals the necessity of changing negative stereotypes and beliefs about children from special populations. Many students are bypassed as competent learners when they are highly talented and gifted.

Bridging Strengths and Weaknesses

One school working with MI theory is founded on the assumption that every child is talented. When teachers refer a student for special education services, they must first provide explicit descriptions of the child's strengths in addition to the reasons for the special education referral. Special education interventions are then based on bridging student strengths to areas of weakness. When schools emphasize strengths, an at risk child does not have to be viewed solely as an individual with problems. Instead, teachers can generate a more comprehensive profile of each student when making educational decisions. MI theory lets us perceive the best in our students and gives us hints about how to intervene in areas where they are challenged.

Changing Classroom Assessment

Assessment practices at nearly all model MI schools have transformed. Four main changes are evident. First, report cards at some schools have been altered to feature the diverse intelligences. Secondly, teachers are using portfolios to capture both the processes and products of student learning. Thirdly, MI-based checklists are being developed and used by teachers to identify a broader range of student talents, and finally, students are becoming actively involved in determining assessment criteria and assessing their own and others' work.

At most MI schools, standardized tests and other traditional assessment measures continue to be administered. Since both new and conventional assessments are employed in tandem, parents and administrators receive information about student progress in familiar ways while learning about alternative measures at the same time. Many parents appreciate videotapes of student projects since they can see what their children learned and how such knowledge was applied.

LESSON #5:
Professional Practice Appears to Transform Developmentally

Some MI teachers experience a developmental progression in implementing Gardner's ideas. While no one individual's experience will adequately explain anyone else's, some MI teachers appear to confront similar challenges in a somewhat predictable sequence. The initial challenge encountered by MI educators is to determine what kind of program model to create for their classrooms. Once they decide how to proceed—whether through learning centers, featuring one intelligence a day, or using multimodal direct instruction—the next challenge is learning how to teach content in new ways. The major focus for many MI educators in the early years of their classroom and schoolwide programs is devising, adapting and/or refining instructional strategies. Time and effort are also spent in gathering new classroom resources such as manipulatives, art, and music supplies. Additionally, some teachers either increase the amount of time they dedicate to student projects or they begin to implement project-based learning in their classrooms. Typically, assessment techniques also become more varied.

Some teachers report that, after the initial year, thinking in seven ways for lesson planning becomes second nature. They sometimes sense new skills developing within themselves and, just like their students, are willing to take risks to explore untapped intelligences in greater depth. Teachers often devise ways to shorten lesson planning time either by relying on strategies they have used previously, by creating long-term projects for students to work at, or by teaming with other colleagues.

Once a degree of comfort has been reached with multimodal instruction, some teachers shift their focus to curricular issues. They attempt to identify truly essential concepts and the most appropriate means for teaching them. Their observation skills of students become more finely tuned, and they may strive to bridge student strengths to weaknesses and to nurture student strengths more effectively. Their ability to teach students how to pursue self-directed learning through projects improves, and they may share their MI efforts and processes with other colleagues formally or informally. Some teachers become dissatisfied with traditional reporting measures and begin altering reports to parents and students that more accurately reflect what students are learning.

Once curriculum and assessment have been addressed, some teachers find that their MI challenge no longer revolves around how to teach and assess through the intelligences but rather how to educate for intelligence. They may begin to identify "intelligence outcomes" for their students to achieve. Some invite individuals with extensive expertise into the classroom or school to provide students with mentoring opportunities. Many teachers who have worked with the Theory of Multiple Intelligences also note significant changes in their professional role in the classroom. Instead of dispensing information, the teachers serve as facilitators, coaches, resource personnel, tutors, motivators, and networkers to support active student learning and to promote diverse forms of intellectual growth. Many experienced MI teachers are also called upon to share what they have learned with others and to help support schoolwide or district-level change.

SIMILARITIES IN MULTIPLE INTELLIGENCE SCHOOLS

While each MI teacher and school is distinct from every other, there are similarities among school programs. All MI schools attempt to teach the multi-faceted minds of their students. To do so, most find it necessary to revise their classroom environments, curriculums, parental relationships, and assessment techniques. The authors have identified ten common characteristics of MI pilot schools which are listed below. Not all schools exhibit all ten, but most include several of the following:

Characteristics of Multiple Intelligences Schools:

1. The learning environment provides all students with easy access to tools that engage each of the seven intelligences.

2. The schoolwide curriculum is well-rounded providing opportunities for each student to explore and develop all seven intelligences.

3. School faculty use the seven intelligences as tools of instruction.

4. Parents and teachers work as educational partners. Parents teach social skills at home as well as take an active interest in their children's

schooling. Such interest may be evident in parents discussing school with their children at home, informing teachers about their children's strengths, participating in assessment questionnaires or conferences, volunteering time in the classroom, serving on school committees, or acting as mentors.

5. Curricular offerings include multi-age groupings so that students observe and work with others of varying abilities. Students learn basic literacies with an infusion of diverse cultural perspectives. Classroom lessons feature activities that extend from the classroom to the home and into the community. At the secondary level, students learn about the core issues and problems of diverse disciplines and have opportunities to explore and challenge traditional knowledge. Their vocational interests are also encouraged.

6. A curricular goal is to teach for student understanding. The curricular scope is narrowed to enable students to achieve in-depth of knowledge of core disciplinary concepts.

7. Students develop autonomous learning skills through initiating and completing projects of their choice.

8. The school program alternates unstructured exploration of student interests with intentional skill development. Both general knowledge and creativity are fostered.

9. Individual talents and interests of the students are identified and nurtured. Students have opportunities to participate in long-term extracurricular, mentoring, or apprenticeship programs of their choice.

10. In collaboration with the teacher, students identify the criteria by which they will be assessed. Students receive feedback and evaluation from numerous sources: from their teachers, from their peers or other individuals, and from self-reflection. In addition, "intelligence fair" assessment tools are used to assess student work. Reports to parents and students include suggestions for follow-up work at home, at school, and in the community for both student strengths and weaknesses.

As is evident in the above characteristics of MI schools as well as in the programs described earlier, much of the schools' efforts are guided in large part by students' talents and interests. Opportunities for gaining general knowledge and specialization, for creative exploration and disciplined skill-building, and for student choice and required study, ebb and flow throughout the school years. When educational institutions transform their environments, instruction, curriculum, and assessment to accommodate intellectual diversity, joy in learning and schooling for intelligence can be realized. And yet, it is the interaction between the teacher and students that is the critical link in student achievement. Those who teach in Multiple Intelligences-based schools must necessarily continue as learners themselves, discovering latent abilities, expressing and refining their talents, and identifying new ones to develop. Ultimately, the greatest influence on student learning is what teachers model in their beliefs, thoughts, and behaviors.

EVALUATING MULTIPLE INTELLIGENCE SCHOOL PROGRAMS

Formal evaluation of Multiple Intelligences pilot efforts around the country has begun. Two researchers from Harvard's Project Zero, Mindy Kornhaber and Mara Krechevsky, have surveyed approximately eleven model programs to determine how school sites are evaluating their efforts and what results they are reporting. The Harvard researchers have learned that most evaluation methods typically consist of teacher, student, and parent interviews. Preliminary findings from these interviews reveal that all groups, teachers, parents and students, claim positive attitudes towards MI efforts.

Teachers and principals state that MI improves the discourse at school as well as

enhances classroom practices. Teachers focus more on student strengths and look at a broader array of student abilities. The language offered by The Theory of Multiple Intelligences enables teachers to describe students and their capacities more comprehensively to students themselves, colleagues, parents, and others. Many schools are altering their report cards to reflect the enhanced views of their students.

A school's commitment to the Theory of Multiple Intelligences usually results in enriched learning environments and experiences for all children. Frequently, arts programs are expanded throughout a school's curriculum. Many teachers feel encouraged to work in teams so that their talents are of service to colleagues and their weaknesses complemented by the strengths of others. In addition, many teachers are inspired to pursue new avenues for their professional growth.

Parents report both academic and affective gains. They explain that their children are taking positive academic risks, that their self-esteem has improved, that they are happy to go to school, and even when ill, students do not want to stay home.

When interviewed, students echo what their parents' state. At MI schools students are proud of their work and are eager to share it with others. Their academic achievement gains have been documented through standardized tests at Cascade Elementary School in Marysville, Washington, The Key School in Indianapolis, and the New City School in St. Louis.

In addition to these preliminary positive results, challenges have been noted. Whatever MI approach an individual teacher or an entire school staff might adopt, pilot efforts have shown that when MI is mandated in a top down approach, some teachers will resist adjusting their curriculums. In those schools where some are working with MI and others aren't, problems arise around special status concerns. It is crucial that teachers dialogue about what they are doing and why, and work to maintain open lines of communication when different methods and philosophies exist among a school's staff. Changing teaching and curricular approaches to MI-based formats is similar to other reform efforts where much depends upon administrative actions, the status of the program, and whether it involves part or all of the school.

Certainly teachers are concerned with the additional time required to change their teaching and assessing practices. Another concern is that while community mentors are invaluable resources, they do not always understand school procedures or child development and successful integration of experts into the classroom can be problematic. It is necessary for school and community members to coordinate their efforts so that mentoring opportunities are developmentally appropriate. Additionally, it appears that several schools may be exhibiting a tendency to create new labels or stereotypes for children claiming that some are visual-spatial learners while others are kinesthetic. Such practices ignore the full richness of the students' Multiple Intelligences and only serve to create unnecessary labels.

Since MI programs have only existed since the late 80's, it is not surprising that evaluation is limited. Certainly, additional evaluation is necessary. Yet, it is evident from the model programs that exist that Gardner's ideas alter how we think about schools. His work questions the familiar structure of schools. How we perceive students, how we teach, organize curriculum, assess student learning, and even who at times teaches our students might all be reconsidered.

WHAT ARE OUR NEXT STEPS?

Gardner's work acknowledges that human development is more complex and flexible than many psychologists or researchers had previously theorized. As we contemplate how to respond to the numerous implications of the Theory of Multiple Intelligences, we can begin looking at our students with a new curiosity and appreciation. We can explain to them as well as colleagues and parents that each of us possesses a unique cognitive profile of individual gifts. We can offer pre-service and in-service staff development to expand our vision of what it means to be human and what it means to be educated. We can design educational programs that nurture individual differences through wholistic offerings. We can share ideas with each other and feel free to discuss both our successes and failures. We can create learning communities that are self-transforming. We can realize that school does not have to be the way we remember it.

And perhaps we might also choose to reflect on the question: What is the mission of education? There is currently no agreement about the mission of education in the United States. Some claim it is to educate for basic skills literacy. Some say it is to ready our graduates to compete in a global market place. Others say it is to pass on our cultural heritage. And some of us might suggest a mission for education is to develop the full range of human capacities, to identify the gifts that our students possess and then develop those gifts through education. All children and adults deserve opportunities to explore their strengths, pursue their interests, and become gifted in their own right. Society can only benefit from such a goal, but to achieve such a mission society will have to participate and support new educational ventures.

To transform schooling as we have known it to what it might become, we will need the support of administrators, parents, business leaders, and policy makers. Others must realize that education is the single most important responsibility of society and be willing to invest the time, money, and creativity to make the development of human capacity our top priority. One example of making human development a governmental priority was pioneered in Latin America. In the early 1980's the small country of Venezuela identified a governmental goal of increasing the intelligence of every Venezuelan citizen. Military, media, business and educational organizations all participated in this venture aimed at achieving this goal. Luis Machado, the Minister for the Development of Intelligence in Venezuela stated

"Today a society of and for intelligence can be consciously and humanly planned. This is not a theory; it is a reality that transforms.....In possession of more developed minds, people will be able to find within themselves the elements needed to build a new society."

Surely if an entire nation can strive to enhance the intelligence of its citizenry and thereby enhance its society, we in our classrooms, schools, districts, and states can do no less.

Part of Howard Gardner's definition of intelligence includes the ability to solve problems. The authors refrain from prescribing specfic approaches to implementing the Theory of Multiple Intelligences. It is through problem-solving ways to better meet the needs of their educational communities that teachers will develop effective model programs while also concurrently developing more of their inherent capacities. Instead of offering prescriptions, we conclude this book with many questions still unanswered:

How might teachers, students, school administrators, parents, and community members become well informed about human competence and its implications for new educational approaches?

How can pre-service, in-service, and staff-development programs incorporate teaching and learning strategies that meet the needs of all students?

How might our school environments be adapted to offer richer programs?

How can our perception of students be improved?

How can instructional and assessment repertoires be expanded?

What are the essential concepts students should learn? Which curricular areas can be eliminated? Which included?

Which community members might be willing to serve as mentors or provide apprenticeships?

How will educators learn to combine the most effective educational strategies with the most practical and intelligent use of technology?

And finally, how will you use the information in this book to stimulate your own inventiveness in finding new ways to develop more fully all of the intelligences of your students?

LESSONS LEARNED REFERENCES

Bolanos, P. (1990). "Restructuring the Curriculum" in *Principal.* January, 1990.

Ellison, L. (1992). "Using Multiple Intelligences to Set Goals" in *Educational Leadership.* October, 1992.

Gardner, H., Krechevsky, M., and Hoerr, T. (in press). "Complementary Energies: Multiple Intelligences in the Lab and in the Field." Manuscript prepared for J. Oakes and K.H. Quartz (Eds.). (In press). *Creating New Educational Communities: Schools and ClassroomsWhere All Children Can Be Smart.* Chicago: National Society for the Study of Education.

Kornhaber, M. and Krechevsky, M. (1993). "Expanding Definitions of Learning and Teaching: Notes from the M.I. Underground." in P. Cookson (Ed.) Creating School Policy: *Trends, Dilemmas, and Prospects.* New York: Garland Press.

Leibowitz, D., and Starnes, W. (1993). "Unmasking Young Children's Gifts" in *Gifted Child Today Magazine.* September/ October, 1993.

Maker, June. (1992). "Intelligence and Creativity in Multiple Intelligences: Identification and Development" in *Educating Able Learners.* Fall, 1992,

Maker, June. (1993). "Creativity, Intelligence, and Problem Solving: A Definition and Design for Cross-Cultural Research and Measurement Related to Giftedness" in *Gifted Education International.* Volume 9, No. 2, 1993.

Sisk, Dorothy. (1993). "A Different Approach Pays Off" in *Gifted Child Today Magazine.* September/ October, 1993.

PERMISSIONS

Excerpts from "Notes for a Preface" in *Complete Poems*, on page 1 Copyright © 1950 by Sandburg, Carl, and renewed 1978 by Margaret Sandburg, Helga Sandburg Crile, and Janet Sandburg. Reprinted by permission of Harcourt Brace and Co.

Portions of the text entitled "Checklist of Verbal-Linguistic Intelligence Qualities" on page 3 and "Finding Materials" on page 19 are from *Planning and Assessing the Curriculum in English Language Arts* by Stephen Tchudi. Alexandria, VA: Association for Supervision and Curriculum Development. Copyright © 1991 by ASCD. Reprinted by permission.

The poem entitled "The Intelligence Rap" on page 9 by is printed with permission of Lisa and Shawna Munson.

Portions of the text entitled "Classroom Discussions" on page 14 were adapted from Richard Arends' *Learning to Teach*. N.Y.: McGraw Hill. This 1994 copyrighted material was reproduced with permission of McGraw Hill.

The section entitled "Reading for Understanding" on page 20 was paraphrased from the book by James Moffett and Betty Jane Wagner entitled *Student-Centered Language Arts, K-12*, 4th ed. Permission granted by Heinemann.

Portions of the text entitled "Categories of Writing" on page 21 were adapted from James Britton's *Language and Learning*. Copyright © 1970 by James Britton. Reproduced by permission of Penguin Books, Ltd.

Part of the section entitled, "Mediating Learning", referring to the Building Blocks of Thinking developed by Katherine Greenberg, Ph.D. on page 44 was adapted from the Cognitive Enrichment Network (COGNET) funded in part by the U.S. Department of Education Follow Through Program (Grant # S014C10013), The University of Tennessee Follow Through Sponsor Project, Katherine H. Greenberg, Ph.D., Director.

"The Questioning Strategies Bookmark" on page 47 was developed by Jay McTighe of the Maryland State Department of Education. Reprinted by permission.

Portions of the text entitled "Definition: Understanding Kinesthetic Intelligence" on page 67 are quoted from *Experiences in Visual Thinking* by Robert McKim. Copyright © 1972. Published by PWS Publishing Company. Boston, MA. Reprinted by permission.

"Classroom Zones" on page 70 is printed with permission from Dr. Ann Taylor, Professor of Architecture at the University of New Mexico, and originator with partner, George Vlastos, of Architecture and Children, 111 South Jackson, PO Box 4508, Seattle, WA.

Text sections entitled "Understanding Bodily-Knowing" on page 75 and "Introduction to Creative Movement Activities" on page 76 were contributed by Peggy Hackney. Printed with permission.

"Elements of Dance Warm-Ups" on page 77 and "A Sequence for Learning through Dance" on page 78 are printed with permission from Debbie Gilbert, Executive Director of Very Special Arts in Washington State, and Co-Director with Joanne Petroff of the Whistlestop Dance Company, PO Box 20801, Seattle, WA. 98102.

The text section entitled "Task Cards" on page 79 is adapted from Kenneth and Rita Dunn's book, *Teaching Students through their Individual Learning Styles*. Copyright © Allyn and Bacon. Reprinted/adapted by permission.

"Characteristics of a Physically-Educated Person" on page 85 reprinted from *The Physically-Educated Person: Outcome and Benchmarks of Quality Education Programs*, 1991, by permission from the Outcomes Committee of the National Association for Sport and Physical Education, Reston VA.

"Local and Global Problem-Solving" on pages 180-183 is adapted from the *Our Only Earth Series* by Linda MacRae-Campbell and Micki McKisson. Copyright © 1990, 1992 Zephyr Press. Used with permission of publisher.

"Teaching with a Multicultural Perspective" on pages 184-185 is adapted from James Banks' *Multiethnic Education: Theory and Practice*. Third Edition. Boston: Allyn and Bacon. 1994. Printed with permission.

"Understanding Cultural Diversity through the Arts" on pages 185-186 is adapted from *Strategies for Culturally-based Art Education: A Qualitative Methodology* by E.M. Andrews, 1980, and *The Innovation Process of Cultually-based Art Education: A Qualitative Analysis of the In-service Programming and Implementation Processes of an Innovative Multicultural Art Curriculum in Canada* by E.M. Andrews, 1983. Reprinted by permission.

"Culturgrams" on pages 186-188 is from the David M. Kennedy Center for International Studies, Brigham Young University, 1981. Reprinted by permission. Culturgrams may be purchased as a full set or individually by country of choice. To order, for pricing information, or for a free catalog, please call 1-800-528-6279.

Quotes from "The Inside World" by Bill Knake on page 194 are reprinted with permission of Bill Knake.

The information on the Apollo program on pages 197-198 was contributed by Brad Greene who may be contacted at 938 Rivera St., Simi Valley, CA 93065

"Olympic Goal Setting" on pages 206-207 is adapted from the work of Marilyn King and her "Dare to Imagine" program. Reprinted by permission.

The summary of "The World Within: Intra-personal Intelligence" on page 225 contains a quotation by Carl Rogers from *On Becoming a Person*, Copyright © 1961 by Houghton Mifflin Company. Reprinted by permission.

The section entitled "Principles of Assessment" on pages 270-278 is adapted from the work of Arts PROPEL of Harvard Project Zero and the Educational Testing Service. Printed with permission.

The information on "Working Styles" on pages 279-280 was excerpted from Mara Krechevsky's article entitled "Project Spectrum: An Innovative Assessment Alternative." *Educational Leadership*, 48, 5. Reprinted with permission of the Association for Supervision and Curriculum Development. Copyright © 1991 by the Association for Supervision and Curriculum Development. All rights reserved.

The Project Spectrum sample report card on pages 280-281 was reprinted with permission of Mara Krechevsky of Harvard Project Zero.

The portion of the text entitled "Multiple Intelligences Report Cards" on page 301 contains a report card from Bruce Campbell's book, *The Multiple Intelligences Handbook: Lesson Plans and More*. Copyright © 1994 Campbell and Associates, Incorporated, Stanwood, WA.

SUBJECT INDEX

Complex Instruction, 167-168

compliment circles, 199

concept maps and mapping, 106-107

codes, 49

conflict

    causes for, 49

    management, 77, 150, 169-170

Control Theory, 198

cooperative learning

    (see collaborative learning)

creative problem-solving, 114

creativity, xvii, 128, 150-151, 313, 316-317

Cubism, 55

culminating essay, 283-284

"cultural detectives", 185

Culturgrams, 186-187

curriculum

    arts-based MI curriculum, 309

    bias, 252

    development, 229-266

    developmentally-based MI curriculum, 309

    differing MI curriculums, 308-311

    education for understanding and curriculum, 258-262

    implications of the Theory of Multiple Intelligences for curriculum, 231

    intelligence-based curriculum, 246, 310

    interdisciplinary curriculum, 239-246

    multimodal curriculum design, 308

    project-based, 253-256

D

dance, 77-78

Dewey Decimal System, 112-113

digestion, 57

dioramas, 80

discussions, 115

    five stages of, 14-15

    whole class, 15

    small group, 16

drama, 71-73

    creative drama, 73-74

Duke Ellington School of the Arts, 141

E

education for understanding, 258-262

Eight Treasures, 88-89

Eleanor Roosevelt Elementary School, 299-300

emotionally intelligent education, 210-214

"end states", 251-252

energizers, 87-89

environment (see separate intelligences)

equity pedagogy, 184-185

essays, 123, 283, 285, 287

eye exercises, 89

exhibitions of student work, 283, 287-288, 302

F

feelings

    engaging feelings in the classroom, 210

    expressing feelings, 212-215

    expressing feelings through the arts, 312-214

    identifying emotions, 211-212

    inventory, 212

field trips, 89-90

flow charts, 100-101

foreign language, 22, 74, 84, 99, 171

Frames of Mind, xvi, 1, 67, 133, 305, 307

Framework for Aesthetic Literacy, 259

games, 82-85

    board, 115-117, 126

    card, 117,

    total physical response games, 84

geometry, 55-56, 58-59, 76, 246

global perspectives, 177-183

goal-setting, 203, 208, 310

graphs, 50, 115

groups, criteria for effective groups, 162

Hart-Ransom School, 308-309

Harvard University, xv, 59, 258

heredity, 195, 278

history

    events, 100, 107, 115

    strategies for teaching history, 9, 22, 26, 71, 74, 79, 82, 90, 100, 144, 150, 176, 244

homework, 234, 275

I

I Can Problem-Solve, 170

imagery, 96-97, 110-111, 112-114, 206,

intelligence

    intelligence-based curriculum, 246, 310

    I.Q. tests, xvii

    categories of, xvii

    criteria for, xv

    culturally-fair testing, 311

    definition of, xv, 316

    measuring, 278-279

    teams, 245-246

    (see also separate intelligences)

instructional menus, 232-233

interdisciplinary education

    planning, 240-245, 307

    schoolwide approaches, 244

    units, 239-245

interpersonal intelligence

    assessment through, 290-291

    checklist of qualities, 160-161

    definition, xvi, 160

    environment for, 161

    learning processes, 161-187

    technology, 188

interviews, 18, 23, 186, 219, 254, 292, 295-296, 300, 314

intrapersonal insights, 218-219

intrapersonal intelligence

    assesssment through, 292

    checklist of qualities, 195-196

    definition, xvi, 195

    environment for, 197-198

    learning processes, 196-224

    technology, 224-225

J

journals, 216-218

junk drawer manipulatives, 80

K

Key School, 231, 245, 247, 256, 259, 296, 302, 310, 314

kinesthetic intelligence

    assessment through, 287-288

checklist of qualities, 68

definition, xvi, 67

environment for, 69-70

learning processes, 69-90

technology, 90-91

L

language, 7, 13, 27-28, 96, 106, 128, 251-252

language arts, 19-22, 76,120-121, 244

　(see verbal-linguistic intelligence)

learning centers, xix, 70, 223, 247-248, 308, 312

learning styles, 79, 174-175

Learning through an Expanded Arts Program (LEAP), 120-122

legends, 5, 9, 11, 185, 220

lessons

　learned from pilot efforts, 305-316

　matrices, 235-238, 242, 262-263

　planning, 14, 182, 209, 249-251, 307, 312

　sample lessons, 237, 238, 243, 248, 262

Lincoln High School, 251, 309

linguistic intelligence (see verbal-linguistic)

listening, 5, 7-12

　active, 47

　guide, 12

　ten keys to effective listening, 6-7

　to lectures, 11-12

　to music, 139-140

　to poetry, 8

　to stories and reading aloud, 7

logic

　deductive, 38, 39-40

　inductive, 38, 41-42

logical-mathematical intelligence

(see mathematics and science)

assessment through, 285-286

checklist of qualities, 35

definition, xvi, 35

environment for, 13

learning processes, 36-62

technology, 58-60

M

Magna Carta, 26

mathematics

(see logical-mathematical intelligence)

　assessment tool, 272

　professional associations of, 36-37

strategies for teaching mathematics, 22, 35, 37, 48-50, 51-56, 76, 118, 144

mathematical intelligence

　(see logical-mathematical intelligence)

manipulatives, 37, 48, 69, 79-81, 91, 93, 282, 288, 312

measurement, 36, 51, 55, 62, 317

Mediated Learning Experience (MLE), 43

memorizing, 16-17, 71, 112, 114,

metacognition, 208

mindmapping, 12, 107-108

mindscapes, 110

mnemonics, 112, 288

Montgomery Knolls Elementary School, 282-283

movement

　creative, 75-77

　zone, 70

multicultural education, 184-187

multicultural storytelling, 9-11

murals, 121, 123, 198

R

reading

    comprehension, 20-21, 111, 122

    finding materials, 19

    for understanding, 20, 143

    motivating students to read, 19

    teaching reading musically, 142-143

    reflecting on classroom reading, 20

Reading Instruction through the Arts (RITA), 120, 122

Rebus stories, 81

reports

    Spectrum reports, 270, 280-281

report cards, 300-301, 303, 312, 314

role-playing, 72, 177

S

scavenger hunts, 82-83

Scholastic Achievement Tests (SAT), 134

science (see logical-mathematical intelligence)

    achievement, 134

    and logical-mathematical intelligence, 35-37, 46, 61

    strategies for teaching, 22, 58, 71, 73-74, 106, 111, 141, 144, 172, 178, 229-230, 237, 244, 248, 251-254, 275, 281, 287, 301, 309, 319

scientific method, 38-39

self-confidence, 2, 5, 171, 200, 205

self-esteem, 183, 195-201, 218, 225, 281, 314

self-directed learning, 222-226, 233, 249, 259, 282, 309, 312

service learning, 171-173

    reflecting on service learning, 172-173

    service resources, 172-173

sequencing, 45, 57, 262

simulations, 74-75, 82, 91

singing, 16, 133-136, 139-146, 149-150, 279

Skyview Junior High, 257

social skills, 160-161, 163, 165-167, 190, 201, 205, 233, 313

social studies (see history), 22, 39-40, 74, 82, 90, 107, 144, 146, 149, 171-172, 176, 184, 186-187, 246, 258, 287

songs

    curriculum songs, 149-150

    in content areas, 140-141

    math, 141

    science, 141

    recorded songs, 140-141, 149

speaking, 13, 16, 27-28, 120, 126, 145, 164, 172, 205, 211, 216, 273

spelling, 16, 24, 49, 51, 65-66, 78-79, 112-115, 140, 142, 301

stamps, 48, 81

story problems, 51, 53, 56-57

storytelling

    cultural dimensions of, 9-11

    guidelines for, 13-14

    multicultural storytelling resources, 10

    resources for, 9

    students as storytellers, 4, 11, 13, 20, 27, 29, 36, 106, 123, 138, 148, 217, 235, 311

    subject matter stories, 9

    teachers as storytellers, 4, 9, 29, 54, 195, 267

strengths, perceiving student strengths, 281-282, 306

syllogisms, 39-40

systems wheel 178-179

T

task cards, 79-80, 165

teaming, 235, 245, 312

technology

    (see separate intelligences)

Ten Shin Go So, 87-88

theatre, 71-73, 75, 282, 309

themes, 58, 143, 167, 186, 246, 248, 252, 259

The Theory of Multiple Intelligences, iii, xvi, xviii, xix, xxi, 231-232, 247, 264, 283, 305-307, 309, 313-316

thinking skills, 52, 58-61, 85, 115, 118, 120-121, 184, 207-208, 224-226, 233, 239, 248, 260-261, 284

Tickle Tune Typhoon, 132, 140

U

understanding (see education for understanding)

    defining, 258

    education for understanding, 260-262

    principles for teaching for, 258-260

    teaching for, 258, 260-264, 310

The Unschooled Mind, 229, 258, 266

V

values

    classroom, 162-163

    common, 215-216

Venn Diagrams, 36, 39-41, 62

verbal-linguistic intelligence

    assessment through, 283-284

    checklist of qualities, 3-4

    definition, xvi, 2-3

    environment for, 5

    learning processes, 4-26

    technology, 26-27

visual accompaniment for lectures, discussions, 115

visual arts, 120,-124, 213, 220, 231, 251, 280-282, 301, 309

visual imagery, 96, 98, 111

visual memory, 112

visual outlines, 98, 100-103, 110

visual peripherals, 126

visualization, 96, 111-112, 220

visual-spatial intelligence

    assessment through, 286-287

    checklist of qualities, 97

    definition, xvi, 96

    environment for, 98-99

    learning processes, 98-124

    technology, 125-127

visual variety in learning materials, 114-115

W

weekly planning grid, 250

Whistlestop Dance Company, 77

wonder, 202, 220-221

working styles, 279-280, 293

writing

    across the curriculum, 22

    categories of, 21

    creative, 21, 151, 213

    groups, 25-26

    journal writing, 216-218

    options for all content areas, 23

    process, 24-25

Y

Youth Summit, 180-183

Z

Zorba the Greek, 65

NAME INDEX

Andrews, E. Margaret, 185
Aristotle, 134
Armstrong, Louis, 135, 155
Asher, James, 82, 84

Bacon, Roger, 61
Banks, James, 184, 320
Bayes, Lorraine, 131, 319
Benzie, Teresa, 77
Bloom, Benjamin, 46
Britton, James, 4, 21, 318
Brookes, Mona, 124
Buzan, Tony, 107, 112

Campbell, Bruce, xix, 255, 320
Campbell, Linda, xviii
Carrol, Kathleen, 141
Carver, George Washington, 7
Chaucer, Geoffrey, xix
Churchill, Winston, 56
Chopin, Frederic, 135
Clarke, John, 103
Cohen, Elizabeth, 164, 167
Confucius, 134
Costa, Arthur, 207
Curie, Marie, 247
Cziksentmihalyi, Mihalyi, 162

DaVinci, Leonardo, 111
Deardorff, Danny, 131, 319
Dewey, John, 82, 253
Dickinson, Dee, xviii-xix, 227
Diamond, Marian, xxi
DeGarmo, Charles, 46
Dunn, Kenneth, 79
Dunn, Rita, 318

Edison, Thomas, 7
Einstein, Albert, 155, 189, 247-248
Eisner, Eliot, 120

Feldman, David, 278
Feuerstein, Reuven, 43
Fitzgerald, Sheila, 143, 319
Flying Karamozov Brothers, 159
Frye, Northrup, 1
Frost, Robert, 27
Fuller, Renee, 193

Galileo, 33
Gandhi, Mahatma, xvii
Gardner, Howard, iii-iv, xv-xvii, 1, 132-134, 189, 229, 231, 258, 267, 269, 278, 305, 316
Gaugin, Paul, 56
Gilbert, Debbie, 77, 318
Glasser, William, 198
Goebbels, Hermann, xvii
Goodlad, John, 2, 68
Gowin, Bob, 106, 319
Greenberg, Kathleen, 43-46

Hackney, Peggy, 75, 318
Hesse, Herman, 139
Hippocrates, 174
Hokusai, Katsushika, 1
Holmes, Oliver Wendell, 193

Johnson, David, 166, 319
Johnson, Roger, 164, 319
Jones, Beau Fly, 103, 319
Jung, Carl, 174

Kazantzakis, Nikos, 65
Kekule, Fredrich, 111
King, Marilyn, 206-207, 320
Knake, Bill, 194, 227, 320
Kodaly, Zoltan, 131, 133
Krechevsky, Mara, 278, 314, 320

Lamy, Stephen, 175
Lincoln, Abraham, 1
Lozanov, Georgi, 99, 138

Machado, Luis, 316
MacLean, Paul, 210
Maker, June, 311, 317
Margulies, Nancy, 110, 319
Martin, Herbert, 220
McKim, Robert, 67, 97, 128, 318-319
McPherson, Kate, iv, 172-173, 319
McTighe, Jay, 47, 318
Mead, George Herbert, 82
Merida, Carlos, 56
Moffett, James, 4, 20, 318
Monet, Claude, 56
Montessori, Maria, 80
Munson, Shawna, 9, 318
Murphy, Nancy, iv

Nelson, Doreen, 119
Newton, Isaac, 155
Novak, Joseph, 106, 319

O'Keefe, Georgia, 95

Pepys, Samuel, xix, 216
Perkins, David, 15, 258
Petroff, Joanne, 77, 318

Piaget, Jean, 31, 82
Picasso, Pablo, 126, 247
Plato, 134, 305

Rico, Gabriele, 109, 216
Rogers, Carl, 225, 320
Rohnke, Karl, 86, 319
Roosevelt, Franklin Delano, 159

Sandburg, Carl, 1, 318
Santyana, George, 147
Shakespeare, William, 247-248
Shure, Myrna, 170
Socrates, 39, 46
Steil, Lyman, 7

Taylor, Ann, 118, 318-319
Tchaikovsky, Peter, 135
Tchudi, Stephen, 3, 19, 318
Thoreau, Henry David, 174

Van Gogh, Vincent, 56
Verney, Thomas, 2
Vlastos, George, 118, 318-319
Vygotsky, Lev, 4, 205

Welsh, Sarah, iv, 107-108
Whitman, Walt, 216
Whitney, Eli, 56